MW01114763

To Dr. Cordesman,

With much appreciation!

Boaz Ganor

The Counter-Terrorism Puzzle

The
Counter-Terrorism
Puzzle

A Guide for Decision Makers

Boaz Ganor

The Interdisciplinary Center, Herzliya

The International Policy Institute for Counter-Terrorism

Transaction Publishers
New Brunswick (U.S.A.) and London (U.K.)

Copyright © 2005 by The Interdisciplinary Center for Herzliya Projects.

All rights reserved under International and Pan-American Copyright Conventions. No part of this book may be reproduced or transmitted in any form or by any means, electronic or mechanical, including photocopy, recording, or any information storage and retrieval system, without prior permission in writing from the publisher. All inquiries should be addressed to Transaction Publishers, Rutgers—The State University, 35 Berrue Circle, Piscataway, New Jersey 08854-8042. www.transactionpub.com

This book is printed on acid-free paper that meets the American National Standard for Permanence of Paper for Printed Library Materials.

Library of Congress Catalog Number: 2004063698
ISBN: 0-7658-0298-8
Printed in the United States of America

Library of Congress Cataloging-in-Publication Data

Ganor, Boaz.
    The counter-terrorism puzzle: a guide for decision makers / Boaz Ganor.
        p. cm.
    Includes bibliographical references and index.
    ISBN 0-7658-0298-8 (cloth: alk. paper)
        1. Terrorism—Prevention. 2. Terrorism—Government policy. 3. War on Terrorism, 2001- I. Title.

HV6431.G267 2005
363.32—dc22
                                                        2004063698

This book is dedicated to two great people who are no longer with us: my late father, attorney David Ganor, who taught me the theory of learning and from whom I inherited my thirst for knowledge; and my teacher, the late Professor Ehud Sprinzak, one of the greatest researchers on terrorism, who instructed and guided me in preparing my doctoral dissertation, upon which this book is based.

Contents

Figures

Acknowledgements

I want to thank sincerely the interviewees who consented to give of their valuable time; my family, who understood and supported me throughout the entire process; and in particular, my wife, Amit, and my children Lee, Tom, and Dan, who had to give up a great deal of "quality time" with their father while this book was being written.

My appreciation and thanks to Irwin Hochberg, Ellie and Mel Dubin, David P. Steinmann, and Eugene M. Grant for their unwavering support in publishing this book.

Preface

On September 11, 2001, international terrorism crossed the Rubicon and became unrecognizable following the attacks in the United States. The force of the attack, the targets chosen, the terrorists' daring and their sophisticated planning, the way in which all accepted conventions were shattered while boundaries and limits were crossed, and most of all, the enormous scope of the damage and the number of victims—all of these turned international terrorism into an immediate, tangible, and existential danger to modern civilization and the entire world.

The attacks of September 11, which were immediately followed by a series of biological terror attacks (anthrax envelopes sent to various targets in the U.S.), marked the beginning of a transition from modern terrorism to unlimited and unrestrained post-modern terrorism. The potential for injuring thousands of people in a single attack, the danger posed by the use of unconventional materials (chemical, biological, radiological, and even nuclear), and the spread of radical Islamic ideology, which perceives anyone who does not share the fundamentalist point of view—be they Jewish, Christian or Muslim—is a heretic who must be fought, have all turned terrorism into an international problem of the highest magnitude. Terrorism is no longer merely a local problem to be dealt with by one country or other. Rather, it has become an unprecedented danger to world peace, resulting from a radical Islamic terror network that has spread worldwide and is focused on fulfilling the divine religious commandment of holy war—*jihad*—by means of terror attacks.

In the face of this grave threat the world stands confused and divided. Most people are unaware of just how great the danger is, and in any case, they lack the skills required to deal with this new breed of terrorism. While soldiers, police officers, and security forces must drill and train long and hard in order to be able to cope with the enemy on the field of battle, it would appear that governmental bodies—ministers and members of parliament, policymakers, and heads of security networks—act and make decisions about terrorism without the proper background, without previous knowledge regarding the major dilemmas they must address, while making decisions under the stress of public pressure and tremendous time constraints.

In today's world it is hard to find a more complex and problematic issue facing decision makers than the need to contend with terrorism. The difficulty in defining a counter-terrorism policy derives, among other things, from the unique characteristics of the phenomenon itself:

A. *Interdisciplinary*—In order to fully understand the phenomenon of terrorism, the tools of a single research discipline do not suffice. Almost all academic disciplines are relevant to one aspect or another of terrorism. In order to understand just how complex this phenomenon is, all we need do is to remind ourselves of some of the disciplines that are directly or indirectly related to terrorism, such as: psychology, sociology, political science, law, economics, computer science, biology, chemistry, etc. To cope effectively with terrorism, therefore, a certain degree of familiarity with each of the aforementioned spheres is required, as is the ability to formulate a situational assessment and make decisions on an interdisciplinary basis.

B. *Ambiguous boundary between the front line and the home front*—By its very nature, terrorism blurs the boundaries between the front line and the home front. Terrorists focus their attacks on the civilian population in an attempt to discover the vulnerable "soft underbelly" of the country and society under attack. Coping with terror cannot, therefore, be based only on police-military skills; rather, it also involves civilian actions in a variety of areas.

C. *The impact of terror*—Terror has both a direct and indirect effect on almost all aspects of a nation's life: the political system (terrorism is likely to affect voting patterns); the economic system (terrorism can undermine various economic spheres, such as transportation, tourism, air traffic, exports and imports, insurance, the stock market, the banking system, etc.); the military (terrorism is liable to divert attention from other, perhaps even more serious military threats and jeopardize the training network of the combat forces); and the education system (which must address the challenge of terrorism and reinforce the public's ability to cope with the phenomenon). Decision makers must, therefore, identify all of terrorism's possible ramifications on these and other spheres, and be prepared in advance to mitigate any possible damage.

D. *Types of terrorism*—Terrorism comprises different and varied types of attacks—hostage situations, suicide attacks, shootings, bombings, etc. Each type of attack has its own unique characteristics and the treatment of each necessitates different behaviors and attitudes, as well as the need to address a host of dilemmas.

E. *Test of leadership*—Terrorism places a tangible and immediate challenge before decision makers: it tests their ability to lead and make decisions in real-time, while under pressure. A leader's ability or inability to deal with the threat of terrorism is quickly exposed, and could have a direct impact on his political future. This often leads to faulty decisions in an effort to offer quick solutions to immediate challenges, sometimes without examining all the alternatives and their possible ramifications. In this context, it should be emphasized that the price of a wrong decision is likely to be high and may be expressed in loss of life, along with collateral economic, political, and international damage.

F. *Conflict of interests*—Formulating a consistent policy in the fight against terrorism can affect a country's other interests, and at times even place these in jeopardy. In their attempts to cope with terror, decision makers must take into account the possible impact of their decisions on the rest of the country's interests— economic, political, and diplomatic.

G. *Levels of the war on terrorism*—The complex nature of the battle against terrorism demands that counter-terrorism policies operate simultaneously on all possible levels: intelligence-gathering, offensive, defensive, deterrent, etc. The desired results cannot be produced by concentrating on one level only. An effective policy for the war on terrorism requires a comprehensive strategic perspective and the ability to manage complex crises, while focusing on a mechanism to control and coordinate between the numerous agencies—both military and civilian—that are taking part in the fight, such as: government ministries, emergency services, intelligence networks, security forces, and others.

This volume will point out some of the major dilemmas facing decision makers in examining the main aspects of the war on terrorism: dilemmas relating to intelligence, offensive, deterrent and defensive activity; dilemmas regarding legislation and punishment, information and education; dilemmas associated with international cooperation, the media, etc. In each of these spheres, several key issues are examined and various alternative solutions are presented. After discussing the advantages and disadvantages of the possible solutions, one alternative is recommended for solving the dilemmas based on Israel's cumulative experience in its fight against terrorism.

This volume is intended to serve as a guide to the perplexed, a tool for decision-maker at all levels—leaders of government and legislators; heads of the security systems and administration; personnel from the military, police and emergency services; as well as academics, students, heads of international companies, businesspeople, and the public at large—which, unfortunately, may occasionally find itself in the eye of a terrorism storm and forced to consider its next move in order to avoid becoming the victim of the next terrorist attack.

The book will examine different models and approaches to decision making. Rather, it provides a knowledge base that will allow for more informed, more effective decisions within the political echelon, within the security and administrative forces, at the municipal level, and at the commercial and individual levels.

Israel is a nation that has been suffering from extensive terrorist attacks for a period of many years, and has often proven its ability regarding various aspects of the war on terrorism. As such, it is a suitable model for examining these key dilemmas. For the purpose of this book, personal interviews were conducted with decision makers involved with combating terrorism—key Israeli figures who served in the past as prime ministers, defense ministers, heads of the Mossad, the Israel Security Agency—Shin Beit (ISA) or the IDF Intelligence Division; advisors to the prime minister on terrorism; or the Counter-Terrorism Coordinators at the National Security Council.

Each chapter deals with a different level of the war on terrorism. Chapter 1 presents the dilemmas involved in defining the threat. This chapter discusses questions relating to the very need to define terrorism and the unique aspects of this phenomenon as compared with criminal activity, political protest, and revolutionary violence. At the end of the chapter there is a proposed definition for terrorism that differentiates between the goals of the activity, the means employed, and the targets of the attack. This definition can serve as a suitable platform for achieving international cooperation in the war on terrorism.

Chapter 2 examines dilemmas in defining the framework of the counter-terrorism. It discusses what the stated goal of the war on terrorism should be, and against this background it looks at the goals that have characterized Israeli counter-terrorism activities over the years. This chapter also discusses the issue that comes up repeatedly concerning the dominance that should be given to the military component of counter-terrorism policy; in other words, can terrorism be defeated using military means? In this context the chapter also deals with the question of the need to define a clear counter-terrorism policy and the question of how public that policy should be.

Chapter 3 discusses intelligence dilemmas in the war on terrorism. It begins with a discussion concerning the importance of the intelligence component on all aspects of the war on terrorism. After clarifying concepts from the intelligence-gathering sphere, issues are discussed relating to the use of human intelligence sources (hereinafter, this will be referred to as "humint"), and the relatively short lifespan of an intelligence source. The problem of international cooperation in this field is illustrated by looking at how intelligence cooperation was conducted between Israel and the Palestinians following the signing of the Oslo Accords. This chapter highlights the need for creating a mechanism for coordinating intelligence and operations, and it discusses the question of how the political echelon treats the intelligence assessments and information it receives.

Chapter 4 deals with the complex question of deterring terrorists and terrorist organizations. The chapter begins by analyzing the complexity of the deterrence element of the counter-terrorism policy. This complexity is presented in the context of Israel's counter-terrorism policy. Later on, the chapter discusses dilemmas relating to degree of rationality of terrorists in general, and particularly of suicide terrorists. In addition, various issues concerning deterrence are discussed—offensive, defensive, and deterring state sponsors of terrorism.

Chapter 5 examines dilemmas regarding offensive and defensive actions taken against terrorist organizations. One of the key questions raised in this chapter concerns the effectiveness of an offensive war on terrorism, and how the value of one action or another can be measured. The problem of offensive actions is illustrated by looking at a particular type of this kind of action—individual offensive action, that is, "targeted killing." A survey of Israel's offensive actions against terrorism presents two key dilemmas, which are discussed in this chapter: the dilemma of the "boomerang effect," in other words, the possibility that a terrorist organization will escalate its activities following offensive action against its activists or facilities; and the dilemma involving the timing of offensive activities against terrorism, that is, when is it best to carry out an offensive action—following a terrorist attack and in retaliation for that attack, as a preventive strike prior to an attack, or in an ongoing, continuous manner. Regarding the matter of the defensive-security level of counter-terrorism activities, this chapter raises the issue of how to divide the overall budgetary pie for the war on terror, and the size of the slice reserved for defensive activity compared with other areas.

Chapter 6 deals with one of the main questions facing a liberal-democratic nation coping with a broad range of terrorist activity—the democratic dilemma in the context of the war on terrorism. The chapter surveys modern counter-terrorism strategy and emphasizes the fact that terrorist organizations take advantage of the values and institutions of a liberal-democratic country, especially the open media, the impact of public opinion on decision makers, the limits of punishment and the supreme value placed on human life—all those factors that constitute a nation's "soft underbelly." This chapter focuses on two main dilemmas: the government dilemma in coping with terrorism, that is, how the government maintains its legitimacy by avoiding certain types of counter-terrorism activity while at the same time, preserving the government without the public perceiving its avoidance as political and personal weakness; and the ethical dilemma—how to be effective in fighting terrorism while still maintaining liberal-democratic values. To illustrate these dilemmas the chapter examines ethical questions relating to information-gathering, methods of interrogating suspected terrorists, and offensive and defensive actions. The chapter concludes by proposing a model for examining the scope of the democratic dilemma in counter-terrorism activities.

Chapter 7 focuses on the legislative and punitive aspects of the war on terrorism. Various types of anti-terrorism legislation are surveyed, and there is a discussion on the issues of shutting off funds, individual legislation against terrorism, emergency legislation, and designating terrorist organizations as illegal, as well as fundamental questions dealing with the publicity of trials and confidentiality of evidence, and the issue of putting on trial those suspected of being involved in terrorist activity. With regard to punishment, the chapter looks at two key questions: that of collective punishment, illustrating the dilemma through Israel's experience with demolition of terrorists' homes; and the issue of administrative punishment, discussing the question of imposing closures and curfews on areas used by terrorists as hideouts and safe havens, or bases that train and dispatch terrorists, and administrative detention and deportation against terrorists who perpetrate attacks and those who assist them.

Chapter 8 discusses the issues involved in the media's coverage of terrorism. The chapter reiterates the importance of the media component in modern terrorism strategy, and describes the reciprocal relationship between terrorists, the media, and public opinion. The chapter maintains that a journalist covering a terrorist attack must find the delicate balance between his professional obligation as a journalist to report about the event in real time and without censorship, and his civic duty not to become a pawn in the hands of terrorists or provide a platform for terrorist organizations. The chapter also discusses the question of broadcasting tapes prepared by terrorists, conducting interviews with them, and the matter of the scope of media coverage of terrorist attacks, the content of such broadcasts and their influence on the regular daily broadcast schedule. Two additional issues examined in this chapter involve the matter of censorship on the media's coverage of terrorist attacks, and the behavior of the media if and when they are invited by terrorists to the site of a future attack.

Chapter 9 deals with a central issue in formulating counter-terrorism policy, and that is the dilemma of coping with the psychological damage of terrorism and its negative impact on morale. The chapter describes the fear of terrorism generated among the public as the strategic weapon of modern terrorism. Against the background of terrorism as a type of psychological warfare, dilemmas are discussed concerning the public announcement of intelligence warnings regarding possible terrorist attacks, and reinforcing the public's ability to cope under the threat of terrorism. Furthermore, the chapter looks at the effect of the fear and stress on the public and the way decisions are made regarding counter-terrorism and the quality of those decisions, as well as the legitimacy and wisdom of using offensive means to combat terrorism in order to boost the public's morale.

Chapter 10 looks at issues related to international cooperation and terrorism. It outlines the characteristics of the threat of modern international terrorism as it appears after September 11, 2001, and derives from this threat the international strategy needed to cope effectively with this type of radical Islamic terrorism. This chapter emphasizes the need to create a league of nations combating terrorism, which can help establish and intensify international cooperation in this sphere by forming a framework for collaborative international activity on each level of the war on terrorism—intelligence, offensive, defensive, punitive, etc.

The final chapter of the book provides a summary and conclusions that focus in particular on the dilemmas relating to Israel's experiences in coping with terrorism, the matter of a clear counter-terrorism strategy in Israel, and Israel's successes and failures in this sphere. The chapter ends with a series of recommendations for formulating an effective counter-terrorism policy and for solving major problems in this regard.

Given the complexities involved in coping with terrorism and the need for solutions to the many and varied dilemmas, the need is highlighted for a suitable government body capable of effectively managing all of the government's activities—both civilian and security-related.

1

Dilemmas in Defining the Threat

In the process of formulating any kind of strategy, especially a strategy aimed at addressing a security threat such as terrorism, it is imperative that the threat be precisely defined and delineated. Therefore this volume, which deals with decision making pertaining to counter-terrorism, begins with the issue of defining the threat of terrorism and its unique aspects in contrast with other phenomena, especially those that are similar or parallel to terrorism, such as guerrilla warfare, political protest, criminal activity, and struggles for national liberation.

The Need for a Definition

Issues of definition and illustration are, usually, purely theoretical and intended to allow the researcher to establish a defined, fixed, and accepted basis for the research he is about to conduct. However, when discussing the phenomenon of terrorism, the matter of its definition is a fundamental and essential element for coping with terrorism, an element upon which we must establish a cooperative, international campaign against terrorism.

Modern terrorism relies more and more upon the support of nations. In certain cases terrorist organizations employ means to realize the interests of states sponsoring terrorism, and in other cases their activities are contingent upon the various forms of economic, military, and operational aid they receive from these nations. Certain organizations rely upon state support so heavily that they become the "puppets" of these nations—in accordance with their decisions and under their direction.[1] At the present time, it is obvious that terrorism cannot be addressed effectively if the close ties between terrorist organizations and the countries that support them are not severed. But it is impossible to sever those relationships without reaching a broad-based, international consensus regarding the definition of terrorism, and from this, a definition of states sponsoring terrorism and the steps that must be taken against them. It is impossible to reach a broad understanding of the nature of different terrorist organizations, outlawing them and effectively preventing their fundraising and international money laundering without defining the term "terrorism." The worldwide awakening against terrorism, which is reflected through international conferences, regional discussions by nations, and the like, cannot yield any genuine results so long as the nations participating in these forums cannot agree to a definition of terrorism. As long as there is no agreement as to "what is terrorism?" it is impossible to assign responsibility to nations that support terrorism, to formulate steps to cope on an international level with terrorism, and to fight effectively the terrorists, terror organizations and their allies. Without a definition of terrorism it is impossible to establish international treaties against terrorism, and if international treaties indirectly relating to terrorism are, in any case, written and signed, attempts to implement or enforce them will be unworkable.

An obvious example of this is the issue of extradition. Many countries throughout the world have signed bilateral and multilateral treaties with respect to various crimes. These treaties do not usually relate to terrorist activity specifically, rather they list ordinary crimes for which the perpetrator must be extradited. A significant number of them state explicitly that when the background of the crime is political, the country is under no obligation to extradite anyone—and the background underlying terrorism is always political. This loophole has allowed many countries to evade their obligation to extradite terrorists even though they have signed treaties that would seem to require them to do so. In the United States, for example, in June 1988, a Brooklyn judge rejected a request by the federal prosecutor to order the extradition to Israel of Abd al Atta (an American citizen suspected of participating in a terrorist attack in the West Bank in April 1986 in which four people were killed). The judge stated that a terrorist attack was a political act that promoted the achievement of political aims and that the action had been carried out as part of the uprising in the West Bank to help realize the PLO's political objectives. According to the judge, this was a political charge that was outside the category of crimes that obligate deportation under the extradition agreement between Israel and the United States.[2]

In fact, the need to define terrorism is reflected at almost all levels of our attempts to contend with terrorism (see Figure 1.1), such as:

- *Legislative action*—The laws and regulations enacted to give security forces the tools with which to combat terrorism. The need to define terrorism in this sphere derives from the desire for legislation specifically related to terrorism, for example, laws that prohibit terrorist activity and aid terrorism, as well as laws that establish minimum sentences for terrorists.
- *Punitive action*—As with legislative action, a definition of terrorism is needed for punishing terrorists if we are interested in imposing specific penalties for involvement in terrorist activity (such as sentences for perpetrators and their assistants, confiscation of finances and equipment, etc.).

  Regarding legislative and punitive action, we must define terrorism in order to distinguish between this type of activity and ordinary criminal activity even though in both cases—terrorism and crime—the act itself may be completely identical. The need for legislation and punishment that distinguishes terrorism from criminal activity stems from the grave danger terrorism poses to society, its values, the government, and the public order (which far exceeds the risk from criminal activity), due to the political nature of such activity.
- *International cooperation*—In order to strengthen cooperative relationships between nations of the world, and to ensure the effectiveness of such relationships, we must reach an international definition of terrorism that will be as widely accepted as possible. This need is reflected, primarily, in the formulation and ratification of international counter-terrorism treaties that prohibit perpetrating terrorist acts, aiding and abetting terrorist activity, transferring funds to terrorist organizations, state support for terrorist organizations, commercial ties with states sponsoring terrorism and, as stated—treaties that stipulate the extradition of terrorists.
- *Offensive action*—The nation struggling against terrorism must be allowed to take the initiative. At the same time, we must ensure that the terrorist organization's operative capacity is as limited as possible. Achieving these objectives requires an ongoing and continuous offensive against terrorist organizations. Naturally, countries trying to defend them-

selves against terrorism win the support of the international community, but countries that launch offensive counter-terrorism attacks are usually vilified and strongly criticized. In order to ensure international support for countries combating terrorism, and perhaps to promote joint offensive action, we must reach an accepted international definition regarding the concept of terrorism.

- *Actions directed towards terrorism-supporting populations*— Often, terrorist organizations need and rely on the assistance of a sympathetic and supportive civilian population. One of the more effective tools for reducing terrorist activity is to eliminate the organization's ability to receive support, aid, and backing from this population. An accepted international definition of terrorism is likely to fulfill this task. When terrorist activity is differentiated from other types of violence, and when it is agreed that terrorism is not legitimate under any circumstances, then it will be possible to insist that these civilian populations withdraw their support of terrorists, and to couple such demands with appropriate punitive and retaliatory measures.

  Defining terror will enable us to define new rules for the domestic and international arena. An organization interested in fighting a state in order to achieve rights or other objectives will have to consider whether to achieve those objectives through terror, or to choose other forms of activity that are not considered illegitimate even if these, too, may very well be violent.

- *Public relations activity*—If terrorism is defined in a way that distinguishes it from other violent actions, it will be possible to initiate an international publicity campaign designed to delegitimize terrorist organizations, cut off their support, and forge a united, international front against them. In order to undermine the legitimacy that terrorist activity enjoys (usually stemming from the world's tendency to identify with some of the political goals of terrorist organizations), we must differentiate between terrorist activity and guerrilla activity, and view them as two distinct forms of violent struggle that reflect varying levels of illegitimacy.

Thus, defining terrorism is aimed at helping the war on terrorism on many different levels. An accepted definition that can serve as a basis for counter-terrorism activity may also motivate a terrorist organization to reconsider its actions and examine whether it truly wants to continue perpetrating terrorist attacks and risk the loss of its legitimacy, the imposition of severe and specific punishment, collaborative international efforts against it (including offensive action), and the loss of its sources of loyalty, support, and aid; or whether it would be advisable for the organization to choose an alternative type of action (guerrilla warfare, for example), for which they would not have to pay such a heavy price.

The need to define terrorism is particularly obvious in light of the deliberate way in which certain bodies (terrorist organizations, states sponsoring terrorism, politicians, journalists, and others) use many different terms to describe, portray, and analyze terrorism. The perpetrators of a particular attack are liable to be referred to simultaneously by different bodies as "terrorists," "guerrillas," "freedom fighters," "revolutionaries," and others—all depending on the perspective of the agency and its interests. For example, when the London *Financial Times* reported on the murderous terrorist attack by Abu-Nidal's group at the airports in Rome and Vienna in December 1985, it used the terms "terrorists" and "gunmen" on the first page of the paper, but on the second page, the term "guerrillas" was used to describe the same incident. This was true for other newspapers in Great Britain as well.[3] This case illustrates the degree to which media coverage can be swayed by the point of view of the journalist reporting on the terrorist activity. Use of the word terrorism is usually reserved for attacks against the population of the reporting agency, while other attacks that take place in foreign countries are often described using different terminology.

Moreover, because there is no clear and accepted definition of terrorism, the term is sometimes used to describe and portray events that have nothing to do with terrorism per se, such as: violence and instilling fear that has no political background, criminal action perpetrated for economic reasons, etc. The use of the term terrorism in those cases is intended to endow these incidents with a negative connotation.

In the past, several attempts have been made to reach an international definition of the term terrorism. It is interesting to note that among the nations that were active in the effort to define terrorism are those known for their clear support of the practice—Syria and Libya. In August 1987, a conference of the Arab League was convened in Damascus in order to formulate a definition of the concept of terrorism for submission to the UN General Assembly. The Syrian foreign minister stated in his speech at the opening session that

Figure 1.1
Defining Terrorism as a Fundamental Counter-Terrorism Measure

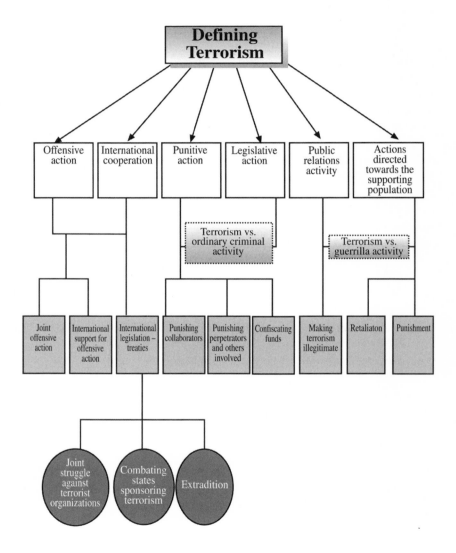

establishment of the committee was "a positive turning point in defending the Arab people from the evil Zionist-Imperialist attacks."[4] In October 1987, the Libyan ambassador to the UN (and chairman of the Legal Committee) officially proposed in the committee that the UN initiate an international conference on terrorism which would be convened, among other things, for the purpose of reaching a new definition of the term "terrorism."[5] Such initiatives are indicative of the tremendous importance that states sponsoring terrorism attribute to its definition, since the attempt to reach a definition will allow them and their allied terrorist organizations to remain free of any direct responsibility for terrorist attacks and to evade punishment.

In January 2001, during discussions of the UN Ad-Hoc Committee on International Terrorism, India submitted a document that attempted to formulate a definition for the term terrorism.[6] In later discussions at the UN, which were held following the events of September 11, that definition was rejected. This example also illustrates the difficulty involved in reaching an internationally agreed upon definition for the term.

According to those who oppose any definition, the decision makers—and certainly security establishments—get along quite well without an accepted definition for terrorism based on the assumption that "when you see terrorism you know it is terrorism." Terrorists, they claim, are essentially committing ordinary criminal acts—they extort, carry out arson, murder, and commit crimes that are prohibited according to the standard penal code. Therefore, they can be brought to justice without needing to define a crime that particularizes terrorism. This argument is also voiced with regard to international legislation. The accepted trend in this sphere during the past decades maintains that terrorism can be addressed more successfully from a legal and normative perspective, through legislation that prohibits specific actions, such as airplane hijackings, diverting shipping and marine piracy, setting off explosive devices, etc.—without the need to define what terrorism is. Nor is there any need to reach agreement regarding the concept of terrorism when it comes to intelligence and military cooperation on an international level, because the discourse between countries focuses on specific organizations and activists, and thus the political dimension of any definition can be avoided.

In contrast with this school of thought are those who support the need for an international definition of terrorism. They believe that not only can terrorism be defined objectively and agreement be reached on the nature of the phenomenon, but that without such a definition it is impossible to mount an effective international fight in this arena. According to this approach, numerous spheres of international cooperation that are not necessarily related just to intelligence or military activity require a consensus on the definition of terrorism. Any attempt to "shut off" the financial sources of terrorist organizations; to prevent the recruitment of new activists to their ranks; to thwart attempts at transferring and "laundering" money; to stop terrorists and extradite them from one country to another; to deal with countries and communities that support terrorism; and above all, to formulate a normative and binding system that defines rules for what is permitted and forbidden, what is legitimate and illegitimate—all these necessitate an unequivocal and objective definition of terrorism based, as broadly as possible, on international agreement.

Without a definition for the concept of terrorism, the world's leaders can gather, as they did at Sharm el-Sheikh in 1996, and in an extraordinary but essentially meaningless gesture, hold each other's hands and wave them aloft and announce together far and wide that they are opposed to terrorism. This, of course, without defining what terrorism is. In the absence of a definition, countries like Syria and Iran can loudly proclaim that they do not support terrorism—they support the "national liberation" of oppressed peoples.

Terrorism and Crime

Before proposing a definition for terrorism based on accepted international norms, we must determine the relevant context for defining the phenomenon. Is it an "ordinary" criminal act that must be judged according to the penal codes? Or is it an act of warfare, and the struggle against it conducted according to the norms and rules relating to war?

Researchers are divided in their opinions of whether terrorism should be considered a criminal act or a political-military act. Brian Jenkins (former head of the Terrorism Project at the Rand Institute) addressed this controversy. According to him, if we look at terrorism as a crime, we will need to gather evidence, arrest the criminals, and put them on trial. This approach provokes problems of international cooperation and is not a suitable response for acts of terrorism perpetrated by a distant organization or a country involved in terrorism. In contrast, if we approach terrorism as warfare, we can be less concerned with the aspect of individual guilt, and an approximate assessment of guilt and intelligence is sufficient. The focus is not on a single perpetrator, but rather on proper identification of the enemy.[7]

Contrary to Jenkins, Gad Barzilai believes that terrorists are, in effect, criminals, and if terrorism-related crimes are treated differently than ordinary crimes, a country's leader could employ tougher, more stringent tools to gain illegitimate political advantage. It appears that Barzilai does not give proper weight to the attribute that distinguishes terrorism from ordinary crime: the political objective that underlies terrorism. As a direct result of the fact that terrorism has a strategic goal, we are left with a situation wherein any step taken to fight terrorism becomes, naturally, a type of political act, although this does not derogate from the legitimacy or need for such an act. Moreover, terrorism as a social crime constitutes a more serious threat to the public order than ordinary crime; it threatens the degree of trust the public places in their system of government, and the citizens' sense of personal and national security, and as such, terrorism must be treated differently from ordinary crime. Barzilai notes the essential and possible danger of the arbitrary use of counter-terrorism measures, but he infers the rule from an exception and in fact, throws the baby out with the bath water. The risk of deliberately misusing counter-terrorism measures for political purposes, as serious as this may be, must not be overwhelmingly translated into foregoing special legislative, punitive or tactical tools to fight terrorism. Quite the contrary, it must force us to be more selective when choosing the steps used to combat terrorism; to find the methods and means that will cause minimum—if any—damage to democratic-liberal values; and to employ certain counter-terrorism tactics to a lesser degree and less often, while making the security network completely subject to public control mechanisms and legal supervision, and creating a system of checks and balances that will prevent decision makers and security agencies from using these steps in an arbitrary and illegitimate manner.[8]

Michal Tzur claims that what distinguishes terrorism from ordinary crime is that it is, in reality, "organized and intelligent crime with totalitarian indications, both in terms of negating the enemy and in terms of the excessive means employed."[9] Tzur also emphasizes the particular difficulty in coping with terrorism using standard punitive perceptions, because the counter-terrorism framework must prevent actions that constitute preliminary stages of the crime and often these are not considered to be crimes in and of themselves, so therefore their perpetrators go unpunished.[10]

The Israeli Supreme Court stated its view regarding the tension between the perception of terrorism as a criminal act or a military act. In its ruling with regard to the Nazal Case (HCJ6026/94 *Abd al-Rahim Hassan Nazal et al. v. Commander of the IDF Force in Judea and Samaria*), Judge Cheshin wrote as follows: "The judge's job is a difficult one. It becomes even more difficult when he must deal with a murderous and despicable attack such as the one before us. The act of the murderer was, in essence—although not in its context nor its formal definition—an act of warfare, and an act that is essentially military in nature must be responded to with action that is also, essentially, military in nature, and by means of warfare." In this context Cheshin was quoting from his previous ruling (HCJ4162/93 *Federman et al. v. The Attorney General et al.*), which referred to the conceptual and legal difficulty in judging someone who caused hundreds and thousands to lose their lives: "The penal code that was created for the daily lives of human society is an inadequate response to this question."[11]

Terrorism and Political Protest

The goal underlying terrorism is always a political goal. Its interest is served by achieving an objective in the political arena: overthrowing the existing government; changing the form of government; replacing officials; revising an economic, social or some other type of policy; disseminating a socioeconomic ideology; religious or nationalistic goals; and so on. Violent actions against citizens with no political agenda is, at most, a purely criminal offense, a felony or simply an act of madness, and bears no resemblance to terrorism. From this perspective, we can, and must, look at terrorism as a brand of extremist political protest.

Ehud Sprinzak concludes, on the basis of academic research conducted over fifteen years, that terrorism is not an unexplained, random attack or the result of some mental disturbance; rather, it is a political phenomenon that can be defined in political terms. Terrorism, according to Sprinzak, is a special case of crisis within the ideological authority, the result of a continuing process of delegitimization of the established society or the government, a process whose beginning is usually neither violent nor based on terrorism.[12] Crenshaw supports this approach, and states that the tendency to employ terrorism or extreme violence against civilian targets is not the outcome of a sudden change in the organization's behavior or the result of a momentary decision by violent individuals, rather it is part of the gradual development that often begins with rhetoric, organizational activity and protest, and escalates to the point of extreme violence.[13]

Looking at terrorism as an extreme form of political protest on the one hand, and as an aggressive act of warfare on the other hand, also influences, among other things, the means needed to cope with the phenomenon – a combination of political, state, social and economic actions in order to address the motives behind the terrorists and their supporters, as well as a military struggle aimed at damaging the operational capabilities of these organizations.

The standard definitions of terrorism currently in use are rife with conceptual difficulties and problems with phraseology. It is no wonder, then, that in an attempt to describe and analyze the activities of terrorist organizations, alternative terms are often used that convey more positive connotations, such as: guerrilla movements, undergrounds, national liberation movements, commando units, etc. Generally speaking, these terms are used unintentionally and without considering the ramifications of the particular definition, but in other cases their use is deliberate and originates with the political and subjective worldview of the one using the definition. With an intentional definition for terrorism, terrorist organizations and their supporters are attempting to distort the unique aspects of their terrorist acts and endow their activities with a legitimate and more positive foundation (using terms that reflect basic values of the liberal-democratic world, such as "revolutionary violence," "national liberation," etc.). Given the attempts to rationalize terrorist activity using political, nationalist or social justifications, we must reiterate that the political goal in and of itself, whatever it may be, does not legitimize terrorist activity. Even when terrorism is relegated to the extreme range of political protest activity, it must be stated that the decision to employ terrorist violence is a deviation from the range of legitimate acts of protest.

An example of an attempt by terrorists to give their activities a positive spin by manipulating their definition is evident in the words of Salah Khalaf, a.k.a. Abu Iyad (former deputy of Yasser Arafat and one of the leaders of the Fatah and "Black September" groups, who was responsible for many terrorist attacks including the death of the Israeli athletes at the Munich Olympics in 1972). Abu Iyad chose to present "terrorism" and "political violence" as two terms that contradict each other, when he said: "By nature, and on ideological grounds, I am strongly opposed to political assassination and more generally—to terrorism. However, unlike many others around the world, I do not confuse revolutionary violence with terrorism, or compare something that constitutes a political act with action that does not…"[14] From Abu Iyad's statement it is possible, once again, to infer that the political motive excuses the activity and that the end justifies the means. Our recognition of the fact that terrorism has a political motivation, and the fact that it is extreme behavior that can be placed along a continuum of expressions of political protest, must not be used in any way to sanction this type of violence.

"Terrorism" versus "National Liberation"

One of the most widespread efforts to forestall a definition of terrorism and to empty it of any meaning, is the attempt to compare terrorist activity with actions aimed at national liberation. Syria, for example, has repeatedly stressed that it does not assist terrorist organizations, rather national liberation movements. According to President Hafez al Assad in a speech made in November 1986 to those attending the 21st Convention of Workers' Unions, "We have always opposed terrorism. But terrorism is one thing and national struggle against occupation is another thing. We oppose terrorism…. Nevertheless, we support the struggle against the occupation being waged by national liberation movements."[15]

The International Islamic League states, in a publication devoted to the definition of terrorism, that terrorism is any injury to a person's body, property, dignity, and even his intellect. Such a blatant extrapolation of the definition effectively drains it of any content or practical meaning. The definition of the International Islamic League adds insult to injury, by stating that when the goal of these acts is justified, the action shall not be considered terrorism. Once again, there is an attempt here to confuse the ends and means in order to justify terrorism. And if that were not enough, the League explains to the readers of its publication that *jihad* will never be considered terrorism because it is aimed at rooting out the expression of terrorism from the world.[16] The League's definition illustrates the need to focus on as narrow a definition as possible, which will stress the most basic, normative common denominator for which broad international consensus can be reached.

The attempt to justify acts of terrorism by using "national liberation" arguments has been reflected in various Arab forums, including also, decisions by the Fifth Islamic Summit Conference held in Kuwait, which stated that "the conference clearly reiterates its absolute faith in the need to differentiate between criminal and oppressive acts of terrorism perpetrated by individuals, groups or states, and between the legitimate struggle by enslaved and oppressed peoples against foreign occupation of any kind. This struggle is sanctioned by heavenly law, human values and international treaties."[17] This, too, is an attempt to justify the "means" (terrorism) by basing it on the "ends" (national liberation). According to this school of thought, the action being carried out is irrelevant—when talking about "liberation from the yoke of foreign conquest" it is not terrorist activity, rather a justified and legitimate act. This background gave rise to the cliché that "One man's terrorist is another man's freedom fighter," which highlights the fact that terrorism is subjective and depends on the perspective and the point of view of the one doing the defining. Leonid Brezhnev, former president of the USSR stated during a visit by Libyan leader Muamar Qaddafi in April 1981, that "the Imperialists have no regard for the will of the people or the laws of history. Struggles for national liberation make them bitter. They call it 'terrorism'."[18]

Surprisingly enough, many in the Western world have accepted the mistaken assumption that terrorism and national liberation are two extremes of a continuum of legitimate use of violence. The struggle on behalf of "national liberation" appears to be the positive and justified extreme of this continuum, while terrorism is the negative and abhorrent extreme. According to this approach, it is impossible for a certain organization to be both a terrorist organization and a national liberation movement.

Those who have failed to understand the difference between these two concepts have actually fallen into the trap set for them by terrorist organizations and their allies, and have tried to cope with the national liberation argument using many different justifications, instead of stating that when a group or organization chooses terrorism, its aim of national liberation does not help it and cannot justify its actions. In this vein, for example, U.S. Senator Henry Jackson stated:

> The idea that one person's "terrorist" is another's "freedom fighter" cannot be sanctioned. Freedom fighters or revolutionaries don't blow up buses containing noncombatants; terrorist murderers do. Freedom fighters don't set out to capture and slaughter school-children; terrorist murderers do. Freedom fighters don't assassinate innocent businessmen, or hijack and hold innocent men, women and children; terrorist murderers do. It is a disgrace that some democracies would allow the treasured word "freedom" to be associated with acts of terrorists.[19]

Benzion Netanyahu also assumed that freedom fighters would not perpetrate acts of terrorism.

> For in contrast to the terrorist, no freedom fighter has ever deliberately attacked innocents. He has never deliberately killed small children, or passersby in the street, or foreign visitors, or other civilians who happen to reside in the area of conflict—the conclusion we must draw from all this is evident. Far from being a bearer of freedom, the terrorist is the carrier of oppression and enslavement.[20]

Naturally, there is no basis for the claim that a freedom fighter cannot perpetrate acts of terrorism, murder, or killing. This approach unintentionally supports the attempt by terrorist organizations to portray the freedom fighter and terrorist as two contradictory concepts, and thus it plays into the hands of terrorists who can argue that since they are acting in order to eliminate those whom they consider to be foreign occupiers, they cannot be considered terrorists.

In fact, the concepts of "terrorist" and "freedom fighter" do not contradict one another. The difference between the two is not a subjective difference based on the definer's perspective, but is an essential difference related to the goals and means used by the perpetrator of the attack. The statement that a particular organization is a terrorist organization is based, as stated, on the way in which the organization's members behave in their attempt to achieve the objectives they have set for themselves, while freedom fighting refers to the goals the organizations wish to achieve. Therefore, a situa-

tion is possible wherein a terrorist organization can also be a national liberation movement working to liberate their homeland from
the yoke of a foreign conqueror.

Injury to "Innocents"

There are times when politicians in countries coping with terrorism also take political advantage of the definition of terrorism. Jenny
Hocking stresses such manipulation by countries in defining terrorism.

> The "threat of terrorism" has two aspects: the general threat to the legitimacy of the
> state, and the more immediate threat—the perception of terrorism as a personal threat.
> The second dimension is the aspect that is manipulated by using the image of terror-
> ism, which is presented by researchers as being "non-discriminatory," "immoral"
> "abusing the rights of non-combatants," "deliberately targeting innocents," and "threat-
> ening the rule of law." Perceiving terrorism in this way has helped enlist public
> support for counter-terrorism measures that may—or may not—protect the public
> from terrorism.[21]

One of the more prominent characteristics of the attempt to endow terrorism with a negative connotation is to describe terrorist
violence as deliberately targeting the innocent. Thus, for example,
Benjamin Netanyahu states in his book, *Terrorism: How the West
Can Win*, that terrorism is the "systematic and deliberate murder,
maiming and menacing of the innocent to inspire fear for political
ends."[22] This definition was changed in Netanyahu's third book,
Fighting Terrorism, where the term "innocents" was replaced by
the term "civilians"—"terrorism is the deliberate and systematic
assault on civilians to inspire fear for political ends."[23]

The problem with using the term "innocents," as well as the sub-
jectivity of the concept, can be found in the statement by Abu Iyad,
who claims that, "as much as we repudiate any action that endangers the lives of innocents, that is, citizens of countries that are not
directly involved in the Arab-Israeli conflict, we feel no pangs
of conscience concerning attacks on Israeli military and political personnel who are fighting and oppressing the Palestinian
people." But at the same time he adds, "Israeli acts of reprisal
usually cause a large number of casualties among Palestinian civilians—particularly when the Israeli Air Force bombs refugee camps
wildly and blindly—and it is natural for us to respond in appropriate ways to prevent the enemy from continuing its slaughter of innocents."[24]

"Innocents" is, indeed, a subjective concept influenced by the point of view of the definer, and thus, it cannot serve as a normative basis for defining terrorism. Anyone who is considered to be innocent by one side, is not necessarily innocent in the eyes of the other side. When defining terrorism, use of the term innocents tenders the definition meaningless, and becomes a tool for political attack. Therefore, we must think of terrorism as injury to civilians, which is an objective term that is defined in international conventions—rather than injury to innocents.

A Proposed Working Definition

In their book *Political Terrorism*, Jongman and Schmid examined 109 definitions for terrorism they received, in response to their request, from leading academic researchers in the field. From these definitions the authors isolated the following definition elements:[25] violence and force—appeared in 83.5percent of the definitions; political goal—65percent; spreading fear and dread—51percent; threat of violence—47percent; psychological impact of terrorism—41percent; discrepancy between targets and victims—37.5percent; degree of consistency, planning, and organization of terrorism—32percent; terrorism as a method of warfare, strategy and tactics—30.5percent.

At the same time, the various researchers were asked to note questions about the definition of terrorism which, in their opinion, were yet to be resolved. The following questions, among others, were received in response:[26] Where is the boundary between terrorism and other forms of political violence? Are state terrorism and resistance terrorism part of the same phenomenon? What is the difference between terrorism and ordinary criminal acts, between terrorism and warfare, between terrorism and insanity? Is terrorism a separate sub-category of violence, oppression, power? Is there such a thing as legitimate terrorism? What aims justify the use of terrorism? What differentiates terrorism from revolution or violent protest? And so forth.

The extent of the confusion regarding the definition of terrorism can be seen from the statement made in May 1989 by U.S. Department of State spokesperson, Margaret Tuttweiler, following a terrorist attack that took place in Jerusalem in which two civilians were killed:

I honestly don't know what the literal definition of terrorism is here. This is undoubt-edly violence…. I don't know how to respond to your question on the definition of terrorism. And I think, if I'm not mistaken, that the State Department has never defined it.[27]

The question that must be asked is: Can we even arrive at an exhaustive and objective definition for the concept of "terrorism?" Is it possible to compose a definition that will facilitate international action against those involved in perpetrating terrorism, and which can serve as an accepted basis for academic research?

The following is a proposed definition of terrorism:

Terrorism is a form of violent struggle in which violence is delib-erately used against civilians in order to achieve political goals (nationalistic, socioeconomic, ideological, religious, etc.).

This definition is based on three elements:

1. *Essence of the action*—the form of violent struggle. According to this definition, any action that does not involve violence is not defined as terrorism (for example, non-violent protest activ-ity, such as strikes, non-violent demonstrations, tax revolts, etc.).
2. *The goal underlying terrorism*, which is always political, that is, a goal aimed at achieving something in the political arena: over-throwing the regime, changing the form of governance, replac-ing those in power, revising economic, social or other policies, dominating and disseminating ideologies. With no political agenda, the action in question is not considered terrorism. Vio-lent action against civilians without a political goal is, at most, a purely criminal act, a felony, or simply an act of insanity that has nothing to do with terrorism. The motive underlying the political end is irrelevant for the purpose of defining terrorism, and it may be ideological, religious, nationalistic, socioeconomic, or anything else. In this context, we should note the remarks made by Stohl and Duvall that motivations are entirely irrel-evant to the concept of "political terrorism." Most researchers do not recognize this, and therefore they tend to present various motives as a necessary explanation for terrorism.[28]
3. *The target of the damage*—civilians. In this way terrorism can be distinguished from other forms of political violence (guer-rilla warfare, popular insurrection, and so on). The proposed definition emphasizes the fact that terrorism is not the result of random damage inflicted on civilians who happened to find them-selves in an area of violent political activity, rather it is directed *a priori* at harming civilians. Terrorism takes advantage of the

relative vulnerability of the civilian "soft underbelly," as well as the tremendous fear and media impact it causes.

For the purpose of achieving as broad an international consensus as possible for the proposed definition, it must be based upon a system of norms and laws of warfare that have already been stipulated through international treaties and have been accepted by most of the world's nations. In other words, in order to reach an accepted definition for terrorism, we must extrapolate from principles of warfare between countries and regular armies with regard to irregular warfare between an organization and a state, or between a regular army and a militia force.

Many nations around the world have agreed on the normative perception (and have even expressed this by signing international treaties) that we must distinguish between two types of personnel involved in military activity. This consensus is reflected in the distinction between "combatants"—military personnel who deliberately target opposing military personnel, and between "war criminals"—military personnel who (among other actions prohibited according to the rules of warfare) deliberately harm civilians (see Figure 1.2). This normative and accepted statement, which relates to military personnel in situations of war allows us to infer the rules of warfare for organizations against a country. The ethical distinction between a fighter and a war criminal requires a similar normative arrangement between a guerrilla fighter and a terrorist. *Terrorism* is, as stated, "a violent struggle in which violence is deliberately used against *civilians* in order to achieve a political goal," while *guerrilla warfare* is "a violent struggle in which violence is deliberately used against *military targets* in order to achieve a political goal."

"Terrorism" and "guerrilla warfare" are often used interchangeably to describe the same phenomenon, but the term terrorism has a negative connotation and seems to involve taking a stand, while the term guerrilla is perceived as being neutral and has a more positive connotation.

One of the problems in using the term guerrilla derives from its ambiguity. Yehoshafat Harkabi distinguishes between "guerrilla fighting" and "guerrilla warfare."[29] In his opinion, guerrilla fighting is a prolonged war of attrition, where the level of violence increases in intensity over time; a war wherein the limitations are blurred with a fluid line of contact; a war that emphasizes the human factor and during which, militia forces become regular forces until victory is achieved, that is, when one side is defeated.[30] Harkabi relates to terrorism as a common element of guerrilla warfare, the starting point of the sequence of violent actions that end with continuous guerrilla warfare against military forces.[31]

Thornton, on the other hand, sees guerrilla war and terrorism as two separate phenomena along a single continuum, and notes five stages in the development of the uprising: pre-violence, terrorism, guerrilla war, conventional war, and post-violence.[32]

Figure 1.2
Definition of Terrorism

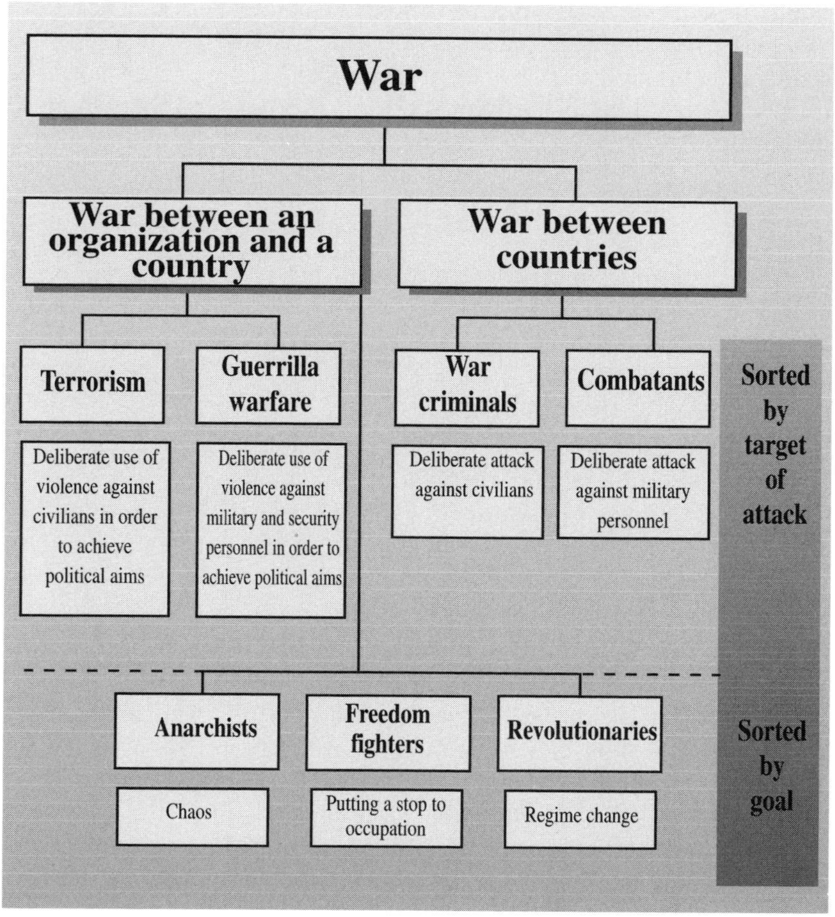

In contrast, Walter Laquer claims that urban terrorism is not a new stage in guerrilla war, but derives from a different tradition. While the aim of guerrilla war is to establish small military units and engage the army in small, local military battles, terrorism operates in the city, clandestinely.[33] Ehud Sprinzak summarizes this concept by saying, "Guerrilla war is a small war, subject to all the rules that apply to big wars. That is where it differs from terrorism."[34] David Rapoport adds that the traditional difference between terrorism and guerrilla warfare is the terrorist's explicit refusal to adopt the accepted, conventional moral limitations that apply to military and guerrilla activity.[35]

As noted, the proposed definition distinguishes terrorism from guerrilla activity according to the target of the attack. The claim that terrorism and guerrilla warfare share a single chronological sequence, although this may have empirical backing, does not contradict the distinction between them on the basis of the proposed definition. An organization may decide to move from the terrorism phase to the guerrilla phase, and thus it will change from a terrorist organization to a guerrilla organization; transition in the opposite direction is equally possible.

For the purpose of defining terrorism, the type of goal the organizations hope to achieve is irrelevant (so long as it is a political goal). Both the terrorist and the guerrilla fighter might strive towards the same goals, yet each one chooses a different means to achieve those goals (see Figure 1.3).

There are several political goals that various organizations (both terrorist organizations and guerrilla organizations) strive to achieve, including: national liberation (liberating territory from foreign occupation); revolution (overthrowing the existing regime); anarchy (creating governmental chaos); changing the accepted economic system, and more. This distinction between means and ends undermines the attempt to consider terrorism and freedom fighting as two different and contradictory phenomena that do not go hand in hand. In effect, according to the proposed definition of terrorism, a certain organization can be both a terrorist organization (if its activities target civilians) and a national liberation movement (if its goal is national liberation) at the same time.

The proposed definition of terrorism is intended to help in the analysis of specific incidents and events, and in determining whether

Figure 1.3
Methods of Operation and Goals in the Violent Struggle
of Organizations against Nations

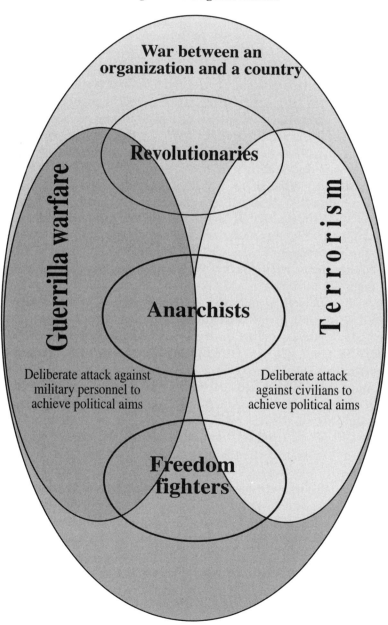

they are terrorist acts or guerrilla actions. The definition therefore, can, and must, serve as a scale for ethical judgment, and a basis for establishing a code of rules, norms, and by-laws for punishing those who perpetrate different attacks.

The question is, does the definition condone guerrilla activity? Indeed, the definition makes a moral distinction between terrorism and guerrilla activity. Presumably, any nation coping with attacks against its military personnel will consider the perpetrators as enemies that must be fought, but it cannot expect the world to come to its aid in a guerrilla war. On the other hand, it can certainly demand that the international community assist in the struggle against terrorism because terrorism constitutes a dangerous breach of international norms and stability, and harms not only the nation under attack, but all nations of the world. Terrorism following the attacks on September 11, 2001, places the peace of the entire world at serious and immediate risk, and obligates the enlightened world to deal with this phenomenon, with no exceptions and regardless of who the perpetrators are and what their grievances may be.

Another question is whether it is possible for nations to employ the methods of terrorism. Many politicians and security personnel in Western and other countries are afraid to adopt a clear and accepted definition of terrorism that is based on the statement that terrorism involves deliberate harm to civilians, for fear that their military actions will also be defined as terrorism under certain circumstances. To all appearances, dropping the nuclear bomb on Hiroshima and Nagasaki could be considered terrorism. In response to the question of the accountability of nations for terrorism, we can state that sometimes nations are no more moral than organizations—sometimes even less so. Yet we don't need the term terrorism to describe the illegitimate actions of countries, because according to international conventions, when a country's representatives deliberately harm civilians in a time of war, they will be defined as war criminals; and when the action takes place at times other than war, we can say that they have committed crimes against humanity. Paradoxically, what is prohibited for nations has yet to be prohibited for organizations. The question of Hiroshima and Nagasaki are irrelevant to the issue of terrorism. The normative test for this action can be found within the context of war crimes. From this perspective, the definition of terrorism neither adds nor detracts, and certainly does not place another normative burden on the country beyond the obligations already placed upon it by virtue of the existing international conventions. The definition of terrorism only allows us to subject the organizations to the same ethical code that determines the rules of war that presently obligate nations.

In an attempt to expand upon the definition of terrorism so that it can also include injury to soldiers, the U.S. Department of State has adopted a definition stating that terrorism is the deliberate use of violence against non-combatants, and not necessarily against civilians. Thus, the United States has extended the definition of terrorism to include injury to military forces that are not on the battlefield, such as an attack against the American warship, the *USS Cole*, in Yemen in 2000, and possibly even attacks against American soldiers in Iraq. Despite the natural tendency of someone who has been injured by terrorism to adopt this broad definition, terrorist organizations and their supporters will argue that in order to achieve their goals, it is impossible to demand that they confront military personnel only when they are armed and ready for battle. According to them, they must have the right to surprise soldiers anywhere they may be found. The State Department's definition of terrorism cannot serve as a sufficiently broad common denominator for international agreement on the definition of terrorism. Only the narrower definition of deliberate injury to civilians solves this problem and enables us to set a clear moral threshold that must not be crossed. This ethical norm is likely to be accepted by both Western countries and Third World countries, and perhaps even by some terrorist organizations.

The proposed definition delineates two phenomena—terrorism and guerrilla warfare—but does not seem to solve the problem of defining the organizations themselves. In order to do so, we may employ either a qualitative or a quantitative index. Those who favor a quantitative index argue that we must consider an organization a terrorist organization only if most of the attacks its members perpetrate, or at least a significant portion of them, can be termed terrorist attacks. Those who favor a qualitative index argue that when an organization deliberately targets civilians, even if it is only once, it has broken a normative rule and regardless of the type of goals it champions and other methods it uses to realize those goals, it should be defined as a terrorist organization.

One way or the other, when organizations perpetrate both terrorist attacks and guerrilla attacks it is, among other things, a direct result of the lack of an accepted, international definition regarding terrorism and guerrilla warfare. If an agreed-upon definition did exist, it would be followed by operational actions by the international community against terrorist organizations, and different types of action against guerrilla movements. If terrorist organizations were forced to deal not only with the nations that oppose them but the entire world as well because they chose to deliberately target civilians, perhaps some of them would choose to suspend attacks on civilians and concentrate on guerrilla attacks against military personnel. If the world learns to employ economic, diplomatic, and military sanctions against states sponsoring terrorism and avoids using these types of threats against those nations supporting guerrilla organizations, then presumably these nations would demand that the organizations discontinue their terrorist attacks and resort to guerrilla actions only, while threatening that their refusal to do so would result in the suspension of the country's support. This demand would change the "cost-benefit" balance for terrorist organizations, which would prefer—or, at least some of them—to abandon terrorism and focus on guerrilla activity to achieve their political aims. Such a change would be a tremendous achievement for the international community in the war against terrorism, and would likely reduce the scope of terrorism around the world substantially, perhaps eliminating it completely.

In conclusion, the proposed definition for terrorism would no longer allow the artificial distinction between "bad terrorism" and "good terrorism" or "acceptable terrorism." In any event, terrorism must be considered a prohibited and illegitimate method of operation, regardless of the intentions and goals of its perpetrators. The ideological underpinnings of terrorism; its religious, political, social or economic motives; the cultural background of its perpetrators—none of this is relevant in determining whether a particular act is to be considered a terrorist act. The principle that guides us, therefore, must be that "terrorism, is terrorism, is terrorism," irrespective of the perpetrator's identity—Muslim, Christian or Jewish—or his motives.

2

Dilemmas in Defining Counter-Terrorism

Any decision maker intending to formulate a counter-terrorism policy must first define the goal behind the war against terrorism—the mission he presents to the security forces and other government bodies taking part in the struggle.

Figure 2.1 illustrates a number of alternative goals that might underlie a nation's counter-terrorism policy. The chart is designed in the shape of a pyramid, divided into three main goals: eliminating terrorism, minimizing damage caused by terrorism, preventing the escalation of terrorism. The pyramid configuration reflects the goal's general outlines and scope (the higher up one goes on the pyramid, the more comprehensive the nation's counter-terrorism goals become). This structure also reflects the premise that if the goal is located closer to the apex of the pyramid, it usually encompasses the goals of the lower levels as well (for example, eliminating terrorism embodies reducing damage from terrorism and preventing its escalation).

Every goal is comprised of a group of several sub-goals:

- *Eliminating terrorism* is likely to be expressed as eradicating the enemy (destroying the terrorist organization itself), removing the enemy's incentive to commit terrorist attacks and use violence against the state and its citizens, or resolving the controversial issue (since the motive behind terrorism is a political one, the solution is also to be found in the political sphere).
- *Minimizing damage caused by terrorism* may include sub-goals such as reducing the number of attacks and/or the number of victims, preventing certain types of attacks (suicide bombings, mass killing, etc.), lessening property damage, etc.

- *Preventing the escalation of terrorism* is based on two sub-goals: (1) *Ensuring that the conflict doesn't spread*—stopping the terrorist organization's growth and development through enlistment of new activists to its ranks, preventing the organization from gaining political achievements in the international arena, blocking or neutralizing support from foreign countries, impeding intensification of the organization's political objectives and efforts; (2) *Making certain the scope of attacks does not escalate*—preventing an increase in the number of attacks and/or victims, stopping more serious types of attacks.

The goals and objectives that decision makers assign to security forces often vary according to changes in the direction of terrorism,

Figure 2.1
A Nation's Strategic Goals in Combating Terrorism

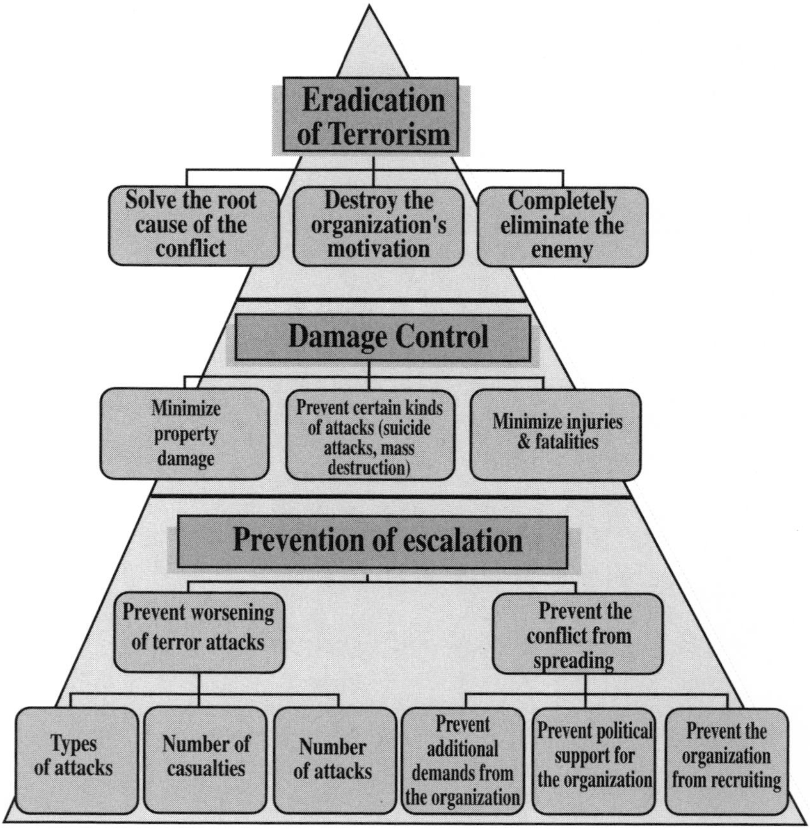

constraints from the international community, multilateral relationships between different nations, and the state's own internal political situation. For example, the strategic goals of Israel's counter-terrorism policy have changed over the years: At the end of the 1960s, immediately following the Six Day War, the goal was to abolish terrorism and uproot it by eliminating the organization's infrastructures and arresting activists in the Gaza Strip and in Judea and Samaria. In the early and mid-1970s, the policy was to deter terrorist organizations from committing terrorist acts by targeting their leaders and activists, including implementing severe reprisals in various countries in the wake of attacks perpetrated against Israel. At the end of the 1970s and in the early 1980s, Israel began to recognize that given the international and regional political constraints as a result of the success of the Palestinian movement on the political level, and in light of the depth and complexity of the Palestinian conflict, it would be impossible to insist on a policy whose goal was to eliminate terrorism solely through military means. Therefore, policymakers sought a more realistic goal—to minimize the damage resulting from terrorism rather than attempting to eliminate the phenomenon itself.

Defining the Goals of Israel's War against Terrorism

In view of the political distinctions between them and their different attitudes towards the threat of terrorism, successive Israeli governments have placed various goals at the root of their counter-terrorism policies.

Examination of the attitude towards terrorism held by Israeli's decision makers over the years shows that they have defined different goals for the war against terrorism, but most of them chose to highlight the limitations behind counter-terrorism objectives and refrained from defining more far-reaching goals such as eliminating or defeating terrorism. In this context, the following goals should be mentioned:

- *Former prime ministers: Yitzhak Shamir*—"simply to prevent and reduce [terrorism]"; *Shimon Peres*—"to place a barrier between terrorism and its people."[36]
- *Former counter-terrorism advisors to the prime minister: Meir Dagan*—"To keep terrorism at a level that doesn't interfere with the public's daily lives"; *Rechavam Ze'evi*—"To keep terrorism on such a low flame that it has no impact on the deci-

sions made by the political echelon"; *Rafi Eitan*—"First of all, prevention...second of all, prevention via counter measures."[37]

- *Former heads of Israeli intelligence networks: Former head of the Israel Security Agency Yaakov Perry*—"A definition we have always used [is]...to eliminate terrorism, to achieve its destruction...everyone knew the truth, that in a proper and effective war we could minimize, but a total solution was impossible";[38] *Former head of the Mossad Shabtai Shavit* believes, on the other hand, that terrorism can be wiped out using offensive means, but the international climate does not allow Israel to do so.[39] Against this background, Shavit explained the goals of counter-terrorism during his tenure as head of the Mossad:

> The hope, and not necessarily at the level of a formal declaration of objectives, but our hope was to exterminate terrorism. We learned and understood that it is really impossible to exterminate terrorism, so the hope—and if you prefer you can call it a strategic goal—was to reduce as much as possible the capability for terrorism and its impact.[40]

With regard to counter-terrorism goals during his tenure as chief of staff, *Amnon Lipkin-Shahak* stated, "our goal, Israel's goal, was, firstly, to reduce the damage to the smallest possible minimum, and hurt them to the maximum." Lipkin-Shahak objects to defining sweeping goals for counter-terrorism, and states that the main goal of the war against terrorism is to keep the terrorism to a level at which it doesn't influence the public agenda:

> Any time that terrorist attacks are kept to a level of sporadic events that don't disrupt the public's agenda or their lives, in my opinion we have won that battle. When terrorism affects the public's day-to-day affairs and the essence of life in Israel, then terrorism has won. Therefore...the goal must be very limited. I would say that preventing terrorist activity is the primary goal.[41]

Former prime minister Benjamin Netanyahu, in contrast with his predecessors, sets the bar higher in the war against terrorism:

> Systematic weakening of Arab terrorism until it has been reduced and suppressed must be, therefore, the main goal of Israel's policy. Any agreement that Israel makes with the Arabs must be adapted to this goal. It must lead to a reduction of terrorism, and not its intensification.[42]

Factors that Influence the Scope of Terrorism and Its Nature

In order to determine the goals underlying counter-terrorism measures, the factors that influence the scope of the terrorism and its nature must first be identified (see Figure 2.2).

Terrorist organizations do not operate in a vacuum—they are influenced by their environment. The surroundings are likely to have an impact on the organization's goals and objectives, its strategy and modes of operation, the motivation and sense of unity of its members. And the scope of the organization's violent activity, its nature and character will also be affected. Among the environmental factors that influence the violent actions of a terrorist organization, the following should be noted:

- *The international community.* Terrorist organizations which, by their very nature, act in order to achieve some political aim, are directly or indirectly influenced by events and processes in the political arena. World wars, local conflicts, the rise and fall of superpowers, economic crises, political and other types of struggles are likely to have an effect on the scope of violent activity committed by a terrorist organization, and the nature of that activity. One of the most important factors in this regard is the amount of support and assistance a terrorist organization receives from state sponsors of terrorism. Many such organizations benefit to a certain degree from the support of various nations. This support may be expressed as political-ideological indoctrination, economic and military aid, operational training and weapons, and even actual assistance in committing terrorist attacks. Any change in the amount of aid the organization receives from the supporting nation can directly influence its capacity to commit violent acts. Removing that support, therefore, can help bring about the elimination of the organization's violent activity, or at least reduce it substantially.
- *Actions of the nation coping with terrorism.* A major factor influencing the scope and nature of terrorism are the steps taken by a nation or regime faced with terrorism. These can take the form of safety and security measures to prevent terrorist attacks, as well as offensive steps carried out against the terrorist organization, its infrastructure, facilities, activists and leaders, in an effort to disrupt and deter the organization's activities. But it is the country's political policy, and not only its operational activities against the terrorist organizations, that is likely to influence the scope and character of terrorism. For example, reaching partial or general arrangements with the organization, gestures and willingness for compromise, and the political positions taken by the government—any of these may motivate the organization to modify its policy.
- *Influence of the supportive population.* Terrorist organizations usually grow and operate within the population whose

aims these organizations claim to represent. This native population serves as the organization's main pool of support and
recruitment. The organizations use these populations to enlist activists, to receive aid and supplies, to seek asylum and
a safe haven, etc. The abetting population allows the terrorist
to behave "like a fish in water," as described in the well-
known essay by Mao Tse-Tung. Therefore, any change in
the support and encouragement the organization receives from
its native population is likely to have a direct impact on the
scope of its violent activities and their nature. (This is why
various actions staged by terrorist organizations often aim to
send a message to the native population, the substance of
which asserts—we are acting in your name and on your behalf, so join in and help us in our activities so we can realize
our shared political aims.)

- *Impact of the interorganizational situation.* In many cases a
single political arena will find itself facing different terrorist
organizations acting to achieve the same political goal, or
similar goals. These organizations may be distinct from one
another, while at other times they are united and cooperate in
various spheres. The connection and reciprocal relations between these organizations (the ideological and personal rivalries between them or, alternatively, the cooperation they
share) have an immediate and direct influence on the scope
and nature of their violent activity.
- Impact of the organization's internal status. One of the most
influential factors on the scope of an organization's violent
activity is its own internal process. This process is affected
by other issues such as personal rivalries within the organization; the establishment and functioning of the organization's
institutions, bodies, and divisions; the sense of connection
exhibited by its members, and the organization's prepared-
ness.

All of these factors have concomitantly influenced the scope and
character of attacks perpetrated by terrorist organizations. This influence is translated, in the final analysis, as an equation with two
variables that determine the level of the organization's violent activity—its level of motivation and its operational capability to carry
out acts of violence.

The motivational component of the terrorism equation is a combination of feelings, desires, dreams of vengeance, on the one hand,
balanced against the rational calculation of interests, external and
internal pressure, and possible outcomes. For example, an organization might decide at a particular point in time to suspend tempo-

Figure 2.2
Factors that Influence the Violent Activity of Terrorist Organizations

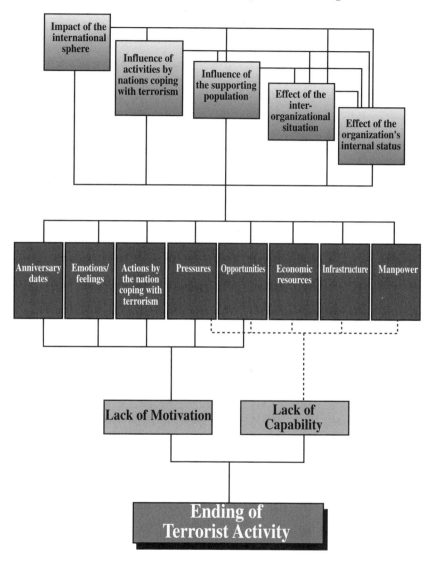

rarily its violent activity for tactical reasons. Alternatively, it could decide to completely abandon terrorism after recognizing the fact that such acts do not promote the interests the organization had hoped to achieve, and may even jeopardize them. Either way, when the organization lacks the incentive to perpetrate terrorist attacks, even if it has the capability to do so, it prefers to refrain from committing such acts.

The second variable that determines the scope of violent activity and its nature is the organization's operational capability. In certain cases, the terrorist organization may endeavor to commit attacks but will not be able to carry them out. Lack of operational capability may be caused by a lack of funding, weapons or fighters, or due to difficulties because of counter-measures being taken against the terrorist organization.

Factors that have a direct impact on the level of the organization's motivation to commit, or refrain from committing, terrorist attacks at any given point in time can be divided into four groups: the impact of pressures brought to bear on the organization, irrational-emotional motives, actions carried out by the nation coping with terrorism, and anniversary dates. To all of the above, we should also add the possibility or opportunity to carry out an attack.

The first group includes, as stated, all of the pressures brought to bear against the terrorist organization, including:

1. *Pressure from the organization's supporting population, that is, the people supposedly represented by the organization*—The native population is likely to have an influence in two opposing directions: support for terrorist attacks at the time in question or a demand that attacks be stepped up, and alternatively, resistance to carrying out attacks at that time. This influence is seen, primarily, with populist terrorist organizations that are very closely connected to the public opinion of its supporting population. Thus, for example, Palestinian public opinion influenced the scope and nature of terrorist attacks perpetrated by the Hamas Movement in the West Bank and Gaza between 1994 and 2004. When public opinion was opposed to carrying out attacks, the Movement was pressured to refrain from committing such action (although this pressure did not always lead to a total cessation of attacks), and when it encouraged and supported terrorism Hamas had an even greater incentive to carry out attacks. The impact of public opinion on Hamas's policy of attacks gave the Palestinian Authority an indirect ability to influence the scope and nature of terrorism through its control of the media and its ability to shape public opinion.

2. *Internal pressures, including those resulting from interpersonal relations within the organization*—that is, the existence of variant ideological streams, differences of opinion regarding the organization's strategic objectives or its tactical goals, arguments

concerning the effectiveness of taking certain political or military steps. Personal competition and rivalries between key figures within the organization are liable to have a tremendous impact on the scope and nature of the attacks of numerous organizations. Thus, for example, personal rivalries in the 1970s between Yasser Arafat's two deputies—Abu Jihad (Khalil al Wazir) and Abu Iyad (Salah Khalaf), who controlled the different terrorist factions within the Fatah organization (with Abu Jihad controlling the Western Sector and Abu Iyad controlling the Special Security Branch and Black September)—led to competition between them and their activists, to see who could perpetrate more significant attacks against Israel.

3. *Interorganizational pressures*—Such pressures are a direct result of competition and rivalry between various organizations operating in parallel within the same supporting population. These organizations, which often claim to represent the same population, compete for the support and public opinion of that population. One of the more prominent examples of this type of interorganizational influence was seen in the late 1980s and early 1990s, between Hamas and the Palestinian Islamic Jihad, which competed for the backing of the same militant Islamic Palestinian public, and tried to win the support of that audience by perpetrating bolder, more elaborate attacks. In fact, one of the reasons for the establishment of the Hamas Movement in 1987 as the military wing of the Islamic Brotherhood movement was the fear by Brotherhood leaders in the West Bank and Gaza that the young, militant organization—Islamic Jihad—would recruit activists from among their ranks who would want to participate in terrorist activity against Israel. Therefore, this such interorganizational competition and rivalry is likely to influence the scope and nature of the organization's terrorist activity. Another type of interorganizational influence could be the attempt by one organization to imitate the success and daring of another organization, even if it has no ideological, nationalist, or other common denominator. Thus we may consider the attacks of September 11 in the United States as symbolizing to other terrorist organizations throughout the world a new, more serious and dangerous threshold of mega-terrorism, which serves to encourage imitation and escalation in various parts of the world.

4. *Pressure brought to bear on the organization by sovereign states*—At times, these may be state sponsors of terrorism who have traditionally aided the organization and who can influence the group's policy of terrorist attacks, or other nations that may exert their influence on the organization, either directly or indirectly, through pressure on state sponsors of terrorism. An obvious example of such power is the influence that Iran—and particularly, Syria—has on the scope and the nature of Hizballah's

activities in Lebanon. Thus, when tensions between Israel and Hizballah intensified, the pressure brought to bear against Syria by Israel, and especially the United States, proved to be effective in preventing escalation and stopping Hizballah's firing of Katyusha rockets from South Lebanon at Israeli civilians in the north. To the impact of pressure from state sponsors of terrorism on the scope and nature of terrorist acts by the various organizations, we can also add pressure that may be exerted on the organization by the nation coping with terrorism. (Due to the substantial impact that all of these pressures can have on the organization's attack policy, we can relate to them as a separate group of pressures and not merely a component of the influence by nations on the organization.)

The second group of influences on the nature of the violent activity of terrorist organizations includes *influences based on the actions of the nation coping with terrorism.* These influences may either be direct and immediate, or indirect and remote. Among these we should note the following:

1. *The scope and nature of offensive and defensive actions taken by the nation against the terrorist organization or other organizations*—the frequency of offensive measures and the degree to which they succeed in damaging the organization's infrastructure, as well as increased motivation for revenge that might be caused as a result of such activity. Thus, for example, Israel's intense offensive activity against Hamas leaders and activists in 2003-2004 led to a serious drop in the organization's success in perpetrating terrorist acts, and the organization's motivation to commit attacks was greater than its ability to act on that motivation. The effectiveness of the defensive actions and the ability to create a barrier between the terrorists' staging areas and populated targets around the country are also likely to reduce the organization's capability to commit mass-victim terrorist attacks. For example, the difficulty that Hamas experienced in perpetrating attacks by moving its activists from the Gaza Strip to Israel motivated the organization in several instances to "import" terrorists from European countries to carry out attacks. In the attack that took place in April 2003, a suicide bomber blew himself up in central Tel Aviv near the American Embassy, and his companion escaped. The two terrorists were citizens of Great Britain, which is where they were recruited by Hamas. They traveled as tourists to Gaza, where they obtained the explosives, and then went to carry out the attacks in Israel, by taking advantage of their ability as tourists to move freely between the Gaza Strip and Israel.

2. *Activity by the nation coping with terrorism*—conducting tactical or strategic negotiations with the terrorist organization, and the country's readiness to make minor or substantial political concessions towards the organization. In this context, we can look at the moderation of terrorist activity by the Fatah organization against Israel between 1994 and 2000, and the self-restraint exercised by the LTTE in Sri Lanka or ETA in Spain after cease-fire agreements were reached with them. At times, the influence on the scope and nature of terrorism is a direct result of alliances the nation signs with neighboring countries in order to cope with terrorism or to block channels of aid and supplies to the organization. For example, pressure exerted by Turkey on Syria that led to the capture of the PKK leader Ocalan, ultimately brought about a cessation of terrorist attacks by that organization.

3. *The country's attitude towards the terrorist organization's supporting population*—humanitarian actions directed towards this population, the ramifications of defensive and offensive assassinations on the civilian population—all these are likely to have an influence on the degree to which the public supports or opposes the terrorist organization, its willingness to contribute and be recruited into the organization, and thus affect the scope and nature of its terrorist acts.

4. *Public statements by political leaders and heads of the security network*—At times, statements coming from key figures in the nation coping with terrorism are likely to be perceived by the terrorist organization as provocations, challenging them to commit terrorist acts in response. On the other hand, moderate statements may be perceived as weakness and could influence the nature of terrorist attacks, causing the terrorist organization to carry out additional attacks so as to force the nation to accede to their demands.

5. *The degree to which the nation can formulate a deterrent force against the terrorist organization*—Deterrence is likely to have a moderating effect on the scope and nature of terrorist acts being carried out against a country because it reduces the organization's motivation—even if only temporarily—to perpetrate attacks for fear of retaliation. However, as we will see below, successful deterrence could have a medium- or long-term effect of increasing the organization's motivation to improve and develop the means, capabilities, and methods that will allow it to ignore such deterrents, and may even tip the scales and serve to deter the nation from acting against it.

The third group of influences is *irrational motives, usually based on the emotions and feelings of the organization's leaders, terror-*

ist activists, and their supporters. This group of motives should include the "boomerang effect"—the desire for revenge following an effective offensive action against the organization. Another motive might be a direct result of feelings of humiliation and anger for nationalist or social reasons, or in light of a personal-family experience.

The fourth group of motives that can influence the scope and nature of terrorism is *anniversary dates.* Various organizations tend to perpetrate attacks at specific times in order to note a historic event; a religious or national holiday; key dates in the organization's past (the day on which the organization was founded, a leader was elected, etc.); significant offensive action that caused serous damage to the organization (the assassination of a leader, a large number of casualties among the membership); large attacks perpetrated in the past by the organization or companion organizations. This is why, for example, some claim that March 11, 2004, the date on which the most serious terrorist attack to take place in Europe's history occurred, the combined railway attacks in Spain, was deliberately chosen to commemorate the date of the most serious terrorist attack in the history of the United States, which took place on September 11, 2001. In many cases, the anniversary is not the actual motive for the attack, but rather, a symbolic link between the date and the operational plan, thereby sending a message to the public while using the date to highlight the attack.

Finally, as stated, in many cases the direct motive for perpetrating an attack in a particular location at a particular time is a result of *exploiting an opportunity*—information collected that points to a possibility for committing an attack, access by one of the organization's activists to a possible target site, operational readiness and having the means necessary to commit the attack. It should be emphasized that the existence or achieving operational capability in itself can serve as an incentive that raises the organization's motivation to perpetrate terrorist acts or to change their nature.

Alongside factors that influence the organization's motivation to commit, or refrain from committing, a terrorist act at a particular point in time, it is important to examine *the factors that influence the capability* of that organization to perpetrate attacks: the quantity and quality of the organization's manpower, the existence of an administrative and operational infrastructure to support the fighting, and the existence of financial means the organization needs to function on an ongoing basis and carry out attacks.

The *manpower* component is one of the basic elements that determine the organization's capability to perpetrate terrorist acts. The organization's ability to recruit activists, to instruct them and train them to carry out their mission, to activate them and send them out to perpetrate attacks—all of this has a direct impact on the organization's success in committing acts of terrorism, and special types of attacks in particular, such as suicide bombings and unconventional attacks. To ensure its ongoing activity the organization needs, in addition to the attackers themselves, professionals in a variety of fields, such as collectors of intelligence information, recruiters, spiritual and ideological leaders, experts to prepare bombs and weapons, as well as administrative and financial personnel, collaborators and supporters.

Another element that affects the scope and nature of the attacks perpetrated by the organization is *the existence of an operational and administrative infrastructure*, such as training camps and bases, recruiting and representational offices, locations where terrorists can escape and hide out, front-line war rooms, administrative and operational vehicles, and various weaponry. Many organizations, such as Hizballah, the different Palestinian groups (e.g., Fatah and Hamas), the IRA and others have had, at various times, an extensive infrastructure and their administrative and military ranks numbered in the thousands. All of these require vast, ongoing financial resources and economic means for the proper management of the organization, in addition to the cost of the organization's operational and administrative activities, which require paying salaries to hundreds and thousands of activists, purchasing weapons, infrastructure facilities, vehicles, miscellaneous operational expenses, etc. Many terrorist organizations place huge sums of money on activities to "win over" their supporting population: activities involving political and religious indoctrination, education, health, welfare, compensating families of terrorist casualties, and various types of humanitarian activities. *Financial resources*, therefore, constitute one of the key factors that influence the organization's capability to perpetrate attacks, and the nature of those attacks.

Thus, any attempt to influence the scope and nature of the terrorist acts of a particular organization by reducing its capability to carry out such acts requires a simultaneous attack on these three factors: the organization's manpower, its infrastructure, and its financial resources.

Dominance of the Military Component in Counter-Terrorism Policy

Terrorism is, therefore, a political-military action that requires simultaneous use of military means, together with state-political-social-economic measures. The question is: How dominant should the military component be within the counter-terrorism policy as a whole?

The level of dominance a nation assigns to the military component of its counter-terrorism policy is a direct result of its overall attitude towards the phenomenon. One school of thought prefers carrying out military actions against terrorist organizations, while another school of thought opposes military action and sees this as an inducement that only escalates and exacerbates terrorism. Between these two attitudes there is a third approach, which maintains that military action and state-political action must be combined in order to form a unified policy that strives to eliminate the problem.

The experience of various countries in contending with terrorism illustrates the need to manage simultaneously an overall campaign in every possible sphere of activity. For example, during the first half of the 1980s, Franco's regime in Spain failed to cope with the rise of Basque nationalism and the growth of the ETA by intensifying its oppressive behavior and using military and security measures. Not only did this policy not eliminate the national hopes of the Basques, it served to speed up the development of the movement this policy had hoped to destroy.[43] On the other hand, the single-minded approach towards international terrorism as a political problem—an attitude that characterized France's policy until the early 1980s—did not prove successful, either. France, which adopted a "doctrine of political asylum" in an attempt to prevent international terrorist attacks on its land by making French territory "neutral," was forced to change its policy after France itself became a target of terrorist attacks.[44] Great Britain, which understood the problem of using military means, tried to avoid involving its military forces in counter-terrorism assignments as much as possible.[45] In Israel, too, this issue has become quite timely and is reflected in the comments made by *Aharon Yariv*, former head of military intelligence, regarding Israel's counter-terrorism policy. In his view, the desired goal of this policy is, naturally, putting a stop to terrorist activity, but since the roots of Palestinian terrorism and its aims are political, it is impossible to eliminate Palestinian terrorism solely by military means, because this requires severe measures that would not meet internal and international legal and political restrictions.[46] In spite of this, the main efforts of Israel's war against terrorism in the 1970s and 1980s were expended in military actions against terrorist organizations and their supporters in various spheres, particularly in Lebanon and the West Bank.[47]

The considerations that have characterized many of Israel's policymakers in the counter-terrorism field on the eve of the war in Lebanon (1982) and in its early stages are reflected in the response given by Rafi Eitan to the question of whether terrorism could be eliminated via military means: "First of all, the answer is affirmative. It depends on what you are up against. If you take the history of terrorism in the world, the answer is affirmative. All of the organizations that arose in the fifties, the sixties and a few in the seventies—were eliminated by force."

Following the war in Lebanon, eliminating terrorism was no longer the declared goal of Israel's policy; this was replaced by the goal of reducing the dimensions of the phenomenon and its ensuing damage. The Palestinian popular uprising (*intifada*) at the end of the 1980s led to a further devaluation in the importance of the military component as part of Israel's counter-terrorism policy, and it seems the political and security echelons came to a sobering realization regarding the possibility of eliminating terrorism through military means.

Former head of the Israel Security Agency Carmi Gilon does not accept the claim that the change regarding the dominance of the military component took place specifically in the wake of the *intifada*. In his words:

For many years the Israel Security Agency—as a professional body—was of the opinion that the Israeli-Palestinian conflict had no military solution. There are those who feel this belief is the result of the *intifada*, but that isn't the case. To the best of my knowledge, the highest professional levels at the Israel Security Agency tended to believe this even during the first few years following the Six Day War. Nevertheless, this thinking did not stop the Israel Security Agency from doggedly and tenaciously fighting Palestinian terrorism, according to the instructions of the Israeli government—and political organization in the West Bank, too.[48]

Benjamin Netanyahu, as an adherent of the hard line, does not ignore the possibility of destroying terrorism using military means. In answer to the question of whether it is possible to eliminate terrorism via military means, Netanyahu said, "Why not? Certainly…you have to ask whether you can eliminate crime using the police? No one would consider asking such a question on criminal issues…"[49]

It appears that the solution to the controversy between these two schools of thought regarding the dominance of the military component and the practical feasibility of eliminating terrorism using military means depends on the nature and essence of the terrorist organizations we are facing, the international and internal-political environment and conditions, and the military-intelligence-operational capability of the nation's security agencies.

For example, when discussing a "skeleton-organization" consisting of several dozen activists, a severe and effective military blow aimed at the organization's soft underbelly—such as the arrest or elimination of the organization's leadership, destruction of its operational infrastructure, etc.—is at times liable to bring about the organization's destruction. This was the case in the 1970s, when Italian security forces began operating against activists from the "Red Brigades," and their German counterparts initiated action against "Bader-Meinhoff." But when the terrorist organization is a popular organization that involves thousands of activists and enjoys an extensive support base—which also serves as a never-ending human pool of manpower reserves—military action may, at most, reduce the phenomenon and its resultant damage, but will not eliminate it altogether. In these cases, the importance of a combined military-intelligence-political effort to solve the terrorism problem becomes even greater.

To sum up, the military component should not be discounted as a legitimate and effective means for eliminating terrorist attacks, reducing their damage, and hurting terrorist organizations. Yet, at the same time, we must examine the terrorists' demands, the degree to which they may be reasonable and legitimate, the extent of the damage that may be caused to the country's vital interests if those demands are not met, the chance for achieving a compromise solution acceptable to all sides, and the impact on any extremist organization that will result from any compromise. Concomitantly, we must assess the nation's capability to prevent terrorist organizations from achieving their interests and goals over the long term. All of these will enable us to determine the relationship between the military and political aspects of the nation's counter-terrorism policy.

The Counter-Terrorism Equation

The terrorism equation is, as stated, a combination of the motivation to perpetrate terrorist acts and the ability to act on that motivation. These two essential conditions determine the scope and nature of past, present and future terrorism. From the terrorism equation, we can extrapolate a counter-terrorism equation. When combating terrorism, one must carry out various types of activities aimed at reducing or eliminating the terrorist organizations' ability to perpetrate attacks, and activities aimed at reducing or eliminating the terrorists' motivation to carry out attacks. Naturally, the hope is to diminish both of these variables, but the principal dilemma in fighting terrorism is the fact that the more successful one is in carrying out actions that damage the terrorist organizations' ability to perpetrate attacks, the more we can assume that their motivation will only increase. Figure 2.3 illustrates this dilemma and presents the necessary counter-terrorism combination between the means to reduce operational capability and to reduce motivation to commit terrorist acts.

The "Terror level" line in the figure represents the line above which it is possible that terrorist attacks will take place, and below which terrorist acts cannot be carried out. The motivation line represents the level of motivation of a particular organization to carry out attacks at any given point in time, while the operational capability line represents the organization's ability to carry out an attack at that particular time.

The figure starts out with the motivation of a group of people to achieve a particular political aim (A). At first their level of motivation is lower than the threshold needed in order to decide to perpetrate terrorist attacks, but, for one reason or another, that group of people decides to employ violent means against civilians, that is, terrorism, in order to achieve its aims. This is when motivation rises above the minimum threshold for perpetrating terrorist attacks (B). At this point, the group of people who have banded together into

Figure 2.3
The Terrorism Equation

Terrorism = Motivation + operational capability

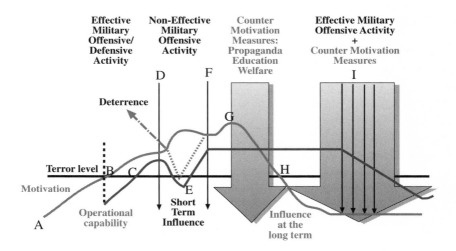

an organization begins to attempt to gain capabilities that will en-able it to act on its motivation to perpetrate terrorist attacks. When these capabilities exceed the minimum required for committing ter-rorist acts (when they cross the "Terror level" line), the organiza-tion is liable to perpetrate attacks (C). At this point, the nation coping with terrorism takes effective offensive activity against the terrorist organization (D). Such activity diminishes the organization's op-erational capability and the more focused and successful this action may be, the more likely it is to reduce the organization's capability below the terror line—to the minimum capability needed to commit terrorist acts (sometimes defensive activity can also reduce the ter-rorist organization's operational capability—for example, the fence that Israel is building, between the west bank and its densely popu-lated areas, has proven itself as a productive defensive measure in reducing the level of terrorists attacks in Israel). But the influence of the offensive activity, no matter how effective it is, is usually short term and after a certain period of time the organization works to repair the damage it suffered and compensate for the damage to its operational capability (E). Then the capability line begins to go up once again, until it crosses the terrorism threshold. At the same time, as stated, the offensive activity raises the organization's motivation to continue perpetrating, and perhaps even to escalate, terrorist activity in retaliation and in response to the country's actions. The rise in motivation stabilizes after some time at a level that is higher than it was prior to the nation's offensive activity.

When the country carries out non-effective offensive activity against the terrorist organization (F), the organization's operational capability is not damaged at all, and its motivation to carry out revenge attacks only increases.

Planning and carrying out effective offensive counter-terrorism activity is a complex task and difficult to achieve, but this difficulty is negligible compared with that of carrying out activity to counter an organization's motivation for terrorism. It would appear that the ultimate counter-motivation measure would be to accede to the political demands of the terrorist organizations. But giving in to terrorism, even without getting into the substance of the organization's demands, cannot and must not be a relevant alternative to coping with terrorism, if only because such compromise could whet the organization's appetite to increase its demands on the nation and encourage other organizations looking to achieve their own political aims to use violence and terrorism in order to achieve those aims. In spite of all this, taking steps to reduce the motivation for terrorism is essential when formulating a sound and effective counter-terrorism policy. Such steps might include: humanitarian actions aimed at the organization's supporting population; social welfare activities; education and publicity within this sector; negotiating with public representatives of the organization's supporting population—those who oppose terrorist activity or who, at least, are not involved in committing attacks and are not secretly in contact with those who are, etc. All these activities are aimed at mitigating the conflict, attempting to bring about a solution or an interim agreement through non-violent means, to win people over, to demonstrate that there is a way out. While the offensive counter-terrorist activities may have immediate, tangible results, counter-motivational activities will make themselves felt only in the long term.

Only in the years—or even generations—to come will it be seen whether these actions were effective in lowering the level of motivation to carry out terror attacks. As far as the country is able to take counter-motivation measures, then the level of motivation to perpetrate terrorist acts drops (G). This drop in motivation doesn't necessarily represent the feelings of the terrorists themselves, but primarily, the feelings of the organization's supporting population. Steps taken to counter motivation must be directed, first and foremost, towards this population in order to prevent their support for terrorism, to isolate the terrorists, and make it easier to undertake offensive measures against the organization's hard core. In essence, the goal of counter-motivation measures is to distance the terrorists from their supporting population. The more effective the counter-motivation measures, as stated, the more we can expect a decline in the level of motivation to perpetrate terrorist attacks over time, until the level dips below the terror threshold (H). However, a decline in motivation does not impinge on the level of capability to commit terrorist attacks. This may be compared with someone sitting on a barrel of explosives, where the lack of attacks is the result of limited motivation but the ability to perpetrate attacks is higher than the threshold needed to carry them out. In this case, any factor that causes a temporary rise in motivation—offensive activity by the nation, interorganizational or intraorganizational relationships, external pressures, etc.—without restricting the operational capability, will lead to a terrorist attack or a series of attacks. Therefore, the combination needed in an effective counter-terrorism campaign is counter-motivation activity to distance terrorists from their supporting population, together with repeated offensive activity against the terrorist organization's hard core, its leaders, perpetrators, and its physical and financial infrastructure in such a way that the organization will not be able to recover and improve its operational capability between one blow and the next (I).

Defining a Counter-Terrorism Policy

After defining the goals of counter-terrorism measures and analyzing the dominance of the military component in a counter-terrorism policy, we come to the question of whether the decision maker should define a specific and clear policy, or whether it is enough to have several plans of action that reflect cumulative experience in the field—a kind of counter-terrorism handbook.

On the one hand, declaring a specific counter-terrorism policy is likely to define for the nation's security forces, in the clearest possible manner, the goals of the war on terrorism and the best way to achieve them. By outlining such a policy, the decision maker conveys a message and a demand for security forces to meet the expectations of the political leader. On the other hand, the very defining of a policy could jeopardize the dynamism needed to adapt the knowledge and experience gained in the counter-terrorism field to changing conditions and to the environment, as well as to the changing nature of terrorism itself.

Those who endorse the approach that decision makers should define a nation's counter-terrorism policy believe that defining the goal will ultimately neutralize, at least to a certain extent, public pressure that is likely to be aimed at the political leader, particularly following a terrorist attack. Crenshaw states that a considerable proportion of counter-terrorism policies are defined and implemented when public emotions are at their peak, in the wake of terrorist acts. In this situation, although the best course of action may be to ignore terrorism, many democratic nations find themselves forced to respond lest they lose credibility among their supporters. According to Crenshaw, "governments cannot refuse to play the game because too many people are watching.[50] It is interesting that Crenshaw actually supports this argument with the Israeli example, where—in her assessment—the Israeli government was forced to respond after each attack due to public pressure. Indeed, an examination of Israel's counter-terrorism activity shows that Israel had no written policy, or even a consistent strategy, when it came to counter-terrorism. Different governments serving in office may have used similar counter-terrorism measures, with regard to offensive, defensive, and punitive actions; but there was a difference in the extent to which these measures were employed, the timing of such activity, and their emphasis. Perhaps avoiding the formulation of a written counter-terrorism policy derived specifically from the need to maintain greater flexibility in decision-making, and the desire not to appear as a government that cannot meet the strategic principles it outlined for itself.

Another question that must be answered when formulating a counter-terrorism policy is whether decision makers should announce the outlines and principles that underlie their policies and decisions. Should a public counter-terrorism policy be adopted? On the one hand, a stated, consistent, and unambiguous counter-terrorism policy would make it clear to the terrorist organizations' activists and supporters that a response can be expected if they deviate from the rules the nation has defined, and this might contribute towards deterring the terrorists and may even prevent attacks. Knowing in advance what the nation's response will be if and when a terrorist act is committed is likely to serve as a "red line" that terrorist organizations might hesitate to cross. On the other hand, however, publicizing the principles underlying the counter-terrorism policy could limit decision makers' discretion to act and maneuver. The public might perceive any change in policy as giving in and "surrendering" to terrorist organizations, and may even make decision makers pay a heavy political price for such action.

It is generally recommended that a nation's counter-terrorism policy not be made public. General guidelines can be defined publicly, explaining to the population the government's goals for anti-terrorism activities, but decision makers should allow themselves sufficient maneuvering room and ensure an appropriate response to the dynamic nature of terrorism, one that can be adapted to changing conditions and circumstances.

Decision makers would be wise to adopt a general framework for a flexible counter-terrorism policy, one that enables rapid transition from one tactic to another, in accordance with needs. This type of policy should allow decision makers, at different times, to place special emphasis on a variety of key counter-terrorism actions—intelligence, offensive or defensive activity, deterrent or retaliatory measures, legislation, education, and international cooperation—all in accordance with the nature and scope of the terrorist acts the nation is facing at that point in time. The decision makers should define the goals of such a policy and formulate rules and preferred methods of operation, without delineating this policy with a rigid, written strategy.

3

Intelligence Dilemmas in the War on Terrorism

Many researchers are at odds over the effectiveness of various counter-terrorism measures, but there appears to be a consensus concerning the supreme importance of intelligence activity for preventing terrorist attacks.[51] In this regard, Alex Schmid states that intelligence activity stands at the forefront of the struggle against terrorism.[52] Ken Robertson considers the advantages of the constant and proper use of intelligence measures in all aspects of coping with terrorism. According to Robertson, intelligence can help to: identify those engaged in terrorism at all levels of involvement and reveal their safe havens and sources of recruitment; track down their weapons, channels of supply, and methods for funding terrorism; warn against future attacks and thus, prevent them; manage crisis situations by transmitting the information decision makers require; provide information necessary to carry out counter-terrorism actions; disrupt terrorist organizations' communications networks; and more.[53]

David Charters, in one of the more prominent articles on this issue, divides counter-terrorism intelligence into three categories: warning intelligence, operational intelligence, and criminal-punitive intelligence. Early warning intelligence is aimed at removing the element of surprise and enabling security forces to organize and safeguard possible targets, and to implement other preventive measures. Operational intelligence includes information that aids security forces in locating and identifying terrorist organizations and terrorists, and recognizing their sources of power and resources in such a way that will allow them to plan operational measures against the terrorists. Criminal-punitive intelligence provides the evidence needed in court in order to convict the terrorists. Charters notes that these three types of intelligence aim at providing answers to the fundamental intelligence questions: who, what, where, when, why, and how. In his view, the focus must be on intelligence-gathering in two domains: strategic intelligence and tactical intelligence. Strategic intelligence includes, among other things, information regarding the identity of organizations; the identity of their leaders, activists, and assistants; the organizations' ideology and motives; hierarchical structure and operational frameworks; their policies and methods for perpetrating terrorist attacks. Charters emphasizes that formulating a strategic assessment is vital for preparing an effective plan of action against the terrorist organizations. However, strategic intelligence plays another key role—it is the starting point for gathering tactical intelligence which includes, among others: details of concrete attacks being planned (type, method, weapons, target, date, etc.). Once the terrorist attack has been committed, explains Charters, it is the criminal-punitive intelligence that becomes most important, in order to locate the perpetrators of the attack and those responsible, and to enable their capture and sentencing in court.[54]

Allan Behm emphasizes a different angle regarding the critical importance of intelligence in counter-terrorism measures. According to Behm, the traditional analytical formula places prevention and response at two opposite extremes in the range of counter-terrorism activity. It would seem possible to define counter-terrorism goals in various places along this range of activity, and to determine the resources to be invested in each channel according to needs and their location within this range. But Behm stresses that in contrast with the common wisdom, the model is not linear and the intelligence component plays a dual role: in preventive action and for responsive-operational action.[55]

Martha Crenshaw notes the need for accurate intelligence in order to facilitate pre-emptive strikes—preventive action against terrorist organizations or reprisals aimed at deterring organizations from committing additional terrorist acts.[56] Shabtai Shavit refers to Israel's counter-terrorism experience and also emphasizes the importance of intelligence as a major element when he says:

> Good intelligence is, in my opinion, more than 50% of the solution to the problem.... The better your intelligence, the more you can diminish or limit the force of the other weapons you employ against terrorism.[57]

Intelligence-gathering is an essential and preliminary step for almost any counter-terrorism activity (see Figure 3.1). Basic intelligence includes collecting information about the structure of the terrorist organizations, their activities, activists, hierarchy, resources, ideology, assistance they receive from state sponsors of terrorism,

Figure 3.1
The Place of Intelligence in Counter-Terrorism Strategy

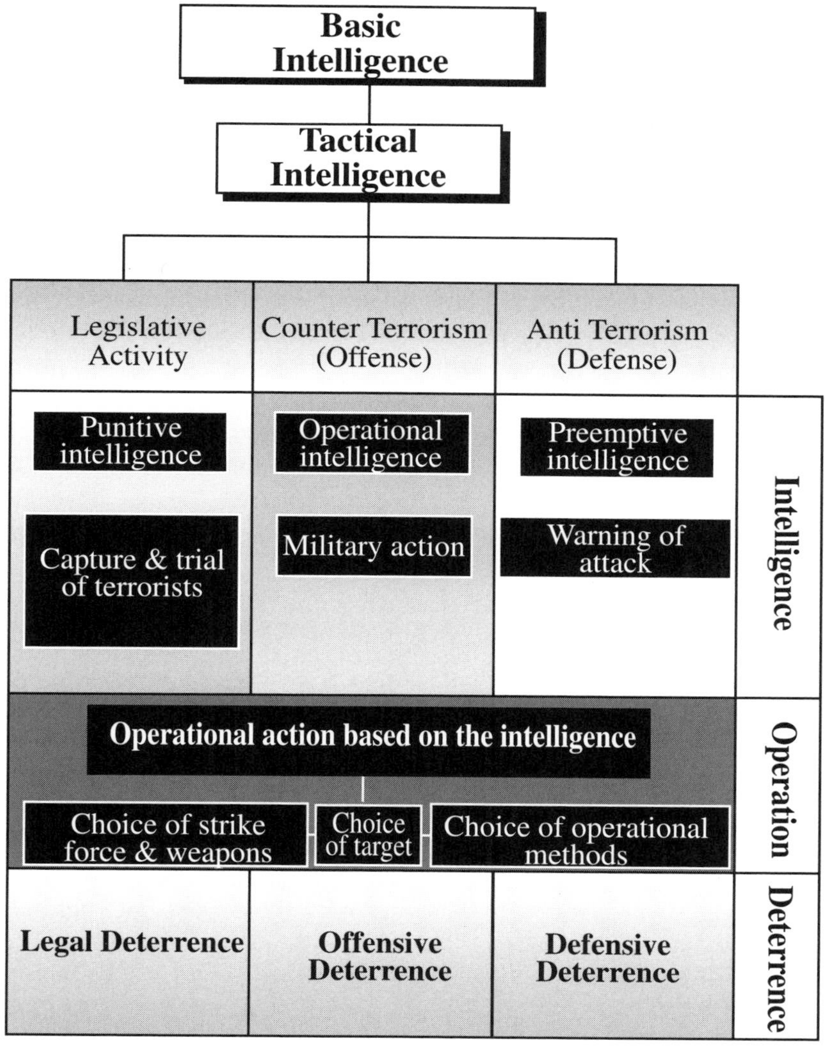

etc., and constitutes an important database with which one can analyze and understand tactical intelligence.

A preliminary requirement for any operational action is tactical intelligence: offensive, defensive, or legal-punitive. In an offensive action, tactical intelligence will be translated into information required for military operations; in defensive action, tactical intelligence becomes preventive intelligence, a means of deterring a particular terrorist attack; regarding legal-punitive action, tactical intelligence is an essential element for locating suspects, bringing them to trial and convicting them. For these three types of activity, tactical intelligence is the basis for defining the planned goal, determining the method of action and readying an operational plan, and preparing the forces and means needed to carry out the mission. It is also an important basis for creating a deterrent with each of the aforementioned actions: offensive deterrence, defensive deterrence, and punitive deterrence. The more accurate the intelligence and the more successful the resultant action, the greater a deterrent that action becomes. A typical example of how essential preliminary intelligence information can be is evident in the cases of individual offensive action—"targeted killings." In these cases, very accurate intelligence data is required, almost intimate information—in real time—in order to ensure the success of the action and reduce the chance that innocent civilians will be injured during its implementation.

Intelligence agencies have a variety of sources for gathering data, and these include:

- "Humint"—intelligence gathering using human sources: agents planted in the terrorist organization; defectors from the organization; special recruits from the organization's operational, political or social frameworks; and activists from the organization who have been captured and arrested.
- Technical intelligence—including aerial photography, signal intelligence ("sigint"), listening in on communications networks, etc.
- Material intelligence—which is likely to include, *inter alia*: fingerprints; blood, hair or tissue samples; examples of clothing, tire tracks, weapons that may have been left behind; documents that were seized, etc.
- Open source intelligence—information from open media-based and academic sources.

Many researchers (see Hoffman and Morrison-Taw, and Carver)[58] emphasize the importance of humint sources in intelligence-gathering regarding terrorist organizations and their intentions, but obtaining information of this type raises special problems that are unique to counter-terrorism.

Employing Human Intelligence Sources ("humint")

The importance of the "humint" aspect (short for *hum*an *int*elligence) of intelligence-gathering for the war against terrorism can, at times, raise moral-legal questions, the substance of which involves the need to use an intelligence source who is, himself, involved in something illegal. It should be recalled that when the intelligence source operates as part of the terrorist organization, he may find himself forced to take part in illegal activity. This requirement might be an "initiation test" or a "test of loyalty" towards the terrorist organization. The desire to establish the source's standing within the terrorist organization and have him rise through the organizational hierarchy may place his handlers in a difficult position—what should or shouldn't intelligence agents do in order to enhance their position within the organization and establish their reliability? Can they be involved in the organization's illegal activity, or even initiate such action? In a secret appendix attached to its conclusions, the Shamgar Commission (an Israeli commission that was established in order to investigate the assassination of the Israeli prime minister, Yitzhak Rabin) stated that in several cases, Israel Security Agency agents operated in contravention of the law, believing that by acting as ISA agents they were exempt from prosecution. In light of this, committee members warned the ISA against "giving intelligence sources in the field a free hand."[59] Such statements were a direct criticism against the actions of ISA agent Avishai Raviv who headed the extreme right-wing movement "Eyal" and who was alleged to have been in contact with the assassin who shot Prime Minister Yitzhak Rabin.

From a moral-ethical point of view, it seems the answer to this issue is that agents should not be employed if their operation necessitates illegal activity or actions that could harm others, unless such actions are carefully controlled and it is clear from the outset that no actual damage will be committed. But a blanket decision of this nature is liable to jeopardize the ability to use such agents, because the terrorist organization may demand an illegal act as an initiation test for acceptance into the organization, in an attempt to rid its ranks of potential intelligence agents. The criteria proposed for solving this dilemma are, therefore—weighing the substance of the crime the agent must commit and the extent of the risk, that this crime may entail casualties or property damage, against the benefit of exposing the organization's activities and preventing its attacks. In the face of such a dilemma, we must enable a high level body with the necessary legal background and operational knowledge, such as the attorney general, to use its own considerations regarding the question of whether to permit the use of the intelligence agent.

The question of Avishai Raviv, leader of the Eyal organization, poses another dilemma—should security forces even be permitted to recruit leaders of terrorist organizations as agents? Are they entitled to use people who, by virtue of their position, initiate and direct terrorist activity and illegal acts? The use of an intelligence agent who serves as head of an organization that perpetrates violent and illegal acts could be considered as direct or indirect involvement in the initiation, preparation and perpetrating of such acts, and as such it is extremely risky. Therefore, operation of agents at this level should be avoided.

In addition to the specific issues associated with using human intelligence sources, the matter of intelligence gathering for counter-terrorism purposes raises several general dilemmas. Head of the Mossad Meir Dagan highlights one of these dilemmas, which he refers to as "the limited shelf-life of the intelligence source." Dagan claims that intelligence which is gathered regarding a hostile nation is saved for a long period of time, and strategic use is made of it on rare occasions, in time of war. This is not true in the war against terrorism. Since the goal in this case is to thwart terrorist attacks, the intelligence use is operational and occurs on a daily basis.[60] The very act of using the intelligence information received, both to prevent intended terrorist attacks and to plan and carry out offensive counter-terrorist actions, presents the tangible danger that the intelligence source will be exposed by counter-intelligence agencies or by the terrorist organization itself. For example, if intelligence information is received that someone intends to commit a terrorist attack against a particular target, and based on this the terrorist is subsequently arrested, or road blocks are placed along the way to the target and security measures are beefed up at the target itself, then this signals to the organization that its intentions were exposed and the enemy managed to place an intelligence source inside the organization. It is no wonder, therefore, that the first thing terrorists often do following an offensive attack by an enemy is to begin a comprehensive and extensive internal investigation to root out the intelligence source that revealed the vital information.

Fundamentally, the dilemma regarding the short shelf-life of the intelligence cannot be resolved. The pressing need to use the existing intelligence source in order to save human lives usually puts the question of the life span of the intelligence source as a second priority. Naturally, one can try to safeguard the life of the source by adhering to strict field security rules and using operational actions aimed at misleading the enemy and protecting the source's life. For example, upon receiving information about plans to attack a particular target, security can be beefed up at several similar targets in different areas in order to limit the fear that such security measures would expose the intelligence source. But ultimately, any operational action that is based on concrete intelligence information involves a risk to the intelligence source himself. A prominent example of this is in the problematic relationship that developed between Israeli intelligence agencies and their Palestinian counterparts following establishment of the Palestinian Authority.

Intelligence Cooperation between Israel and the Palestinians during the 1990s

With the founding of the Palestinian Authority in 1994, the importance of intelligence information increased dramatically. So long as the IDF controlled the areas in which the terrorists had organized and prepared their attacks (the West Bank and the Gaza Strip), it was capable of preempting their actions during the preliminary preparation and organization stages. Furthermore, ongoing security activity in the area under IDF control (without intelligence reports) often prevented attacks. But once the IDF left the territory of the Palestinian Authority during implementation of the Oslo Accords with the Palestinians and 1994, and free passage was permitted for almost all people and goods between the West Bank and Israel, in many cases the security forces had to rely solely on intelligence in order to avert terrorist attacks.

Moreover, prior to the establishment of the PA, Israel could gain the cooperation of the Palestinian intelligence agents by offering them benefits, permits, and jobs, or by threatening to revoke certain privileges. Control of the territory for Israel's intelligence services made it possible to gather vital information in the war against terrorism. But Israel's withdrawal from the autonomous areas turned the tables. The Palestinians' motivation to pass along vital information to Israeli intelligence services disappeared completely, certainly in light of the bitter fate of those who were suspected of collaborating with Israel during the intifada years (1987-1990) and were hounded by terrorist organizations, and due to efforts by Palestinian intelligence services to track down Israeli agents in the West Bank following the establishment of the PA.

In January 1995, Chief of Staff Lipkin-Shahak was already prepared to admit that "we have no response for dealing with suicide bombers. Eight months have passed since we left Gaza and we have fewer intelligence sources."[61] In September 1995, the head of the Research Department of Military Intelligence, Brig. Gen. Ya'akov Amidror, was more decisive than his predecessors when he said, "Israel's intelligence capability in the Gaza Strip has dropped to zero, and a similar situation is likely to take place in Judea and Samaria when we hand over control to the Palestinian Authority."[62]

This serious blow to the intelligence capability of Israel's security forces in the territories controlled by the PA made them highly dependent upon the PA's intelligence and security services. This is apparent in the statements made by official spokespersons that, following the Oslo Accords, repeatedly stressed that cooperation with the PA on intelligence issues was necessary during this period of time. The vast number of Palestinian security and intelligence forces; the employment of numerous people in these organizations; the inclusion of these organizations within the Palestinian social fabric, which constituted their very own native population; and the group structure of Palestinian society in which some family members may have been active in Hamas, for example, while their relatives served in one of the Palestinian intelligence organizations—all these gave the PA extensive intelligence knowledge in real time. In February 1995 Maj. Gen. Uri Sagie, head of Military Intelligence, appeared before the Knesset (Israeli parliament) Security and Foreign Affairs Committee and said, "The Palestinian police has the intelligence and combat capability to reach every terrorist headquarters and every terrorist's home, and they do so when they are given the appropriate orders."[63]

In light of the drastic decline in Israel's intelligence capability, it was only natural for them to use their Palestinian counterparts to obtain advance intelligence information regarding terrorist attacks. But there was a catch: the Palestinian intelligence agencies usually avoided passing along advance information to Israel regarding terrorist attacks, and if they had such information then, in the best case, they acted on it themselves to prevent the attack (if such action coincided with the PA's interests at that time). On occasion, the Palestinians refused to use the information even after they had received it from Israel. In a meeting of the Knesset Labor Faction in September 1994, Prime Minister Yitzhak Rabin stated:

> If they don't take action against terrorism and if they don't make a reasonable effort, it will have a very negative impact on the process. We demand that they meet their obligations. The steps they have taken to date have been more like warnings, not counter-terrorism measures. We demand that Arafat take action against the organizers and perpetrators of terrorist attacks. We cannot accept a situation where, even when we have given them information and even when they are aware, they do not do what they can.[64]

In a number of cases, as previously stated, Palestinian security services acted to prevent certain terrorist attacks, or they stopped perpetrators in light of intelligence information they received from Israel,[65] but such cooperation meant seriously jeopardizing Israeli intelligence sources. Thus, when they received information from Israel regarding an intended attack, the Palestinian security agencies would sometimes give advance warning to the planners and perpetrators of the attack, and at other times they would prevent the attack, arrest those involved for a short while, and immediately afterward they would attempt to identify the Israeli intelligence source and neutralize him.[66]

The attitude of the Palestinian preventive security forces towards those suspected of collaborating with Israel is obvious from the statement by Muhammad Dahlan, Palestinian security chief in Gaza, who said, "There are those who gave information that led to the assassination of a Palestinian, or those who killed their own people. If we catch them, we will cut their heads off."[67] But the Palestinian security service didn't stop at locating and killing Israeli intelligence agents. In some cases they even turned them into double agents, and exploited them to gather information about Israel's security services. In April 1995, it was discovered that an Israeli intelligence agent who had been exposed by Jibril Rajoub's intelligence force was compelled to continue pretending to work with Israel and extract information from the Israeli ISA about others who had collaborated with Israel.[68] Individuals suspected of collaborating with Israel so feared the Palestinian intelligence forces that at times, in order to clear their names and that of their families, they were even prepared to volunteer to commit suicide attacks in Israel.[69]

The special relationship between the Israeli ISA and the Palestinian security forces is evident from the following statement by Carmi Gilon:

> In my opinion even in all the rationale surrounding Oslo, the five years, there was a transition period in an attempt to build a trusting relationship.... I remember some early meetings with Dahlan, with Jibril and Amin al-Hindi, and Nasser Yusuf. They were the ones who were around at that time. And the suspicion that was felt specifically, I believe, among the security people, dissipated very quickly. And I don't mean me. I mean the level of the coordinators, the division commanders, the level of field personnel who met with their equivalent levels in the security forces they had set up, and in this regard there were excellent relationships.[70]

But this positive relationship also had other sides to it. The IDF and the Israel Police criticized, for example, the "free hand" the ISA gave to Jibril Rajoub's people to act throughout the West Bank after Rajoub, they claimed, recruited Fatah activists from all over the West Bank in contradiction to the signed agreements into the ranks of the Palestinian security forces, to the point where the Palestinian security force had a foothold in every village.[71] Nor was this a one-time criticism. At the end of 1994 the heads of the ISA pressed for enhanced cooperation with the Palestinian security force in East Jerusalem, arguing that Rajoub's people contributed to the enforcement of order in the city. On the other hand, the minister of police and the attorney general opposed having Palestinian security forces operating in this area.[72] About a year later, in September 1995, the ISA wanted to remove a senior police officer from his job in the capital's police force because of a dispute regarding the approach to use Rajoub and his people in Jerusalem. The ISA believed that Rajoub was a strong man that "we could do business with," and that Israel had a clear interest to cooperate with him. The police, on the other hand, believed it was necessary "to act tough with Jibril Rajoub when he breaks the law in Jerusalem."[73]

International Cooperation in the Intelligence Domain

The tangled web of intelligence relationships between Israel and the Palestinians suggests another dilemma in the intelligence domain—the question of international cooperation.

The terrorist attacks of September 11, 2001, in New York and Washington exposed the extent to which world peace is threatened by international terrorism. The spread of the fundamentalist Islamic terrorist network throughout the world, and the chance that these activists—who are experts in terrorist and guerrilla tactics—are filled with fundamentalist religious motivation to use terrorism and chemical, biological, radiological, and even nuclear materials in their attacks, illustrates the critical need to intensify international cooperation in the intelligence arena. In this context, it should be emphasized that most major terrorist attacks defined as "international terrorism" (that is, an attack that involves more than one nation, either in terms of national identity of the perpetrators or victims, or when the attack is committed on the territory of a third-party country, or if a state sponsor of terrorism is involved in the attacks), such as the attacks in the United States (2001), Bali (2002), Mombasa (2003), Istanbul and Madrid (2004), necessitate an extended period of preliminary operational preparations in various countries, including moving activists from one state to another, renting flats to serve as hideouts and front-line headquarters, and more. The attempt to prevent attacks of this magnitude ahead of time requires ongoing international intelligence cooperation—both bilateral and multilateral.

But there is one catch: this vital cooperation naturally leads to a genuine danger of exposing the intelligence sources working for the countries cooperating with one another. In the face of this risk, countries are less motivated to share sensitive information they may have about terrorist organizations with other nations, and this jeopardizes the international intelligence cooperation so crucial to identifying and preventing potential terrorist attacks and worldwide terrorist networks.

The solution to this lies in establishing an intelligence bank—an international framework for gathering and processing intelligence and information on terrorist infrastructures. This intelligence bank would be based on open sources of information found on the Internet, in journals and publications, and various databases, as well as on concrete intelligence data transmitted by nations who are members of this bank—information with low sensitivity, or a paraphrased version of highly sensitive information in a way that neutralizes the identity of the intelligence source—to the extent this is possible. In addition, the new international intelligence apparatus should operate its own intelligence capabilities, which will enable it it gather genuine information on terrorist organizations.

Coordinating Intelligence and Operations

Another issue to be addressed when coping with terrorism involves the various agencies involved in intelligence-gathering for the nation. Duplication of efforts can, at times, generate negative competition and jeopardize the effectiveness of the activities. Many researchers emphasize the need for a coordinating body to work with the various intelligence agencies, to enable decision makers to obtain a comprehensive intelligence picture, and to ensure greater efficiency for the intelligence forces.[74] Some recommend not only concentrating the communication between intelligence forces in the hands of such a coordinating body, but also granting such an agency the authority to make decisions and deploy resources among all the different operational branches that are relevant to counter-terrorism activity. Crenshaw states that the policy's effectiveness depends on the nature of the intelligence and to what degree implementation of such of policy is coordinated.[75] Hoffman and Morrison-Taw add that with regard to intelligence-gathering, there must be coordination between the military, police, and other security forces. In their opinion, the plan's success relies not only on the type of intelligence obtained and its quality, but also on its effective circulation in the shortest time possible among all agencies involved. Without such a coordinating framework, the security forces' efficacy is compromised. Hoffman and Morrison-Taw note that this lesson was learned from the British experience in Malaysia, Kenya, and Cyprus. Nonetheless, they highlight the difficulty in establishing such a coordinating body with decision-making and executive authority because in democracies, duly elected officials cannot be replaced by an appointed body; therefore, government agencies cannot be made subject to the authority of such a body.[76] Following the terrorist attack at the "Grand Hotel" in Brighton during the Conservative Party conference on October 12, 1984, which killed five people and injured scores of others, Great Britain decided to establish an interministerial committee with a view towards improving intelligence activities and coordinating between the various intelligence agencies.[77]

Uberoy discusses the question of whether the coordinating body should be limited to merely coordinating intelligence, or whether it should coordinate all of the agencies and authorities engaged in the war against terrorism as a whole. He proposes establishing a special body to coordinate among the numerous agencies and departments engaged in applying counter-terrorism strategy at the local and national level. This body would be comprised of experts and professionals from fields related to the measures employed, including: intelligence, police, psychological warfare, communications and public relations, foreign affairs, etc.[78]

Allan Behm delineates the principles he believes can guarantee effective coordination:

- Defining clear roles and areas of responsibility for the various agencies. Agencies should understand the boundaries of their responsibility, as well as the legal and administrative limitations within which they must act.
- Policy formulation and operational responsibility must be clearly separated—coordinating bodies and policymaking agencies must leave operational matters to the executive branch, and the executive branch must go to the coordinating body with any questions relating to policy.
- The coordinating body must focus on strategic issues at all times. This body must not allow operational activity to distract it from strategic goals. It is very tempting for coordinating bodies to become involved in the operational aspect, but resisting such temptation will enhance the agency's efficiency.
- The coordinating body must promote cooperation among the various agencies—not control them.[79]

In 1996, Israel established the Counter-Terrorism Bureau, with the aim of providing a solution to the question of coordinating counter-terrorism activity. This office replaced the prime minister's counter-terrorism advisor, a position that had existed in Israel for the previous twenty years. Benjamin Netanyahu, serving as prime minister at that time, stated in reference to this coordinating body, that

This is a body to coordinate all the branches. It has no authority. The coordinating body can instill order by reporting to the prime minister. On many occasions the coordinating body was able to divide things well and resolve conflicts; problems were raised and a decision was made. In Israel, this is the framework we need. Meir Dagan's [the first Counter-Terrorism Coordinator] job was functional and practical, and it helped me as a decision-maker. It helped clarify decisions and things didn't fall between the cracks.[80]

Netanyahu believes that the need for coordination is not necessarily reflected in the intelligence domain, but primarily in other areas related to counter-terrorism:

The problem is the order in which things are performed, not coordinating the intelligence. The prime minister also receives raw intelligence, albeit the information is screened, but he obtains the data. There's no way that something can be developing and you don't know about it. But there can be a situation in which the one agency clashes or overlaps or conflicts with another agency. When there is such a coordinating body, organization is much easier. It has no executive authority. The prime minister is the one who makes things happen, and this reduces competition among the agencies.[81]

Yaakov Perry feels that Israel has no problem when it comes to coordinating intelligence and even states, unlike Netanyahu, that Israel has no need of a coordinating body with regard to counter-terrorism. He says:

In the operational sphere—Israel is one of the world's leaders when it comes to coordination. Defining responsibility is where there are problems—can the ISA actually use agents outside [i.e., outside of Israel—BG], and should the Palestinian Authority be under the authority of Military Intelligence or of the ISA, etc. Therefore I think that an advisor on counter-terrorism as well as a coordinator are unnecessary bodies. We didn't need them to begin with. They were personnel-related solutions, and didn't contribute anything from a professional point of view.[82]

Meir Dagan, in contrast with Perry, believes that the unique characteristics of terrorist organizations and the way in which they operate, necessitates cooperation between numerous and varied government, security, and civilian agencies. Such cooperation requires coordination among the different bodies. According to Dagan:

The body that must begin looking at it in a comprehensive way is the coordinating body…because democratic societies are built on a separation of powers, so you start out with a coordination problem. This is a given: the judiciary branch won't necessarily yield to the dictates of the executive branch, and as a result there may be difficulty in unequivocally enlisting all the different forces to serve a single purpose.

In connection with the way things operate in other countries, Dagan explains that "each country has addressed this differently.

The Americans have a National Security Council, and that makes it easier for them. The American system of government allows them to act directly to implement policy, but even then, rivalries between the organizations can interfere at times.... The British method is that of the committees. They have no council, but rather a coordinating committee." To illustrate the need for a counter-terrorism coordinating body, Dagan actually looks at areas that are not directly related to neutralizing the violent actions of the organizations, and in particular—financing by terrorist organizations:

> What nation has acted against the financing? None. The most advanced nation in this regard is Israel. Why? Because a coordinating body was established that undertook, and succeeded, in enlisting the Ministry of Justice, police, Income Tax Authority, Treasury, the army.... Anyone who just coordinates among the intelligence bodies doesn't understand the problem.[83]

To sum up the issue of coordination, and based on the experience of nations contending with terrorism, especially nations with democratic regimes based on the principle of a separation of powers, it would appear that establishing a coordinating body for counter-terrorism is vitally important. This body should do more than just deal with the matter of coordinating intelligence. The profusion of government agencies involved in coping with terrorism in all realms—intelligence, offensive, defensive, punitive, legislative, etc.—demands that such a coordinating body create a detailed intelligence concept based on all the information in the possession of the state's intelligence agencies, and to translate this into operational action against the terrorist organization. The coordinating body must draw its authority and power from its proximity to the government leadership, and must be faithful to that leadership; at the same time, it must be acceptable to the heads of the security forces, the intelligence, and the administration involved in all aspects of the nation's war against terrorism.

Decision Makers and Intelligence

Even when the intelligence network operates properly, that is, it gathers and processes data, draws operational conclusions, and makes recommendations to the decision makers, the process still requires willingness, understanding, and openness on the part of the decision makers—the consumers of the intelligence data—in order to understand the intelligence picture and act accordingly.

Former Prime Minister Shimon Peres used to criticize the Israeli intelligence network, saying that it failed to foresee dramatic events that took place all over the world.

> I just never found experts when it came to the future. If you can find someone who is an expert on the future, I'll speak with them. I claim that most of the events that took place were not predicted by the experts, and most of the things that were predicted by the experts—never happened. Take the last decade, analyze it event by event; not only the 1973 War, not just the revolution in Moscow, even Khomeini—none of it was anticipated.[84]

This criticism compares intelligence to a narrow opening, a peephole that sheds a focused beam of light but doesn't let you see the whole picture. Intelligence information, reliable and accurate though it may be, is liable, therefore, to lead to a distortion of reality, and to bad decision-making. In this context, there is a distinction between defensive and offensive tactical intelligence, which is based on concrete intelligence information, and between strategic intelligence, which is primarily based on intelligence assessments and data processing. When this strategic intelligence is presented to decision makers, it must indeed be treated critically because it also reflects the interpretation and assessment of those engaged in the intelligence work at any given point in time. Even when these agents do their job faithfully and do not employ inappropriate considerations and personal judgments or beliefs in their work, they simply may be wrong in their assessments. Since the responsibility for a comprehensive counter-terrorism policy ultimately rests upon the shoulders of elected government leaders, they must seriously weigh all the intelligence and strategic information that reaches them. When necessary, they must even demand the raw intelligence data upon which the assessment was based in order to try and confirm or refute the opinion that has been presented to them. But decision makers must take care not to throw the baby out with the bath water by ignoring the intelligence information they are given, especially when it contradicts their own political beliefs and point of view.

4

Dilemmas in the Deterrence of Terrorists

The question of deterrence in the international arena is a complicated and problematic issue within the context of the relationship between two nations, but is even more difficult when it comes to a struggle between a group of people or substate organization and a sovereign state.

In commenting on deterrence at the level of conventional and nuclear warfare, Yehudah Wallach states that in the nuclear age the strategy has become the art of prevention. We endeavor to avoid war by threatening to retaliate against any provocation with violence. Thus, he believes, instead of the art of using the force of weapons, the strategy now is the art of threatening to use the force of weapons, or the art of deterrence. It is interesting to see how appropriate this definition is for the two extremes of military conflict—nuclear war and low-intensity struggle. Wallach notes that deterrence is a threat against an opponent to prevent him from employing certain means, lest such action lead to fatal retaliation. He claims that in order to achieve such an outcome, the opponent must understand that his losses will outweigh any possible gains.[85]

Yehezkel Dror maintains, in this regard, that deterrence is a matter of image, and thus is more suited to the same discipline as psychology, anthropology, and cultural research than the theory of warfare.[86]

Various studies on deterrence as part of a counter-terrorism policy highlight the importance of the issue and the difficulty involved in realizing an effective deterrent policy against a terrorist organization. On the one hand, a substantial part of the offensive and defensive military and punitive actions taken against terrorists are directed at preventing these organizations and their activists from continuing to perpetrate attacks in general, or a certain type of attack in particular. At the same time, it is difficult to deter a terrorist organization. It is much easier to deter a sovereign state, if only because a state has sensitive targets and numerous interests that can be attacked if the state crosses a particular "red line." In contrast, a terrorist organization is, by its nature, clandestine. In most cases its activists are out of sight and organized in such a way that harming one part of the organization will not strike a severe blow to other parts of the organization. According to Lesser, the main difficulty with deterrence is when dealing with individuals and networks, rather than with nations or terrorist organizations with a hierarchical structure.[87]

Moreover, any attempt to deter a terrorist organization presupposes the assumption of rationality on the part of the organization. Any organization that fails to operate on the basis of rational cost-benefit considerations will not calculate the benefits or costs from its actions, and will not be deterred from perpetrating terrorist acts and attacks that have been defined by the nation as crossing red lines.

In considering Israel's policy towards its Arab neighbors, Dror raises several doubts as to the advantage of establishing red lines. In his view, it might not be wise to announce in advance clear red lines which, if crossed, would supposedly lead to an automatic response that had already been stated, or at least hinted at, in advance.[88]

The problems in formulating a deterrent policy are particularly evident with respect to terrorist organizations. Crenshaw stresses the difficulty, stating that the terrorist must be convinced that the price he will have to pay for his actions will be high, and the punishment severe. But it is hard to assess how messages of deterrence will be received by and impinge upon the terrorist organization. Their values are usually different from the values of their adversaries. They have other frames of reference and above all, another attitude towards risk factors. In Crenshaw's view, there may be a misconception when it comes to imposing deterrent measures against terrorist organizations, among other things, because the terrorists' motives are misunderstood and because it is assumed that their activities are based on a strategic rationality.[89] Jessica Stern adds that although the traditional response to threats involving risk and uncertainty is to convince those that are threatening you to stop carrying out their attacks by creating a convincing deterrent force, it is particularly difficult to deter perpetrators whose identity, motives, and possible response are unknown. According to Stern, groups that do not measure their success in terms of a desired political change, but rather by the extent to which they are able to sow fear, injure the populace, and humiliate the government, have very little to lose and it is therefore extremely difficult to deter them. It is also hard to deter groups that seek to put an end to the world or whose activists are prepared to commit suicide for religious or other reasons.[90]

The difficulty in deterring terrorist organizations derives, therefore, from the specific characteristics of the terrorist organization (in contrast, for example, with the characteristics of a state supporting terrorism). A terrorist organization is usually composed of a group of people infused with an extreme ideology or religious belief, or a combination of the two, who are faithful to their goal and prepared to sacrifice personal and common resources, their personal well-being and on occasion, even their lives, in order to attain their goal. Since the goals of the terrorist organization and the indicators it defines for success are usually different from those accepted by sovereign nations, sometimes even the ability to threaten the organization with actions that would prevent it from achieving their goals is debatable.

The degree to which the deterrent is relevant for the terrorist organization depends, among other things, on an assessment of the organization's response to the deterrent. But it is difficult to formulate such an assessment, and the possible margin of error is great due to the organization's special decision-making processes; because of the great impact a charismatic leader is likely to have on the organization's response; and because of the ethical, cultural, and social variables that are unique to the organization. These variables could have an influence on their cost-benefit calculations and it is difficult for the deterring body, whose ethical-cultural-social point of view is different, to understand them or even guess what they might be.

Figure 4.1 illustrates the complexity in deterring a terrorist organization. The deterrent policy, as shown in the illustration, relies on an assumption according to which the opponent is rational, that is, he can weigh cost-benefit considerations and then formulate his policies and actions accordingly. On the basis of this underlying assumption a nation establishes its deterrent policy, which is comprised of two key elements: the ability and motivation of the deterring body—the ability to carry out the threat in case a red line is crossed by the terrorist organization; and their motivation and determination, when necessary, to meet their obligation and undertake the action that was decided on.

However, as shown in Figure 4.1, the deterred organization's perception of the capability and motivation of the deterring body to carry out its threat is even more important than any actual capability and motivation. Even if the deterring body lacks the ability or is not resolved to carry out the stated threat, the deterred organization may assess the situation differently, in which case the deterrent is likely to achieve its goal. Conversely, when a deterring body has both the ability and the motivation to carry out the terms of its threat but the deterred organization doesn't perceive it in this way, then the deterrent policy will presumably not achieve its goal. It should be emphasized that the perception of the deterrent, both in terms of capability and motivation, is greatly affected by cumulative past experience—to the degree that the deterring body has proven its

Figure 4.1
Deterrence of Terrorist Organizations

ability and its resolve to use its power in similar situations in the past. Because of the fact that the deterrent is based on the world of images, in reality, this is a long learning process rather than a momentary decision made by a particular decision maker.

The success of a deterrent, then, depends upon the image transmitted to the deterred organization. No less important, however, are the nature of the deterrent threat and the means used to communicate it. The method by which the message is transmitted is particularly critical in this context: is the method public or private, direct or indirect? The nature of the threat being used against the deterred body is even more significant—is it a realistic threat, that is, can it be carried out? Does it reflect a genuine consideration of the cost-benefit aspect by the deterring body? Another pivotal issue is the degree to which the threat has been used before. Oft-repeated threats against the deterred organization are liable to diminish the threat and reduce its effectiveness. Moreover, long-term deterrence may cause a feeling of humiliation and even the desire for revenge. In any case, it is almost certain that the deterrent will motivate the deterred organization to develop new capabilities—means and methods that will allow it to overcome its inferiority in the face of the deterring nation, and thus, neutralize the deterrent. Finally, the deterrent's success is also contingent upon the extent to which the threat is relevant to the organization being deterred—to what degree is it important to them to prevent the threat from being carried out?

Since we are dealing with the world of images, and since building or altering an image involves lengthy and cumulative processes, there is a reciprocal influence between a nation's deterrent image at the various levels of intensity (see Figure 4.2)—low intensity, conventional intensity, and non-conventional intensity. When the deterring nation's image is undermined at a particular level of intensity, this also affects its deterrent capability at the other levels. Conversely, when a nation proves its capability and determination and achieves deterrence at a particular level of intensity, occasionally this also has an influence on that country's deterrent image at other levels of intensity. For example, the response by Israel's home front to Iraqi rockets fired during the Gulf War influenced the image created among Palestinians and other Arab countries regarding Israeli society's ability to contend with other security crises that involve risk to the home front. Failures by the Israeli Mossad in various overseas operations (the capture of Mossad operatives during surveillance operations in Cyprus or during wiretapping attempts in Switzerland, and the failed assassination attempt against Khaled Mashaal, Hamas leader, in Jordan) have also undermined Israel's image regarding its ability to carry out other special operations using specialized units, and have thus undermined Israel's overall deterrent image. It should be noted that Israel's deterrent image is influenced not only by different levels of intensity, but also by past experience in other spheres of endeavor. Israel's unilateral withdrawal from South Lebanon, for example, was regarded by the Palestinians as Israel's failure and therefore influenced the country's deterrent image in the Palestinian sphere, which contributed to the start of the Intifada in September 2000.

A nation's cumulative experience, its level of determination and ability to act against a terrorist organization has a significant impact on the world of images and the sense of security felt by that country's public at large.

When we examine the effectiveness of a deterrent against a terrorist organization, we must recall that the deterrent is likely to be expressed in different forms: from a "general deterrent," which is aimed at causing a terrorist organization to renounce its terrorist ways and to completely stop perpetrating terrorist attacks, or avoid certain types of attacks, to "defensive deterrent," in an effort to stop terrorists from perpetrating attacks against particular targets because of the defensive measures taken at the site, which narrow the chances for success, to "punitive deterrent," which aims at deterring the organization's activists from participating in terrorist activity.

Overall deterrence is, as stated, a difficult and complex task that cannot be applied long term against a terrorist organization. A defensive deterrent, on the other hand, is sometimes likely to achieve its objectives, especially when the terrorists are not suicide terrorists. However, it must be remembered that this deterrent will prevent, at most, terrorist activity in a particular place and at a given time, but it is liable to cause the terrorists to divert their activity to another time or location. The effectiveness of a punitive deterrent is also doubtful. It would appear that the means of punishment available to a nation (from imposing monetary fines and restrictions on terrorists and their supporters, to prison sentences, administrative

Figure 4.2
Components of Israel's Deterrent Image

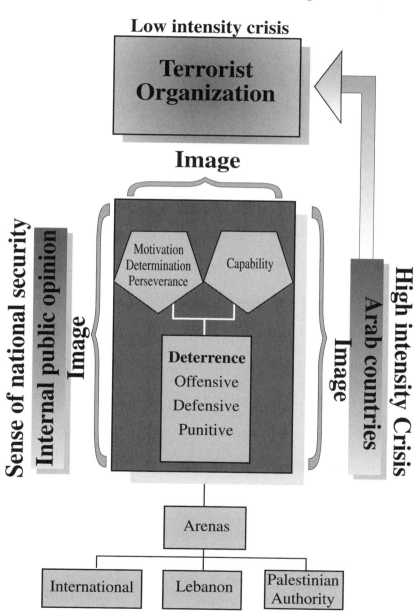

detention, and sealing or demolishing homes, to deportation, closures, etc.) might succeed at temporarily removing some activists
from the overall threat and removing them from society, but in many
cases these actions do not succeed in deterring others from becoming involved in terrorism, particularly when terrorist organizations
work to minimize the damage to terrorists and their families by
offering financial support, building replacement homes, and so on.

Israel's Policy of Deterrence

As part of its efforts to cope with terrorism, Israel has acted
throughout the years to deter terrorist organizations, their activists,
leaders, and assistants from continuing their activities against Israel, and to deter nations that support these organizations—by providing them with money and weapons, offering "a safe haven" and
a supportive environment, and by allowing terrorists to cross their
borders on their way to carrying out attacks in Israel. (Even in the
early days of the state, Israel had a strong retaliation policy against
Arab countries that sponsored and assisted Palestinian terrorist organizations in an effort to deter them from continuing to do so.)

Indeed, Israel's counter-terrorism policy and statements made
by official Israeli spokespersons following an Israeli offensive action coincided with the main points of this approach, that is to say,
Israel could raise the price that the organizations would have to pay
up to the specified deterrent limit of each organization. This attitude is reflected in various spheres of Israel's counter-terrorism activity, its air strikes, individual attacks, and severe punishments such
as deportation and destruction of homes.[51]

Operation "Defensive Shield" in March-April 2002 is an example
of offensive action Israel undertook in response to the numerous
terrorist attacks carried out during March 2002. Following the operation, the head of the IDF Intelligence Division, Maj. Gen. Ze'evi,
claimed during a discussion held in the Knesset Committee on Foreign Affairs and Security that "Operation Defensive Shield was effective in terms of IDF deterrent capability. The operation proved
itself and the Palestinian Authority was prevented from firing mor-
tars and Kassam rockets from the Gaza Strip for fear of a similar
campaign in the south."[92] This was apparently true regarding
Katyusha shelling from the Gaza Strip. Operation "Defensive Shield"
created a deterrent for a certain period of time, but it would seem

that the impact of the offensive campaign in the West Bank did not serve as a deterrent with regard to suicide bombings.

Figure 4.3 clearly shows the effective impact of the campaign conducted in March 2002 (and which, in fact, resulted in the reoccupation of certain West Bank cities) on reducing the number of actual suicide bombings in Israel and the West Bank during the period following the campaign. However, according to the large number of suicide bombings that were foiled following the campaign, it would seem that motivation to perpetrate suicide attacks was not reduced—and even rose immediately afterwards. Thus, the campaign was proven to be effective and contributed much towards preventing terrorism—but it did not achieve any deterrent objective with regard to this type of attack.

Regarding punitive measures pursued by Israel, then Defense Minister Binyamin Ben-Eliezer stated that there had been a sharp drop in the number of terrorists attempting to perpetrate suicide attacks. The decline, according to Ben-Eliezer, was the result of deterrent measures such as demolishing homes and deportation. Furthermore, he announced, "we intend to intensify the deterrents by dealing with the families of suicide terrorists."[93]

Voices were heard from the opposing side as well, admitting that "the IDF has succeeded in hurting us"—as expressed by Hamas spokesman Abdel Aziz Rantisi in an interview with the Danish pub-

Figure 4.3
Suicide Attacks in Israel 10/2000-12/2003

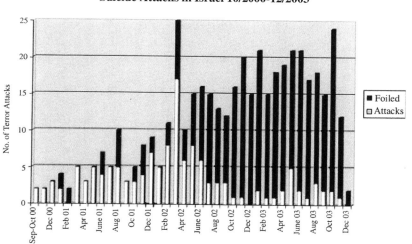

lication *Jyllands-Posten*, adding that the curfew policy and closure made it very difficult for those he called "Hamas fighters" to penetrate the Green Line and carry out attacks. "I cannot help but admit it, there is an impact from the killing and arrest of Hamas leaders on our operational capability." However, Rantisi tempered his remarks by saying that "once we become accustomed to the curfew and closures we will renew our activities."[94]

Thus, retaliation is aimed at deterrence, but the best deterrent doesn't involve force at all—instead, it generates the fear of the use of force. Israel's policy of periodic reprisals in the late 1960s and 1970s actually illustrate the failure of deterrent measures. Frequent retaliation indicates an attempt to summon a deterrent capability that does not exist, and this becomes more and more difficult and complex the more often it is used. Furthermore, the very use of frequent retaliation jeopardizes its deterrent value. The body that is supposed to be deterred becomes used to it and either learns to live with it or learns how to overcome the deterring body.

To illustrate, Israel's deterrent policy against terrorist organizations in the Lebanese sphere in the 1990s, which was based on frequent use of air raids against terrorist bases, raised doubts concerning the effectiveness of this method. Gordon argues that in the Lebanese arena there was a drop in Israel's deterrent capability resulting, according to him, from the lack of a consistent and stated deterrent policy.[95] But the erosion in Israel's deterrent capability should not necessarily be attributed to the lack of a consistent and stated policy, rather primarily to the terrorist organizations adapting to this continuous offensive activity. The extensive use (sometimes, overuse) of air strikes against terrorist targets leadterrorist organizations to formulate procedures aimed at reducing the number of their wounded, and to make it more difficult for the air force to carry out its mission. Among these procedures we should mention:

- *Relocating near civilian populations*—in an attempt to make it more difficult for the air force to hit terrorist targets without risking civilian lives and causing damage to civilian property.
- *Prohibiting terrorists from remaining on the bases*—occasionally, especially following an attack in Israel with multiple victims, the terrorist organization has felt that an air response from Israel is imminent and organizations have in-

structed their people to temporarily abandon their bases until tensions have been diffused.

- *Digging underground and building subterranean terrorist facilities*—in an attempt to minimize possible damage from Israeli air raids, some terrorist organizations have chosen to locate their sensitive facilities in underground tunnels. The most prominent organization to employ such tactics is the "Popular Front—General Command," headed by Ahmed Jibril, who created a sophisticated network of tunnels beneath the village of Na'ama, south of Beirut.

As terrorist organizations adapted to Israel's air tactics, this actually served to jeopardize the deterrent effect of the strikes, and at certain times the policy was amended by shifting major efforts from damaging the organizations themselves and their infrastructures, to damaging Lebanese infrastructures, in order to generate a chain reaction of pressure from the local Lebanese population and government against the terrorist organizations, thereby forcing them to stop perpetrating terrorist attacks against Israel.

Although the stated Israeli position following an offensive action repeatedly emphasized its deterrent nature, "so that they shall see and be fearful," it appears that policymakers and heads of the security network themselves were not entirely convinced of the country's ability to deter terrorist organizations, and many among them chose to stress the limitations of these measures. The head of military intelligence, Maj. Gen. Ze'evi, for example, claimed in the Foreign Relations and Security Committee that even if the terrorist infrastructure was severely damaged following Operation Defensive Shield, the various organizations were motivated to perpetrate large-scale attacks in order to prove their operational capability even after the campaign, rendering the deterrent no lasting value. The terrorist infrastructure may have been temporarily damaged, but the organizations would soon recover and be fully active once again.[96]

The wave of terrorist attacks that took place in Israel during the mid-1990s heightened the argument concerning a country's limited ability to deter attacks. In contrast with previous assessments, there was a growing feeling among Israeli decision makers that it was impossible, and that a suicide terrorist determined to carry out his plans could not be deterred, even at the price of his own life. Expression of this can be found in the government meeting following the bombing of the No. 5 bus on Dizengoff St. in Tel Aviv in October 1994. When Minister Shimon Shetrit proposed that Israel increase its deterrent capability against terrorism, Prime Minister Yitzhak Rabin responded, "There is no deterrent capability against terrorism."[97] In answer to a question on whether a nation could deter a terrorist organization, Carmi Gilon, who served as head of the ISA at that time, replied:

> Deter? Very little.... Look at the Lebanese example, first and foremost. Just as terrorism is the weapon of the weak, it is the Achilles heel of the strong. Take the mighty IDF. The mighty IDF doesn't know how to respond to two Katyusha incidents, or LAW rockets. It knows how to respond to three divisions marching from right to left, but that isn't helpful against Bedouin shepherds.[98]

Shabtai Shavit also believes that the nation faces essential difficulties in its attempts at deterrence. When asked a similar question his response was as follows:

> Yes, if the nation is prepared to go all the way. But in today's normative world, not only in Israel but also the British in Northern Ireland, the answer is no. The cost the nation might have to pay—and not necessarily in military or economic terms, but rather in terms of public opinion and international relations—is such that it will think twice before making any decision to ignore criticism and go all the way.[99]

The Issue of the Rationality of Terrorist Organizations

All types of deterrent measures are based, as stated, on an assumption of the enemy's rationality. How can we make it clear to an opponent that he isn't using rational cost-benefit considerations because a particular act or failure to act will cause him tremendous damage, and consequently he shouldn't implement them? This assumption of the opponent's rationality is apparently doubtful when it comes to terrorist organizations.

It is a common error to judge the enemy's rationality through the subjective mirror of those coping with terrorism. Cost-benefit considerations are the result of several variables—history, culture, sociological and psychological aspects, etc. An act that is perceived as beneficial by one, may not necessarily be perceived as such by someone else. The rational judgment must be based, therefore, on the cost-benefit considerations as perceived by the enemy alone. In Palestinian society, for example, the value of honor is important and very central, and many who have been brought up on Arab tradition are prepared to kill and be killed if their honor is violated. This is perceived by them as an effective option, and therefore, as a rational act. But not so in Israeli society. Irrationality is expressed, therefore, in choosing an option whose damage, in the eyes of the decider himself, outweighs its benefit.

Meir Dagan differentiates between two types of deterrents against terrorist organizations—the "tactical deterrent" and the "strategic deterrent." Dagan believes that it is possible to deter terrorist organizations from perpetrating attacks against a certain type of target or in a particular place (tactical deterrent), but he warns against engaging in the question of a strategic deterrent against an organization, because organizations are different from countries. According to Dagan:

> One of the greatest errors people make is to relate to a terrorist organization as if it were a terrorist state, which weighs its actions according to the rationale of a decision-making process. Therefore, they express the system of rules and the organizational language of the war on terrorism using military motifs: concentrated effort, damage to channels of communications, etc. When you look at a terrorist organization, it doesn't work that way.[100]

In discussing the question of the rationality of terrorist organizations, Shimon Peres states: "They are rational, according to their own rationale. It is not an objective rationale. There is a rationale that is also partly emotional."[101]

Yaakov Perry adds:

> I think that in recent years there has been more rationalization…there were periods when it was less rational and more emotional, as a result of fewer serious discussions concerning: whether to do it, how to do it, and who should do it. As the years passed, it has become more rational.[102]

We may ask, is it really impossible to deter terrorists? Is their system of considerations really so different from that of other groups of people?

One of the key arguments that highlight the difficulty of deterrent measures is that terrorists "have nothing to lose," and therefore it is impossible to deter them. Is this argument valid? Terrorists may, indeed, be lacking in individual or group means, they might come from populations with poor socioeconomic status, and perhaps they represent oppressed people fighting for their independence, etc. But even in these cases (which are not typical for all terrorists), they do have something to lose, even if it is only certain accomplishments in the future or resources that are non-tangible and unquantifiable, such as: respect, prestige, legitimacy, carrying out God's will, and the like.

In general, terrorist organizations usually conduct rational considerations of costs and benefits, but they often attribute different weight to the values taken into account in their cost-benefit calculations, and occasionally, may even consider values that are different from those of the ones coping with the terrorism, thus making a decision that appears irrational to an outside observer. In most cases, though, the leadership of a terrorist organization will not make a decision whose cost is perceived to outweigh its benefit, that is, an irrational decision. The state contending with terrorism, therefore, is faced with a difficult task—becoming familiar with the terrorist organizations, their ideology, their heritage, culture, motives and objectives, their decision-making processes and their cost-benefit considerations, in such a way that will enable that nation to assess and project in advance the outcomes of the organizations' cost-benefit considerations, and plan its counter-terrorism strategy on the basis of these assessments.

Deterring Suicide Terrorists

The dilemma involved in deterring terrorists reached its peak following the phenomenon of suicide attacks. If the rationality of terrorists in general is doubtful, then the rationality of people who carry out suicidal acts is even more difficult to grasp. How is it at all possible to deter a suicide terrorist who is willing to sacrifice his life for some goal?

Deterring suicide terrorists is a complicated issue that requires, first of all, a profound understanding of the phenomenon of suicide terrorism. We can already state here that within terrorist organizations, the number of those who are willing to commit suicide is usually relatively small: most activists in terrorist organizations and most of those involved in perpetrating terrorist attacks do not belong to this group, and are not suicidal. The same is true for the organizations' leaders, who are usually older, and have a higher social status, families, and a career. These people usually carry out rational cost-benefit considerations. Heads of terrorist organizations who send suicide attackers on their missions do, indeed, take pride in their willingness to die on behalf of the goal they have staked out, but these statements are, in most cases, merely lip service. The proof of this—the tremendous efforts invested by leaders of terrorist organizations in close personal security and changing their daily routines (including, for example, sleeping somewhere else every night), because of their constant fear of assassination.

Beyond their small numbers, there is another characteristic that typifies suicide terrorists. In contrast with the person who chooses to end his life in order to avoid disappointment, failure, difficult or tragedy in this world, or because of a physical or emotional problem, the suicide terrorist is not committing an act of suicide at all, according to his perspective; rather, he is committing an act of self-sacrifice in order to achieve a concrete goal he believes is worthy. In many cases this action is supported by religious reasoning, a "martyrdom in sanctification of God's name"—"*istishad.*" From the point of view of the *shahid*—the suicide terrorist himself—the suicide attack has several advantages. The attack reflects for him, and for all of his population of origin, a willingness for supreme self-sacrifice—a demonstration of personal determination, social loyalty, national patriotism, and religious zeal.

Consequently, a suicide attack allows the terrorist and his family to climb the social ladder of his society from their present place—usually on the fringes of society—to a place of honor. If these rewards are not sufficiently tangible, the family of the *shahid* (martyr) is given a very tangible reward of thousands of dollars (until the Al Aksa *Intifada*, the amount that the family of the Palestinian *shahid* received from the terrorist organization was some $5,000 and during the *Intifada*, when Iraq allocated huge sums of money for this purpose, the amount awarded to the family of a suicide attacker rose to $25,000—an enormous sum compared with the average yearly salary in the West Bank). From this perspective, perpetrating suicide attacks could be considered by a youngster from a large family as an altruistic act for his family's benefit. Another tangible reward is in realizing the desire for revenge. The suicide terrorist may want to avenge the death of a friend or someone close to him, or what he perceives to be the maltreatment of his people. But above all, the suicide attacker earns, according to his Islamic beliefs, numerous heavenly rewards: his act allows him to ascend straight to heaven, skipping over the painful and difficult purification stage in the grave following his death; as a *shahid* he is able to gaze upon the face of Allah and serve as a heavenly advocate for seventy of his family members who will also earn the right to enter heaven, when the time comes, by virtue of his act; and above all, in heaven he will have seventy-two virgins at his beck and call, who will provide for all of his needs. Anyone who comes from Western culture will find it difficult to understand how real these rewards seem to a suicide terrorist, who is usually a young person without any sexual experience in his puritan society. But as strange as it sounds to the Western ear, this is even true of the nineteen suicide attackers who carried out the 9/11 attacks in the United States, who did not share the same sociological profile as the Palestinian suicide attackers since they came from middle-class families, were educated and non-fundamental Islamists, and some of whom studied in Western countries in various universities. Even they were probably driven by the concrete belief in the heavenly benefits that they would receive after committing the attacks. This is the reason why Muhamad Atta wrote to them in the last letter (which was found in the vehicle that they left in the airport parking lot)—"Do not forget the *Hurias*" (the beautiful black-eyed virgins waiting for the suicide bombers in heaven). From this we can conclude that even for the so-called secular Islamic terrorist, the heavenly benefits are very concrete and are taken into consideration. All of these rewards are so tangible that they can make an essentially irrational act—the act of suicide—into a rational act whose benefit is many times greater than its cost.

Given that the *shahid* does, indeed, naively believe in so many rewards for his act, and this belief serves to motivate his action, this belief can also be used to deter him from carrying out his plan. Any action that will deny him these rewards, or at least undermine his belief that they will be awarded to him and his family in the end, can serve as a deterrent factor. For example, if leading Muslim religious figures were to be enlisted in a campaign against suicide attacks and would highlight the fact that this action was not a holy war but rather an act that contradicts religious values and God's will; and if political and social leaders were to wholeheartedly reject any type of attack with the argument that it doesn't serve their national interests, but rather jeopardizes them—that would certainly be a deterrent measure. No one doubts the fact that the suicide terrorist is prepared to sacrifice his life in order to perpetrate an attack, but the advance knowledge that his action is liable to seriously harm his family, his loved ones, and his peers, might deter him from carrying it out.

The above illustrates the option for deterring the suicide attacker himself, but we must remember that terrorist organizations side with these attacks by initiating, preparing, and perpetrating them. One should bear in mind that the terrorist organizations themselves certainly have no suicidal tendencies. In general, it is possible to classify all terrorist action into two types of attacks—"individual initiative" and "organized" attacks. Attacks perpetrated through individual initiative are attacks that are usually carried out by a single party as a result of a momentary whim, generally motivated by a desire for revenge, without any prior planning and without any third party initiating or preparing the attack. In these attacks, the terrorist usually decides to take whatever weapon he may have in his possession and go out on a killing rampage. In contrast with this type of attack, organized attacks are initiated, prepared, funded, aided and perpetrated by some terrorist organization. These attacks are usually more complicated and lethal, causing much more damage. A look back at suicide attacks perpetrated in Israel from 1993 until the present shows that all of them, without exception, were organized attacks, and not personal initiative attacks. In other words, these attacks were perpetrated in order to realize the objectives of a terrorist organization and to serve its goals. That being the case, deterrent measures can be aimed against the terrorist organization itself, making it clear to the organization's decision makers that this type of attack (in contrast, perhaps, with other types) will result in a response so severe that their loss would exceed any benefit they had hoped to gain from the attack.

Deterring State Sponsors of Terrorism

Yet another dilemma involved in the question of deterrence of terrorism is the ability to deter state sponsors of terrorism. For years, terrorism has been perceived as a struggle between two adversaries: a group of people or an organization that is not a country versus a sovereign state. But in the second half of the twentieth century, various states have increasingly used terrorist organizations to promote their own interests in the international arena. In many instances, terrorism has gone from being "the weapon of the weak"—a minority group, liberation movement or revolutionary organization—

to a tool in the hands of nations, and even superpowers. In certain cases, states have initiated the establishment of terrorist organizations to serve as their messengers ("puppets"), perpetrating terrorist attacks on behalf of the state, promoting their interests in the international arena, and representing their positions in the internal or regional sphere. In other cases, these nations have sponsored and supported existing organizations, thereby creating mutually beneficial relationships.

For their part, terrorist organizations have asked for and received from these states political support, financial assistance, and sponsorship in order to help them preserve their very existence, continue their operations and expand their struggle until their aims are achieved. The state sponsors have helped these organizations perpetrate terrorist attacks as means for spreading their ideology throughout the world. (Occasionally, the nations expected the terrorist organizations to ultimately achieve power in their country, or to imprint their ideology among the public at large.) According to Cline and Alexander, "they aim to achieve strategic ends in circumstances where the use of conventional armed forces is deemed inappropriate, ineffective, too risky or too difficult."[103]

The rising cost of modern warfare, the cold war, and fear of escalation to non-conventional weapons, as well as the risk of defeat and the desire to refrain from appearing as the aggressor, have made terrorism an efficient, expedient and usually discreet weapon for achieving a state's interests in the international sphere using violent means, within having to "pay the price" and be held accountable for the results of the violent action.

At first it was the Soviet Union that, either directly or through other Communist Bloc nations, sponsored and aided various terrorist organizations. Later on, with the fall of the Soviet Union, Iran became involved in a greater share of the world's terrorist attacks, and quickly became the leading state in terms of the level and scope of its involvement.

Recognizing the central role played by state sponsors of terrorism and their tremendous influence on this issue, the United States constantly monitors these countries' involvement in terrorism, and publishes an annual report highlighting their activities during the preceding year. American companies are prohibited from trading with nations appearing on this list, and they receive neither military nor economic aid from the United States, except for humanitarian aid. The chapter "Patterns of Global Terrorism—Overview of State Sponsored Terrorism" in the report for 2003, states:

> State sponsors of terrorism impede the efforts of the United States and the international community to fight terrorism. These countries provide a critical foundation for terrorist groups. Without state sponsors, terrorist groups would have a much more difficult time obtaining the funds, weapons, materials, and secure areas they require to plan and conduct operations. The United States will continue to insist that these countries end the support they give to terrorist groups.[104]

Until the campaign in Iraq (2003) and the recent development in Libya, which renounced terrorism, the U.S. list has not changed, and includes: Cuba, Iran, Iraq, Libya, North Korea, Sudan, and Syria.[105] Is it possible to take action against these nations such that they will stop aiding terrorist organizations and desist from perpetrating attacks themselves? The question of deterring state sponsors of terrorism is also relevant to the question raised earlier regarding their degree of rationality. A policy of reward and punishment aimed at an irrational nation is liable to be irrelevant, and may even escalate the situation. In his book entitled *Crazy States*, Dror stressed the weakness of deterrence as a strategy against "crazy states" because goals that are important to the deterring nation are likely to be meaningless for the "crazy" one. Furthermore, such a nation tends to take risks in any case. Nevertheless, Dror states that except for extreme cases in which nations are prepared to sacrifice themselves, deterrence may be the preferred sub-strategy to combat their craziness.[106]

Most nations supporting terrorism do so out of choice. In an effort to achieve aims and interests, they weigh the price they will have to pay for their actions. These nations usually employ a system of considerations involving cost v. benefit, that is, essentially rational considerations. However, most states sponsoring terrorism have not been blessed with a democratic regime, and decision-making processes at the national level often rely upon the fevered mind of a single ruler. The variables that go into the cost-benefit equation in such cases are sometimes likely to be perceived by those in the West as irrational and capricious, variables that give disproportionate weight to ideology, religion, and emotion, variables based on a different value system than that accepted in the Western world, with less weight being given to the value of human life than in the West.

But even the decision maker in a state sponsoring terrorism examines the degree to which his actions will ultimately promote his goals, and how much the sanctions, which will almost certainly be imposed against his nation when its involvement in terrorism is exposed, will endanger his basic interests and those of his nation.

From this perspective, the campaign in Iraq towards state sponsors of terrorism is an important milestone in American policy, and perhaps that of the entire Western world. Before and during the campaign in Iraq, the question was asked over and over again—Why Iraq? Isn't Iran, for example, or Syria, or others countries that sponsor terrorism more dangerous than Iraq and therefore, based on international priorities, shouldn't they be called to order first? If we ignore cynical arguments relating to oil prices and settling family scores, we can state that Iraq was worthy of its rightful place on America's list of State Sponsors of Terrorism, and of being counted among the countries constituting the "axis of evil" as defined by President George W. Bush. Iraq met two criteria that justified its inclusion—it supported terrorism, and at the same time, at least according to the United States and Great Britain, it was perceived to have non-conventional weapons capabilities. The combination of these two variables created a dangerous prospect that such a state might arm terrorist organizations with non-conventional weapons, a threat that has become very real following the events of September 11.

But even taking these two criteria into consideration, Iraq was not necessarily the most dangerous country of all. What made it the most dangerous among its counterparts on the list was one more criterion—its leadership and their "irrational" decision-making process. The combination of "irrational" decisions, non-conventional capabilities, and involvement in terrorism made Iraq the most dangerous.

Moreover, the campaign in Iraq had the clear objective of transmitting a deterrent message to other countries on the list. In this context, it is significant to note the fact that the United States decided to go to war despite widespread international criticism, public non-support by the United Nations, and outspoken opposition by some European countries, including mass demonstrations. This American resolve—the fact that none of this discouraged President Bush from taking what he believed to be the proper and necessary step—only reinforced the deterrent significance towards other state supporters of terrorism (but not necessarily terrorist organizations). It appears that Libya's decision to disarm from non-conventional capabilities and to make overtures to the West reflects, among other things, an understanding of the deterrent message in Iraq. In any event, America took a big gamble. If the Iraqi campaign had been drawn out and produced too many casualties—either American or even Iraqi civilians, the deterrent message would have lost much of its value and perhaps, the damage caused by the war in terms of deterrence would have exceeded the benefits.

The American military presence in Iraq is still quite massive, and a stable Iraqi regime has yet to be set up in its place. These problems must be resolved in order to establish the deterrent message towards fundamentalist Muslim countries and states sponsoring terrorism, and in order to illustrate to them that the damages they could incur from being involved in terrorism are liable to far outweigh the benefits. Ongoing injury to American soldiers stationed in Iraq is also likely to be an anti-deterrent, especially if these injuries seriously impair the soldiers' morale, and may even lead to a decision to withdraw from Iraqi soil before a stable regime is set up.

Most state sponsors of terrorism calculate costs and benefits, and take into account the international response to their actions. Every nation determines a certain price that it will not be willing to pay for its continued involvement with terrorism. This "price scale" differs from nation to nation, as does the "breaking point" of each country. For this reason nations coping with terrorism must raise the price of a country involved in terrorism so high that it will not want to continue, to a point at which it will decide it no longer pays to be involved in terrorism.

What is the range of activity that can be undertaken against a state sponsor of terrorism? What is that "price scale" the international community must employ in order to change the balance of interests of a state supporting terrorism?

Figure 4.3 outlines the punitive and deterrent measures that may be taken against states involved in terrorism. The figure reflects a sliding scale of international steps against such nations. The first part includes warnings and demands to stop their activities, followed by international condemnation, and later on, cultural sanctions (including exclusion from international events, removal from international cultural and education programs, and deporting its citizens who live, work or study in foreign countries).

The next step is diplomatic sanctions against the state supporting terrorism: beginning with expulsion from international institutions, to revoking its membership in UN institutions or even removal from the UN assembly, to discontinuing the nation's relationship with UN members.

The following step (or in parallel with the previous) involves imposing economic sanctions on the state supporting terrorism: from limiting its ability to purchase sensitive weapons or advanced technology that may aid in its violent activities (either military struggle or involvement in terrorism) to preventing the export of products to this nation and preventing the purchase of its products with a view towards causing economic damage; and freezing and confiscating its assets around the world (for the creation of an international fund to aid victims of terrorist attacks who have been injured in actions perpetrated by organizations who are supported and assisted by this nation); to a physical blockade of its land, sea, and air borders in order to prevent the transportation of goods to and from the country. As a complementary step, a secondary embargo may be imposed against nations and commercial companies that defy the economic sanctions imposed against the state supporting terrorism and continue to maintain economic ties with that nation.

The next stage of activities against a nation involved in terrorism is legal: defining heads of state and heads of security agencies of that nation as "war criminals" or charging them with "crimes against humanity," and afterwards, to conduct international tribunals in order to convict them and determine their sentences (even if they, themselves, do not attend.)

The uppermost level of sanctions and deterrent measures against states supporting terrorism involves joint military action by the international community against terrorist facilities located in the nation offering them sponsorship, as well as military installations of the sponsoring nation itself.

A one-time action against a nation, the lack of international coordination and cooperation against states involved in terrorism, and half-hearted declarations by the international community only strengthen the belief held by states supporting terrorism that they can continue their activities with impunity, or that the price they

Figure 4.4
Sanctions against States Supporting Terrorism

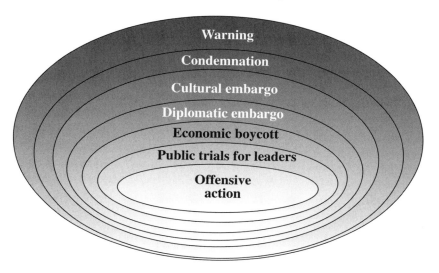

will have to pay is tolerable. This trend is evident in the attitude of the Iranian Foreign Ministry to American legislation that attempted to force international companies to refrain from trading with state supporters of terrorism—Iran and Libya.[107] The Iranian Foreign Ministry stated, "the Clinton decision lacks international support and therefore, is doomed to failure."[108]

States involved in terrorism will use any means to try and find cracks in the wall of international sanctions, and will look for nations who are willing to maintain cultural, diplomatic, and economic relationships with them in spite of the sanctions, covertly as well as overtly. States supporting terrorism are willing to pay a high price for this, and grant those who cooperate with them economic and other types of benefits. Alternatively, they are liable to threaten to harm foreign investments and assets on their territory, to perpetrate massive terrorist attacks or even engage in all-out war against countries that participate in the sanctions against them. In an attempt to break an international boycott, state sponsors of terrorism may attempt to use ethnic, religious, national, or other types of relationships with nations that are also members of various forums (a joint league or organization of nations) and request relief from international legal institutions.

In 1992, for example, the United States and Great Britain accused Libya of bombing two Western passenger planes and charged them with being responsible for the deaths of 440 people. They submitted a proposal to the UN Security Council that included, among other things, an air and military embargo against Libya. These sanctions included the discontinuation of air transport, a decline in the echelon of the diplomatic representation, and an arms embargo against Libya. After the proposals made by the United States and Britain had been accepted by the Security Council (Resolution 748), Libya appealed to the International Court at the Hague requesting that implementation of the decision be prevented. The International Court rejected their petition, *inter alia*, because the sanctions against Libya were accepted under Paragraph 41 of Article 7 of the UN Charter. This section grants the Security Council sweeping authority to act so as to maintain world peace and security, even when these outweigh considerations of law and justice.[109] Col. Qaddafi, the Libyan leader, announced that his country would refuse to succumb to possible sanctions from the UN. He sent messages to kings, presidents, and sultans throughout the world in order to protest against the proposed UN Security Council resolution, in which he stated:

> If the world accepts such a distortion of the UN Charter, and agrees to publish such a resolution, then it will become a world of natives and primitives. And if we are different, we must leave New York, "beg for mercy" for the UN, and withdraw from it as we previously did from the League of Nations. It is obvious that this is not a legal matter. We are standing before a new age of Colonialism in the Third World.[110]

In light of an appeal by Libya, its ally, Syria, came to its aid and introduced an initiative to ease the sanctions against Libya. Syria proposed to the Council of Ministers of the Arab League, which convened in Cairo, that the Security Council release Arab League nations from having to enforce Resolution 748, which imposed sanctions against Libya. This request was made on the basis of Article 50 of the UN Charter, which states that in a case where measures are taken against a member state, any other state confronted with special economic problems arising from the carrying out of those measures shall have the right to consult with the Security Council with regard to resolving those problems. Syria claimed in this matter that "being Arabs, we stand beside Libya, following our proposal which was accepted by the Arab ministers. It agreed to turn over the two Libyan nationals who were suspected of being involved in the Lockerbie incident to a neutral country, so they could stand trial."[111]

The international community cannot stand by while international sanctions are flouted. The effectiveness of international punitive and deterrent measures is severely compromised when nations are willing to defy international sanctions in order to promote their own private interests, or in order to maintain solidarity with their terrorism-supporting allies. To prevent this, the international community must make it clear that any nation that deliberately violates international sanctions will be subject to secondary sanctions against it.

In the past, such measures were used against nations whose involvement in terrorism was exposed. Generally speaking, these steps were employed randomly, either by one nation or several nations (sometimes relying on the support of UN resolutions and occasionally, independently), rather than part of a permanent, recognized and predefined "price scale." In 1986, following revelations that Syria had been directly involved in dispatching the terrorist Hindawi, who had planned to blow up an El Al plane en route from London to Tel Aviv, the federal government in Bonn decided to adopt a series of measures against Syria, including supervising the Syrian embassy, Syria's airlines and Syrian nationals in Germany; and suspending a decision to send a German ambassador to Syria. France and Germany decided to impose punitive measures against Syria after Great Britain's motion for joint sanctions against Syria was rejected at the EU Foreign Ministers' meeting in Luxembourg.[112] At the same time Britain vetoed a five-year aid package, valued at $140 million, which the EU had intended for Syria. Geoffrey Howe, the British Foreign Secretary, said, "Britain is not prepared to continue financial aid to Syria given the present circumstances."[113]

Some of the more prominent measures adopted against states involved in terrorism have been imposed against Libya. In light of knowledge regarding Libyan involvement in various terrorist attacks (including acts in which American military personnel had been injured), American fighter planes bombed various targets in the Libyan cities of Tripoli and Benghazi in 1986. In April 1991, at the initiative of the United States, the UN imposed sanctions against Libya due to its continued involvement in terrorism and primarily because of its refusal to extradite Libyan security personnel suspected of involvement in two attacks on passenger planes (the Pan Am flight over Lockerbie and the French UTA flight over the Saharan Desert in Niger), both of which took the lives of hundreds of victims. The sanctions were tightened when the UN decided on an air blockade against Libya because of its continued refusal to hand over the suspects. UN Resolution 748 required Libya to declare its commitment to desist from terrorist activity and to stop aiding terrorist organizations. The Security Council also called upon member states to stop supplying Libya with all forms of weapons, to reduce the number of Libyan diplomats, and to restrict their movements within the host countries.[114] For the first time, the UN used its power to impose sanctions against a country accused of international terrorism (a resolution that was passed by a majority of ten nations, with five abstentions).

In November 1993, the UN adopted Resolution 883, which ratified the previous decision (this time, with a majority of eleven with four abstentions). Among other things, the decisions called for a freeze on funds and economic resources owned and controlled by the Libyan government, and prohibited nations from supplying Libya with oil drilling equipment. The resolution stated that the sanctions would be lifted if Libya met the Security Council's demands, that is, ensuring that the suspects in the Pan Am Flight 103 bombing attended their trial, and cooperating with French agencies investigating the UTA incident.[115]

However, the struggle against states supporting terrorism reflects numerous conflicts of interests between the various actors on the international stage: nations, superpowers, alliances, leagues of states, groups and organizations. Occasionally, the struggle against terror creates conflicts of interests even within a state—between security and economic interests. Until the September 11 terrorist attacks on the United States, it seemed that economic interests had the upper hand while security interests, expressed as the desire for a more effective struggle against states involved in terrorism, had been pushed aside.

Based on the international measures taken over the years against states involved in terrorism, it seems that most nations are unwilling to sacrifice their interests (in particular, trade and economic relations) in order to force these nations to reduce their involvement in terrorism. The most prominent example of this double standard (which is a direct result of economic interests) is the relationship between European countries (headed by Germany and France) and the leading nation involved in terrorism—Iran. Contrary to the American position, which is aimed at restricting Iran's involvement and forcing it to abandon terrorism through the use of economic and others sanctions (based on Iran's shaky economy), these nations have found many different excuses in order to justify their extensive commercial and economic ties with Iran.

As opposed to the American claim, countries that maintain extensive economic ties with states involved in terrorism do not use economic terms to excuse their policies; rather, they use international utilitarian explanations. They argue that imposing sanctions will not make these states reduce their involvement in terrorism. Instead, these nations will be pushed to the extreme and become even more radical so that at the end of the day, policies involving sanctions will only lead to an escalation of international terrorism. In their opinion, a policy of "critical dialogue" should be used with states involved in terrorism—maintaining open channels with them through commercial, economic, cultural, and others ties. Through these channels it will be possible to criticize the behavior of state supporters of terrorism, to influence them to abandon terrorism. Naturally, the critical dialogue approach does no more than pay lip service to support for counterterrorism measures by employing a hypocritical policy aimed at hiding the importance of economic interests over security interests.

The international community's hypocrisy in the struggle against state supporters of terrorism is evident from the critical words of Margaret Thatcher, former prime minister of Great Britain, in a speech delivered at the fourth summit conference of the International Democratic Union in 1989. She stated that the international community was prepared to forgive certain nations "as if civilized behavior were not expected from them." According to Thatcher, the international community is not aggressive enough towards governments that support terrorism. "A state cannot support terrorism and also enjoy the treatment afforded to a regular member of the international community."[116]

Geoffrey Howe, British foreign minister at that time, explained the disparity between demonstrative statements of Western countries against international terrorism in general, and against state involvement in terrorism in particular, and the translation of these declarations into concrete action. He said, "It seems that terrorist actions perpetrated in one European country do not resonate in other European countries."[117]

Yet even some nations opposed to "critical dialogue," such as the United States and Israel have, at times, used the services of countries that maintain commercial and economic ties with states that sponsor terrorism, particularly when they want to negotiate the release of hostages or need those countries to put pressure on terrorist organizations they support in order to prevent attacks. In this regard they undermine the moral basis for their opposition and render meaningless any criticism against countries that endorse such a policy.[118]

The mediation tasks placed upon these nations ostensibly give them permission to pursue their extensive economic and commercial ties with states involved in terrorism, but actually frustrate any effort at reaching a joint international strategy against state supporters of terrorism.

In order to examine the claims of nations who maintain "critical dialogue" policies one must return to the underlying assumption, according to which states involved in terrorism conduct a rational decision-making process using cost-benefit considerations. When those supporting a "critical dialogue approach" state that one must avoid demanding that these states pay a price for their involvement in terrorism, the cost component of the cost-benefit equation does not increase and thus that nation's balance of interests doesn't change in a way that will motivate it to restrict its involvement in terrorism.

Nations that maintain relations with state supporters of terrorism sometimes use moral grounds as justification. Their reasoning is that it is immoral to target entire innocent populations because of the policy of a corrupt, violent, and extremist regime. At the summit meeting of the industrialized nations (G-7) held in Paris in August 1996, France and Germany argued that U.S. measures designed to "turn entire populations into hostages" were cruel.[119] Yet if the issue is about justice, then the suffering of populations in states involved in terrorism must be measured against the suffering of the population in a nation under attack. Thus, if the damage to the former will restrict or stop the state's involvement in terrorism, thereby limiting the damage to citizens in the state suffering from terrorism, then such action may be justified. Moreover, the damage suffered by the population in nations contending with terrorist attacks is greater than the damage suffered by the population in the state supporting terrorism. Compared with the inconvenience and economic problems that may be caused to the latter due to economic sanctions, the population coping with terrorism faces a life and death situation. In the balance of justice and morality, the right to life takes precedence over well-being. Therefore, the moral claim countries use to defend their ties with state supporters of terrorism is unsubstantiated.

The question arises as to whether it is reasonable to expect that pressure brought to bear on the population of a state supporter of terrorism will change its policy or reduce its involvement in terrorism. Nations opposed to economic sanctions contend that states that are recognized as being involved in terrorism have autocratic or dictatorial regimes, and public opinion does not necessarily play a key role in their internal political systems. Therefore, it would appear that pressure brought against their populations would not achieve the desired results. On the contrary, they claim, such pressure could lead citizens to take an even more radical position and encourage additional volunteers to join the circle of violence. Furthermore, residents in these countries are used to a lower standard of living and the domestic economy is usually capable of providing for the basic needs of its people (in contrast with Western populations). Thus, they can withstand the pressure of economic sanctions for longer periods of time; hence, the effectiveness of economic sanctions is doubtful.

Such arguments are inaccurate. Firstly, sanctions are not directed at influencing public opinion, but rather the government. Economic sanctions are meant to cause serious damage to the nation's economy and limit its ability to direct economic resources towards supporting terrorist organizations or perpetrating terrorist attacks. Before sanctions would impact the population's shopping basket, they might affect the government's ability to carry out expensive economic, military, and other projects, and force the regime to invest its time in finding solutions for the country's economic difficulties. Moreover, civilian populations in states that sponsor terrorism do not necessarily constitute a source for recruiting terrorists to carry out international terrorist attacks. So even if the population becomes angry against the nations imposing sanctions, these feelings will be translated, first and foremost, into organized demonstrations within the country itself, and not necessarily international terrorism. There is also the possibility that such unrest will provide fertile ground for the growth of opposition groups against the present regime, which may eventually overturn the government and adopt new policies that will renounce terrorism.[120]

During the early 1990s, Iran was at the height of an ongoing economic crisis. Although oil production increased from 2.5 million barrels per day to 4.1 million, Iran could not afford to repay short-term loans it had taken in the amount of some $3 billion, and thus access was denied to lines of credit needed to import technological products and industrial raw materials.[121] Iran's total foreign debt in 1993 was estimated at around $40 billion.[122] The Iranian regime was saved from economic collapse only thanks to the willingness of countries that maintained commercial and economic ties to reschedule its debts (Germany agreed, for example, to reschedule Iran's debt totaling approximately $5 billion).[123]

To sum up, in order to formulate an effective international policy against state supporters of terrorism, the international community must take the following steps: arrive at an accepted and comprehensive international definition of terrorism; classify nations according to the nature of their involvement in terrorism and its severity; recognize the need and the obligation to impose sanctions against states involved in terrorism; publicize an up-to-date list of state supporters of terrorism, according to their various types of involvement; impose secondary sanctions against nations and companies that continue to maintain economic ties with states against whom sanctions have been imposed because of their involvement in terrorism; establish a permanent, international counter-terrorism mechanism, one of whose goals will be to monitor the implementation of punitive measures against states involved in terrorism, and to warn of any nation that deviates from the measures imposed (see chapter 10 for a more in-depth discussion of the issue of international cooperation).

Only full compliance with the aforementioned steps will ensure effective action against states involved in terrorism, will change the balance of interests for these countries, reduce their involvement in terrorism and, ultimately, reduce the scope of terrorist attacks around the world and their resulting damage.

Defensive Deterrence

Defensive-security action is one of the crucial elements in counter-terrorism policy. This component includes defending the nation's borders and providing security for sensitive installations, traffic arteries, symbolic targets, population centers, and the like. The security network's goals with regard to counter-terrorism policy include: preventing the infiltration of terrorists into the country, identifying and neutralizing terrorists as they travel about the nation's roadways, preventing penetration into secure installations or areas, and finally—deterring terrorists from carrying out their attacks because they fear injury, capture, and punishment.

The defensive action component of a counter-terrorism policy consists of two key elements: actual prevention of attacks by making it difficult for the terrorist to reach his intended target, through early identification and neutralization; while at the same time, deterring terrorists from carrying out their attacks at well-protected facilities by generating the feeling that any action they may undertake is doomed to failure, and thus making them fearful regarding their own fate. Crenshaw, however, emphasizes the fact that even when a nation conducts an effective war against terrorism, in many cases this does not eliminate terrorism, and may not even prevent certain attacks, but only serves to divert terrorism towards alternative methods, means and targets.[124] In other words, defensive means may redirect a terrorist attack towards a different target at a different time, which would then prove to be an unexpected surprise for security forces—for example, a target that is not adequately protected or is not considered by security forces to be a potential target. Consequently, defensive deterrence might prove to be a double-edged sword within the context of a nation's counter-terrorism policy.

This critical approach, correct though it may be, is futile because its adoption may lead to a decision to reduce or completely avoid defensive actions, even in the face of assessments or information regarding an intended attack against a particular target, for fear that the terrorist organizations will be deterred from one target and choose another. The advantage of having an opportunity to stop an attack through effective defensive action offsets any speculative consideration regarding the possibility that the attack will not be stopped, but rather, merely redirected to another place or another time. A bird in the hand is worth two in the bush. Moreover, even if the defensive deterrence doesn't stop the attack, merely delays or diverts it, this could still give security forces the time needed to identify the alternative intentions and thwart the attack or carry out an offensive action. Decision makers must allocate the defensive means needed to defend potential terrorist targets, both in light of specific intelligence information and on an ongoing basis, in order to ensure a defensive deterrent.

Drawing "Red Lines" with Regard to Terrorist Activity

A nation attempting to deter a terrorist organization draws, as it were, a "red line"—a deterrent ceiling that the terrorist organization must not cross. If the terrorist organization ignores this line, it can expect to suffer retaliation and punishment from the deterring nation. But a nation that wishes to maintain its credibility, in the eyes of the terrorist organization, its own population, and international public opinion, may find itself having to act upon its threat when deterrent measures have failed and the terrorist organization has crossed over the red line. At times, it may be necessary to act on the threat, even if it contradicts the nation's desire or its immediate interests, in order to maintain its present and future deterrent credibility. On the other hand, it should be recalled that without a public and clearly defined red line, the terrorist organization might not understand the nation's retaliatory and punitive actions, and might continue perpetrating attacks or even escalate them in order to test the limits of its action, and the ability of the deterring nation and its population to withstand the attacks.

There is also another dilemma: once the deterrent ceiling has been made public, any action that does not reach the defined deterrent ceiling is liable to be considered acceptable and permitted by the terrorist organization, because such activity will not result in a response from the nation under attack, or at least not a strong response.

As part of the considerations relating to these dilemmas, decision makers must take into account that proclaiming red lines obligates them to take action when these are crossed, and therefore such public pronouncements should be avoided when security decision makers lack the ability, commitment, and resolve to carry out the threat. Moreover, in order to avoid a situation wherein actions that fall below the deterrent ceiling are tolerated, it is recommended that the deterrent consist of stages based on a range of severity, with possible, alternative responses that correspond with the scope of damage caused to the nation, even if it is lower than the deterrent ceiling (that is, below the red line that would obligate the nation to act on its threat). In this way a nation's response to the terrorist organization crossing the red line would, of necessity, be different from its response to terrorist activity below that ceiling, but a response would be forthcoming in any event. In short, there is zero tolerance for any level of terrorism.

Escalation and Efficiency of Terrorism as a Result of Deterrent Activity

Deterrent activity against terrorism may entail losses. When a terrorist organization feels it cannot respond to the deterrent it is facing, it could become motivated to develop new, more dangerous, methods using weapons that are more lethal, or it may attempt to attack more sensitive targets. In this way the organization may turn the tables and instead of being deterred by the nation, it could actually escalate the violence in attempt to discourage the nation from undertaking punitive and deterrent measures.

According to Israel Tal, overuse of deterrent means and measures causes the enemy to experience humiliation, arouses feelings of revenge, and demonstrates its military inferiority and helplessness. According to Tal, the sense of inferiority urges and motivates the organization to draw conclusions and increase its efforts at empowerment and military capability. Tal agrees that "effective deterrent measures in the present are liable to make the enemy stronger and more determined, and weakens the effectiveness of the deterrent in the future."[125] In essence, then, deterrence sows the seeds of its own failure. An outstanding example of this can be found in Crenshaw's attitude towards hostage situations. According to Crenshaw, following Israel's success with the action it undertook in Entebbe in 1976, most Western countries established elite rapid-response units. This greatly increased the degree to which governments tended to use the military means at their disposal in hostage situations, despite the risk this imposes for the hostages. Terrorists adapted to this policy and very quickly developed new methods for making rescue difficult, such as hiding hostages in different locations, or making such units irrelevant, for example, by using suicide tactics.[126]

We cannot ignore the dilemma relating to the terrorist organization's efficiency as a result of effective deterrent measures. Although this dilemma does not negate the advantages of deterrents nor does it reduce their importance, it does signal a warning to a nation's security forces coping with terrorism because they must not allow themselves to rest on their laurels. Even in times of relative calm and quiet as a result of effective deterrent measures used against terrorist organizations, security personnel must try to anticipate the efficiency measures the terrorists will follow next, the innovative methods they will employ, the weapons they will have in their possession and the targets they are liable to focus on. Early assessment of the directions in which terrorism could develop are likely to help minimize the general impact of the terrorists' efficiency measures, particularly with the existence of an effective deterrent, and will enable security forces to stay one step ahead of the terrorists.

Summary and Conclusions

Given the controversy pertaining to the effectiveness of counter-terrorism deterrent measures, and based on Israel's experience in this sphere, we can define the various dilemmas relating to deterrence and articulate them as a model of stages that decision makers can use to assess in advance a deterrent's effectiveness before carrying out any action (see Figure 4.5). Although this model does not elaborate on when terrorists are likely to be deterred and when they are not (among other things, because it is impossible to give a general answer to that question since such a response would be derived from the characteristics of each organization and the specific circumstances), it does offer tools and principles that may reduce the margin for error when choosing the best deterrent framework to be used against terrorist organizations.

The model must be based on determining the purpose of the deterrent. Is the goal a "comprehensive deterrent," that is, to prevent all terrorist activity against the nation, or is it only a partial deterrent? And if it is a partial deterrent, is the goal to reduce the scope of terrorism, to prevent a specific attack, or to force the terrorist organization to refrain from a specific type of attack, or its time or location?

Figure 4.5
Formulating Deterrence against Terrorist Organizations

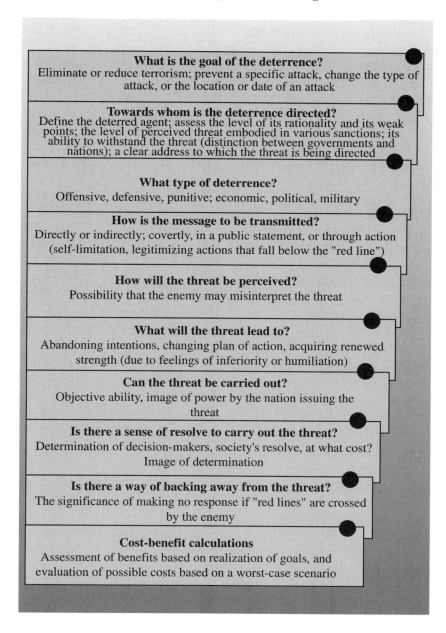

What is the goal of the deterrence?
Eliminate or reduce terrorism; prevent a specific attack, change the type of attack, or the location or date of an attack

Towards whom is the deterrence directed?
Define the deterred agent; assess the level of its rationality and its weak points; the level of perceived threat embodied in various sanctions; its ability to withstand the threat (distinction between governments and nations); a clear address to which the threat is being directed

What type of deterrence?
Offensive, defensive, punitive; economic, political, military

How is the message to be transmitted?
Directly or indirectly; covertly, in a public statement, or through action (self-limitation, legitimizing actions that fall below the "red line")

How will the threat be perceived?
Possibility that the enemy may misinterpret the threat

What will the threat lead to?
Abandoning intentions, changing plan of action, acquiring renewed strength (due to feelings of inferiority or humiliation)

Can the threat be carried out?
Objective ability, image of power by the nation issuing the threat

Is there a sense of resolve to carry out the threat?
Determination of decision-makers, society's resolve, at what cost? Image of determination

Is there a way of backing away from the threat?
The significance of making no response if "red lines" are crossed by the enemy

Cost-benefit calculations
Assessment of benefits based on realization of goals, and evaluation of possible costs based on a worst-case scenario

The next step is to define precisely the target against which the deterrent is to be directed—a state sponsor of terrorism, terrorist organization, group of terrorists, or a single terrorist—and to assess in advance the rationality of the deterred agent. Similarly, the character of the deterred agent must be analyzed and evaluated (based on intelligence data). What is its weak point? How threatened will the deterred agent feel by various types of threats of sanctions imposed against it? And to what extent is it able to withstand such sanctions? Decision makers must also examine whether there is a specific address against which the threat should be directed.

Afterwards, and based on an analysis of the aforementioned assessment of characteristics, the type of deterrent measure to be employed must be selected: offensive, defensive, or punitive. What type of threat is being formulated? Does the threat involve political or economic sanctions, or the use of military force in the event that red lines are crossed?

Once the goal of the deterrent, the identity of the deterred body, and the preferred type of deterrent measures have been defined, decision makers must determine how to transmit their message: Should the message be transmitted directly, or indirectly through a intermediary? Will the message be transmitted secretly, through public declaration, or using practical action? (Decision makers must take into account the advantages of a public deterrent, the main aspect of which involves setting an unequivocal limit for the deterred agent while minimizing interpretation and misunderstanding versus the disadvantages of such a deterrent—the danger that the nation will be hampered by "tolerating" an activity level that falls below its stated red line, as described above.)

Once the basic steps for the deterrent have been completed, decision makers must project how the threat will be understood by the opponent: What is an acceptable margin of error regarding the threat as perceived by the deterred agent?

In the next step, decision makers need to assess what response the threat will trigger: Will the threat achieve its goal—abandoning a plan to perpetrate terrorist attacks, or change or divert an attack—or will the threat only incite the organization's feelings of inferiority and humiliation, and motivate the terrorists to enhance their capability? In this context, the deterring nation must consider the ramifications of the deterrent not only in the short term, but for the long term as well.

Now the decision maker must examine whether he has the power and the resources needed to realize the threat in the event the deterred organization crosses the red line. If the answer to this question is affirmative, he must assess the appearance of capability as perceived by the deterred agent, and whether that image corresponds to reality.

In a similar fashion, decision makers must then appraise the determination of their fellow leaders to realize the threat in the event of a violation by the deterred agent. In addition, they have to examine whether the sphere of action—on both the domestic and international levels—will allow decision makers to act on their threat. (Is the public prepared to withstand the possible ramifications of the steps they take against the terrorist organization?) In this case, too, it is very important to analyze the appearance that has been perceived by the deterred agent regarding the nation's resolve to carry out the threat.

At this point, decision makers must consider the significance of not carrying out the threat if a red line is crossed. They must ask themselves whether the deterrent, as it was formulated, provides the decision makers with a way out that will enable them to refrain from acting on their threat if the deterrent ceiling is crossed without seriously jeopardizing their overall deterrent capability.

At the end of the decision-making process described above, and given the nature of the deterrent measures being formulated, decision makers must calculate the cost-benefit values of the deterrent, regarding both its success and its failure. Failure must be measured on the basis of a worst-case scenario, that is, what would the damage be if the worst possible option actually came to pass?

5

Dilemmas Concerning Offensive and Defensive Counter-Terrorism Actions

One of the key elements in the war against terrorism is offensive action, that is, action initiated by security forces against terrorist targets, carried out in areas where the terrorists deploy and operate. Offensive action usually takes place on the territory of a state sponsor of terrorism or, alternatively, on the territory of the attacking nation—in areas that are not controlled by security forces, or against clandestine bases throughout the country. In regions where terrorist organizations enjoy full or partial control, or at least have relative freedom of operation, offensive action will be based on land incursion operations, air bombardment and artillery fire, naval activity and special operations aimed at specific targets within the organization.

Assessing the Effectiveness of an Offensive Action

At times it appears that the offensive action undertaken by a nation coping with a terrorist organization is the result of a momentary whim by decision makers, or the outcome of internal pressure on leaders following a mass-casualty terrorist attack and the desire for revenge. The question is: Can objective criteria be devised to assess the need and the effectiveness of carrying out various counter-terrorism measures and, in particular, offensive action?

It is usual for a nation that pursues offensive action as part of its counter-terrorism strategy to very quickly encounter severe criticism, both internal and external. Moreover, offensive action aimed at terrorism is a complex undertaking that could have a negative impact, with both short-term and long-term consequences. Therefore, decision makers must attempt to assess ahead of time the degree to which the use of offensive measures will be effective.

In order to examine the effectiveness of the offensive action we must first define the goals underlying these initiatives, and decide whether these goals can be achieved using the methods and means chosen.

Goals of the Offensive Action

The goals that underlie offensive action may include: preventing terrorist attacks; disrupting the organization's activity; revenge and punishment; deterrence; damaging the morale of the organization's activists and supporters; raising the morale of the nation's residents; and occasionally, there may be other considerations, such as internal political circumstances, upcoming elections, etc. (see Figure 5.1).

Preventing terrorist attacks—One of the crucial goals behind offensive action is to prevent terrorist attacks. This goal is based on the belief that damage to the terrorist organization's activists and infrastructures will disrupt one of the necessary preparatory stages: The planning of the attacks, training the terrorists, preparing the explosives and weapons, and other support activity.

Sometimes the offensive action is designed to prevent a specific attack and not necessarily to disrupt the organization's ability to perpetrate attacks in general.[127]

Among all the goals underlying an offensive action, that of preventing attacks is the one most likely to be acceptable even to those opposed to such actions, because its purpose is to save lives in a concrete and immediate fashion by thwarting a terrorist attack. However, precisely for that reason, decision makers may claim they are engaged in genuine prevention even when the real goals underlying the attack are different. Moreover, it is sometimes very difficult to prove that attacking a particular terrorist target will necessarily thwart a terrorist act and, as stated by opponents, the offensive action may only motivate the terrorist organization to escalate its activity. In this way, the offensive action can become a losing proposition. Nonetheless, even when there is a reasonable likelihood that the terrorists will react, offensive action should not be rejected out of hand and the benefit of such action should be exam-

Figure 5.1
The Effectiveness of Offensive Actions

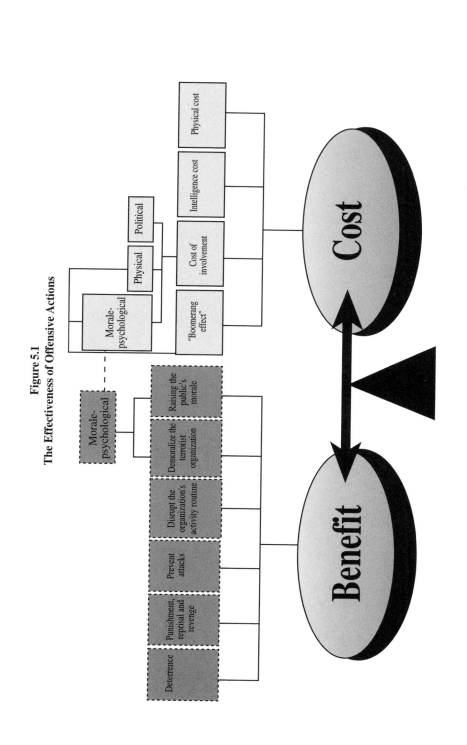

ined in relation to the long-term scope and nature of the attacks perpetrated by that organization.

Disrupting the organization's activity routine—One possible goal of an offensive action is to disrupt the organization's routine of activities. This goal can be achieved, for example, by killing one of their top-level activists, following which there will be a "power struggle" among other activists eager to inherit his place; or by destroying the organization's infrastructure, which will force members to allocate resources, manpower, and time to restore the situation to the way it was.

Revenge and punishment—The special nature of coping with terrorism, the tremendous cruelty of the attacks, and the people's weakened sense of security can, at times, leave decision makers and the public at large with a strong urge to seek revenge and punish those involved in the attacks. Therefore, some offensive actions carried out by the state may be attributed to this desire.

Deterrence—Along with punishment, the goal of deterrence underlies offensive action. These two goals often coincide with each other, such that those responsible for the terrorism will pay the price while others will be taught a lesson. This message was sometimes transmitted by Israel's leaders and the heads of its security forces. For example, following the assassination of Abbas Musawi, secretary-general of Hizballah, Minister of Defense Moshe Arens said, "This serves as a message to all terrorist organizations...whoever starts something with us, we will finish it for them. This must be made clear to all the gangs, terrorist organizations and their leaders."[128] Several years previously, after the elimination of Abu Jihad, Arafat's second-in-command, then-Prime Minister Yitzhak Shamir declared at a ceremony marking Israel's Memorial Day to fallen IDF soldiers, "Let us hope and believe that our enemies will come to realize and understand that the People of Israel know how to fight back and that anyone who causes us injury—will be injured sevenfold."[129] And a short time following the assassination of Fathi Shekaki, Shimon Peres, who was serving as foreign minister at that time, said at the Jerusalem Business Conference, "Islamic Jihad is a murderous organization and he, Shekaki, was its leader. Anyone who engages in murder risks assassination."[130]

Demoralizing the organization's activists and supporters—Leaders of terrorist organizations and top-level activists are constantly aware of the possibility of an individual attack against them, or against their organization's infrastructure. At times this may impinge on their ability to function, their behavior, and daily routine. However, offensive action takes its toll not only on senior members of a terrorist organization, but rather on all of its members, as well as those who support and sympathize with its activities and aims. Demoralization among the organization's activists is a consequence of the damage caused to the organization by the offensive action; the way in which the action demonstrates the nation's technological, operational, and intelligence superiority; and the fear that the information used to carry out the operation came from a "mole" within the organization. This fear sometimes leads to a campaign to "purify" the organization. For example, Hizballah Secretary-General Sheikh Hassan Nasrallah (who inherited the position from his predecessor, Abbas Musawi, who was killed by Israel), announced that his first task after inheriting Moussawi's position would be to find out whether there was an Israeli spy ring within the organization.[131]

Lifting the morale of the nation's populace—Offensive action is sometimes accompanied by another goal—lifting the morale of the people living in the nation rocked by terrorism. As stated, the primary damage caused by terrorism is not necessarily physical, but rather psychological damage. Terrorism engenders fear, a feeling of helplessness. A successful and complicated armed operation that reflects great military capability, daring, determination, imagination and, above all, technological and intelligence superiority, is likely to enhance the public's sense of security and reinforce their ability to confront terrorism.

Yet carrying out an offensive action for the sake of "morale-building" is often perceived by those engaged in this sphere as forbidden, an act to be condemned. How can one even consider endangering human life for such an "unworthy" and "populist" goal as "morale-building?" Things are not so simple, however.

In considering the impact of the morale-psychological variable on the "effectiveness scale" of offensive actions, it would appear that the morale-psychological element is significant. Nevertheless, it must not be the only variable, or even the primary variable, when making the decision to carry out actions of this type, *inter alia*, because we must also take into account revenge attacks following an individual assault, which will damage public morale once again (see below, the "boomerang effect").

Improper considerations—The issue of morale is occasionally—and erroneously—thought to be an "improper consideration." There is a small but important difference between the desire to "raise morale" with an offensive action and illegitimate considerations, such as the desire to influence the results of upcoming elections, the desire to distract the public from urgent political, social, or economic crisis; the leader's desire to "score points" at the expense of his opponents, either within his own party or rival parties, etc.[132] But while these latter goals are not a legitimate part of the decision to initiate some type of offensive action, raising morale is a legitimate and true need facing the strategic risk of counter-terrorism—the public's demoralization. As such, it is important to carry out offensive actions that will strengthen the public's resolve in the face of terrorism.

To sum up, there are many and varying goals underpinning offensive actions. These goals are usually interconnected and their importance varies in accordance with circumstances of time and place. In any event, the effectiveness of an offensive action is a direct result of the degree to which the action succeeds in achieving all, or at least some, of its objectives.

The Cost of Offensive Actions

Against the benefits of offensive actions, decision makers must weigh five possible costs:

- *Intelligence cost*—The nation initiating the offensive attack may have to pay the price of exposing the intelligence source that provided the information needed to carry out the action. Offensive action requires accurate preliminary information in real time in order to guarantee its success, but that information can lead to exposing and neutralizing the intelligence source by the enemy shortly thereafter.
- *Physical cost*—The offensive action requires the allocation of tremendous resources, at all stages of intelligence-gathering, planning and training, and implementation. When added together, these costs constitute the physical cost of the action.
- *International cost*—Offensive actions, particularly those carried out on foreign territory, usually attract widespread inter-

national censure, particularly from countries that identify with the terrorists' cause or actually sponsor the organization. In many cases this type of activity is considered to be in violation of international law and a danger to regional stability.

- *Cost of possible complications*—Decision makers must consider the possibility that the military operation might fail or that things may not go as planned. Such a situation could have diplomatic and international consequences, or military complications if the combat force requires a dangerous and difficult rescue operation, and may even develop into direct military conflict with hostile forces.
- *The cost of reprisal ("boomerang effect")*—As mentioned above, decision makers must consider the possibility that an offensive action may heighten the motivation of terrorist organizations to perpetrate revenge attacks. Once the organizations are capable of acting on such motivation, the nation may have to pay a high price for the offensive action it took.

In light of the above, decision makers and security agencies looking into the possibility of initiating an offensive action against terrorist organizations must first take several issues into account:

- *Frequency (quantitative parameter)*—Decision makers must bear in mind that excessive use of offensive action jeopardizes its effectiveness. Repetition of similar attacks aimed at the same areas will cause terrorist organizations to adopt a defensive routine.
- *Screening (qualitative parameter)*—Offensive action should be aimed primarily at crucial targets whose elimination will likely prevent terrorist attacks, disrupt the organization's activity, deter the terrorists from perpetrating attacks or demoralize them.
- *Weighting*—Decision makers must calculate the cost-benefit analysis before each such action, and assess possible damage based on the worst-case scenario.
- *Alternatives*—Because of the high price the state may have to pay for taking offensive action, decision makers must consider all possible alternatives that could achieve the same goals (or at least some of them) but at a lower cost.

Other Considerations for Assessing the Effectiveness of Offensive Action

It is not enough to do a cost-benefit analysis when assessing the effectiveness of an offensive action, for there are other dimensions that are germane to the issue of effectiveness. Horowitz and Aronson propose examining the effectiveness of Israeli reprisals by looking at immediate impact and long-term effect; influence on the situation along the borders and on the attitude of the super-powers; the impact on the Arab world and on Israel's internal policy. On the basis of such variables the authors examine several of Israel's major reprisal operations and emphasize that although such retaliation served to maintain and enhance Israel's deterrent capabilities, thereby creating a "safety valve" that prevented the need for all-out war and in the main, strengthened the public status of Israel's political elite, it is difficult to establish ironclad rules regarding the effectiveness of any reprisal action because we cannot know what the situation would have been had that action not been carried out.[133]

Zachi Shalom believes that underlying the controversy between supporters and detractors is the question of the effectiveness of Israeli reprisals. While the opponents, who were represented in the 1950s by Moshe Sharett, believe that retaliation increases the Arabs' hatred and loathing of Israel in the long run,[134] those who approve of reprisals feel that Arab hatred of Israel and their desire for its destruction is a given, and thus reprisals neither intensify nor weaken these sentiments. In contrast, Israel's reprisal policy does, indeed, influence and reduce the Arab countries' willingness to act on their intentions.[135] In Shalom's opinion, in examining the effectiveness of reprisals we must look at two key criteria: the goals this policy is supposed to achieve, and the alternative situation that would result in its absence. In his view, policymakers did not originally tend to attribute far-reaching goals to the reprisal policy, but primarily perceived it as a tool to prove they were undertaking security activity against infiltrations during the 1950s, and this goal seems to have been achieved. But Shalom concludes: "The debate on the efficacy of the reprisal policy as a means of deterring Arab nations is the type of debate that has never been resolved, and will apparently never be."[136]

Hanan Alon examined Israel's counter-terrorism policy up to 1978 using the criterion of the cost-benefit analysis. The main parameter chosen in his study to examine the "benefit" was the risk to human life as a result of counter-terrorism measures.[137] Alon proposed a technique for comparing physical damage from terrorism with physical damage caused by other factors (such as traffic accidents) and stated that resources should be distributed according to the outcome, such that the lion's share of resources would be allocated to the plan that copes with the factor responsible for the highest number of injuries.[138]

The question becomes, Is "saving human lives" the only or best index for examining the effectiveness of counter-terrorism activity, or are there other quantitative and/or qualitative factors that should be taken into account?

During the first intifada (1987-1990), a new variable was added into assessing the effectiveness of Israel's offensive counter-terrorism activities. The Israeli government's policy in the West Bank during the early part of the intifada, which was dictated by the Minister of Defense at that time, Yitzhak Rabin, changed from time to time according to the degree to which certain actions were beneficial, the level of public criticism in Israel, and the pressure put on the government by friendly nations. Decision makers quickly learned that it wasn't enough to examine the effectiveness of Israeli policy in empirical terms, that is, the degree to which the number of Israeli and Palestinian injuries declined as a result of some action or other. Now Israel also had to consider how its actions were being photographed in the media, and what message they transmitted to public opinion in Israel and throughout the world.

When examining the effectiveness of the war against terrorism, it is therefore important to consider four main indices: operational capability, motivation to perpetrate terrorist acts, internal morale of the terrorists and their supporters, and the morale of the people coping with terrorism (see Figure 5.2).

- *Capability*—This index examines the degree to which counter-terrorism actions damage (or enhance) the terrorists' ability to perpetrate attacks. There are several possible results that counter-terrorism activity can have on the terrorist organization's operational ability:
- *Damage to its internal image*—damage to the organization's status among its native population, from which it draws its strength, personnel, and ability to act;
- *Damage to its international image*—damage to the organization's status in the international domain, the organization's political achievements in this area, or its political plans and goals;
- *Damage to its fundraising process*—from its various sources of financing, laundering the money, and transfer of funds to them;

Figure 5.2
Indicators for the Effectiveness of Counter-Terrorism

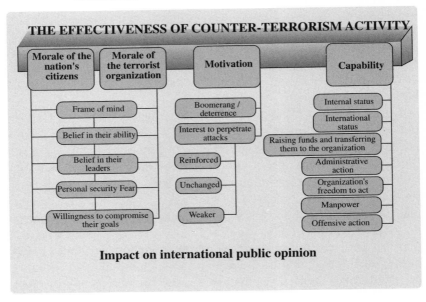

- *Disrupting the organization's administrative activities*—interfering with the organization's activities with regard to enlisting manpower, field preparations, arming, training, and practice, and structural or technological development; or damage to personnel or facilities the organization needs for its ongoing operations;
- *Damaging the organization's freedom of movement*—the terrorist organization's ability to commit terrorist attacks will be compromised following an offensive action if, as a result, the organization's freedom of movement in its staging and training areas has been restricted;
- *Damage to personnel*—the organization's ability is likely to be reduced when its numbers have dwindled due to killings or widespread arrests;
- *Damage to the organization's operational capabilities*—direct damage to the organization's operational facilities that were specially prepared for committing terrorist acts, or to its infrastructure—its bases, headquarters, explosives laboratories, etc.
- *Motivation*—This index examines the effect of offensive counter-terrorism measures on the organization's motivation to commit terrorist acts (either because of the impact such

measures have on the organization's decision makers and their feelings and desires for revenge, or as a result of a change in the organization's balance of interests). In this context we must consider that the offensive activity is liable, at times, to actually cause an increase in the terrorists' motivation to perpetrate revenge attacks (see the "boomerang effect" following).

- *Internal morale of the terrorists*—Offensive counter-terrorism measures may have an effect on the internal morale of the terrorist organization's activists and abetting population. This may be expressed in several ways: undermining the belief in the organization's ability to achieve its goals; undermining the belief in the organization's leadership, weakening their personal feeling of safety and spreading fear among the organization's activists and supporters. These expressions of internal demoralization could lead to a willingness to compromise on the organization's goals and objectives. (Here, too, we must take into consideration that the response may be just the opposite.) Internal morale is therefore likely to be one of the factors that diminish the organization's motivation to perpetrate or intensify terrorist acts (alongside its other considerations and interests).
- *Morale of the people suffering from terrorism*—The fight against terrorism should also influence the morale of the public suffering from terrorism and reduce—even if only in part—the morale-psychological damage that terrorism has created. Thus, counter-terrorism activity (when it succeeds in achieving its goal) should enhance individual and national morale; bolster the public's belief in the nation's ability to achieve its goals and bring calm and safety; enhance the people's individual belief in the nation's leadership; and intensify the nation's resolve to stick to its national goals and defined objectives. (It should be emphasized the such achievements are possible when counter-terrorism measures are successful in the field, but if they fail, they may have a completely opposite effect.)

Accurate assessing the effectiveness of offensive activity is a particularly difficult task, if only because it is impossible to know how many terrorist attacks have been prevented because of the action taken and what could have happened had those actions not been carried out. It should be pointed out that at times, actions that may appear to be successful in the short term are liable to be revealed as long-term failures—and vice versa.

Only when security forces and decision makers have considered all the issues and assessments discussed above and the benefit still outweighs the cost, will it be possible to consider positively carrying out an offensive action against a terrorist organization. Mordechai Gur, former Israeli deputy defense minister, remarked in this regard:

> When you're talking about an enemy whose terrorist activities cannot be stopped by a single action or series of actions, we must examine the ramifications of each response in order to ascertain that it justifies the outcome, including injuries, losses and political fallout. Woe to the government that does not take all of these factors into account.[139]

Targeted Killing—
The Normative-Moral Dilemma

Individual offensive action ("targeted killing") spearheads offensive activity within the context of counter-terrorism policy. With this type of action, a nation fighting against terrorism attacks an activist, or a group of activists within an organization, who are engaged in initiating, directing, preparing, recruiting, training or aiding in attacks, for the purpose of killing—or at least neutralizing—the terrorist. Individual offensive action raises two dilemmas that are interconnected: the moral-normative dilemma, and the question of the effectiveness of such action or, in other words, the justification and the wisdom in implementing an individual offensive action. The question of the effectiveness of "targeted killings" is inextricably linked to the general dilemmas regarding the effectiveness of offensive action, and was examined above. Therefore, the following section will examine the normative-moral issue.

Moral questions are, by their very nature, culturally dependent, and it is difficult to reach a consensus because moral values are not absolute. Instead, they are values that vary among different cultures, at different periods of time, and even between diverse groups and individuals within the same society.

With regard to the morality of targeted killings, there are those who believe that human life is a supreme value, and there is no justification for taking a human life. This axiom applies to anyone who has committed a serious crime, including criminal or political assassination. According to this perspective, no matter how heinous the terrorists' activities they may not be sentenced to death, and certainly not via a process that falls outside the normative judicial framework and whose legality is questionable. Moreover, opponents of targeted killings claim that if a nation possesses incriminating information about a terrorist then, as would be the case for any other criminal, he should be arrested and tried, criminal evidence should be presented in court, and if there is a conviction then execution might be permitted under certain circumstances. But a criminal cannot be killed without due process at the whim of a particular decision maker.

In contrast, those who support targeted killings argue that the killing of a terrorist who is personally responsible for serious, mass-casualty attacks and who is still capable of spilling the blood of innocent civilians is not only justified and moral, it is even essential for saving human lives. Supporters of this approach also cite the value of human life, and claim that in the name of the sanctity of life, decision makers must be allowed to do everything they can to prevent the few from harming the many—terrorists killing civilians and endangering world peace—and therefore individual attacks are permitted, moral, and justified.

In this context it is interesting to listen to the statement made by Israel Air Force Commander Maj. Gen. Dan Halutz in an interview conducted one month after the killing of Salah Shehade (in July 2002), one of the leaders of the Izzadin al-Kassam Brigades (Hamas's military arm), during an attack in which civilians were killed:

> I am prepared to discuss a fundamental question: Is there a situation where it is legitimate to strike at a terrorist when you know that such action will carry a price in terms casualties to civilians and uninvolved agents—I have no doubt about this, the answer is affirmative. Weighed against a man who has committed, or is known for certain to be planning, a "mega-attack," my answer is categorically "yes." [140]

In another interview with him, Gen. Halutz related to the same topic, saying:

> Each time we carry out a killing we also think about the 29 fatalities from the Park Hotel, and the 22 dead at the Dolphinarium and about the bus that blew up in Jerusalem. We take that into account as well. This is our war and anyone who thinks this isn't war—is mistaken. [141]

The moral dilemma regarding killing these individuals becomes, in effect, superfluous when these acts are thought of as warfare as opposed to criminal-punitive measures. Indeed, the "war against terrorism" is a form of undeclared war; moreover, this is a war without borders in which the front lines and the home front are intertwined.

However, even though a terrorist perpetrates attacks against citizens at random, anywhere and anytime, the state that contends with terrorism must not extrapolate from this as to what is permitted or forbidden to do. It should be demanded that sovereign nations act within the framework of accepted rules of war, that is, that they exercise caution concerning offensive activities and refrain from deliberately injuring civilians, even when coping with an organization or faction of people, rather than with an enemy state.

This restriction raises the question of whether the targets of targeted killings are civilians, or whether they are military personnel (or combatants), who are part of a military-operational framework and the combative and violent struggle of the terrorist organization. The answer to this question will change, naturally, according to the identity of each target. There is almost no question that physical damage to terrorists before they embark on an attack is legitimate and constitutes an act of self-defense aimed at saving lives. In similar fashion, any operational activity aimed at activists involved in the chain of command, or planning and carrying out attacks, must also be considered a legitimate action in the context of the war against terrorism.

The targeted killings Israel has committed over the years against various terrorist organizations have been directed towards several types of activists: leaders of organizations, senior members of the organizations' military branches, activists who initiate terrorist acts, activists who plan and organize attacks, heads of terrorist cells and members of terrorist cells. In this context, MK Yossi Sarid, who served on the Sub-committee on Intelligence and Secret Services of the Knesset Foreign Affairs and Defense Committee stated in November 1997 (following the failed attempt on the life of Khaled Mashaal, a Hamas activist in Jordan), that the only reason that could justify targeted killing is the need to prevent an actual terrorist attack. This need, he said, is subject to several tests, including "clear and present danger" and "proven certainty," and identifying the target as "an active perpetrator of terrorism" (that is, not a religious or ideological leader).[142]

The question becomes, therefore, whether harming leaders and senior activists of non-military or non-operational branches of the organization is equally legitimate. Here, opinions are likely to differ. One school of thought claims that this group deserves the immunity awarded to civilians during time of war, while the other school of thought believes that the terrorist organization should be considered as a single entity—a quasi-military body that perpetrates terrorist attacks as part of a common effort by various groups and personnel. According to this approach, there is no reason to differentiate between administrative and political personnel, and military-combat personnel because, ultimately, they are all working to enhance the organization's ability to perpetrate terrorist attacks against the state's civilian population. Moreover, with many terrorist organizations the areas of accountability are not so clear or absolute. At times, the one in charge of the organization's political branch is a member of the organization's administration, and as such is also responsible for formulating its terrorism policy; and at times may officially hold several positions, some administrative and some operational.

In the public and media debate following the foiled attempted killing of Abdel Aziz Rantisi (the spokesman of Hamas and a member of its leadership, who after the killing of Ahmed Yassin was appointed as his successor as the leader of the organization in Gaza), the argument was raised that this was a "quantum leap" in Israel's policy of "targeted killings." It has been argued that Israel does not distinguish between an organization's military echelon and its political echelon. When the director of the Prime Minister's Office, Dov Weisglass, was asked to justify the killing attempt on Rantisi, he said that Rantisi "had placed himself at the forefront of initiating terrorist activity against Israel," and that according to information in Israel's possession, Rantisi was leading the extremist line within Hamas, ruling out any dialogue with Abu Mazen (the Palestinian Authority's prime minister at that time).[143]

Because of the problems inherent in the targeted killing approach, it seems that the decision-maker would be best served by not employing this method against a terrorist who is not explicitly affiliated with the organization's military branch, or who is not personally involved in one of the stages of committing a terrorist act. Focusing only on military activists and operational terrorists may meet with somewhat less international censure, and in any case should be seen as a legitimate "pre-emptive strike." Moreover, just as the definition of terrorism attributes a certain measure of legitimacy to guerrilla activity against military and security forces, as opposed to the non-legitimate terrorist activity that targets civilians, thus targeted killings of terrorists should be considered at least as legitimate as guerrilla activity.

Any examination of the legitimacy of individual offensive action must also deal with the concept of the action itself. Compared with any other offensive action against terrorist organizations, including some administrative punishments, targeted killing is much more selective because it is supposed to harm only a particular individual. In other words, criticism of and opposition to targeted killings for fear of injuring innocent bystanders would eliminate most of the offensive actions carried out against terrorist organizations (air bombardment of bases, camps and headquarters, artillery fire, etc.), because in most cases the terrorist facilities are deployed in civilian surroundings and these methods are much less selective. This attitude actually restricts the war against terrorism only to a passive sphere—a dangerous and impossible step in light of the scope of the threat and the risk terrorism poses to nations and peoples in this modern era.

But the moral question of targeted killings not only involves the legitimacy of injuring the terrorist activist. This issue also entails questions related to processes of decision-making, implementation, and monitoring: Who decides to go ahead with the killing? Who authorizes its implementation? Who monitors the action? Who carries it out? Is there a judicial or quasi-judicial procedure prior to the decision? And so on.

Answering these questions with reference to Israel's counter-terrorism policy is by no means a simple matter, both because of the "policy of vagueness" Israel employs in this matter, and because of the fact that the decision-making processes and other details involving actions of this type are sensitive and usually classified.

In the Israeli decision-making process regarding targeted killings as seen from foreign publications, it appears that the final decision regarding such action is made by a single person—the prime minister, after he receives the information required and has consulted with relevant security agencies, and at times, even with a special ministerial committee authorized for this purpose. The decision-making process is likely to vary at different time periods (in accordance with the prime minister's policies and work methods) and under various circumstances (based on the target's identity, the degree to which the information about him is up-to-date, character-istics of the attack, and the planned location).

According to some publications, it appears that in the past there had been some quasi-judicial procedure prior to the decision to kill a terrorist. It was claimed that in the 1970s, when Golda Meir was prime minister, the Mossad had prepared a list of candidates for killings and prior to its implementation, the entire plan was presented before the Committee of Secret Service Chiefs (CSSC or *varash* in Hebrew). Later on it was sent for approval by "Committee X."[144] (This operated during Golda Meir's administration as a court for terrorists. Minister-Without-Portfolio Yisrael Galili served as "prosecutor" and brought the heads of Military Intelligence, the Mossad, and the ISA as witnesses; the justice minister acted as "defense attorney" and raised arguments why the individual should not be killed; and the prime minister, defense Minister, and opposition leader were the judges.)[145] If such a "Committee X" did, in fact, exist, and if this was how it operated, then this represents an attempt to solve the apparent moral dilemma of endangering human lives without trial, by conducting a quasi-judicial proceeding. However, it is highly doubtful that such a procedure, wherein the accused is not informed of the fact that he is standing trial, is not given an opportunity to defend himself, and where some minister is forced to serve as his defense counsel, would pass any type of test for proper judicial proceedings.

One of the questions that must be examined in order to make a moral-ethical determination in cases of targeted killing operations is whether such actions can be implemented using a different judicial process, one that is more systematic and subject to judicial controls. Individual attacks usually entail an operation carried out deep in enemy territory, or in some friendly or neutral foreign country. Therefore, it is a highly sensitive action that must be veiled in secrecy. With operations of this nature it is essential that the numbers of those who are privy to the secret be kept to a bare minimum, and it is certainly impossible to conduct a public proceeding. The legality of the action and the fear of possibly jeopardizing the sovereignty of other countries actually prevent the nation's executive and/or judicial institutions from making an official decision.

Moreover, as stated previously, the need for a proper judicial process in order to authorize a killing of an active terrorist is related to how the action is defined. When a targeted killing is not essentially a punishment, but rather an action aimed at achieving a purely military objective—preventing terrorist attacks, deterring those who perpetrate attacks, disrupting the enemy's activities, etc., and when this action is carried out in a state of war against terrorism (whether declared or undeclared) between the nation and the organization, then it is a legitimate military action and the need for a judicial proceeding is superfluous.

Another question, which complements the moral dilemma, is the legality of the targeted killing. On this issue, Louis Rene Beres presents a clear and unequivocal ethical position when he states:

> Eliminating terrorists is mandatory under the law…. There is no "international court" where one can go to complain about what a terrorist may be planning in his country of asylum. If there is a nation that shelters terrorism, the only way the victim can protect himself is to eliminate the terrorist…. In 1945 the Special Tribunal for Nazi War Criminals at the Nuremberg trials stated that in the case of heinous crimes such as those, adhering to a conventional judicial procedure may be a greater injustice than skipping the entire process. A terrorist is recognized under present international law as "an enemy of humanity," and just like the pirates of the 18th century, should be hanged by the first person who catches him. And if that person is also the victim—all the more so.[146]

But it isn't necessary to go to such extremes as Beres; rather we can say that when it is a matter of self-defense or a military action within the framework of warfare, it is a legal and permissible action. In any case, even if we accept Beres's ethical and judicial conclusion regarding the legitimacy of killing terrorists, we must recall that the legitimacy of killings does not only rely on the identity of the victim, but also on the means used to kill him and where the event takes place. Therefore, international legislation must be promoted that distinguishes between a killing that does not violate the sovereignty of a foreign nation and an action carried out on the territory of another sovereign nation without its permission, thereby jeopardizing its sovereignty. In that case, one must take a different approach towards various types of states:

- *States that are in a state of war with the state that attacks the terrorist*—A targeted killing on the territory of this state is likely to be considered a component of the state of war between the two countries (particularly if the nation whose sovereignty was compromised exploits the terrorist organization to harm the attacking state).

- *States that sponsor and aid the terrorist organizations* (especially a state defined as such through international forums)—Such a state has no one to blame but itself if its sovereignty is compromised by a state defending itself from terrorism by damaging terrorist targets located on the sovereign territory of the former.
- *States that do not support terrorism*—If this is a state that does not sponsor terrorist organizations, and the terrorist passes through its territory or remains there without the knowledge of the state's official agencies, then any damage to its territory without its permission is an illegal violation of its sovereignty, unless a request had been made through the country's official channels to arrest, try or extradite the terrorist, and the request was rejected.

The legality of a targeted killing is, therefore, a thorny issue when it involves compromising the sovereignty of another state. In that situation, it may be wise to first consider demanding the terrorist's arrest, trial, or extradition. Such a step is likely to be perceived as an attempt to employ all other means available to neutralize his activity before carrying out a targeted killing against him. Concomitantly, this request may draw the nation's attention to the fact that the terrorist is located on its territory, and can serve as unofficial warning that if the individual is not extradited, or if legal measures are not taken against him, a direct-targeted killing may be considered on that nation's territory. In such a case, the nation requesting the extradition must naturally supply clear proof of the terrorist's guilt, and present this to the relevant court. This task may be difficult and complicated, while killing does not necessitate presentation of such evidence.

Finally, there is disagreement over the effectiveness of targeted killings. According to Crenshaw, security agencies are tempted to try and eliminate a terrorist leader on the assumption that the organization will collapse without his leadership. However, this may have the opposite outcome: an increase in the level of violence. For example, in the 1970s the Red Brigades in Italy began murdering government officials following the arrest of one of their leaders. The movement escalated its activity in order to demonstrate that it was not defeated because of those arrests. Crenshaw adds that when an organization breaks down into sub-groups because its leadership has been neutralized and is left without any central control or communications, this may cause an escalation in violence, difficulty in locating activists, intensify their motivation, etc.[147] In other cases, such as the case of the PKK, it seems that the arrest of the leader narrows down or even stops the organization's terrorist activity. The connection between the moral dilemma and the benefit dilemma is reflected in the question of whether a level of effectiveness similar to that of a planned targeted killing can be achieved using some other method, which may be considered more moral (such as kidnapping, deportation, etc.). The answer to this question is, of course, a direct result of the concrete characteristics of the planned operation, and is likely to change from operation to operation. At any rate, this issue must be examined as soon as any action is in the planning stage.

Targeted Killing as a Component of Israel's Counter-Terrorism Policy

The conventional wisdom is that one of Israel's first decisions to carry out a targeted killing was made following the murder of the Israeli athletes at the Munich Olympics on September 4, 1972. But Merari and Elad point out that actions of this type were carried out prior to Munich, and demands to harm the leaders of Palestinian terrorist organizations had been voiced in Israel since mid-1972, in the wake of the attack at Lod Airport. Indeed, three weeks after the attack, the spokesperson for the Popular Front for the Liberation of Palestine, Ghassan Kanafani, was killed, when his car blew up in Beirut. His replacement, Bassam Abu Sharif, was seriously injured when a bobby-trapped book exploded, and other Palestinian leaders were also hurt after opening booby-trapped envelopes that had been mailed to them.[148]

In any event, there is no doubt that the brutal attack in Munich, which was covered extensively in real time by all the international media, shocked the Israeli public and required decision makers to demonstrate resolve and undertake new, severe measures. The solution, among other things, was to begin a worldwide campaign of individual attacks, focusing on the elimination of anyone involved in initiating, planning, preparing, directing, and carrying out the slaughter in Munich. The opening signal was given by Golda Meir, prime minister at that time, when she announced following the attack:

Our war against the Arab terrorists…cannot be limited to defensive means, to self-defense and safeguarding, but it must be pro-active as far as identifying the killers, their leaders, their actions and perpetrators, thwarting their plans and, in particular, destroying their organizations.[149]

Israeli intelligence services followed these activists, and when an operational plan was prepared, the terrorists were killed once authorization came from the political echelon. Salah Khalaf (Abu Iyad) attributes to Israel a long list of assassination attempts against Fatah activists and PLO representatives in Europe. He states:

> This war of shadows intensified. The intelligence services of the Zionist State sent bobby-trapped packages to a large number of our activists, among others, in Beirut; Algiers (where PLO representative Abu Khalil was mortally wounded); Tripoli (Mustafa Awad Zaid, a PLO representative, who was blinded and paralyzed); Cairo (Farouk Qadummi and Hayal Abdal Hammid, Fatah leaders who escaped unharmed); Stockholm (to Omar Sufan, director of the "Red Crescent," who lost the fingers on both hands); Bonn (Adnan Hamad, from the Palestinian students' organization who was seriously wounded); Copenhagen (to Ahmed Awadallah, a student, whose arm had to be amputated). Following the assassination of the PLO representatives in Paris and Rome— Zuwaiter and Hamshari—our representative in Nicosia, Hussein Abu al-Khair was murdered on January 25, 1973.... "Black September" fought back as best as it could, and doubled the number of assassinations...[150]

Establishment of the Palestinian autonomous area in the West Bank essentially changed the rules of the game with regard to offensive action against terrorism, which had been standard operating procedure during previous administrations. Chief of Staff Ehud Barak referred to this issue in September 1994:

> It was clear from the outset that the IDF would not carry out actions to prevent, thwart, or otherwise deal with terrorism in the autonomous areas. That was handed over to a very clear address, and that address is currently being tested in Gaza and Jericho.[151]

The decision to leave responsibility for counter-terrorism activities in the autonomous areas in the hands of the PA derived from several considerations: the complexity of operating in these areas (among an armed and hostile population); unwillingness to jeopardize the sovereignty of the Palestinian Authority, which was given security responsibility for the area only a short time beforehand; and the reluctance to compromise Arafat's status and image in the eyes of the Palestinian public, lest that jeopardize the ongoing peace process. But this government policy did not endure for very long. When decision makers realized that the fundamentalist-Islamic organizations were continuing their brazen terrorist attacks in Israel and that the PA was not materializing its operational capabilities (or was unable to do so, as some policymakers believed), Israel's policy apparently changed and policymakers instructed security forces to operate inside the autonomous areas as well, although discreetly at first.

This activity was assigned to undercover units and special forces, and focused on eliminating senior activists in the terrorist organizations who were wanted for initiating, planning, preparing, and perpetrating terrorist attacks in Israel. Following a suicide bombing in the heart of Tel Aviv in October 1994 in which twenty-one persons were killed and thirty-four were injured, Yitzhak Rabin announced that he had directed security forces to assassinate terrorist leaders: "We must seek out, find and arrest or eliminate those who organize this terrorist activity."[152] According to the British weekly, *The Observer*, these instructions were given at an emergency cabinet meeting attended by the head of the Mossad and the heads of the ISA and Military Intelligence. Fifty-one days later one of the leaders of the Palestinian Islamic Jihad was killed—Hanni Al Abed. Israel did not claim responsibility for his killing, but the Palestinian Islamic Jihad blamed Israeli security forces. In January 1995, Foreign Minister Shimon Peres reiterated the government's commitment to employ offensive means against terrorist organizations, and told the Knesset Foreign Affairs and Defense Committee that:

> We must use every means, including draconian methods, to find the terrorists and harm them before they have a chance to perpetrate their evil deeds. We must act against them at every opportunity, without limiting how or where we act...[153]

One of the most daring targeted killings in recent years was one that actually failed, and for which Israel's responsibility was made public: the attempted assassination of Khaled Mashaal, head of the Hamas political bureau. A study of this episode reveals many details regarding the characteristics of the killings Israel has committed, especially processes involving those of decision-making, preparing, and carrying out this type of action.

On September 25, 1997, the attempt to kill Khaled Mashaal via lethal injection in Amman, Jordan, failed after his personal driver and security guard intervened. The security guard stopped a passing automobile and began pursuing the agents, without their noticing that they were being followed. After about 300 meters, the agents stopped their car and got out. The security guard went after them, accosted them, and with the help of a plainclothes policeman who happened on the scene, managed to overcome them and arrest them. When word of their arrest was received in Israel the head of the Mossad went to Jordan with an antidote for the poison that had been injected into Mashaal's body. In the negotiations with Jordan, it was concluded that the agents would be released in exchange for Sheikh Yassin and several additional prisoners.[154]

When the failed operation became known, the Israeli public began asking several questions: Why was the decision made to kill Mashaal particularly, who was apparently a political activist for Hamas? Why was Jordan, which has a peace treaty with Israel, the specific location chosen for the killing? Why were such unusual methods employed for this operation? And why did it ultimately fail?

Regarding the first question, security forces and decision makers in Israel stressed the fact that Khaled Mashaal was, indeed, officially the head of the political bureau, but he could not claim to be free of any involvement in terrorist activity. From his office in Jordan, Mashaal had been involved in ordering numerous terrorist attacks against Israel, directed the perpetrators of such attacks, and sent them money to finance their operations.[155] When discussing the choice of Mashaal as the target of a killing, Netanyahu said, "I definitely wanted to kill Khaled Mashaal. I felt that Jordanian terrorism was a center of the agitation in Judea, Samaria and Gaza. I wanted to do it regardless of the terrorist attacks."[156] While Netanyahu attempted to downplay the impact of terrorist attacks on the decision to commit the assassination, former head of the Mossad, Dani Yatom, stated, "it was important to me to stop the series of terrorist acts, when it became known that orders for such attacks came from Hamas headquarters in Jordan..."[157]

Jordan was chosen for the location of the attack due to the fact that Mashaal's permanent place of residence was Amman, and perhaps even because of the desire to send terrorists a message that there was no place in the world they could hide, and that Israel's long arm would find them anywhere.[158]

The decision to kill senior Hamas activists was made at a meeting of the security cabinet that was convened shortly after the attack at the Mahane Yehuda market in Jerusalem in July 1997. The recommendation to kill Mashaal came from the Mossad, and was approved by Prime Minister Netanyahu. The special means chosen for this was a syringe that would inject a poison into Mashaal's body through his ear. This method was chosen in order to hide Israel's "fingerprints" and make Mashaal's death appear natural, rather than the result of an assassination attempt. Had the operation gone off as planned, Israel's responsibility for the attack would not have been detected. In fact, his death would not have been considered an assassination at all, and thus no damage would have been caused to relations between Israel and Jordan.[159]

The gross failure in Amman signified the beginning of a process of internal criticism in Israel, dealing not only with the incident itself and the decision-making process that preceded the event, but also concerning the way in which the crisis following the failed operation was managed, including knowledge of the special methods that had been used and how this information was transmitted to Jordan, how Mashaal was treated and his life saved, and exposure of the responsibility of the political echelon for the incident.

Regarding the decision to give the Jordanians the antidote enabling them to save Mashaal's life, former Mossad chief Dani Yatom explained that after he had found out that the operation had failed:

> I proposed that I travel to Jordan in order to meet with the King, in attempt to minimize the damage. Actually, the idea of offering Jordan an antidote that would bring Mashaal back to life was Netanyahu's.... Someone said about this that it was the first time in history that we killed a person, and also brought him back to life. But from the moment things went awry, I feared for Mashaal's health. It was obvious to me that if Mashaal remained alive, we could solve the problem between us and Jordan relatively easily.[160]

The Ciechanover Commission, which was established on October 6, 1997 to investigate the Mossad's failure in Jordan, met forty-seven times, heard thirty-five witnesses, and examined hundreds of exhibits and documents. All of the commission's meetings were held behind closed doors. In the public portion of its report, the Ciechanover Commission placed the primary blame for the failure on

> the conceptual fixation prevailing in the Mossad, at the various levels involved in planning, approving and carrying out the operation, who believed that the weapon in question and its mode of use could guarantee a "silent operation" without risk; in other words, that the weapon was "silent" and had no immediately evident effect upon the target. It was assumed that the proposed operation would be effective without anybody being immediately aware of it. This concept of a "silent operation," with the

assumption that chances of failure were minimal, hardly took into account the possibility that it could fail for any reason, and turn into a "noisy" one...[161]

Concomitant with the Ciechanover Commission, the Sub-committee for Intelligence and Secret Services of the Knesset Foreign Affairs and Defense Committee also began to look into the fiasco in Amman.[162] The committee met twenty-seven times on this matter, and heard twenty-eight witnesses. It stated that for many years successive Israeli governments had failed to formulate a policy for fighting terrorist organizations, "based on organized thinking and on a continuous and consistent defensive line."[163] The committee declared that "lacking a suitable doctrine for counter-terrorism activity, the aspect of responding to terrorist attacks became an important and dangerous factor." Thus, the committee criticized the procedure for initiating offensive actions in the wake of massive terrorist attacks, rather than on an ongoing basis or according to genuine needs in the field.[164]

The diplomatic fallout and hurdles following the failed killing attempt on Mashaal went way beyond the relationship between Israel and Jordan. For example, in the light of knowledge that Mossad agents had used Canadian passports, the Canadian government blamed Israel for violating its commitment not to use Canadian passports and documents in committing intelligence operations, and the Canadian ambassador to Israel was recalled for consultations.[165]

The Mashaal Affair clearly illustrates the problems with targeted killings in general, particularly when the targeted killing is carried out on foreign territory (not to mention an Arab country that maintains a sensitive peace treaty with Israel). This episode highlights the vital need for prior consideration and assessment, before any action is undertaken, of all the possible risks in the event of the worst-case scenario. On the surface, it appears that in this case the cost component of the cost-benefit equation was not properly taken into account during the planning phase. According to the Ciechanover Commission, this was the result of an overly optimistic opinion regarding the chance for success of such a "quiet operation" that would not be identified with Israel. Another question regarding the logic behind the decision to specifically target Mashaal stems from the fact that several months prior to this Israel had withdrawn its request to extradite his predecessor, Mussa Abu Marzuk, who had been arrested by the United States and was about to be extradited to Israel.

Differences of opinion in Israel on the moral question of targeted killings often cut across political lines. For example, in July 1994, Yossi Sarid, then minister of the environment, stated, "terrorism is a dirty war and that is how it must be fought." He added that he had no moral problem with eliminating terrorists in a process that is not based on criteria of law and democracy, so long as "there is positive identification of the terrorists and on condition that they cannot be brought to trial, and there is the risk that they will perpetrate more attacks." Sarid added, "I fear the consequences, but I am more afraid of a bomb killing dozens of innocent people." Shulamit Aloni, on the other hand, who was at that time head of Sarid's party and minister of communications, science and art, justified her opposition to this method by saying, "We are a nation of laws and a member of international organizations, not a gang of pirates."[166]

The subjective nature of the issue, and the lack of rules and accepted universal values make it difficult to try and form an ethical judgment vis-à-vis targeted killings. The challenge of imposing a moral-ethical viewpoint on these activities can be seen from the words of Zvi Zamir, who served as head of the Mossad from 1968 to 1974, under the government of Golda Meir, among others, regarding the claim that the Mossad pursued and killed the perpetrators of the slaughter in Munich. Zamir is quoted as regretting this: "I am not proud of this, neither as a human being nor as a Jew. Part of me is even ashamed of it. But you have to understand that there was no other way." Zamir remarked that Prime Minister Golda Meir had opposed the "killing of the individuals" on the claim that "Jews simply don't do things like that," but she changed her attitude and authorized these activities when Palestinian terrorism increased.[167]

In contrast with Zamir, many decision makers and heads of security services supported the individual attacks against leaders of terrorist organizations, although not without reservation. When asked about his approach to this type of counter-terrorism, Netanyahu responded:

> I have no objection. Terrorist leaders should not be immune. I was cautious about injuring people who had reached the political echelon, but not about operational leaders. With regard to operational leaders, it is obvious.[168]

The head of the Counter-Terrorism Bureau during Netanyahu's term of office, Meir Dagan, responds:

I'm in favor of it, but we need to put some restriction. We must always examine this against the benefit—what purpose does it serve? One goal is prevention. If injuring someone prevents an attack, then that is certainly a goal. A second goal is deterrence. Third, I think we should also be using these acts as punishment.... Would I go and harm a religious figure who was not involved in terrorism but was merely an authority? The answer is no. That would be counterproductive...[169]

Lipkin-Shahak does not believe that targeted killings deter terrorists in the sense of preventing future terrorism, although they are likely to deter certain types of terrorist activity. In any event, Lipkin-Shahak feels that this type of warfare is a kind of "eye for an eye, or some kind of abstract justice, or revenge."[170]

The day on which two senior-level Shi'ite activists were injured in southern Lebanon when a side bomb exploded near their car by the village of Nabatiye (December 1994), Ehud Barak, chief of staff at the time, declared:

Members of Hizballah should fear for their lives, anytime, anywhere. The policy is that they have no immunity anywhere, but the IDF will act wisely and will do what is necessary.[171]

According to Aharon Yariv, former head of Military Intelligence and the prime minister's advisor on counter-terrorism during Golda Meir's administration, the goal of deterrence through individual offensive activity was achieved, at least with regard to assassinations against senior PLO operatives during the 1970s following the attack in Munich. According to Yariv, "The impact was very significant because they were top-level officials in sensitive positions, and suddenly felt as if they weren't safe even in their own homes."[172] In contrast to him another head of Military Intelligence, Uri Sagie, following his retirement from the IDF, expressed his doubts regarding the effectiveness of the targeted killings policy as a deterrent measure against terrorist organizations. He said, "Even this assumption, that these actions serve as deterrents, has not been proven. Although in principle leaders of terrorist organizations should be killed, replacements always spring up from within the organization."[173]

In reference to the assassination of "The Engineer" Yihye Ayyash, Shlomo Gazit wrote:

The message is also for the murderers themselves. When it comes to certain terrorist acts, those that are particularly "dirty" and bloody, perpetrated against innocent civilians, you cannot just say, "Time out, we're not playing!" These rules are not acceptable to Israel. And these evildoers will remain on Israel's "Wanted" list until their final day.

There is a chance that this knowledge may deter some of them and keep them out of the cycle of terrorism…[174]

In a lecture he gave at the American Solidarity Conference held on September 11, 2002, at the Herzliya Interdisciplinary Center, a representative of the military echelon, Chief of Staff Moshe ("Bogie") Ya'alon referred to the "Al Aksa intifada":

> The idea that you have to hunt down the terrorists, and catch or kill them before they can take action, is the essence of preemption—the policy of targeted killing for example, has become a tactic requiring no explanation.[175]

Decision makers are thus divided as to the effectiveness of targeted killings. However, we can conclude by stating that when the goal is to deter an organization from terrorist activity and to obstruct its actions, it would appear that this goal can be achieved by hurting a senior terrorist in that organization, which will then embark on a "power struggle" among those eager to fulfill his role. The difficulty in finding another leader with professional skills, charisma or other positive characteristics to fill the position left by the dead activist could interfere with the organization's activities. Disrupting the organization's routine is liable to have ongoing consequences, rather than merely a short-term effect. The organization might then have to invest considerable resources—financial resources, manpower and time—in defense and ongoing protection for its senior officials.[176] In certain cases, the organization's senior activists take preventive steps and long-term security measures, and may even adopt new behavior because of their fear of personal attack.[177] At times they alter their activities due to information or rumors they have heard about Israel's intentions to kill them soon, or in light of a killing of another activist in that same organization, or from another organization.[178] Thus, following the attempted killing of Dr. Abdel Aziz Rantisi, Hamas spokesman and head of the movement's political leadership, the Izzadin al-Kassam Brigades organization issued instructions to its activists not to travel in private cars because of the fear against killing attempts by Israel.[179] "Injuring the *mujahaddin* became very easy for the Zionist adversary and its agents because of improper use of vehicles. In the past 26 hours Israel has succeeded in killing six activists from the Izzadin al-Kassam Brigade by targeting their cars."[180]

Security arrangements are a serious hardship on terrorists, their families and their neighbors.[181] The constant fear of killing among PLO officials, for example, led to the establishment of a special department within Fatah—"Force 17"—and one of its major jobs was to provide security for the organization's senior officials.[182] Its members were specially trained for these assignments, and they served as security escorts for senior Fatah members.

The degree to which targeted killings are effective in terms of disrupting the organizations' activities must be examined therefore, among other things, according to the level of fear felt by terrorist leaders by the threat of their assassination. It should be noted that in the past, several terrorist leaders have expressed anxiety over Israeli action against them personally, and their belief that it would come eventually.[183]

The "Boomerang Effect"

Advocates of the "tough policy" approach to counter-terrorism feel that the nation should be more proactive and initiate offensive counter-terrorism action. In contrast, others believe that not only is aggressive action ineffective because it is difficult to locate specific targets within the terrorist organization whose injury will paralyze its activities, but that such offensive action is also dangerous because it is actually liable to reinforce the terrorist organization's motivation to perpetrate revenge attacks that are more heinous than previous attacks (hereinafter, this will be referred to as "the boomerang effect"). Bandura explains this by saying that the response to harsh counter-terrorism measures could have a more serious impact than the terrorist acts themselves.[184] Crenshaw emphasizes that in weighing the considerations taken into account prior to initiating counter-terrorism measures, the government must also assess how the organization will respond to the policy carried out. On the basis of this assessment, the nation must then decide what types of policies would be appropriate for various situations. Crenshaw states that policymakers must understand the advantages and disadvantages, as well as the "final outcome" of their policy choice.[185]

According to the boomerang effect theory, a serious blow to a terrorist organization is liable to be followed by an escalating response from the terrorists, so that nothing will have been gained from the counter-terrorism measures taken. Proponents of offensive measures claim that the boomerang effect argument doesn't hold water, since the variable that limits the scope and nature of terrorist attacks is the organizations' operational capability to perpetrate attacks, and not their motivation. According to them, the motivation of terrorists is always high and attacks are committed solely as a result of "operational readiness." A serious blow to the terrorist organization's infrastructure will jeopardize its operational capability, and even if it elevates the organization's motivation to commit a counter-attack, it will not be able to act on it. Those who favor offensive action claim that the boomerang effect is merely the invention of terrorist organizations, as part of a sophisticated and calculated strategy of psychological warfare aimed at ensuring their immunity from military attack. On the other hand, those who oppose offensive action believe that the boomerang effect should be taken seriously, and that it actually dictates a policy of restraint and avoiding offensive action against terrorist organizations.

One of the most prominent examples of the boomerang effect was the attack on the Israeli Embassy in Buenos Aires, which was carried out following the assassination of Abbas Musawi, secretary general of Hizballah. In April 1992, a car bomb exploded in front of the building, causing it to collapse upon its inhabitants. Dozens of people were killed in the attack, and hundreds were injured. This was a clear case of the boomerang effect. When asked, "What terrorism-related event do you recall most from your tenure as Minister of Defense," Moshe Arens responded, "The thing that bothers me most to this day was the attack on our embassy in Buenos Aires, which was apparently supposed to send us a message."[186]

Ariel Sharon emphasizes in this context, "the most dangerous thing is to do something, and then they do what they do and you are deterred and you no longer respond."[187] Yigal Pressler, former counter-terrorism advisor to the prime minister, continues his thoughts in a similar direction:

> When terrorist organizations respond to our actions, we must continue hitting them while boosting the level of our response. We must not leave an attack unanswered. This campaign is judged in the long term, and what counts is consistency in the response and sending messages.[188]

Another example was the assassination of Hamas activist Yihye Ayyash, known as the Engineer, and the suicide attacks that followed. Ayyash was the most senior figure wanted by Israel for his extensive involvement in suicide bombings. He was the first one to perpetrate these types of attacks on Israeli territory, and was involved in almost all of the suicide bombings committed by Hamas, until his elimination. He himself prepared the bombs, planned the attacks, directed the terrorists, and trained others in committing suicide bombings. Ayyash was killed in Gaza by a booby-trapped cellular telephone that was given to him, apparently, by ISA agents.

Ayyash's assassination took place after a period of approximately six months when there had been no suicide bombings in Israel (although security forces claim that during this period of time a significant number of attacks were averted). The lack of suicide attacks during this period can be attributed, among other things, to the temporary agreement between Hamas and the PA to avoid such attacks on the eve of Israel's elections.[189] About two months after the Engineer's assassination, the relative lull in terrorist attacks was shattered, and within a period of a week, there were four serious attacks in Israel (including three suicide bombings in Jerusalem and Tel Aviv), in which dozens of people were killed and hundreds injured. Uri Savir talked about the mood of Prime Minister Shimon Peres and the Israel public following these attacks:

> As soon as we returned to Israel I met with the prime minister, who looked as if he had aged 10 years during the 10 days since we had last seen each other. Four times during the past week he had visited the sites of attacks, and went among the victims while listening to cries of anger and hatred.[190]

Peres rejected the claim that the four terrorist attacks constituted a boomerang effect of Ayyash's assassination, and he had this to say in a personal interview:

> This is a journalistic dilemma. You have the story about "the Engineer" and the telephone. To me that is foolish because we knew that "the Engineer" was going to perpetrate more attacks. Let's say we hadn't killed him and he would have carried out those attacks, what would they say then? You could have prevented it. It's all about media descriptions. I know the truth, I know he was about to commit more attacks…[191]

Savir supports Peres's assessment that there was no connection between the two events. "I don't think that killing Ayyash led to what happened afterwards. The motivation for terrorism was and remains strategic—and it is not seriously based on revenge."[192] The head of the ISA at that time, Carmi Gilon, agrees with this assessment when he says:

> I recall, following Yihye Ayyash, that they criticized me for "not thinking"—look what you created—revenge attacks! At the time I was truly a lone voice in the dark, when I said, "Excuse me, but you aren't looking at the Hamas seriously enough." It was true that Hamas used [the assassination of] Yihye Ayyash for its own internal political needs.... They spoke from the gut and said, "We are avenging the death of the *shahid* Yihye Ayyash." But years have passed, and they have already perpetrated all the possible revenge attacks, but still they continue.[193]

Gilon admits that he had "serious discussions with the intelligence community, especially with Military Intelligence, which vociferously claimed that the Hamas attacks "were motivated by a desire to avenge the interception of wanted terrorists."[194] Gilon denied the boomerang effect in the case of Ayyash by explaining the attacks of February-March 1996:

> At that time [the end of 1995—BG] Arafat was conducting intensive negotiations with the internal leadership of Hamas (Sheikh Yassin was still being held prisoner), in an attempt to convince them to stop using terrorism and to content themselves with political action.... After an agreement had been reached between them the Hamas internal leadership had to leave the Territories in order to obtain the agreement of the external leadership. The meeting was held in Cairo in December 1995, under Egyptian auspices, and was a total failure. The external Hamas leadership refused to lay aside the weapon of terrorism. In my opinion, the practical expression of the negotiations and the final decision in Cairo was the explanation for the fact that between August 1995 and February 1996 Hamas had refrained from terrorist activity, and the Cairo decision explains the renewal of full-blown terrorist activity in February-March 1996.[195]

Meir Dagan denies in principle the existence of a boomerang effect. "In my opinion the 'boomerang effect' doesn't exist. What does exist is a strategy of psychological warfare by the other side in order to create the 'boomerang effect.'" Dagan claims that the terrorist organizations invented the boomerang effect only to generate a deterrent balance against Israel, and he believes that the blatant attacks carried out in the past and attributed to the boomerang effect because they took place following painful Israeli attacks, would have been perpetrated in any case, although perhaps at a different time and in a somewhat different fashion. Dagan admits that, indeed, Israel's offensive action is liable to increase the terrorist organizations' motivation to perpetrate revenge attacks, but according to him, the question of motivation is secondary; largely, it is a question of capability and capability certainly doesn't increase in the wake of a successful Israeli attack. Dagan summarizes:

> Therefore, the bottom line is we need to act as if "the boomerang effect" doesn't exist.... Israel should define the goals of its war by ignoring the "boomerang effect."

Israel must always ask itself what the enemy wants to do next, but the question has nothing to do with the "boomerang effect."[196]

This approach, which was common among many Israeli decision makers, must be re-examined. Dagan's distinction between the two components of a terrorist attack—capability and motivation—is still valid, and thus, so is the claim that Israel's offensive actions may increase motivation but certainly do not increase capability to carry out attacks. However, in this context we must distinguish between two types of terrorist groups: organizations whose motivation to perpetrate terrorist attacks at a particular point in time is higher than their capability to act upon that motivation (usually smaller organizations with limited resources, such as the Palestinian Islamic Jihad); and organizations for whom motivation is the factor that limits their attacks at a given time, rather than capability (this usually refers to larger organizations with more activists and which rely on a vast audience of supporters, such as Hamas and Hizballah). Dagan's analysis is correct and relevant with respect to the first type of organization, but does not hold true for the second type. When an organization has the capability to perpetrate terrorist attacks but, for various reasons that are ultimately interpreted as motivation—such as interests, internal and external pressures on the organization, cost-benefit considerations, etc.—the organizations' leaders decide to refrain from attacking during certain periods of time, or avoid particular types of attacks. Offensive action against the organization is liable to increase its activists' motivation for vengeance and because the capability is already there, the organization's leaders are likely to decide to perpetrate an attack that may have previously been held in reserve, or plan a new attack. This is when we can expect the boomerang effect.

The following chart illustrates the probability of the boomerang effect in the wake of a planned offensive action.

In order to evaluate the chance of a boomerang effect ahead of time, it is possible to state that, as mentioned, with regard to terrorist organizations whose motivation prior to any offensive action was higher than their operational capability—that is, the factor that limits their attacks is their operational capability—the chance of there being a boomerang effect is quite low. The offensive action might, indeed, reinforce their desire for revenge, but their limited capability (which may be even more limited following the offen-

Capability	Motivation	
	Higher than capability	**Lower than capability**
Damage to capability following action	The chance of a "boomerang effect" is low	There is the chance of the "boomerang effect" unless there is serious damage to the organization's capability and it prevents them from acting on their motivation
No change in capability following action	The chance of a "boomerang effect" is low	High chance of the "boomerang effect." Recommend that the planned offensive action be examined very critically.

sive action) does not enable them to act on their desires. Yet we can reasonably assume that the organization will attempt to link the attacks they commit in the future with the offensive actions carried out against them, and present them as a "boomerang"—but in such a case, this isn't a genuine boomerang effect.

However, when the organization's motivation before any attack against it is lower than its operational capability—that is, the organization is refraining from perpetrating attacks because it isn't interested in attacking just now and not because it is incapable of carrying out an attack—then the effect of the planned offensive action on the organization's operational capability must be assessed in advance. If the action will not reduce the organization's operational capability, then the possibility of revenge attacks as part of a boomerang effect must be taken into account. If the assessment indicates that the planned action will, indeed, damage the organization's operational capability, one must try and surmise the extent of the expected damage and whether such damage will jeopardize the organization's ability to perpetrate revenge attacks. It should be emphasized that even in cases where the decision maker feels that the planned offensive action may, indeed, lead to a boomerang effect, such offensive action should not necessarily be rejected. The advantages of the offensive action should be weighed against the possible damage, and the final decision should be made accordingly.

On the one hand, decision makers should take into account that revenge attacks and escalation following a successful offensive action may render the benefits accruing from such action insignificant. However, on the other hand, being overly fearful of the boomerang effect is liable to make the country become too passive and refrain from any counter-terrorism initiative. In this context, we should recall that the boomerang effect, to the extent it exists, is a dynamic phenomenon that changes from organization to organization, and from one period of time to another. An organization that, at a particular point in time, uses its operational capability following an offensive attack aimed against it, may find itself at a different point in time, incapable of acting on its motivation for revenge attacks. Therefore, actions must be directed towards a particular time frame in which the organization being attacked cannot respond with a boomerang effect, despite the possible increase in its motivation.

Timing Offensive Actions against Terrorism

Decision makers who determine a state's counter-terrorism policy must consider, *inter alia*, when and under what circumstances to carry out an offensive action against a terrorist organization. There are several approaches that characterize different nations with regard to their timing of counter-terrorism measures: one approach favors *continuous* action against terrorist organizations based on the state's offensive capabilities and the intelligence in its possession, rather than as a direct or indirect result of terrorist attacks; another approach supports *pre-emptive* measures with a view towards averting a particular attack on the basis of intelligence that has reached security forces; a third approach is the *reprisal* approach, which states that the nation must concentrate its counter-terrorism efforts after the attacks occur, whether to deter the organizations from continuing their attacks or to appease the public. Alongside these three approaches, there is one more approach that represents the passive extreme of counter-terrorism policy—the approach of *restraint*. According to this latter approach, the nation must refrain from attacking the organization even in the wake of serious terrorist attacks, because the benefits to be reaped from such an attack will, in any event, be overshadowed by the losses.

O'Brien states that following a terrorist attack, there are two possible courses of action: reprisal and prevention. In both cases, the principle of punishing the terrorists underlies the action, and in both cases the target is likely to be any one of the following three options: the terrorists themselves and their infrastructures, facilities belonging to the nation that sponsors the organization, and the population that supports the terrorists. O'Brien emphasizes that in order to be effective, preventive actions must cause significant, long-term damage to the terrorists and their infrastructures and should not be thought of as a response to the terrorist attacks. Preventive action is aimed at removing the initiative from the hands of the terrorists and forcing them to defend themselves.[197] Crenshaw adds that in order to guarantee the effectiveness in preventing terrorism—both by means of "preemptive strikes" against the organizations and by means of reprisals—the nation must ascertain that the punishment is directed solely against those responsible for the terrorist attack.[198]

Allan Behm states that looking at preventive measures and response in the counter-terrorism domain as if there was a linear connection between them is an erroneous approach that doesn't take into account the complex and mutual relationship between the two types of measures. Behm maintains that in many cases prevention is a response, and vice versa.[199]

Charters presents an interesting argument to explain why some nations assume a policy of responding to terrorism, rather than initiating "pre-emptive strikes." He claims that governments or societies are likely to relate to terrorism the same way they relate to organized crime. This approach dictates the use of "low enforcement" measures against terrorism; that is, security forces must wait until a crime has been committed before they can take any steps against the organization and its activists.[200] George Carver supports Charters's argument by referring to the American model. He claims that given American society and its legal system prior to 9/11, it is impossible to arrest a person for something he is about to do, even if that something could endanger the lives of innocent civilians. In America you must wait until the individual commits an act, and even then you must grant him every protection under the law, including the assumption of innocence.[201] This analysis was correct until the "USA Patriot Act" was adopted by the United States in 2001, which virtually changes the statutory circumstances in the United States and greatly expands the powers given to security and intelligence forces with regard to preventive measures and obstructing terrorism.

Wilkinson, in contrast, proposes classifying the various types of actions a nation can take against terrorism into four policy-type groups: *reprisal*—involving the use of force based on the principle of "an eye for an eye;" *no compromise*—a policy based on the assumption that giving in to terrorist demands only leads to additional demands; *pragmatism*—a policy based on covert support of the terrorists, which is likely to be combined with concessions and emergency measures; and a policy of *concession* to the terrorists. Each of these types is accompanied by diplomatic steps, economic actions, preventive and deterrent measures—within the context of existing legislation, enhanced international cooperation, and police and intelligence activity. These all lead to a situation where it is difficult to imagine two nations reacting to the threat of terrorism in exactly the same manner.[202]

It is important to note that a nation is likely to change its counter-terrorism policy and the timing of its actions against terrorist organizations according to the changing needs and circumstances of different periods of time. One of the more interesting test cases in this sphere is Israel's policy. Lesser and Hoffman note that the Israeli counter-terrorism policy is perceived as one of reprisal and escalating response. But they contend that this is an unfounded myth since not every terrorist attack in Israel is following by a response, and a significant portion of Israel's war against terrorism is aimed at preventing and disrupting the terrorist organizations' activities, rather than generating any escalation.[203]

Israel's policy with regard to the timing of offensive actions against terrorism has changed from time to time, in accordance with changing circumstances and the attitudes of decision makers. Lustick states that between 1949 and 1956, Israel's policy was based on reprisal and escalation, which included hundreds of actions beyond its borders that led to thousands of Arab injured.[204] In response to an attack by George Habash's "Popular Front" organization on an El Al plane in Athens, Israel decided to conduct a dramatic action in southern Lebanon. On December 12, 1968, IDF forces raided the Beirut airport and blew up thirteen passenger planes belonging to Arab airline companies. The action was planned so as not to cause injury to human life, but would cause serious damage to Lebanon's air transportation. In response to a question posed by a foreign reporter, Chief of Staff Bar-Lev replied, "Our safety is more important than our desire to be popular," and in a meeting with military journalists he added:

> I hope and believe that the IDF raid on the Beirut airport will make Arab airline companies and Arab governments do everything possible to ensure that the various terrorist organizations stop targeting our aircraft, and not only our aircraft, but every possible target abroad. That was the objective of this action and I hope it achieved its goal.[205]

Merari and Elad note that the raid in Beirut had two goals: deterring terrorists from perpetrating additional attacks against air transportation to and from Israel, and putting pressure on Lebanon so that it would suppress terrorism originating from its territory. According to them:

> At the end of 1968 a policy of deterrence and reprisal was chosen, which held the Arab governments accountable for terrorist activity outside of Israel. This was, in reality, a continuation of the attitude during the early years of terrorist activity against Israel, when the Israeli leadership warned Arab nations that they would be considered responsible for any action carried out from their soil.[206]

But Merari and Elad remind us that Abba Eban, Israel's foreign minister at that time, attempted to present the action as part of Israel's fight for existence:

> In response to an interview question on whether the international reaction to the raid in Beirut would have any influence on Israel's policy of reprisal, Eban replied, "We have no policy of reprisal. We have a policy of survival. If reprisal helps us survive, then I am in favor of it."[207]

Notwithstanding these statements, due to international criticism in the late 1960s and early 1970s, Israel preferred to focus on reprisals against targets belonging to the terrorist organizations themselves, rather than on the infrastructures of their host nations. Following the Munich attack, Israel decided to conduct extensive reprisals against terrorist targets in neighboring countries. Four days after the events in Munich, the Israeli Air Force bombed eight terrorist bases in Syria and three in Lebanon. In a television interview, then-Chief of Staff David Elazar said that the action against terrorist bases in Syria and Lebanon was not only a response to the murders in Munich, but was part of a war that we must conduct against terrorists so long as they continue to hurt us: "We operate in accordance with circumstances and using all means, and air strikes are not the only response. In this case it was a very effective response."[208] The IDF did not settle for this response only, and several days after the air strike IDF ground forces went into Lebanon and blew up about 150 houses of terrorists and their assistants in the central sector of southern Lebanon.

In the wake of the multi-victim attacks in Munich and at Lod, the opposition Herut party reiterated its long-standing demand not to be satisfied with reprisal attacks against terrorist organizations, but rather to initiate a far-reaching action in order to force Arab countries to evict terrorist organizations from their territory. In his speech to the Knesset in September 1972 following an air strike in Syria, Minister Haim Landau proclaimed, "Sporadic actions do not achieve their objective.... We struck yesterday in Syria and it's a good thing we did, but we must continue with persistence...[209]

IAF commander Ezer Weizman who, at the time, was one of the shapers of the security approach espoused by the Herut party, recommended that the air force bombard the centers of Cairo, Damascus, Tripoli, and Beirut, because "they are the right addresses to submit the bill for war crimes committed by the terrorists." Weizman recommended that the IDF conquer southern Lebanon and remove the PLO from there, and did not dismiss the possibility of initiating a war to eliminate terrorism. According to Weizman, "The state doesn't go to war only when the danger of immediate destruction hangs over our heads."[210]

The rise of the Likud to power during the second half of the 1970s allowed the party's leaders to change Israel's counter-terrorism policy in every domain. For the first time the government was able to implement on the Lebanese front the policy that Likud leaders had preached during the Labor Alignment governments since the 1950s: the use of military force to eliminate terrorism, or at least to remove strongholds of the Palestinian organizations from Israel's borders.

The first expression of a significant change in Israel's policy came on March 18, 1978, with the launch of the Litani Operation. Seven days earlier, one of the worst terrorist attacks in Israel had taken place: the slaughter of the public bus passengers on the Coastal Highway, which ended with numerous fatalities and atrocities perpetrated by the terrorists. The shock and tremendous anger that gripped the nation following the attack forced the government to take unprecedented steps against terrorist organizations in Lebanon. According to Government Secretary Aryeh Naor:

> The IDF plan was unanimously approved.... The goal was to destroy terrorist bases, infrastructures and weapons all along Israel's border with Lebanon.... It was clear that

in the wake of such an extensive operation there would be a new situation in southern Lebanon, which would perhaps pave the way for fundamental change, for the creation of a buffer zone and unification of the Christian enclaves under a leadership that was friendly towards Israel.[211]

A similar position is presented later on by the defense minister during the Unity Government—Yitzhak Rabin, who explained in mid-1986 Israel's policy in this regard:

Gone is the system of reprisal for each and every attack. The war against terrorism is global and demands both defensive means and offensive means. We employ offensive means when we can. These measures are not related to any particular incident.[212]

To sum up the question of timing of offensive action as part of a counter-terrorism policy, decision makers must determine when and under what circumstances offensive action should be carried out against terrorist organizations. Will the war against terrorism be a defensive campaign, that is, to be carried out only in the wake of mass-casualty terrorist attacks? Will offensive actions be carried out on an ongoing basis, regardless of terrorism? Will such measures only be employed for the purpose of preventing particular attacks about which the government has been warned? Or should there be a policy of restraint, ignoring these attacks completely? On the surface it seems that responsible action following a mass-casualty terrorist attack is particularly problematic, if only because often, the number of victims in the terrorist attack is simply an arbitrary result of the event itself. Moreover, an almost automatic response of being dragged into offensive action following severe terrorist attacks compromises the effectiveness of the nation's counter-terrorism efforts. This was the case when Israel's various governments, following a familiar script, ordered Israeli planes once again to bomb terrorist facilities in Lebanon whenever there was an attack against IDF soldiers in Lebanon or against civilians in Israel. This clear policy, as stated, quickly motivated the terrorist organizations to take defensive measures, which actually weakened the effectiveness of Israel's airborne response capability.

In conclusion, policymakers must formulate the timing of offensive actions according to the nation's short-term and long-term interests, and on the basis of regional and international circumstances, the scope and nature of the terrorist act, intelligence information concerning the terrorist organizations, etc. The nation must avoid automatic responses that follow on the heels of a mass-casualty terrorist attack, if they are not aimed at achieving specific, operational-preventive goals.

Defensive Action in the War against Terrorism

Defensive action covers all the various steps taken within a nation's borders, along its traffic arteries and at sensitive targets. Defensive-security actions are one of the most vital elements in counter-terrorism, and the primary aim is to thwart terrorist attacks, whether by preventing them from infiltrating into the country, by locating and arresting terrorists on their way to the target, or by minimizing the potential damage from an attack. In addition to concrete prevention, defensive action can have other goals as well, such as: deterring the perpetrators from realizing their intentions, and enhancing the sense of personal safety felt by the nation's citizens. With regard to timing the action, as offensive actions are directed mainly at averting terrorist attacks before they are carried out, while still in the planning stage, defensive actions are aimed at disrupting efforts to carry out an attack when they are already in various stages of implementation (see Figure 5.3), that is, from the moment the terrorist cell leaves its base, while on their way to the target, to their arrival in the vicinity of the target and preparing to perpetrate the attack.

Christopher Davy feels that most terrorists can be deterred through defensive actions, when it is clear to them that they cannot easily overcome the security measures, or that there is a good chance they will be caught (for a discussion on defensive deterrence, see chapter 4).[213] Crenshaw feels that a lack of sufficient security at potential targets may, at times, serve as an incentive for a terrorist attack.[214] When speaking about Israel's policy, Yariv stated that a purely defensive strategy is liable to have a dangerous outcome, because it leaves the initiative solely in the hands of the terrorists. In spite of this, he claims, experience has proven that defensive tactics are likely to deter terrorist organizations, and disrupt and limit their activity.[215] O'Brien illustrates the problems involved in using security measures when he states that even if all the security measures were used and succeeded in reducing the number of attacks, some attacks would still be perpetrated.[216]

To achieve the goals of defensive action, security forces conduct patrols, ambushes, and roadblocks, and enhance physical security

Figure 5.3
Timing and Location of Offensive and Defensive Actions

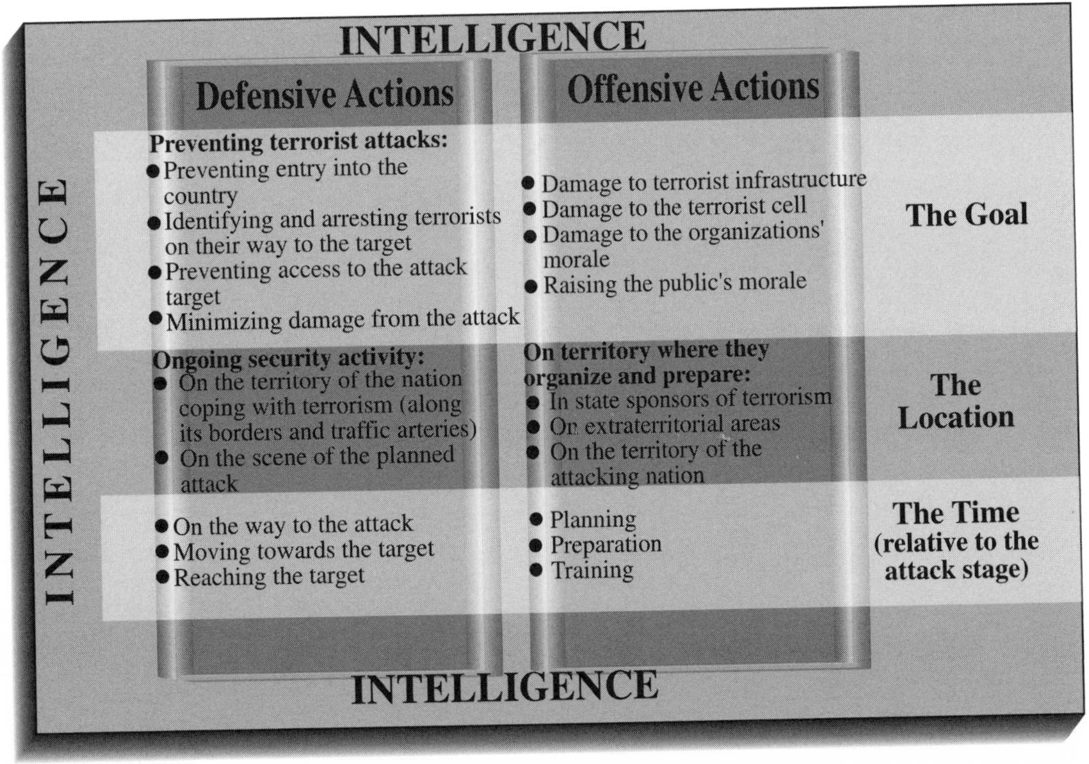

INTELLIGENCE

	Offensive Actions	**Defensive Actions**	
The Goal	• Damage to terrorist infrastructure • Damage to the terrorist cell • Damage to the organizations' morale • Raising the public's morale	**Preventing terrorist attacks:** • Preventing entry into the country • Identifying and arresting terrorists on their way to the target • Preventing access to the attack target • Minimizing damage from the attack	
The Location	On territory where they organize and prepare: • In state sponsors of terrorism • On extraterritorial areas • On the territory of the attacking nation	**Ongoing security activity:** • On the territory of the nation coping with terrorism (along its borders and traffic arteries) • On the scene of the planned attack	
The Time (relative to the attack stage)	• Planning • Preparation • Training	• On the way to the attack • Moving towards the target • Reaching the target	

INTELLIGENCE

INTELLIGENCE

measures (fences, land mines, metal detectors, sensors, radar, "sniffer" detectors for explosives and chemical weapons, video cameras, etc.), based on the special conditions of the border or the protected target. Sometimes security forces will have a specific warning with regard to an impending attack, which will enable them to beef up security at the time and place necessary. But most defensive measures are carried out under conditions of intelligence uncertainty, that is, without any concrete intelligence warning of an intended attack and solely on the basis of prior experience and a general assessment concerning the terrorist organization's intentions.

Due to the need to plug up many security breaches along the nation's borders, traffic arteries, and at specific targets, defensive actions require extensive manpower, and numerous technological means and physical obstacles. All of these make this type of action very expensive, and generate disputes with regard to their effectiveness. It should be recalled that the security network must sometimes be deployed over extensive areas of hundreds and thousands of kilometers, and for long periods of time, while the terrorist organization can concentrate most of its efforts and resources at given point in time and in one location.

The argument concerning the use of defensive-security measures becomes even sharper in light of the cost of the means needed to secure numerous targets, and due to the fact that even maximum security of any target doesn't guarantee absolute prevention of potential attacks against it.[217]

When we take into account the limitations of a "zero sum game" with regard to the nation's budgetary pie, it is obvious that investment of security resources will be made at the expense of other aspects of counter-terrorism, and this is the source of the dilemma over the effective use of national resources and their application to the most efficient channels in the counter-terrorism domain. Bandura notes in this context that since there are few terrorist incidents, the widespread fear of terrorism and the high cost of means for combating terrorism are problematic issues.[218]

In conjunction with the dilemma of dividing up resources due to the high cost and complexity of defensive-security activity, such action also carries with it several ethical-moral dilemmas (which will be discussed in chapter 6—The Democratic Dilemmas).

Israel, as a nation that has been forced to cope with extensive terrorist attacks of a wide variety for many years, must invest tremendous resources in the defensive-security component. Israel's topographic conditions—being very narrow and long—have required Israel to secure lengthy borders without necessarily being able to rely on natural physical obstacles. Moreover, the task of securing the border and preventing infiltration by terrorists into Israeli cities is an almost impossible task because there is no border between Israel's territory within the "Green Line" (1967 borders) and the West Bank, which include a hostile Palestinian population living alongside an Israel-Jewish population, and who may serve as a source of terrorist organization and activity. In this regard, Prime Minister Yitzhak Rabin said in December 1994, following the murder of an Afula resident by an axe-wielding terrorist:

> He crossed the roadblock with an axe with the intention of hurting Jews. We must investigate how he managed to cross through. If only we had more roadblocks, better roadblocks...but even with effective roadblocks it is difficult to locate a lone killer. Traffic there is heavy and there are also many Jews passing through so it is difficult to identify a car; not to mention the fact that thousands of East Jerusalem Palestinian residents have cars with license plates like ours, and those opposed to peace use these types of vehicles.[219]

Israel's tremendous investment in security has, at times, spawned criticism and questions. This was the case regarding the special effort invested in protecting Israeli targets overseas during the 1970s—Israeli embassies, Israeli interests, El Al aircraft and facilities, etc. Shlomo Gazit says:

> I'm not sure that if we would have lowered the volume of all these arrangements by 80% we would have come out with more or less the same amount of damage, but we would have saved ourselves from this terrible burden...[220]

In contrast with his view, Rechavam Ze'evi attributed our successful halting of the wave of air transportation terrorism to Israel's efficient security activities. According to him, "We succeeded in establishing a secure national carrier."[221]

In any event, no one denies the fact that massive security efforts by the national carrier gave El Al passengers a feeling of security, and helped neutralize the fear which, in and of itself, could have caused serious damage to Israel's airline, and perhaps its complete paralysis. Merari adds that:

The terrorists were facing a situation where they found it increasingly more difficult to smuggle weapons into the attack site, move about freely, gather intelligence and escape quickly from the site of the incident. The preventive means were a serious component of the counter-terrorism policy outside the nation's borders...[222]

The defensive action component of Israel's counter-terrorism policy, and Israel's security forces, have had many triumphs over the years in preventing terrorism and reducing its resulting damage. A prominent example was the suicide bombing at the Dizengoff Center shopping mall in Tel Aviv, in March 1996. The attack, which was carried out on the Purim holiday, was supposed to have taken place inside the enclosed mall, and if that had happened, we can assume that the number of victims would have numbered in the hundreds. But the suicide bomber decided to change his plans and explode himself in the open street outside the mall, apparently because of the guards posted at the mall entrances to check the bags of those who went in. Thus, although dozens of people were killed and wounded in the attack, the outcome was less fatal than its planners had originally intended. The effectiveness of Israel's security proved itself in other attacks where the terrorist was deterred from entering a bustling target—a shopping mall, marketplace, etc.—and chose to carry out the attack somewhere else that was not secure.

In spite of Israel's geographic and demographic limitations that make it difficult to create an efficient security network Israel has, in recent years, made a significant effort in erecting a land obstacle—a separation fence—between the West Bank and Israel proper. Israel's security experts have stated that this land obstacle, with proper crossing points, will solve Israel's thorny border problem and prevent terrorism. Indeed, there is no doubt that such an obstacle is a practical necessity if Israel wants to stop the intolerable ease with which suicide bombers and terrorists can enter Israeli territory. Despite international criticism aimed against Israel, this is a fundamental and legitimate self-defense measure. Nevertheless, Israel should assume that even when construction of the fence has been completed, this will not bring an end to terrorism, to infiltrations into Israel and definitely will not prevent Katyusha rockets being fired from the PA into Israeli territory.

In conclusion, defensive action is, by and large, the final link in the chain of terrorism prevention. The importance of this element becomes central when the intelligence network fails and the deterrent policy collapses. Therefore, it is necessary to have a security network that corresponds in size, capability, methods, and means with the terrorist threat, while focusing on safeguarding the nation's borders, traffic arteries, population centers, and other objectives that have been defined as potential terrorist targets on the basis of threat assessments, prior experience, and concrete intelligence warnings. Since security activity demands enlisting extensive personnel, the security network must be based—at least partially—on recruiting volunteers that can serve to back up the regular security forces following a concrete intelligence warning and during periods of heightened tension. Using volunteers in a defensive counter-terrorism activity would serve to enhance the force behind tedious security activities, reduce security costs, and would help, among other things, to strengthen public morale in coping with terrorism. The involvement of volunteers in efforts to prevent terrorism would reduce their fear of terrorism, and perhaps even that of their acquaintances.

6

Democratic Dilemmas in the War against Terrorism

On of the most crucial and most difficult dilemmas for Western societies coping with terrorism is the democratic dilemma. This dilemma derives, first and foremost, from the desire to reach maximum effectiveness in the fight against terrorism (including punitive measures, deterrence, offensive action, defensive action, and intelligence-gathering), while maintaining the nation's liberal-democratic character and without compromising on fundamental democratic values—human rights and civil liberties, respect for the rights of minorities, avoiding harm to innocents, and the like (hereinafter, "the ethical dilemma"). But the democratic dilemma is reflected on another level—the government's concern for its status. On the one hand, democratic government is obligated to safeguard liberal values; and damage to those values during the struggle against terrorism is liable to compromise its legitimacy. On the other hand, the government is required to do everything in its power to protect the lives of its citizens, otherwise the voting public will think of its leaders as not having done their utmost to thwart terrorist attacks, and they will not last long in office (hereinafter, "the governance dilemma").

One of the more prominent arguments found in the professional counter-terrorism literature deals with the relationship between modern terrorism and the liberal-democratic form of government. Many researchers believe that terrorist organizations have found in the liberal democracy a suitable platform to grow and operate. The values of the democratic regime and democratic means of governance provide a convenient medium in which the activities of terrorist organizations can develop, yet they also hamper the government from taking certain actions that could be effective in coping with terrorism.[223] This school of thought tends to represent the characteristics of the liberal democracy, its values and institutions, as an incentive for terrorist attacks.

Another school of thought states that democratic values and institutions actually constitute an obstacle and drawback to terrorist organizations. Yehezkel Dror claims that democracies have managed to cope with terrorism relatively well, and to limit its damage. Moreover, Dror presents a far-reaching position in an attempt to "play the devil's advocate," according to which it is possible that terrorism has a positive role in a democracy. Terrorism may serve as a safety valve that prevents the buildup of dangerous pressures, and provides political drama that helps maintain solidarity with the forces of law and order, and support for the government. Terrorism keeps governments on their toes, and enables them to experience crisis situations and learn from them, at quite a low cost.[224] Schmid claims that democracy has several characteristics that reinforce it and prevent violent eruptions, such as: mechanisms for regime change that are generally non-violent, the existence of a free press, a legal system that can address matters between a person or group of people and the government, etc.[225] According to Schmid, although there is the impression that terrorism is more widespread in democratic nations, this impression is very misleading because democracies have a free press that report on political violence against the nation, without any government-imposed restrictions, and that is why the phenomenon appears more prominent in a democracy.[226]

Another group of researchers who base their theories on comparative statistical data claims that modern terrorism is perpetrated primarily against nations with democratic forms of government, and not in vain.[227] Wilkinson explains this by saying that "in a liberal democracy terrorists can fully exploit democratic freedoms in order to spread slanderous propaganda and undermine values, the purpose of which is to destabilize the institutions and leaders of the parliamentary democracy."[228] We can point to many characteristics of liberal democracy that are likely to have a direct impact on the scope of terrorist activity and its nature. The values upon which liberal democracy is based—particularly freedom of speech, assembly and movement—allow for the growth of the terrorist group and organization of its activists, facilitate their free movement from place to place in order to perpetrate attacks, and enable them to transmit their terrorist message.[229]

The controversy between these two schools of thought can be resolved by understanding the essence of modern terrorism. The phenomenon of terrorism is not unique to democratic and liberal regimes. But with modern terrorism, which is essentially random, the victim's identity is irrelevant; the only aim is to instill anxiety that will be directed later on towards changing attitudes and political processes. Consequently, modern terrorism truly does find liberal democracy a convenient arena for its activities because it is an open society that has public opinion channels through which the public can influence decision-making processes, there are restrictions on punishment and security forces activity, the media is uncensored and competitive, etc.

Public Opinion in the Liberal Democracy

A terrorist organization usually strives to influence decision makers to adopt a policy that will coincide with its political, ideological, or religious aims. In the modern age and in democratic society, the path towards achieving this goal is via pressure on public opinion. The public, fearful for its personal security in the wake of terrorism, is likely to pressure decision makers into acceding to the demands of terrorist organizations. Naturally, this strategy can achieve something only in a state where the political system listens to public opinion and acts accordingly. Although the public's level of influence on foreign affairs and security matters is open to debate, one may assume that if such influence does, in fact, exist it will certainly be expressed within a democratic regime because the liberal democracy, in contrast with other forms of government, has many and various channels whereby the public can express its opinion and influence decision makers.[230]

Former CIA Director Stansfield Turner cites the decision by President Reagan to pull marine forces out of Lebanon in 1983 as an example of the influence terrorism can have on decision makers through public opinion. Although the president called the pull-out a "redeployment," the world understood that terrorism, or the combination of terrorism and public opinion, led to the withdrawal of

U.S. marines from Lebanon. Reagan was unable to withstand the pressure from the democratic society, despite his personal position with regard to terrorism.[231] A more recent example is the results of the elections in Spain, which were held after a series of terrorist attacks on the railway system in Madrid on March 11, 2004. Although most of the Spanish public opposed their country's involvement in Iraq and the assistance that the Spanish government gave to the United States in that campaign long before the attacks, public opinion polls nevertheless showed that the Spanish government was expected to be reelected—if not for the terrorist attacks which took place three days before the elections. The change in government in Spain and election of the opposition leader, who immediately declared after taking office that his new government would recall its troops from Iraq, all these were a direct and almost unprecedented strategic success of modern Bin Laden-style terrorism.

The influence of terrorist organizations on public opinion in a country under attack can be illustrated using the "balance of necessities" theory, formulated by Yehoshafat Harkabi in his book on guerrilla warfare. The theory states that it is possible to examine and even to predict the results of a conflict between states by analyzing the essential nature of the interests of both sides that are at stake (on the assumption that whichever of the parties has the more essential interest involved in the conflict most probably will win). According to Harkabi, "the balance of necessities is liable to influence the willingness to continue with the war, and the attitude towards defeat."[232] We can also use Harkabi's theory to clarify the principle that underpins the impact terrorism has on people's attitudes towards issues of public and national importance. Terrorist organizations use attacks to generate a sense among the public that the national interest being attacked is less important (at least, at the personal level of each individual in the society) than the personal safety of the individual and his family. The message being transmitted to the public is that in order to safeguard personal security and prevent terrorist attacks, the terrorists' demands must be met and they must be permitted to achieve their goals.

However, as noted above, there are differing views regarding the influence of public opinion on decision makers. Some contend that there is no certainty that a terrorist strategy, which perceives public opinion as a crucial element for achieving its aims, can be effective. The disagreement between these two schools of thought raises four key questions: (1) In a democracy, to what degree does public opinion have an impact on shaping the policies of decision makers? (2) To what extent does such influence exist regarding foreign policy and security issues? (3) Are decision makers influenced by genuine attitudes of the public, or do they act on the basis of an appearance or reflection of public opinion as they perceive it? (4) And finally, are decision makers influenced by public attitudes with regard to coping with terrorism, or do the former actually impinge on the latter?

On the surface, "public opinion" fulfills a central and important role in shaping policy in a democracy by a variety of ways, and primarily—via elections. But while the mechanism of elections ensures the public's participation in determining fundamental policy directions regarding how the nation will act at a given point in time, there are differing views regarding the impact of public opinion on government activity on an ongoing basis. In any event, the influence of public opinion on shaping policy is derived from the political culture and tradition of the particular nation, the issues that are at the focus of public attention, and the existence and functioning of strong and active mediating institutions.

The assumption that public opinion, which represents the will of the people, influences decision makers is particularly problematic with regard to issues of foreign policy and security.[233] Here, the public doesn't usually possess all the relevant information needed to make a decision: such information rests in the hands of security and assessment agencies entrusted with advising leaders on these matters. Elitist and Marxist approaches in political science state that public opinion is irrelevant since decisions are made by elite groups on the basis of their influence, and not by the masses. Either way, the impact of public opinion on shaping policy, particularly with regard to security issues and foreign affairs, is not sufficiently clear. And as if this were not enough, it appears that sometimes leaders are likely to include in their considerations what they perceive to be "the attitude of the public" while the public's true sentiments on the issue at hand are completely different. This question is at play in full force in times of crisis following terrorist acts, and especially in hostage situations, where the government is forced to give in to kidnappers' demands in order to secure the release of hostages. At such times, government leaders are prone to make decisions that are the direct result of their assessment of the public will and desire, even if this assessment does not correspond with reality. This has motivated many terrorist organizations who have abducted civilians and soldiers, to use psychological warfare aimed at the entire public—particularly the families of the kidnap victims—and force them to apply pressure on decision makers to meet the kidnappers' demands. This was also true regarding the negotiations conducted between Israel and Hizballah, for the return of the bodies of three Israeli soldiers and the release of the civilian, Elchanan Tannenbaum, during 2003-2004.

Moreover, in many cases—particularly relating to security and foreign policy—it isn't public opinion that shapes the attitudes of decision makers, but just the opposite—leaders shape public opinion through their actions and statements. A study conducted by Asher Arian in 1985 on the topic of public opinion in Israel and the war in Lebanon demonstrated that Israel's political culture tends to give credit to leaders when they are in key positions.[234]

With regard to counter-terrorism, it actually appears that the public has a great deal of influence on decision makers in Israel, compared with other security and foreign affairs issues. Yigal Pressler stresses that public pressure has an impact on decision makers when it comes to coping with terrorism.

> I remember that public discussion following the attack in Argentina influenced decision-makers. The public outcry for decision-makers to conduct counter-terrorism actions had an effect on them. In my opinion, the public influence in this sphere is problematic. Counter-terrorism requires cold calculation, free of public pressure.[235]

Rafi Eitan also believes that the public does actually influence decision makers, and supports this with his own personal experience when he says:

> Absolutely. I think that many times, when I sat with Begin and with Shamir or with Yitzhak Rabin when he was Defense Minister, the question of how it would look in the eyes of the public was a concern.[236]

Yaakov Perry, former head of the ISA, believes that the public influences not only the decision-making process with regard to counter-terrorism, but even the judicial process:

> In general I would say that the public, public opinion, has an impact. I wouldn't say that it has a decisive impact. Nevertheless, there is no judge who is "utterly" isolated

from the world, [who] looks only at this "case." He reads the papers and he listens to discussions, and that has a certain effect.[237]

In this context it should be noted that, at times, terrorist attacks are perpetrated in conjunction with the electoral process that is taking place in the targeted nation, with the declared or undeclared goal of influencing the outcome of the election, by intimidating the voters to withdraw their support from a particular candidate or political party. In addition to the recent terrorist attacks in Madrid, of note are the terrorist attacks carried out in Israel prior to the 1996 elections, the year in which the Labor Party government was replaced by the Likud government, as well as the murderous attack carried out on the 2003 election day at one of the polling stations in Beit She'an.

In addition to the element of public opinion, the following aspects will be discussed as having an impact on terrorist activity in democratic countries.

The Existence of an Independent, Developed, and Competitive Press

The liberal democracy usually has an extensive and competitive network of numerous and varied media. This network is not subject to the government and is not forced to censor the information it transmits. A free and well-developed media in a democratic nation can serve as a platform for terrorist organizations to disseminate their messages from the area of an attack into the homes of every citizen (see a more extensive analysis of this in chapter 8).[238]

The Limitations of Punishment

The fundamental values of the liberal democracy prohibit the state from taking all possible steps that may be effective in capturing and punishing terrorists. The democratic government, itself subject to the nation's laws, cannot use a punishment that is not stipulated in the law or which conflicts with democratic values (such as collective punishment). The strength of democracy hinges upon its legitimacy. When the regime itself upholds the state's laws and democratic values, it earns legitimacy. Any deviation from these standards is liable to lead to the regime's delegitimization.[239] According to Clawson, law enforcement is effective in a democracy only when it enjoys widespread support from both the decision makers, who must allocate resources to this effort, and the public at large, whose cooperation is necessary for both decision makers as well as the security forces.[240] Schmid adds to this the restrictions in coping with terrorism imposed by the judiciary system in the democratic state, which requires solid and admissible facts as evidence to convict a suspect of terrorist activity.[241]

The Value of Human Life

Human beings have joined together in human society in order to ensure—first and foremost—their physical existence and individual safety. Therefore, the primary requirement of any nation and any form of government is to protect the lives of its citizens. Damage to their existential safety is liable to be translated in a liberal democracy into political change, government change, and in more severe cases, even a change in the type of regime. Therefore the "price" that terrorists can demand in exchange for not harming human lives in a democratic nation is unquestionably higher than the "price" they can demand and obtain in nations with other forms of governance.[242]

The Governance Dilemma

A democratic regime's legitimacy is based on the principle of majority rule, while safeguarding the rights of the minority. The liberal democracy is obligated to ensure a person's freedom and civil rights, with tolerance towards political rivals. At the same time, however, every regime is naturally obligated to protect the personal and physical safety of its citizens, and sometimes these two objectives can conflict.[243] A concrete and ongoing threat to the lives and property of its citizens is liable to jeopardize the legitimacy of a regime and endanger its leaders' continued hold on the reins of government.[244] Hoffman and Morrison point out in this context that terrorists push governments into a struggle for political legitimacy.[245]

Terrorists are likely to present the democratic government with an almost impossible dilemma: tenacious counter-terrorist action using violence and measures such as emergency legislation, punishment, and deterrents are likely to reduce the scope and damage of terrorist attacks; but in many cases these steps are not compatible with fundamental liberal-democratic values and could contribute towards severe domestic and international censure.[246] In contrast, avoiding such steps while zealously safeguarding the values and principles of the liberal-democratic form of government may lead to a continuation—or even escalation—of terrorist attacks against the nation's citizens, and jeopardize the people's morale and personal safety. All of these might, in the best of circumstances, leave the democracy unscathed but destroy the ruling party politically; in the worst case, they could lead to the rise of a "strong man" who will establish an authoritarian-dictatorial regime while promising to "destroy terrorism at any price." According to George Carver, "we tend to avoid recognizing the fact that in order to fight terrorism we must wrestle with thorny issues that may be difficult to deal with in a democracy; this is particularly true with regard to elected officials trying to keep their jobs."[247]

Bandura emphasizes the fact that the use of counter-terrorism measures is usually justified in terms of their benefit, since counter-terrorism reduces the overall level of personal suffering.[248] On the surface, jeopardizing the rights of a few innocent people is justifiable in order to save the lives of many others. Hoffnung states in this context that:

> The assumption underlying all the agreements and charters regarding security considerations is the recognition of the supremacy of the state over any other competing consideration. Recognizing the nation's supremacy derives from the ethical priority of the benefit of the organized public over the right of the single individual or group of individuals to fulfill their wishes or desires.[249]

Indeed, decision makers and security agencies that employ a variety of measures to fight terrorism, some of which may impinge on individual rights at times, justify the use of such measures with the phrase "defensive democracy," the thrust of which is the right and obligation of a democratic regime also to use extreme measures, when necessary, in order to protect the existence of the democracy itself. In other words, safeguarding democracy should not be a recipe for suicide in an attempt to preserve all the rules and values of liberal-democratic government.

Gad Barzilai, on the other hand, takes exception to the concept of defensive democracy and states that this is an erroneous and misleading expression that "creates a deceptive awareness of a reality that doesn't exist."[250] Barzilai claims that the term "terrorism" enables decision makers to isolate individuals and groups, to remove them from the public collective deserving of tolerance, to torture them and ignore their demands without any substantive discussion, while at the same time absolving the state from any wrongdoing or essential infringement of the law.[251] Pnina Lahav supports Barzilai's arguments with a quasi-deterministic presentation regarding the actions of security forces fighting against terrorism. According to Lahav, "this body ultimately stops defining its identity as an emergency weapon created to safeguard society and begins to blur the boundaries between its own benefit and that of the public."[252] Lahav relies on the research by Ehud Sprintzak regarding the legalism and illegalism of Jewish society in Israel, which states, *inter alia*, that the current Israeli leadership inherited the mentality of illegalism that once characterized those who founded the Yishuv during the struggle with the British. The research further claims that this political culture, in which the state stands above the law, was the basis for creating the legal norms that allow for far-reaching counter-terrorism measures.[253]

One of the possible serious ramifications of this "democratic dilemma" in general, and the governance dilemma in particular, is extremism on the part of the citizenry. When the government's counter-terrorism policy is perceived by certain strata of society as insufficient, incorrect or irresponsible, they might, as stated, act to change the regime (either democratically or through violence); alternatively, they may "take the law into their own hands," that is, respond against the terrorists in ways they believe are correct in an attempt to resolve the terrorism problem once and for all, or force the government to do so. Indeed, counter-terrorism is one of the dangers of the democratic dilemma.

The Ethical Dilemma

The ethical dilemma is intertwined, as stated, with the governance dilemma, the main point being—the effectiveness of the war against terrorism compared with the degree to which the steps taken jeopardize liberal-democratic values. Many researchers offer proposals and recipes to fight terrorism, which guarantee, so they claim, minimal damage to liberal-democratic values. Robert Moss argues in this regard that those combating terrorism must demonstrate great restraint when mounting counter-terrorism operations in cities. According to him, it is very easy for military personal "to step on the toes of innocent civilians" when conducting searches and pursuits in crowded, impoverished neighborhoods. Therefore, it is essential to avoid arousing the public's hatred; to reduce the number of persons defined as "the enemy" to the lowest possible minimum so as not to alienate public opinion; and not to restrict the right of legitimate criticism of the government.[254] Wilkinson adds in this context that

> Repressive measures should not be used indiscriminately. The government must prove that the steps it employs against terrorism are solely directed towards restraining the terrorists and their collaborators, and protecting society from them.... All aspects of the counter-terrorism policy and operations must be under civilian control and democratic supervision...[255]

Sthol claims that counter-terrorism should not be discounted as a method for coping with terrorist activity, because of its tremendous effectiveness. In his view, though, this method can be justified only on the basis of saving democracy.[256] Charters notes that historical experience teaches that terrorism can be fought without seriously jeopardizing liberal-democratic values. As proof he cites the success of Italy, France, and West Germany in drastically reducing terrorism without jeopardizing democratic principles and processes. For him, this is the true criterion for success in the war against terrorism.[257]

In several instances, the nation coping with terrorism will attempt to minimize the damage to liberal-democratic values by stating in advance that the harsh counter-terrorism measures will only be temporary, and will be undertaken only in an effort to eliminate or minimize the phenomenon. Democratic nations that are not targets of terrorism are freer to criticize those nations that suffer from terrorism. The former claim that liberal-democratic values should be safeguarded under any conditions or circumstances, even if this seems to compromise the effectiveness of counter-terrorism measures. According to this approach, the nation's willingness to compromise these values gives the terrorist organization an essential victory, because it is interested in damaging the nation's legitimacy and its democratic nature; therefore this must be avoided at all costs. Many nations are attempting to find the "golden path" between these two approaches, which will ensure that the nation's values are safeguarded without jeopardizing the effectiveness of its counter-terrorism efforts.

The Democratic-Intelligence Dilemma

Decision makers in Israel, as the leaders of a nation suffering from relatively extensive terrorist acts of various types, have constantly found themselves confronted with the "democratic dilemma."[258] This dilemma is a common thread running through Israel's various governments and it becomes stronger or weaker according to the scope of terror at any given time. The democratic dilemma is reflected in various issues and spheres, primary among them being means of gathering intelligence, interrogating suspects, procedures for standing trial and acceptability of evidence in terrorism-related trials, controversial methods of punishment (such as demolishing or sealing houses, or setting curfews), various types of offensive action (such as targeted killing, which involves killing terrorist activists without due process), censorship of the media with regard to terrorism, and more.

A key manifestation of the democratic dilemma involves intelligence gathering. At times, this process is likely to necessitate illegal actions, while in other cases—actions that may not be illegal but may compromise liberal-democratic values. One of the more controversial topics is the question of gathering intelligence by interrogating those suspected of terrorist involvement. Over the past decade, interrogation methods have become a key issue troubling Israeli policymakers (this highly important topic will be discussed later on in a separate section), but the democratic dilemma surrounding intelligence is not only reflected in the methods used to interrogate suspects, but in other intelligence gathering measures as well, such as surveillance, wiretapping, handling intelligence agents, and so on.

With regard to *monitoring*, Benjamin Netanyahu says that, "democracy must have a variety of methods for monitoring and means to gather intelligence that will enable it to pursue terrorists, try them and convict them."[259] Martha Crenshaw, however, highlights the fact that democratic regimes will not usually monitor their citizens in order to follow all the plots and know in advance when groups or individuals in society decide to go from legitimate protest to violent activity.[260] Schmid also emphasizes the difficulty involved in collecting intelligence against terrorism in democratic regimes, because the private lives of the citizens are none of the state's business.[261]

The thorny nature of the democratic dilemma comes to the fore with regard to *wiretapping* of suspected terrorists. An example of this problematic usage of information, which was apparently gathered through wiretaps and had internal political ramifications in Israel, was the episode in which Defense Minister Ezer Weizman was fired from the Shamir government in January 1990, following phone conversations he had with Yasser Arafat in Tunis.

The difficulty with wiretapping in the context of intelligence gathering on terrorist organizations can be gleaned from decisions handed down by the Supreme Court, such as the decision by Judge Dorner, stating that the Israeli courts were not authorized to permit wiretapping in areas that are under Israeli control but are not part of the state's territory, except for wiretaps against Israelis.[262] (It should be noted that this decision did not prohibit wiretapping in the West Bank.) This is also reflected in the amendment to the Wiretapping Law which was approved by the Knesset Constitution, Law and Justice Committee on March 27, 1995, which states that the ISA is not permitted to eavesdrop on Muslim religious figures in East Jerusalem and within Israeli territory, including those from Hamas and Palestinian Islamic Jihad, without receiving approval from the president of the District Court. Within this context, it was stated that the ISA would be required to present to a secret committee (to consist of heads of the Knesset Security and Foreign Affairs Committee, and the Constitution, Law and Justice Committee) the criteria used to define who could be wiretapped and the parameters by which the wiretapping would be carried out. The decision also extended the types of media for which it was prohibited to eavesdrop without receiving court approval, and these included cellular phones, facsimile, intercomputer communications, and wireless communication.[263] Prime Minister Yitzhak Rabin disagreed with the sweeping decision that was included in the aforementioned amendment, according to which all wiretapping carried out by the ISA would be subject to judicial review. In a letter to the chairman of the Knesset Constitution, Law and Justice Committee, MK Dedi Tzucker, Rabin stressed the fact that he was not prepared to accept the required extension of judicial review on all wiretaps carried out for security purposes, since this would jeopardize national security. Rabin explained his objection to the extension with the following reasoning:

> Wiretaps for reasons of state security are essentially different in nature from wiretaps to prevent crime or to expose criminals.… This has to do with acquiring sensitive and

vital intelligence information of the utmost importance, which will have an effect on people's lives and the chances for achieving peace in the region, and the authority that should bear this heavy burden of responsibility should be the prime minister, who is in charge of such sensitive matters.[264]

Methods of Interrogating Terrorists—
Example of a Democratic Dilemma in Counter-Terrorism

One of the more concrete examples of the democratic dilemma in Israel within the context of counter-terrorism is, as stated, the issue involving methods for interrogating terrorists by the ISA. Between 1987 and 1994, members of the Interrogation Division at ISA facilities interrogated more than 25,000 people suspected of hostile terrorist activity (an average of 3,125 interrogations per year), several dozens of which submitted complaints concerning the means of their interrogation. These complaints are first examined by the internal auditor of the ISA, and since the early 1990s, by the State Prosecutor.[265]

The question of interrogation methods illustrates the dilemma between possible harm to the rights of the suspected terrorist, to the point of torture and physical harm to the suspect, versus the possibility of obtaining vital information that would allow security forces to prevent terrorism and save many human lives.[266] This matter is a common theme that has run throughout Israel's various governments, and illustrates the sensitive and difficult relationship between the government and the entire executive branch (primarily the security forces and the ISA), and between the legislative and the judicial branches. Over the years, governments have usually supported the work methods employed by the ISA, legislators have avoided passing laws that would establish the interrogation procedures defined by commissions of inquiry, and the judicial system has permitted the ISA to continue with the interrogation methods it was using, although it expressed repeated dissatisfaction with the fact that there was no legislation in this regard. One of the more serious episodes in this context, which raised profound questions regarding the interrogation methods used by the ISA and the manner in which it would obtain confessions, was the "Nafsu Episode." Nafsu was a Circassian IDF officer who was convicted of contact with enemy agents after terrorist organizations had tried to threaten him in order to force him into working for them. Nafsu refused to give in to their threats, but he did not report to his superiors about his meetings with the organizations' representatives. In April 1987,

Nafsu appealed his conviction to the Supreme Court. The Supreme Court deliberations, which were held behind closed doors, exposed improper ISA procedures, including the destruction of investigation tapes and notes.

In its ruling, the court included a severe censure of the behavior of Nafsu's interrogators, and stated that they gave false testimony to the military tribunal. The court emphasized the need to define rules for ISA interrogation procedures. During the trial the sides reached a plea bargain, through which the state waived its accusations—major espionage, treason, providing information to the enemy, transferring weapons to the enemy, and moving terrorism materiel into Israeli territory on his behalf. These were replaced with the relatively lesser crime of "deviating from authority."[267] In the wake of Nafsu's release there was a demand for a state commission of inquiry to examine the ISA interrogation methods. An investigative team was appointed to look into the matter of ISA interrogation methods in the war against terrorism, a team that included Attorney Yitzhak Tunik, former head of the Israel Bar Association; and Gen. (Res.) Zvi Zamir, who had served as head of the Mossad. This team did not last long and quickly fell apart.[268] Attorney General Yosef Harish instructed the police to open an investigation against the ISA interrogators who had been involved in the Nafsu episode. Prime Minister Shamir understood that only a state judicial commission of inquiry could prevent a police investigation and, on May 31, 1987, it was decided to form Israel's ninth commission of inquiry, following the announcement just one day earlier regarding his opposition to such a committee. The Landau Commission included, along with Judge Landau, Judge Ya'akov Maltz and Gen. (Res.) Yitzhak Hofi.[269]

Yaakov Perry, who served as deputy director of the ISA, was appointed to formulate and prepare the ISA position for presentation before the commission. On October 30, 1987 the Landau Commission completed its report, after holding forty-three sessions and hearing forty-one witnesses, including past and present prime ministers, members of the civilian and military judicial system, experts in various fields, and people who had been interrogated by the ISA. From the Commission report we learn that: "...Under these circumstances the Commission completely agrees with the ISA position that without some form of physical pressure no effective interrogation would be possible (Section 2.37).[270] According to Perry, the Commission stated, "there are cases when it is necessary to use some type or other of physical pressure when interrogating suspected terrorists." Perry adds that:

> This was the first time a senior echelon—a state commission of inquiry—approved the distinction between a police investigation to obtain evidence, and an intelligence interrogation whose goal is to prevent terrorist activity. This point of view was reflected in the series of detailed instructions contained in the Commission's confidential appendix. It contained general guidelines for behavior during interrogations, defined a series of prohibitions, outlined the authority of the various levels in the service to permit different interrogation methods, which were called "moderate physical pressure," such as sleep deprivation, isolation, handcuffing, shaking, covering the head, and other such methods—and maximum time frames for their use. Among other things, the Commission even defined that slapping the face of a disrespectful suspect required prior approval from a higher authority. The Commission also recommended establishing a ministerial committee to discuss unusual cases and implement the guidelines included in the confidential appendix. The government adopted the recommendations in their entirety...[271]

And so, pressure on the suspect was permitted, but the Commission stated, "the means of pressure should principally take the form of non-violent psychological pressure through a vigorous and extensive interrogation, with the use of stratagems, including acts of deception. However, when these do not attain their purpose, the exertion of a moderate measure of physical pressure cannot be avoided" (Section 4.7). The Commission added that "ISA interrogators should be guided by setting clear boundaries in this matter, in order to prevent the use of inordinate physical pressure arbitrarily administered by the interrogator" (Section 4.7).[272]

The Landau Commission Report created and established a system of norms and rules for interrogating terrorists, and in practice, recognized the need to interrogate using moderate physical pressure in cases of "a ticking bomb"—interrogation under time constraints, when the detainee is likely to possess important information that could prevent a future attack.[273] At the same time, the commission set down clear restrictions with regard to interrogation methods and the use of violence. Years later, these principles serve as a basis for examining the behavior of ISA interrogators when investigating terrorists, and deviations from these guidelines have even led to indictments being handed down against the interrogators.[274] Pnina Lahav summarizes her conclusions regarding the Landau Commission, stating, "the Commission's recommendations were based on a recognition of the reality of counter-terrorism, and the understanding that moral behavior and fighting terrorism do not always go hand in glove."[275]

Alan Dershowitz, in his book *Why Terrorism Works,* claims in this context:

> Several important values are pitted against each other in this conflict. The first is the safety and security of a nation's citizens. Under the ticking bomb scenario this value may require the use of torture, if that is the only way to prevent the bomb from exploding and killing large numbers of civilians. The second value is the preservation of civil liberties and human rights. This value requires that we not accept torture as a legitimate part of our legal system.[276]

The Supreme Court ruling HCJ 5100/94 *The Public Committee Against Torture in Israel et al. versus The Government of Israel et al.*, deals with several appeals submitted by public bodies and suspected terrorists, and can tell us a great deal regarding the physical means included under the heading of "moderate physical pressure":

- *Shaking*—the forceful shaking of the suspect's upper torso, back and forth, repeatedly, in a manner which causes the neck and head to dangle and sway rapidly. In its reply the state argues that the shaking method is only used in very special cases, and only as a last resort.
- *Waiting in the "shabach" position*—the suspect has his hands tied behind his back. He is seated on a small and low chair, whose seat is tilted forward, towards the ground. One hand is tied behind the suspect, and placed inside the gap between the chair's seat and back support. His second hand is tied behind the chair, against its back support. The suspect's head is covered by an opaque sack, falling down to his shoulders and very loud music is played in the room. The state claimed that both crucial security considerations and the investigators' safety require tying up the suspect's hands as he is being interrogated. The head covering is intended to prevent contact between the detainee and other suspects; the loud music is played for the same reason.
- *The "frog crouch"*—this refers to crouching on the tips of one's toes, for five-minute intervals. According to the state, this interrogation practice has ceased.
- *Excessive tightening of handcuffs*—excessive pressure on the hand or leg cuffs, resulting in serious injuries to the suspect's hands, arms, and feet, due to the length of the interrogations.
- *Sleep deprivation*—the state agreed that suspects are at times deprived of regular sleep hours, but it argued that this does not constitute an interrogation method aimed at causing ex-

haustion, but rather results from the prolonged amount of time necessary for conducting the interrogation.

According to the state, use of these methods was not a question of "torture," that is, cruel and inhumane or humiliating treatment, which is illegal under international law. In its ruling, the Supreme Court referred to the matter as the need to strike a balance between two opposing values: the obligation to protect human dignity and the need to effectively fight the phenomenon of crime in general, and terrorist attacks in particular. The Supreme Court ruled that the legality of the interrogation derives from its worthwhile purpose and methods, and thus it concluded that an effective interrogation could be conducted but without violence, and at most through the use of deception. Given this, the court revoked the use of shaking as a violent method that should not constitute part of a legal interrogation, as well as the "frog crouch," which it deemed a humiliating method that damaged human dignity. The court did not accept the need to handcuff the suspect in the shabach position in order to protect the interrogators, and stated that it was neither a fair nor reasonable method of interrogation and impinged upon the detainee's dignity, his bodily integrity, and his basic rights beyond what is necessary. The Supreme Court also attacked the need to put a bag over the suspect's head while awaiting interrogation, because these are opaque bags that cause suffocation and are unnecessary in order to avoid eye contact with other suspects. Thus, the covering of the head, as distinguished from the covering of the eyes, is outside the scope of authority and is prohibited. The court added that sleep deprivation should not be used as a goal in and of itself, beyond being a side effect of the interrogation. Finally, the court prohibited the playing of loud music. The Supreme Court was willing to recognize the fact that if a ISA interrogator were to be brought up on criminal charges for using one of these forbidden interrogation methods he could avail himself of the "necessity" defense, but the judges stressed that one should not extrapolate from this a source of authority for ISA interrogators to employ such physical means during their interrogations.[277]

Given the court's position, it is particularly interesting to note the perspective of those figures who were the decision makers during the Shamir government and the National Unity Government with regard to the matter of the democratic dilemma in general, and especially concerning the question of interrogation methods in "ticking bomb" situations. With respect to the latter, Yitzhak Shamir states that "we need to find the best way to prevent dangerous killings such as these and save human lives, and on the other hand, not to jeopardize the fabric of democratic life."[278]

Shimon Peres stated:

> Ultimately, I tried my best not to deviate out of ethical considerations. I thought that every war is waged twice: once on the battlefield and once in the history books. I didn't want to lose even the war in the history books.... I tried to make decisions that would not shame the state the morning after.[279]

Yaakov Perry believes in this context that

> Fighting terrorism using the tools of a democratic state is almost impossible.... I think that on the whole, Israel should get positive marks in this regard.... It certainly wouldn't be acceptable to many bleeding-heart liberals. But I think that Israel has tried its best to do what it could. You can't be a hypocrite and say "we do it only democratically, that is, only using democratic tools."[280]

Carmi Gilon explains very well the serious dilemma involved in defining a ticking bomb situation, and the difficult decision the head of the ISA must make in granting special permission to interrogate and permit the shaking of suspects:

> What is a "ticking bomb?".... If the interrogator knows that in another two hours a bomb will definitely explode and all he needs to know is whether it will go off at 39 Rothschild St. or 38 Rothschild St., then it doesn't matter what the law states. The interrogator will risk prison and shake him [the suspect—B.G.] as necessary. But these are not the situations. The situations we face are that you have intelligence and knowledge, a suspicion that perhaps Mustapha knows about Ahmed who recruited a suicide bomber whom he doesn't know, who is now doing penance and preparing to be a *shahid*. That's the best intelligence you can get. This is what you know. And that's what I call "a ticking bomb, [even though] ultimately the information may not be true, or that Mustapha isn't even Mustapha and that Ahmed only heard the name Mustapha.... These are cases where you don't know whether to interrogate them or not. You cannot go to the interrogator and say that if necessary you will convince the Attorney General about the "necessity." The interrogator is not a jurist. Give him an order as to what is permitted and what is prohibited, and don't tell him anything beyond that. The result is that they don't interrogate. Unequivocally they don't interrogate! Therefore, my opinion on this is clear and well known. I think that the special permits were used on about 8% of the Hamas and Islamic Jihad detainees, and in 90% [of these cases—B.G.] they also led to results...[281]

Lipkin-Shahak, who also emphasized the ticking bomb dilemma, said:

I have no doubt that a "ticking bomb" justifies interrogations that employ physical pressure, if that is the only way to prevent the "ticking bomb" from exploding and killing innocent civilians. The question is whether this is a "ticking bomb," when, how do you know, and this is the dilemma.... Maybe it will go on ticking for two more months and you have a month to prevent the explosion? Therefore, the dilemma is extremely complicated.[282]

Ruth Gavison emphasizes the quandary involved in using these interrogation methods when she states:

The recommendation to accelerate the creative attempt to change the nature of the security services and establish more effective services that do not employ physical pressure...this is perhaps a somewhat frightening recommendation. Won't we be creating a heaven for terrorists while threatening the personal safety of Israel's residents and the continuation of the entire peace process? On the other hand one could say that we've already tried the option of moderate physical pressure. For us, and throughout the entire world, it has produced only rotten fruit.[283]

Dershowitz, on the other hand, sums up the dilemma in this way:

The simple cost-benefit analysis for employing such non-lethal torture seems overwhelming: it is surely better to inflict non-lethal pain on one guilty terrorist who is illegally withholding information needed to prevent an act of terrorism than to permit a large number of innocent victims to die. Pain is a lesser and more remediable harm than death; and the lives of a thousand innocent people should be valued more than the bodily integrity of one guilty person.[284]

During the years when Israel was striving towards peace with the Palestinians through the Oslo Accords, the governments of Yitzhak Rabin and Shimon Peres (1992-1996) were faced with numerous quandaries concerning the conflict between the effectiveness of counter-terrorism measures versus liberal-democratic values. The horrific terrorist attacks perpetrated in Israel at that time, and particularly the wave of mass-victim suicide bombings, severely undermined the feeling of personal security of Israel's citizens and endangered the continuation of the entire peace process. This is reflected in statements made by those who were involved at that time in thwarting terrorist attacks and dealing with their aftermath. For example, Yigal Pressler, who served as counter-terrorism advisor to the prime minister, said, "anyone who wants to fight terrorism must make cold calculations, even at the expense of liberal values."[285] Shabtai Shavit, head of the Mossad at that time, stated his position somewhat differently:

Given a choice between being less democratic and surviving, and dying democratically, I prefer the first [option]. And in the intellectual discussion of the democratic dilemma we ultimately reach this point, and we must face up to it. Mrs. Thatcher said that in order to protect democracy, you sometimes have no choice but to use undemocratic means.[286]

Carmi Gilon, head of the ISA, added: "In this matter I follow [Justice] Barak, who said, 'Democracy is not a recipe for suicide.'"[287]

Dershowitz, in reference to possible damage to democratic principles, chose to quote Floyd Abrams, an important defender of civil rights, who said, "in a democracy sometimes it is necessary to do things off the book and below the radar screen."[288]

During the Rabin government, the ISA operated according to rules set forth by the Landau Commission and in accordance with special authorization given to its interrogators to use "moderate physical pressure" in cases of a ticking bomb. These authorizations were given by a special ministerial committee, headed by the prime minister, and they were renewed every three months.[289] In April 1993, due to the increase of terrorist acts in Israel, the ministerial committee agreed to institute changes in the instructions issued to ISA interrogators, which eased some of the interrogation restrictions but without deviating from the guidelines set forth by the Landau Commission. The ministerial committee also stated that if any harm is caused to the suspect during an interrogation conducted according to the instructions, the interrogator could not be held criminally accountable.[290] In a deposition submitted to the Supreme Court as part of an appeal regarding the use of physical force when interrogating a terrorist, and given the background of the allowances given to the ISA, the ISA director stated:

> I am convinced that we will not be able to thwart the activities of terrorist elements in an effective manner using interrogation without security services being able to employ, in certain cases and within the restrictions of the law, the special interrogations procedures recommended by the Landau Commission.[291]

The updated interrogation procedures also stipulated actions that were forbidden in any event when interrogating a suspected terrorist, including depriving the suspect of food or drink, preventing him from going to the bathroom, and exposing him to heat or cold. Generally speaking, it stated that "the interrogation directives do not authorize the use of forbidden measures or pressure that constitute torture or that involve severe degradation or jeopardy to human life." The procedure also stated that:

The interrogator must exercise caution, that is, he must first conduct the interrogation without using any unusual means, and only when he is convinced that without the means included in the procedure he will not obtain the information he needs, can he employ unusual pressure as outlined in the procedure.[292]

Given the restrictions placed on the ISA, the director of the ISA at that time, Carmi Gilon, stated:

Israeli society has undergone a revolution, going from a security-oriented society to a normative civilian society, and this compromises the abilities of the ISA, which are in danger of being undermined, and its ability to interrogate is one of the first victims.[293]

Gilon explained the importance of interrogating suspects in foiling terrorist attacks:

The terrorist cells fall like dominoes. Each one who falls takes someone else down with him, each cell means another cell. This is due to effective interrogation, and there is no such this as effective interrogation without the use of special authorization. The one who understood this very well was Yitzhak Rabin. He knew that interrogation is a weapon of war in the hands of the ISA, a weapon without which it is impossible to effectively fight terrorism, and he supported the proper use of this weapon with all the political, governmental and moral force he had.[294]

Dershowitz raises another argument that justifies the use of torture—the simple fact that it achieves its objective. "It is precisely because torture sometimes does work and can sometimes prevent major disasters that it still exists in many parts of the world and has been totally eliminated from none."[295]

The need to use "moderate physical pressure" while interrogating activists from Hamas and Palestinian Islamic Jihad derives, *inter alia*, from the fact that these movements have trained their members in how to withstand various ISA interrogation methods, as they are very familiar with the interrogators' methods and limitations.

As a result of the authorizations given to ISA interrogators by the ministerial committee, several terrorist attacks were prevented. In December 1994, for example, it was reported that a planned suicide bombing by the Hamas in the Petah Tikvah market and on a bus driving along the Trans-Samaria Highway had been prevented. Some members of the terrorist cell who had been specially trained to withstand ISA interrogations, were arrested by the ISA and for a long time they did not give up the information they possessed, until the interrogators had received special authorization from the Ministerial Committee on ISA Affairs to employ "increased physical pressure."[296] In August 1995, the ISA publicized another case where an interrogation using moderate physical pressure led to the prevention of terrorist attacks. The ISA arrested terrorist Abdal Nasser, who sent two Hamas suicide bombers to the No. 26 bus in Jerusalem that month, and after he refused to cooperate with his interrogators for two days, the head of the ISA decided to authorize the interrogators to use "moderate physical pressure." In this way the ISA found out about a car bomb and three other terrorist bombs that were ready for operation, and arrested the members of the terrorist cell who had been planning to kidnap soldiers for extortion purposes. Prime Minister Yitzhak Rabin referred to this when he said:

> The laws exist, what can you do, and they are well and fine, but they are not suited to fighting terrorism and preventing suicide bombers…. If they would permit the ISA to interrogate suspects as it wanted, without being subject to the restrictions impost on it by the Attorney General and other "bleeding hearts," we may have been able to prevent the attack in Jerusalem.[297]

The force of the democratic dilemma is reflected in the conflict between the approach of ISA director Carmi Gilon and the approach of Attorney General Michael Ben-Ya'ir. Gilon had this to say:

> The root of the problem…[between us] was based on the fact that Ben-Ya'ir, in my opinion, didn't find the necessary balance between maintaining the law and providing the ISA with the legal and judicial tools to cope with Islamic terrorism…. Ben-Ya'ir's extreme position was particularly prominent because traditionally, the Israeli judicial system led by Meir Shamgar and later on by Aharon Barak, tried to find the proper balance.[298]

Ben-Ya'ir objected to the fact that the special authorizations were being given automatically and were renewed every three months. According to him, the authorizations were supposed to be specific, and their use by ISA interrogators was meant to be monitored. According to Gilon, Rabin had given the ISA unequivocal support in the face of Ben-Ya'ir's demands, and even resulted in open confrontation with the attorney general because of it.[299]

Within the context of the prime minister's sweeping opposition, as stated, to placing additional restrictions on the ISA above those that had already been ordered by the Landau Commission, Rabin was also against the proposed legislation according to which the Parliament would supervise the activities of the ISA and its leaders.[300] The determined opinion of the prime minister, who sided with security forces when it came to interrogation methods, led to critical statements aimed at him by Justice Minister David Libai: "The prime minister is bound by legal means and he cannot do what he wants regarding the war against terrorism," and "this government has someone whose eye is on security matters, but not on the legal aspects."[201]

Yet the use of moderate physical pressure and shaking did not achieve only successful results. One of the most outstanding failures of this method, which was widely publicized and led to the imposition of further restrictions on the activities of ISA interrogators, was the death of the suspect Abed Harizat in April 1995. The findings of the coroner's report on Harizat's body stated that

> The deceased did not die of natural causes.... Death was caused as a result of trauma to the brain. The shock was caused by deliberate shaking of the head and not as the result of direct blows to the head. The wounds in the shoulder area are the result of being held strongly or from repeated blows. The type of wounds in general point to death as the result of violent shaking.[302]

Following the death of Harizat, the ISA was under tremendous pressure to avoid using physical pressure on suspects. Beside the ethical-moral arguments that the use of physical force during interrogations damaged fundamental democratic values, some critics emphasized the fact that violent interrogation could lead to false information, which would not only not aid in preventing terrorism, but might even cause grave damage. Regardless of the ethical question, or the issue of the benefit of torture, there were those who criticized the recommendations of the Landau Commission and saw them as attempting to have it both ways—to prohibit the use of torture during interrogations and to enable interrogators to use physical pressure on certain occasions. Professor Ruth Gavison, for example, argued:

> The Landau Commission's distinction between permitted moderate physical pressure and prohibited torture is a risky distinction: we cannot be complacent when someone dies under questioning, but it is also difficult to try and convict someone who innocently, and with a sense of duty, employed—albeit, unusually—the rules of action with which he was instructed and that were approved by both the judicial and political echelons.[303]

Carmi Gilon admits:

> True, in Harizat's case we had a professional malfunction, but one cannot ignore the statistics. The ISA shook some 8,000 people during interrogations and nothing happened. In Harizat's case there was an unusual set of circumstances, from his physical data to his physiological condition during the interrogation. His death, I claimed, is not a reason to revoke a special authorization that isn't necessarily one of the most harsh.[304]

Regarding the impact of Harizat's death, Gilon says the following:

In light of the Harizat episode, Ben-Ya'ir decided that the Ministerial Committee for Security Affairs must be acquainted with the details of each and every authorization. In other words, how many times it is permitted to shake each suspect, the height of the stool, the volume of the music (in decibels) played for the suspect, etc. Naturally I argued with him about this, but it didn't do any good. We had to explain each authorization, to detail how each thing was done. It was simply grotesque.[305]

Yitzhak Rabin was forced once again to assist the ISA, and in August 1995, after most of the members of the Ministerial Committee for ISA Affairs refused to extend the special interrogation authorizations, Rabin exploded: "I will tell the Knesset and the government that I can no longer be responsible for security." Rabin added, "the attempts to restrict the ISA are a grievous error." Regarding the Harizat episode, Rabin stated, "there was an slip-up in the interrogation method. They used it with 8,000 suspects and there was never a problem except for one suspect." Rabin ended by saying that "anyone who prevents the ISA from using the means presently at their disposal, will bear the responsibility on his own conscience for reducing our ability to fight terrorism."[306]

In spite of the attorney general's uncompromising attitude in favor of prohibiting any physical pressure during ISA interrogations, it seems that the Supreme Court sometimes tended to give security agencies a relatively free hand in this regard, most likely due to the appalling terrorist attacks that were being perpetrated in Israel at that time. In September 1995, the Supreme Court permitted the ISA, for the first time, to deprive a suspected terrorist of sleep, when his interrogation justified such action.[307] The court rejected the appeal of Hamas suspect Iman Adal Hijazi, who was suspected of making contact with the operator of a suicide terrorist cell, who complained to the court that his interrogators prevented from getting at least six consecutive hours of sleep per day. In January 1998, in a 5-4 decision, the court decided not to issue a temporary restraining order against the ISA, prohibiting them from using physical force to interrogate Abd al Rahman Ganimat, the head of the "Tzurif" terrorist cell that murdered eleven people and injured fifty-two others. Thus, the judges actually approved the suspect's interrogation when he was tied to a chair, his hands in cuffs, his head covered with a sack, and loud music playing in the background.[308]

In conclusion, we can learn a good deal about the democratic dilemma as it relates to interrogation methods of terrorists from the end of the decision of the Supreme Court *HCJ 5100/94 The Public Committee Against Torture in Israel et al. versus The Government of Israel et al.*:

> We are aware that this decision does not ease dealing with that reality [Israel's difficult situation—B.G.]. This is the destiny of democracy, as not all means are acceptable to it, and not all practices employed by its enemies are open before it. Although a democracy must often fight with one hand tied behind its back, it nonetheless has the upper hand. Preserving the Rule of Law and recognition of an individual's liberty constitutes an important component in its understanding of security.... Deciding these applications weighed heavy on this Court.... We are not isolated in an ivory tower. We live the life of this country. We are aware of the harsh reality of terrorism in which we are, at times, immersed. Our apprehension that this decision will hamper the ability to properly deal with terrorists and terrorism, disturbs us. We are, however, judges.[309]

The Offensive Democratic Dilemma

The democratic dilemma is also reflected in another type of activity undertaken as part of a nation's counter-terrorism strategy— offensive action; that is, action initiated by security forces against terrorist targets carried out in their staging areas and regions in which they live.

The issue of offensive action is liable to involve ethical-moral questions, and highlight the democratic dilemma particularly when damage to terrorist targets involves damage to those who are not directly involved in terrorism, when the offensive action infringes upon the sovereignty of a foreign nation, or when it involves the use of extreme force against terrorists in contravention to international charters and accepted rules of law:

- *Direct or indirect collateral damage to those not involved in terrorism* (such as neighboring civilian populations, another country, passersby, etc.)—Most offensive actions, including air bombardment, artillery fire and the like, are—by their very nature—liable to harm people who are not involved in terrorism, particularly when the targets are located in populated areas, that is, when the terrorists themselves or their facilities are located near or within concentrations of civilian populations. The more collateral damage generated by the attack among the civilian population, the less legitimate it becomes. According to Turner, when counter-terrorism becomes more arbitrary and less selective, it assumes the characteristics of terrorism itself.[310] This is precisely the reason many terrorist organizations locate their bases, explosives laboratories, and operational headquarters in populated areas, and the more death there is among this civilian population, the better. Refugee camps, schools, and hospitals are often chosen as proper cover for terrorist organizing and activity. Injury to civilians as a byproduct of offensive action is supposed to serve the goals of the terrorist organization by creating a negative image in international public opinion and could lead to censure of the attacking nation, perhaps even to the point of imposing sanctions against them; it demonizes the attacking nation among the terrorist organization's native population, an audience that was never politically involved to begin with and at most, provided passive support for the organization; it generates controversy among the public of the attacking nation on the question of the legitimacy and effectiveness of such offensive measures, to the point of a political schism and undermining the belief in the reasoning behind the struggle.

- *The use of force in contravention of accepted rules of law*— One type of offensive action that has recently been exposed to widespread public and international criticism, and which has been a fundamental element of Israel's counter-terrorism policy in recent years, is "targeted killing." The normative-moral dilemma with regard to offensive action in general, and targeted killing in particular, has already been discussed in the previous chapter. There, we highlighted the arguments used by opponents of this type of action, who stated that targeted killings violate legal norms as it imposes and carries out a death sentence on someone without the benefit of a trial, with all this may imply (see the discussion of this dilemma in chapter 5).

- *Damage to the sovereignty of foreign nations*—Many terrorists hide in the territory of a third nation, whether the state is aware of the fact that it is sponsoring a terrorist organization or not, or whether it ignores the fact because it is unable to act against the terrorist organization. As a result, the responding nation must, at times, carry out offensive actions beyond its own borders and on the territory of another nation. Such action may be considered an act of war against that nation, and may have serious international consequences for the responding nation.

In response to these three arguments against a nation using offensive action, a broad-based, uncompromising international front must be formulated to establish that whereas terrorism is a blatant violation of all the normative international rules, and that since September 11, 2001, it constitutes a direct and essential threat to the peace of the entire world, the responsibility for the lives of civilian bystanders rests, first and foremost, with the terrorist organization that uses them as a "living shield" and chooses to establish its bases precisely in the midst of densely populated areas. It must be stated that placing a military-terrorist base within or near a civilian target is prohibited, and that the responsibility for any possible collateral damage to this target falls squarely with the terrorist organization. Such a clear statement would probably place public pressure on the organization to avoid locating its facilities close to or inside civilian populations.

Offensive action against terrorist organizations is a permitted combat action—a pre-emptive attack aimed at preventing a combative terrorist action against that nation, and as such should be considered an act of self-defense. But even in the case of self-defense, the nation must safeguard some of the rules, including avoiding deliberate damage to civilians and maintaining the balance between the need to hurt the terrorist organization and collateral damage that may be caused to the surrounding civilian area that isn't related to the terrorism. In other words, the nation must choose methods of offensive action that will minimize the expected collateral damage as much as possible.

Finally, with regard to damage to the sovereignty of another nation as a third party, as stated, if this nation is one that supports terrorism or ignores terrorist activity on its territory, and if this nation was warned and asked to act against those agents but refused to do so, then offensive action against terrorist organizations on its territory must be considered permitted and legitimate—an act of self-defense.

The Defensive Democratic Dilemma

On the surface, defensive action does not compromise liberal-democratic values, if only because it is passive and should be considered as an integral part of the right to self-defense enjoyed by individuals and whole communities. But in reality, as seen in the Israeli case, some defensive actions against terrorism infringe on the rights of individuals and groups in society, and place certain restrictions on civilians. These are usually the result of the fundamental need of a police officer or security guard to identify the terrorist, to search his belongings and prevent him from entering the target area. The attempt to locate a terrorist in a large crowd can be compared to trying to find a needle in a haystack, and requires security checks among very large groups of people. The democratic dilemma regarding defensive action is reflected on several levels:

- *The need to identify oneself*—Nations contending with terrorist attacks are forced to conduct identity checks on the nation's citizens at roadblocks, entrance points to well-populated or sensitive facilities, and via random inspections along highways. The very demand for identification constitutes a restriction of one's civil rights. Since terrorists often belong to a particular ethnic group, national minority or religious sect, the need to identify often makes one particular group of the population more suspect than other groups within the same nation. When such suspicion includes external or physical identifying signs as part of a suspected ethnic profile, there may be potential damage to the liberal-democratic values of that nation.

- *Searching personal objects and belongings*—The citizens of a nation contending with terrorism are required to expose the contents of their personal bags and objects to everyone when entering shopping malls, places of entertainment, airports, and other well-populated areas. Ostensibly, this jeopardizes a person's right to privacy. At times, the damage is even more severe, for example, when a person must submit to a search of his clothing or his own body, whether he is a suspect or whether as part of routine security procedures at a sensitive target. The scope of such damage can be minimized by technological developments that enable security forces to locate and identify materials and devices in a person's handbag or on his person, such as metal objects (by using metal detectors), and explosives (using "sniffers"—odor sensors). But we cannot rely solely on security procedures and technology, and there is no substitute for the professional security guard trained in identifying suspicious objects or behavior. Furthermore, technology itself may jeopardize a person's privacy by identifying objects in handbags or by exposing physical features and private body parts with invasive visual technology.

- *Obligation to bear the burden of security*—The citizens of a nation coping with terrorism are often required to bear the cost of the security burden. This may fall upon the citizens directly, through the imposition of a special tax aimed at financing security and counter-terrorism activity, or indirectly, when shop owners are required to enhance their security measures and they pass the financial burden on to their customers by raising prices. In certain instances, as is the case in Israel, citizens are sometimes asked to take part in security activity itself, by enlisting to guard certain facilities such as schools and kindergartens. This does not constitute voluntary activity, such as the Civil Guard, but rather an obligation that is a direct result of emergency legislation or an administrative order.

Damage to liberal-democratic values in the wake of security-defensive activity dramatically illustrates the democratic dilemma in coping with terrorism, that is, the difficulty in effectively preventing terrorism without infringing on liberal-democratic values.

Considerable criticism is heard against one type of offensive action or another due to the damage this may seem to entail to liberal values and norms. But in the case of defensive action, given the fact that no one can deny the need and the obligation to save human life, even detractors find it difficult to demand that nations refrain from such action. The democratic dilemma involved in defensive steps illustrates that in the lion's share of counter-terrorism activity, whatever it may be, there is some measure or other of damage to democracy's values. Decision makers must be aware of the fact that when deciding to carry out counter-terrorism measures, whether offensive or defensive, there is a reasonable possibility that liberal values will be jeopardized—although that does not necessarily preclude such action. The questions that must be asked are the degree to which such action harms these values, how essential is the action, and to what extent the damage can be minimized by choosing a less detrimental alternative.

A Theoretical Model for Examining Democratic Dilemmas in Counter-Terrorism Activity

In order to define the scope of possible damage in the democratic domain for each aspect of counter-terrorism, we can use the model proposed in Figure 6.1, which establishes two extremes for such damage: one—no damage at all, the other—physical damage to "innocents." Between these two poles the model proposes various indicators regarding the level of harm in the democratic domain, arranged in ascending order: damage to rules for proper governance (including damage to judicial procedure); actions that contravene international charters; actions that are in breach of the

Figure 6.1
Indicators of the "Democratic Dilemma"

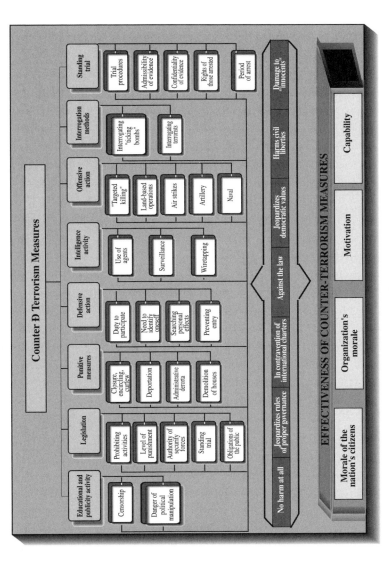

laws of that nation; damage to liberal-democratic values (such as minority rights, civil rights, etc.); damage to basic human freedoms (freedom of expression, movement and assembly, freedom of employment, the right to possess property and the right to defend said property, human dignity, etc.); and finally, on the opposite extreme—damage to "innocents" (that is, physical harm to people who are not involved in terrorist activity). At times these indicators are liable to overlap, and in other cases only one of them will be directly affected. The severity of the damage in the democratic domain caused by a counter-terrorism measure (intelligence-gathering, defensive or offensive operational measures, punitive and legislative measures, etc.), will be defined according to the following parameters: nature of the damage (according to the proposed range of severity), the number of indicators affected by the aforesaid action (one indicator or several at the same time), and finally, the frequency of the damage and the scope (that is, how many people is this action likely to harm, and how often).

The proposed model is, therefore, a qualitative model that can be used by decision makers when determining what type of counter-terrorism action to undertake, with the hope of minimizing the scope of any damage to the democratic domain. It should be emphasized that it is difficult to establish ironclad rules regarding the absolute damage from each counter-terrorism measure in this context, and a new ethical-moral assessment should be made on the basis of the proposed model whenever a decision needs to be taken regarding any type of counter-terrorism measure. This reassessment should be conducted in accordance with prevailing conditions, the severity of the threat and the expected damage according to the model. In addition, decision makers should understand that these indicators represent only one side—the cost—of the democratic dilemma equation. On the other side of the calculation are the expected benefits, that is, the effectiveness of the proposed counter-terrorism measure.

Summary and Recommendations

To sum up, the issue of the democratic dilemma is one of the fundamental questions affecting counter-terrorism policy in a democratic state. Terrorist organizations are aware of the ethical-moral dilemmas involved in employing various counter-terrorism measures, and they attempt to heighten these dilemmas by exploiting various techniques to jeopardize the legitimacy of the government they are fighting. The main question is, as stated above, whether a terrorist organization can be fought effectively without seriously damaging liberal-democratic values. It would appear that the answer to this question is positive, although it is not an easy task. In facing governance and ethical dilemmas in counter-terrorism, the best practices will be those that strike a balance between the extremes in each dilemma (see Figure 6.2).

Given Israel's cumulative experience in coping with terrorism, and in an effort to minimize damage from the democratic dilemma we propose some of the following rules for counter-terrorism action:

- *Government commitment*—The government should define its commitment to do everything possible to protect the lives and well-being of its citizens within the boundaries of the law. If a persistent and pressing need arises to fight terrorism

Figure 6.2
The "Democratic Dilemma" in Counter-Terrorism

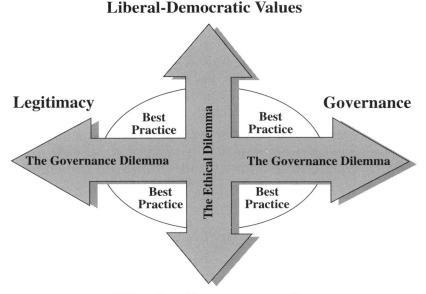

Liberal-Democratic Values

Effective Counter-terrorism

and this entails violating the law, the government must strive to amend the laws in compliance with the indicators specified above. In any case, any counter-terrorism measures used must not violate the law.

- *Emergency legislation*—Counter-terrorism legislation that may conflict with liberal-democratic values must be supported by an absolute majority of Parliament members. Such laws must be limited to a specific time period, at the end of which they automatically expire. They should include provisions as to when and in what cases they are applicable, and an independent supervisory mechanism should be set up to oversee implementation. In general, the use of emergency legislation should be kept to a minimum wherever standard legislation can suffice (see the next chapter for a detailed discussion of this issue).
- *Control*—It should be explicitly stated that all security agencies shall be subject to constant and ad hoc control by the legislative branch of the government.
- *Judicial review*—It should be determined that all operational actions undertaken as part of the state's counter-terrorism activity are subject to judicial review.[311]
- *Remedies*—Anyone who considers himself to have been injured by counter-terrorist activity has the right to seek relief through the courts.
- *Definition of a terrorist organization*—Clear and explicit definitions should be provided for including groups in the list of terrorist organizations.
- *Offensive action*—Such steps should be used to thwart certain attacks, to disrupt the activities of terrorist organizations and damage their infrastructures, to deter them from perpetrating terrorist acts, etc., but not purely as punishment. Security forces should use selective means and methods that can keep collateral damage to uninvolved civilians to a minimum.
- *Intelligence gathering*—It should be stipulated that permission to collect intelligence by means that are liable to infringe on civil rights (surveillance, wiretapping, etc.) can only be granted by a judge and only in advance.
- *Indictment procedures*—If different judicial procedures than those applying to criminal offenders must be established for terrorists, an independent external agency must be appointed to monitor implementation from the moment an arrest is made (see the next chapter for a discussion of this topic).
- *Interrogation methods*—The various methods must be established within the law, as should supervisory mechanisms to prevent violations (this supervision can be technical or

through an independent agency that would monitor the interrogation process, even without the suspect's knowledge). Special interrogation methods must be provided for ticking bomb cases, subject to the approval of a special independent committee and Parliament supervision. In general, the objective should be to use advanced interrogation techniques rather than torture.

- *Administrative punishment*—All types of administrative punishment must be subject to judicial review. Where the evidence justifying the punishments includes privileged information that cannot be revealed to the suspect or his counsel, this evidence must be brought before the court. One can consider establishing a special department within the Public Defender's office with high security clearance, which would review the material and provide the judge with an educated opinion regarding its validity, without notifying the suspect himself or his lawyer (see the discussion on this question in the following chapter).

- *Collective punishment*—Collective punishment should be avoided. Any action whose impact extends beyond the terrorists themselves (including closures, curfews, encirclement, etc.) must only be used for specific operational purposes, and for a limited period of time, not as punitive measures (see the discussion on this issue in the following chapter).

- *Defensive measures*—The use of security and defensive measures that could potentially infringe upon civil rights should be kept to a minimum. If such means are nevertheless required, they should be approved by the Parliament. In any event, restrictions stemming from security measures must not single out any minority group within the general population; however, comprehensive inspections of suspects should not be avoided when necessary, even if their common denominator is based on ethnicity, nationality, religion or some other criteria.

- *Censorship*—Media coverage of terrorist attacks must not be censored. Nonetheless, the media should be encouraged to formulate rules for professional conduct that would avoid playing into the hands of the terrorists. If the media fails to do this voluntarily, public pressure should be applied to motivate it in this direction (see chapter 8 for a discussion of this topic).

7

Dilemmas in Legislative and Punitive Policies

One of the most problematic issues in the war on terrorism, inextricably linked to the democratic dilemma, is the question of legislation—that is, passing special laws in order to promote counter-terrorism and aid in its effectiveness. In practice, such laws have usually been enacted as emergency laws or special regulations, due to a need that has arisen or in response to the demand by security forces for a legal foundation for a particular counter-terrorism measure. These counter-terrorism laws and regulations can be classified into sub-groups as follows (see Figure 7.1):

- Legislation prohibiting terrorism—laws that define terrorism and terrorist organizations and prohibit membership in terrorist organizations, terrorist activity, and assistance, support, encouragement, identification with terrorism, and incitement to carry out such acts;
- Legislation regulating special legal arrangements for prosecuting suspected terrorists;
- Legislation defining the types of punishment to be imposed on crimes relating to terrorism and their severity, and laying down minimum sentences for people convicted of these crimes;
- Legislation requiring the public to participate in the war on terrorism—legislation making it compulsory to pay for or participate in security and defensive measures, such as special protective apparatuses, payment of a tax to finance the cost of security, etc.;
- Legislation stipulating the authority of security forces within the context of counter-terrorism measures—rights of search, surveillance, wiretapping etc.

Nations dealing with terrorism around the world have legislated a wide variety of laws against terrorist activity and against those

Figure 7.1
Counter-Terrorism Legislation

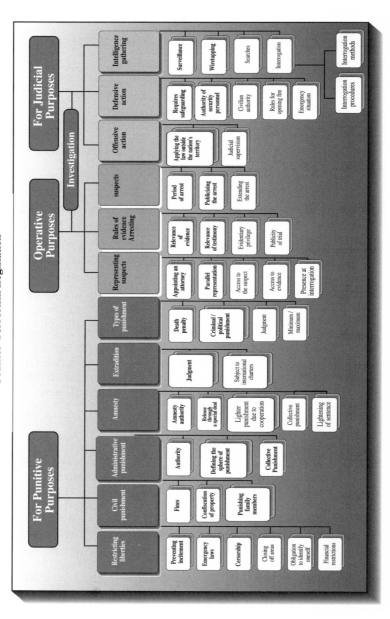

who perpetrate terrorist attacks: from declaring a state of emergency and military administration; through counter-terrorism legislation and strengthening the authority of enforcement agencies, intensifying the punishment policy for terrorism, restricting the rights of those suspected of terrorist activities, etc.; and up to easing the requirements of admissibility for legal evidence in everything relating to terrorism. In this context, Hoffman and Morrison point out a special kind of legislation in the domain of terrorism—"Penitence laws." Laws of this type have been passed in Italy, Britain, and other countries, and mainly involve clemency or restricted punishment for terrorists who "repent," who give themselves and their friends up to security forces, and who are willing to testify against them in court. These laws are not uniformly effective—in some cases they have been relatively successful, but in Britain, for example, they have proved to be ineffective or even damaging.[312]

Indeed, one of the most notable nations that has engaged in anti-terrorism legislation is Great Britain. Over the years, Britain has enacted stringent laws and regulations aimed against Irish terrorism.[313] In 1971, for example, the government expanded the authority of security forces to detain people without trial in cases where they were suspected of involvement in terrorism, but these measures failed and were eventually suspended by the government only seven months after coming into force. In the same way, as noted, British attempts to make use of terrorist "collaborators" who would agree to testify against their friends also failed (trials that became known as the "Supergrass" trials). In the emergency legislation of the Northern Ireland Law (1973) and the Terrorism Prevention Law (1974) it was set forth that terrorist trials would be conducted by a single senior judge, and would not be jury trials. The police were given the right to detain suspects for up to seven days without a warrant, and soldiers had the right to stop and search even without reasonable suspicion. In 1975, following a serious attack in Birmingham that led to the deaths of twenty-one people, Britain passed an amendment to the Terrorism Prevention Law. This amendment gave the Home Secretary the authority, among other things, to deport people suspected of involvement in and support for terrorism. Furthermore, the burden of proof devolved to the person accused, rather than the state.[314] In 1988, the British government proposed an amendment to the law revoking the suspect's right to remain silent. With regard to this amendment, the Home Secretary at the time, Douglas Hurd, stated:

> Democratic governments must consider long and hard before proposing measures of this kind, even when they are dealing with the enemies of democracy. We have done so. Our conclusion is that is we must not take away from the courts the authority required to identify and stop the fuel driving the engines of murder.[315]

In 1989, what is perhaps the most far-reaching law of all was passed, prohibiting media interviews with terrorists and their supporters. At the same time, a law was also passed enabling the confiscation of bank accounts believed to serve terrorist organizations.[316]

Hoffman and Morrison present the British example as proof of the problems involved in emergency legislation and far-reaching anti-terrorism laws, and the danger that lies in the overuse of such legislation. According to them, 4,345 people were arrested on the basis of these laws between 1975 and 1980. Only 205 of them were deported, 381 were detained by means of an application submitted to the Home Secretary, forty-six were charged with crimes set forth in the law, and a further 187 were charged with other criminal offenses.[317] The vast majority of the detainees were never convicted and their guilt was never proved. Even the British legal system criticized the rigid legislative policy with regard to the detention, interrogation, and punishment of terrorism suspects. In the Bennett Report, drawn up by Supreme Court Justice Harry Bennett in 1981, severe criticism was leveled against violent interrogation methods, following which changes were made in Britain. Some of the steps taken by the British were proved, as noted, to be ineffective and damaging. Alongside the Supergrass trials, attempts were also made by British security forces to obtain intelligence information on the IRA by arresting young Irishmen, putting pressure on them to give up information in exchange for their release and dropping the charges against them. Sometimes, in particularly grave cases, suspects were threatened that if they refused to give information, rumors would be spread that they were collaborating with the British—rumors that were liable to jeopardize their lives. The use of intelligence of this kind compromised the government's legitimacy, and in effect, aided the IRA.[318]

The legal situation in the United States was different from that in Britain. The Comprehensive Anti-Terrorism Act of 1986 states that a terrorist attack on American citizens outside the country would be considered a federal crime, and suspects may be arrested outside the country and brought to trial in an American court. U.S. courts do not usually inquire as to how the suspect was brought to court. Patrick Clawson notes that the FBI used the extended authority it was granted in order to capture, for example, the terrorist Fayez Yunas, who was tempted into international waters off the coast of Lebanon. According to Clawson, the main problem in America's legal confrontation with terrorism was the need to examine the evidence against the suspected terrorist according to the stringent standards accepted in the United States, including the right of the suspect's attorney to examine the evidence even if this is liable to reveal intelligence sources and information gathering methods, and to endanger national interests.[319] This state of affairs changed following the attacks of September 11, 2001, when the "Patriot Act" was passed by the United States and effectively gave American security forces many powers they had not had previously, in order to enhance their ability to deal with the threat of international and domestic terrorism in the United States.

Seton-Watson says that the authorities and political parties in Italy grasped the seriousness of terrorism more slowly than other Western European countries, but in one domain they acted quite rapidly—that of legislation.[320] Public Order Act No. 152, passed in Italy on May 22, 1975, enabled the police to conduct searches without a warrant, prohibited citizens from participating in demonstrations wearing a helmet or mask, and more. Following the kidnap and murder of Aldo Moro, further legislation was passed in 1978 increasing the severity of the punishment for kidnapping and blackmail for terrorist purposes, particularly in cases when the hostage died in captivity, while easing the punishment of terrorists turning state's evidence, expressing remorse for their involvement in terrorism and helping free hostages. The law also enabled junior judges to authorize telephone wiretapping verbally and not in writing. After a series of harsh terrorist attacks, another law was passed in Italy in December 1979, allowing the police to arrest suspects "for security reasons" and to carry out a search without a search warrant if there was "reasonable suspicion" of involvement in terrorism. But the law that apparently helped, more than anything else, to halt the terrorist activity of the Red Brigades was Law No. 304 passed in March 1982. This law gave benefits and clemency to repentant terrorists (who were called *Pentiti*). The law stipulated that a person would not be punished for membership in a terrorist organization, nor would it be mandatory to impose a prison sentence on terrorists who voluntarily gave themselves up to the authorities. The law made it possible to reduce considerably the sentence of imprisoned terrorists who chose to cooperate with authorities. Terrorists who cooperated also received better conditions and protection from revenge.[321] This law, which was of considerable help in the fight against Red Brigades terrorism in Italy, illustrates just how complex it is to formulate a punitive policy regarding terrorism, since a similar policy used in Britain, and manifested in the Supergrass trials, failed miserably and caused tremendous harm to the counter-terrorism activity in Britain. The reason for the different success of these legal steps lies in the social and cultural differences between the two countries, and the differing circumstances under which the steps were taken.

In Germany, too, security forces relied on legislation to expand their counter-terrorism strategy and make it more effective. In 1971, a law was passed in Germany increasing the punishment for skyjacking and the murder of hostages. The ability to conduct a trial in the absence of the accused was extended in 1974 and, in 1976, a law was passed prohibiting the support or encouragement of severe violent crimes. The law also prevented representation by a lawyer suspected of being involved in the crime with which his client was charged, or one representing a number of people accused of the same crime. Following the kidnapping of the industrialist and president of the Employers Union in Germany, Hans Martin Schleier, emergency regulations were passed in Germany allowing security forces to conduct searches in residential neighborhoods and to require citizens to identify themselves. A law passed in 1986 enabled the police to collect information on the movement of people in Germany in order to create a database of information for tracking terrorists.[322]

The democratic dilemma in Israel with regard to legislation is mainly focused on emergency legislation. In practice, there are three types of emergency legislation in Israel, each of which draws its incidence from a difference legislative entity: Mandatory emergency legislation (Defense [Emergency] Regulations—1945), administrative legislation (emergency regulations enacted by government ministers for a period of three months under Section 9 of the Law and Order Ordinance, 5708-1948); and Knesset (Parliament) legislation (primary legislation that is liable to be limited in time or contingent on the continuation of the state of emergency).[323]

The main sources of legislation relating to terrorism are the Defense (Emergency) Regulations, the Prevention of Terrorism Act (hereinafter: the "Act") and criminal legislation, mainly the Penal Code.[324]

The Act was passed when the state was established (1948) in the form of the Mandatory laws of pre-state Israel and, in fact, has been valid ever since, with certain amendments and changes.[325] Gad Barzilai says that the Act was used in 1948 as a tool by the new government, primarily to restrict underground movements (especially the "Stern gang"—"Lehi"), which did not accept the authority of the state, and to help delegitimize them in an effort to concentrate the military power of the IDF and security forces under state and party control.[326] Barzilai points out two major problems with the Act: one—it gives the state a special right, against which there is almost no appeal or possibility of reversal, to determine that a particular group of people constitutes a terrorist organization;[327] and two—the normative, broad application of the Act not only to people involved in terrorism and terrorist organizations, but also to those who support, sympathize with, identify with or encourage terrorist organizations.[328] Barzilai presents examples of cases wherein the Act was used for political purposes (among others, by means of an amendment to the Act in 1986 and the prohibition against Israelis meeting with the PLO).

With regard to the Defense (Emergency) Regulations, many researchers criticize the fact that Israel, throughout its years of independence, has not succeeded in passing primary legislation to replace the mandatory regulations, and has chosen to make use of appended amendments and adaptations to suit the times and the requirements. Tzur says in this context, that the Defense (Emergency) Regulations, which have long since been revoked and replaced in Britain, do not strike a balance between security needs and human rights, nor do they contain a review mechanism to prevent abuse of the powers given by virtue of the regulations.[329] Even the passing of the Basic Laws, especially the Basic Law: Human Dignity and Liberty, did not detract from the power of the executive branch because of the provision regarding upholding the rules of this Law, which, in practice, stated that the legality of laws and regulations legislated prior to the Basic Law, including the Defense (Emergency) Regulations, would not stand the test of the Basic Laws (although their interpretation would be in the spirit of the Basic Laws).

Barzilai maintains that criticism should be leveled not only against the political system in Israel, but also against the judicial system, which usually avoids intervening in the considerations of security forces on security matters involving interpretation of the Prevention of Terrorism Act:

> The liberal dialogue, which has many limitations and problems, stops at the threshold of the Prevention of Terrorism Act. The Supreme Court tends not to intervene.... Furthermore, Jewish public opinion in Israel has always tended to object to real judicial supervision in matters of security, and to a large extent the elite and public opinion have objected to judicial intervention in matters defined as "terrorism."[330]

According to Barzilai, instead of fostering a well-oiled mechanism of legislation to prevent terrorism, a culture of tolerance should be developed which will, of necessity, make it harder for terrorist organizations to develop and operate in a democratic country.[331]

The late prime minister Yitzhak Rabin took the opposite stand to that of Barzilai, and at the meeting of the Knesset Foreign Affairs and Defense Committee in March 1993 said that the Defense (Emergency) Regulations were complex, and that the legislation restricted the actions of security forces. Rabin also protested against the intervention of the Supreme Court in security matters, and even called for legislation restricting its ability to intervene.

Forfeiture of Funds to Terrorist Organizations

One example of the problematic nature of using legislation to thwart and prevent terrorism is the issue of forfeiture of funds to terrorist organizations. In the modern era, managing a terrorist organization requires a broad economic base for the organization's ongoing operations. The large majority of Palestinian terrorist organizations maintain an administrative and command network made up of "professional terrorists," and while they are usually motivated by ideological considerations, they also earn their living from this activity. During the 1970s and 1980s some Palestinian terrorist organizations, particularly the PLO, maintained a large network of hundreds—and sometimes thousands—of activists in the framework of their "military forces" in Lebanon and other places, paying them a monthly wage. Beyond paying salaries, the terrorist organization naturally requires large sums of money to purchase and construct infrastructures, acquire weapons, train and drill its members, perpetrate terrorist acts, and so on. Therefore, one of the most effective ways of dealing with terrorist organizations is to block the flow of money to the organization, or at least place obstacles in its way.

These activities, as noted, require specific legislation and international cooperation (especially in view of the fact that terrorists use Western banks in order to transfer and launder their money, and the banks tend to preserve confidentiality regarding their customers).[332] Regulation 74(2) of the Israel Defense (Emergency) Regulations allows—in fact, even requires—confiscation of any object relating to the implementation of a security-related crime (for this purpose, "object" can also refer to money). Sections 32-39 of the Penal Code also allow forfeiture of assets pursuant to security-related crimes, but here confiscation of assets is not a requirement. In any case, an owner of rights in the property who was not a partner to the crime is entitled to appeal to the court to revoke the forfeiture.[333]

The law therefore allows the security agencies to use the sanction of property forfeiture in cases of security-related crimes and terrorism. The problem arises when the money and assets in question belong to terrorist organizations operating also in an apparently humanitarian guise, whose legal activities conceal regular or ad hoc financial aid to terrorist organizations, which is hard to identify and prove using legal means. In this regard, in May 1989 the government brought before the Knesset a draft bill to amend the Prevention of Terrorism Act, making it possible to forfeit property with any connection at all to "a terrorist organization, terrorist activity or the promotion of terrorism." The bill was intended to enable the confiscation of money and assets belonging to philanthropic, welfare, and health organizations, mainly in East Jerusalem, which serve as a cover for transferring money to terrorist organizations, terrorists, and their families. The draft bill stated that in court cases with respect to this crime the court would not be subject to the usual rules of evidence and would be able to invoke privilege with regard to the evidence and not show it to the defendant or his counsel. In bringing this draft bill for its first reading in Knesset, then Justice Minister Dan Meridor said that he was presenting it "with a heavy heart" and that it was "a result of the state of emergency, not that declared in 1948 but that of the recent severely deteriorating situation."[334]

Definite Anti-Terrorism Legislation

This legislative dilemma touches on another problem discussed in this book—the definition of terrorism (see chapter 1). The belief that it is not possible to define terrorism, nor is it necessary to do so, also asserts that it is possible to prohibit terrorist activities without needing to define the phenomenon, since terrorists carry out activities that are similar or even identical to the prohibited activities of "ordinary" criminals, that is—murder, extortion, incitement, threats etc. Just as it is possible to put the heads of the Mafia behind bars without having to prove their involvement in Mafia activities, but merely based on tax evasion and other felonies, it is also possible to remove terrorists from society and judge them for their acts. The argument is, therefore, that the penal codes in force in different countries should provide a sufficient response to the judicial requirements needed to bring terrorists to trial, without it being necessary to define the term "terrorism." This approach relates to terrorism as a type of purely criminal felony, and it is valid, according to its supporters, not only for internal legislation within one country or another, but also in the framework of international legislation. Proponents of this approach feel there is no need for international agreement on the definition of terrorism in order to achieve international cooperation. The obligation of different countries to act against terrorists, to seize them and extradite them is derived from the crimes they commit, which are prohibited in themselves under international norms. Therefore, according to the supporters of this approach, the charters that exist in the criminal domain are sufficient because they prohibit the acts attributed to terrorists. At most, it is possible to develop and expand the international framework agreement to include acts such as suicide bombing, firing at aircraft, etc. In any event, the normative international system can continue to be effective even without recourse to a definition of the term terrorism.

On the other hand, those who oppose this approach hold that even if terrorists carry out acts similar to those of criminals, the crime of terrorism is essentially different and even more serious than criminal offenses, because it is an attack on society as a whole, it endangers the public, and potentially threatens the stability and security of the entire world. If only for this reason, terrorism should be distinguished from "ordinary" crime, and special legislation should be devoted to this phenomenon, to define binding norms and prohibitions both within the country itself and in the normative international system.

In a manner similar to the solution proposed for the dilemma of defining terrorism, it appears that relating to terrorism as a particular type of war crime also solves the legislative dilemma and, in deciding between these two schools, favors the approach that terrorism must be defined and given different legislation. As terrorism is an act of war in every respect, the accepted criminal laws and norms do not apply to it as do the laws of war. As such, on the face of it terrorism cannot be punished, but since terrorism is a war crime, a blatant breach of the rules of war, terrorists can be judged and punished just as war criminals are punished. However, for this purpose it is necessary to designate concrete domestic and international legislation to enable people to be brought to trial and convicted for acts of terrorism and involvement in acts of this kind.

Emergency Anti-Terrorism Legislation

The dilemma of emergency legislation is directly related to the dilemma of specific legislation. The school of thought that maintains there should not be special laws devoted to acts of terrorism generally is of the opinion that the ruling authorities, when dealing with terrorism, should act in the framework of existing legislation and if it is necessary to change and expand this legislation, this should be done as part of primary legislation and in accordance with regular legislative procedure, not as emergency legislation.

Others, in contrast, believe that the severity of the threat of terrorism and the urgency of the problem do not usually allow for a slow and drawn-out process, which is likely to take weeks or months of political negotiation between parties, interest groups, and various other entities. The threat of terrorism requires a rapid response, and those who are engaged in the important task of defeating terrorism should be given all the legislative tools they need for effective prevention. This is true even if it necessitates taking shortcuts or circumventing regular legislative procedures and employing emergency legislation and temporary orders.

The threat of international terrorism, as manifested in the September 11, 2001 attacks in the United States and the events that followed, reinforced the claims of those who support the need to extend the authority of the security and intelligence services by means of emergency legislation. However, it appears that alongside defining the need for legislation of this kind, it is essential to set rules to limit the danger of arbitrary legislation that may be used by the authorities for illegitimate purposes deviating from the original intention of the emergency legislation, and which will remain in force long after the problem for which they were enacted has disappeared. For this purpose, it should be determined that emergency legislation of this kind can only be passed by an absolute majority in parliament, and for a period of time that is fixed and predefined, at the end of which it will expire automatically unless a decision is taken to extend it—once again, by an absolute parliamentary majority. Furthermore, there must be parliamentary supervision of the manner in which such legislation is implemented by the executive branch and the security forces.

Outlawing Terrorist Organizations

One of the main dilemmas with regard to counter-terrorism legislation, which comes up time and again in different countries, is the question of outlawing terrorist organizations. On the one hand, supporters of such legislation believe that the seriousness of terrorism and the danger to human life require fundamental treatment of the problem and its prevention from the earliest possible stage. Terrorist organizations must be prevented from gathering strength and power, and should be neutralized while they are still small and transient, lacking operational capability, and while their supporters and associates are still limited in number. Accordingly, the organization should be outlawed as early as possible, as soon as the political tendencies of its members are identified as turning to the use of violence against civilians in order to achieve their aims. In this approach, the assessment is that outlawing the organization will prevent its active members from operating freely and legitimately to disseminate their dangerous ideas; prevent the organization from enlisting sources of financial and other support from various entities; reduce its ability to recruit new members to its ranks; and oblige its leaders to return to the framework of legitimate action or alternatively, to run and hide from the law.

Furthermore, this view considers that outlawing these organizations will also make it easier for the security services to locate terrorists and foil their activities, *inter alia*, because it will prevent them from receiving support, assistance, and refuge among citizens who support the organization's aims but fear they will get in trouble for this support. Legislation of this kind will also make it easier for the security forces to act against the illegal terrorist organization, using legislative and punitive tools that were not available to it prior to the organization being outlawed. It will also remove the cloak of seeming legality and legitimacy from the organization's activities.

Others, on the other hand, are of the opinion that outlawing a terrorist organization will simply make it harder to foil terrorism because in practice it will drive the group's activists underground and prevent their public activities, making it harder for the security forces to follow their actions, movements, and intentions. Penetrating an underground organization is considerably harder than penetrating an open organization holding public activities. Furthermore, outlawing the terrorist organization will cause it to become more extreme: it will strengthen the radicals among its ranks, who will soon go over to the use of violence, escalating the group's violent activity. In practice, from the moment it is outlawed all the group's resources will be directed towards planning and carrying out attacks. Even those resources that were previously used to finance non-violent and legal activities will be used for terrorism from now on. Outlawing will also block all channels of dialogue with the organization and its members, which will prevent the possibility of moderating its position and solving the dispute peacefully. Finally, the special right granted to the government of placing certain organizations outside the law is liable to be exploited for political ends by the ruling party, enabling it to neutralize political rivals.

In the effort to resolve this dilemma, it may be stated that there are extreme situations with which society cannot come to terms. The use of violence deliberately aimed at civilians, that is, terrorism, is an example of such a situation. The artificial separation between the political, social, and economic activities of a terrorist organization and its use of terrorism to achieve its political objectives only plays into the hands of the terrorists, who hurry to set up a separate political wing and military-terrorist wing and claim that there is no connection between these two, and that the supposedly legal activities of the political arm should not be prohibited. Sometimes, to keep the organization out of danger, terrorist leaders decide to set up two, ostensibly separate, apparatuses—one engaged in terrorism and the other operating within the accepted political arena and even participating in parliamentary elections, in an attempt to enjoy the best of both worlds.

Different countries, including prominent countries in the West, often fall into this trap of separating an organization's political—economic—social activities from its terrorist activities. These countries often do not define one organization or another as a terrorist organization because of its social and political involvement, or alternatively recognize the right of the organization's political wing to operate. A striking example of this is the Hizballah movement in Lebanon, which in the 1980s became the spearhead of Iranian terrorism in the Middle East. Hizballah has carried out cruel attacks causing large-scale casualties against many countries—including the United States, France, and Israel—and serves as a guide and an economic, military, operational, and ideological hinterland for many other terrorist organizations, especially Palestinian organizations. At the same time, it carries out political activity in Lebanon, and its members have even been elected to the Lebanese parliament. For this reason, at least outwardly, many countries, until recently led by Britain, have refrained from defining Hizballah as a terrorist organization and treating it accordingly.[335]

Because of the need that arises from time to time to outlaw organizations of this kind, and against the background of the danger of improper use of this process, it should be determined that an organization will be declared illegal on the basis of a detailed and reasoned application by the security forces, after considering all the advantages and disadvantages of this action. The application will be submitted directly to Parliament, which will consider all the ramifications of taking the decision to outlaw the organization. If the application relates to a group of people who are citizens of the country itself, and not to an external terrorist group—international or foreign—the application should only be passed by an absolute majority in Parliament.

As a precondition for the decision to declare a particular organization illegal, a number of clear and fixed criteria should be formulated for defining a certain association as a terrorist organization; this must, of course, be on the basis of an agreed definition of the term "terrorism." These criteria will be defined in primary legislation and organizations meeting all these cumulative parameters should be outlawed.

Public Trial and Evidentiary Privilege

The principle of a public trial is intended to ensure that justice is not only carried out, but is also seen. The public must know that the law is implemented efficiently and fairly, impartially and without discrimination.[336] In Israel, the "Basic Law: The Judiciary" defines in Article 3 the principle of publicity of court hearings, unless determined otherwise by law or unless the court has legally instructed differently. According to Moshe Negbi, Israeli legislators and courts have taken excess advantage of the final section of Article 3, and in too many cases have prevented coverage of events occurring in court. In this context, Negbi mentions Article 68 of the Courts Law (Combined Version), authorizing all judges to hold sessions *in camera* in a wide range of cases, including those that would endanger national security.[337] The question of media coverage of court hearings on security issues in general, and issues relating to terrorism in particular, has been discussed by the Israeli Supreme Court. One of the main complaints was directed against the advisory committees appointed to discuss the question of deportation of Palestinians from the territories under Regulation 111(4) of the Defense (Emergency) Regulations 1945, who hold their discussions *in camera*. In HCJ 103/92 *Jouad Boulus et al. v. The Advisory Committee et al.,* the court accepted the position of the plaintiffs and determined that in general, the committee's discussions should not be held behind closed doors, other than the privileged part of the case. The State Prosecutor's office claimed that it was necessary to invoke privilege for the hearings because of the difficulty in allocating forces to maintain order and bring in the candidates for deportation, locating halls that were large enough to contain all those interested in the discussions, and preventing the entry of strangers into military facilities. However all theses claims were not sufficient to counter the principle of public debate, which was defined by the Israeli Supreme Court as "a fundamental value in our justice system."[338]

Another type of privilege in the course of the trial of suspected terrorists is evidentiary privilege, that is, the decision not to allow a suspect or his attorney to examine incriminating evidence brought before the court—in whole or in part. The reason for invoking such privilege is usually the desire to protect the source of the evidence, since in certain cases it is feared that revealing the information to the suspect and/or his attorney will endanger the life and activities of this source. In HCJ 672/88 *Muhammad Abdullah al-Labdi v. The Commander of the IDF Forces in the West Bank,* the advisory committee for appeals against deportation orders explained the reasons for invoking evidentiary privilege, which included: preventing revealing sources, preventing the "leak" of information of any kind to terrorist organizations, avoiding revealing the methods of operation of the security forces, and so forth.[339]

Evidentiary privilege is liable to be invoked in Israel under various different laws. In practice, it involves a problematic balance between two public interests. This was well explained by Justice Dov Levine, in HCJ 672/88 *Muhammad Abdullah al-Labdi v. The Commander of the IDF Forces in the West Bank*, who said:

> ...These two aspects, which should guide the court when dealing with confidential material, are of equal importance.... We try to help petitioners obtain information relating to their case, and at the same time prevent the exposure of the sources of confidential information on which the government relies.... The balance between these conflicting interests is delicate and sensitive.... It is therefore necessary to treat confidential material with great caution, understand its implications and allow the controlled disclosure only of those details of the information in the privileged evidence that will not create the above risk.[340]

Justice Gabriel Bach, in HCJ 19/86 *Dr. Azmi Alshouebi et al. v. The Military Supervisor for Judea and Samaria,* adds:

> In order to reject the application of the person in question regarding disclosure of the evidence that exists against him, the court must be convinced that the qualified authorities, genuinely and in good faith, fear that revelation of the evidence involved in disclosing the information is liable to expose and endanger confidential sources of information, and that this fear on the part of the authorities is not unreasonable.[341]

The question of evidentiary privilege is not unique to crimes relating to terrorist activity, but due to the fact that intelligence is the very lifeblood of preventing terrorism, and since terrorism threatens the lives of many people, the dilemma and the need to find a balance between these two interests is more critical in these cases. Therefore, when arguments against evidentiary privilege are brought before it, the Supreme Court frequently tends to propose to the two parties that its judges will study the confidential evidence and examine whether it is indeed appropriate for this evidence to be privileged. However, this willingness on the part of the court often meets with a refusal on the part of the petitioner or a stipulation that the discussion regarding disclosure of evidence take place before a judge who is not one of the panel of judges discussing the appeal itself.[342]

Prosecution of Those Suspected of Involvement in Terrorism

Between anti-terrorism legislation, which lays the legal and judicial groundwork for counter-terrorism measures, and the punishment of terrorists, which translates this legislation into action and punishes those convicted of terrorist activity, lies the thorny issue of prosecuting those suspected of involvement in terrorism. In many countries (Britain, Spain, Italy, and others), laws have been enacted at different times setting out special procedures and making it easier for the security forces and the prosecutor to bring terrorists or those suspected of abetting terrorism to trial. These special procedures relate to all stages of the prosecution, from the moment the suspect is stopped and arrested until his conviction in court, and relate to the following factors:

- *Period of detention*—according to the special procedures, the period of time it is permitted to detain a person suspected of terrorist activity without the need to obtain a court extension is usually longer than the accepted period in regular criminal cases.
- *Admissibility of evidence*—the special procedures are liable to make it possible to present incriminating evidence regarding terrorism obtained in ways that are not permitted by law, such as eavesdropping, surveillance, and searches not conducted according to proper procedure.
- *Privilege*—by contrast with the principle of public trial, in certain cases privilege is invoked in the course of the trial of suspected terrorists. Privilege is likely to be invoked regarding evidence presented to the judge, so that the accused and his attorney are not permitted to see it. In other cases, a gag order is imposed on publishing the fact that the suspect is in detention and that the trial is being held.
- *The rights of a person detained on suspicion of involvement in terrorism*—suspected terrorists are sometimes denied the basic rights afforded to those detained on other charges, such as the right to meet with a lawyer, to hold telephone conversations, and so forth.

- *Legal proceedings*—in certain countries special legal proceedings are implemented for terrorists. For example, in countries where it is usual to hold hearings in front of a jury in the case of serious crimes, it is sometimes decided to deviate from this custom and try terrorists before a professional judge.

Among the reasons brought up by the security forces to justify the need for special trial procedures are:

- *The difficulty in obtaining evidence of the illegal activities of terrorist organizations*—terrorists operate clandestinely and underground, and therefore it is particularly difficult to penetrate their ranks, to follow them, and to obtain evidence of their illegal activity. This situation sometimes requires special means and an easing of the requirements of prosecution.
- *The need to obtain warning information from suspects*—this sometimes necessitates, according to the security forces, holding a suspect in detention for a time without bringing him before a judge and without permitting him to meet his lawyer. This psychological pressure on the suspect is liable to encourage him to cooperate.
- *The serious nature of terrorism*—the grave threat posed by terrorism necessitates denying suspects the right to silence and relating to their silence under interrogation as evidence of their involvement in terrorism. In other words, the silence of a person suspected of terrorist activity in effect negates his claim of innocence.
- *The need to protect sources of information*—in many cases, it is necessary to invoke privilege regarding evidence brought to court, if its disclosure to the suspect and his lawyer is liable to endanger the life or existence of the source of information, whether this involves a human source of intelligence (humint) or signal intelligence (sigint).
- *The fear that the suspect's partners will go underground*—this fear sometimes requires obscuring the fact that the suspect is in detention until his partners are caught.
- *Fear on the part of judges and juries of revenge by terrorists*—this fear sometimes leads to revocation of trial by jury in terrorist trials and the appointment of special judges in these trials.

Summary of the Legislative Dilemmas

It appears that the solution to the democratic dilemma in connection with legislation lies along the axis between the two extreme positions—the one stating that there is no benefit to special anti-terrorism legislation, and the other holding that existing legislation hampers the prevention of terrorism.

There is no disputing the fact that special anti-terrorism legislation always raises the slippery slope of potential harm to liberal democratic values and human and civil liberties. However, the question is whether it is possible to fight terrorism within the framework of regular criminal law. Do not the unique characteristics of terrorism and the dangers it involves require legislation enabling the security forces to use special counter-terrorism measures? Hoffnung proposes three tests to examine the reasoning of decision makers in security issues: (1) What is the interest being protected? (2) How serious is the danger? (3) How immediate is it? According to him, the higher the correlation between the seriousness of the danger, the likelihood of it occurring and its immediacy, the greater the justification for restrictions imposed with respect to the danger.[343] However, it seems that the tests proposed by Hoffnung are not sufficient. In all matters relating to the danger of terrorism, it is also necessary to take into consideration the following factors: the scope of the terrorism, its immediate and long-term possible damage, its characteristics, and the physical danger and harm to morale it poses to the country and to society in general. When a country is forced to cope with wide-scale terrorism, it must establish a special legal foundation enabling it to take the necessary steps (offensive, defensive, legal, and intelligence) to effectively fight. However, even when this vital need exists, legislation should be limited in scale, in the degree to which it harms liberal and democratic values, and in duration. Legislation should be for a defined period of time, in the hope that this will suffice to overcome terrorism altogether, or at least reduce its scale and damage to a level enabling society to continue to function.

Yet temporary legislation is not sufficient. As part of the emergency legislation it is necessary to define a clear and defined system of checks and balances, to enable effective supervision by the judicial and legislative branches over the actions of the security forces. This type of supervisory mechanism will enable a critical examination of the war against terrorism and serve as an address for complaints by those who consider that they have been injured by arbitrary use of the legislation. The complexity of the task facing legislators and the legal system in finding the necessary balance involved in this democratic dilemma is attested to by the words of the president of the Israeli Supreme Court, Justice Aharon Barak:

> I hope that Israeli society will not find a naïve judge who sees everything as a security problem. The rule of law is the country's guarantee. I hope that Israeli society will not find an innocent judge who sees fundamental rights as the be all and end all. A constitution is not a prescription for suicide. I hope that Israeli society will find a reasonable and cautious judge who tries to see all aspects of the picture, who is aware of his creative role, who tallies the different interests objectively, who applies the fundamental principles in a neutral manner and tries to find the delicate balance between majority rule and the basic rights of the individual, a balance that represents the democratic equation of the regime.[344]

Types of Punishment for Terrorists

Punitive policy goes hand in hand with legislative action. In fact, legislation is a preliminary stage preceding punitive action—in legislation, the decision makers define the crimes relating to terrorism that are punishable, and the severity of these crimes, and determine a minimum sentence or range of sentences for specific crimes.

One of the important tiers in shaping the policy for fighting terrorism is formulating punitive policy for involvement in terrorism, participation in carrying out attacks, helping terrorists, and so forth. Crenshaw states that the answer to terrorism is essentially simple: enforcement of an effective and well-adapted law. The security forces prevent terrorism by preventing access to targets, and when this fails, they identify and detain the perpetrators, and deter others.[345] Punitive steps are intended, among other things, to remove dangerous people from society and thus ensure public welfare; to take revenge on those responsible for and involved in carrying out attacks for the damage they have caused to society; to confound the activities of terrorist organizations so that their leaders and activists are kept busy with solving problems and do not have the time or means to carry out terrorist acts; and, finally, to deter others from similar activities.

Many countries tend to use numerous punitive means against terrorist organizations, among other things, because this enables the decision makers to give the public a message of effective counter-terrorist activity, to demonstrate that they are meeting goals and to initiate actions emphasizing their determination to combat terrorism. In the relationship between the terrorist organization and the state, the state is usually forced to be the side that responds, but with regard to punishment the state is able to appear as the side that takes the initiative.[346]

As a rule, the punitive strategy of different countries can be divided into two main groups: offensive punishment and judicial punishment. Offensive punishment is punishment of the leadership or the activists of a terrorist organization, or alternatively punishment of a state that supports terrorism, using offensive means. In offensive punishment, the state carries out actions against terrorist organizations and against prominent members of the organization, with the aim of punishing those responsible for terrorist attacks and avenging their actions, in order to deter their partners or alternatively, to harm their morale and raise the morale of the population in the country targeted by terrorist attacks. This kind of punishment is usually the result of an administrative decision by a leader, security body, or entity belonging to the operative arm of the country, and it could be carried out without any preliminary legal process. Judicial punishment is the punishment of terrorists who have been caught prior to carrying out attacks, in the course of an attack or after an attack, and punishment of their collaborators, commanders, and anyone else involved in one way or another in the terrorist action. Judicial punishment is carried out as part of a regular or special judicial process, under the law of the nation.

The special characteristics of terrorism sometimes require serious punitive measures that differ from those that are usual in regular criminal punishment. In some cases, punitive measures that are taken also have a direct or indirect effect on people who are not involved in the terrorist activity. These steps (such as curfew, closure, the demolition or sealing of houses, and so on) are sometimes defined as "collective punishment," which appears to conflict with liberal democratic values.[347]

Collective Punishment

One of the main subjects of public and professional debate is the use of collective punishment, that is, punishment that is not directed against a single person or group of activists but against a large group of the public, with the aim of creating pressure to prevent this group from supporting the terrorist organizations, helping them or even sympathizing with them. The aim of collective punishment is to isolate the terrorist, cutting him off from his sources of support, denying him assistance and the supply of weapons, food, equipment, intelligence, and refuge. The reasoning in support of these measures holds that it is necessary to prevent what is described by Mao Tse-Tung as the terrorist moving among the population "like a fish in water." According to supporters, the state must stir up these waters and dry up the swamps to make terrorist and guerrilla activities harder and root out the phenomenon.[348] This approach is expressed in the words of the former leader of the German SPD party, Willi Brandt, in September 1977, when he spoke of the kidnapping and murder of Hans Martin Schleier—president of the Employers Union in Germany. According to Brandt, terrorist sympathizers are even more responsible for this act than those who pull the trigger. Without them, the terrorists would be helpless. They are the ones who create the encouraging environment in which murderers can act as heroes. Without psychological support and covert habitat, it would not be possible to carry out the murder.[349]

On the other hand, the approach that opposes the use of collective punishment holds that this type of punishment strengthens public support for the terrorist organization, harms the image of the country as a liberal and democratic state, and leads to a loss of international legitimacy.[350] Bruce Hoffman and Jennifer Morrison-Taw consider that steps intended to prevent active or passive support for terrorist organizations have been shown to be ineffective, and in the end have led to a increase of public support for the organization, because of the inconvenience and disturbance caused to the entire population.[351]

In Israel, there have been those who have recommended using collective punishment against the Palestinian population in order to put across the unequivocal message that they should not enlist in, collaborate with, or assist violent action against Israel in general, and terrorism in particular. For example, Rehavam Ze'evi, who served as the prime minister's adviser on the war against terrorism and later as minister of tourism, claimed that:

> We must look for what hurts them, and we do not do this. We are scared, for example, of collective punishment, despite the fact that it works exceptionally well. Disturbances in Beit Fajar will lead to a prohibition against exporting stones via the Allenby Bridge. If there are disturbances in Hebron, the grapes from the Hebron vineyards will not be sent to Jordan! If you say this is immoral, I will answer that it is more than moral, because in this way we cause less blood to be spilled, both Jewish and Arab alike. But people object to taking these steps, because it is collective punishment. The

government lives in fear of the media and under the threat of criticism by parliament and by its own members...[352]

Yitzhak Shamir's support for collective punishment (with an understanding of Israel's restrictions in applying these measures) can be seen from his comments on the subject:

> I would like to remind you that acts of retribution were always effective. The Arabs never had any difficulty in understanding that these acts were a direct response to their acts of terrorism. The dastardly murder of Jews stopped. The Arabs understood our message...and yet today I would not suggest such things. Israel is a state of law and cannot take steps that were appropriate for an underground movement during the pre-state period.... Without the constraints of policy, we could "finish off" Islamic terrorism easily. Nothing would be left of it. It is only because of the force of circumstance that we have to take into account other countries of the world, and the United States, which is a true friend of ours.[353]

Ariel Sharon presented a different position, by which collective punishment of Palestinians in the territories should actually be reduced. According to him, in order to put an end to the Intifada (popular uprising) it is not necessary to take more stringent steps, but different steps:

> I have often recommended taking different steps. The most important thing is to distinguish between Palestinians Arabs working against us and the non-active part of the population, and then fight against them.[354]

Mao Tse-Tung repeatedly warned his people against causing physical harm, damaging the property or insulting the honor of the citizens. Mao understood how dangerous such actions were likely to be to his guerrilla movement, provoking the wrath of the masses and their desire for revenge. To this end, he even published "do's and don'ts" for his people covering all aspects of their contact with the population. What was true for the Chinese guerrilla in the days of Mao Tse-Tung holds true today for countries fighting against terrorists and guerrillas, who are required take care of the honor, property, and person of those who are not involved directly or indirectly in initiating, guiding, assisting, planning, and implementing terrorist attacks. Decision makers in countries fighting terrorism must remember that in order to create significant deterrence by means of collective punishment, they will have to carry out actions that have no place in the normative liberal-democratic environment, actions that will neither be accepted nor tolerated by international public opinion.

Acts that can be carried out by shady regimes and dictatorships, which are not committed to the international environment and to democratic values, cannot be carried out under a liberal-democratic government. In other words, it will be hard for a democratic country to achieve the cost threshold required to deter terrorists and their allies by means of collective punishment without losing their democratic character and risking their international status; and as long as the cost threshold is not achieved with regard to the terrorist organizations, in terms of benefit, too, the damage caused by collective punishment is greater than the benefits. Nonetheless, it is a country's right to punish not only those who carry out the attack themselves, but also those who are directly or indirectly involved in putting it into practice. Harming all those who knew about and did not prevent an attack, and certainly those who participate in the preparations and planning, should not be regarded as collective punishment.

One of the questions that needs to be answered when discussing the question of punishing terrorists is where does individual punishment end and collective punishment begin? In fact, we are speaking of a range of actions (as described in Figure 7.2), and between the two ends of the range—individual punishment and punishment of the general public—it is also possible to punish a group of people whose common denominator is connection of one kind or another with those who carry out the attacks, or involvement in one of the stages of implementing the attack. Should punishment aimed at such a group—that is certainly not innocent of all wrongdoing—be regarded in the same way as collective punishment of civilians who have nothing to do with terrorist attacks or who are, at the most, passive supporters of the actions or objectives of the terrorists?

Demolishing Terrorists' Homes

In an attempt to increase the effectiveness of punishment, security forces in Israel and around the world have sought additional means of punishment over and above arrest and detention for defined periods of time. One method that is considered by security forces and decision makers in Israel to be effective is demolition of the home of the person carrying out the attack, or of buildings used to carry out the attack. Actions of this kind are not arbitrary actions, nor are they indiscriminate punishment, but they certainly cause harm to a wider group of people than just the attacker himself, and of course represent, on the face of it, a type of collective punishment.

Israeli demolition orders are issued by the military commander and are usually carried out swiftly, immediately after arrest of the suspect. These orders are apparently intended to deter family members and acquaintances of the terrorists from helping them, and to make it clear to terrorists that their families will be forced to pay the price for their actions. According to the former head of the Israel Security Agency Yaakov Perry, "the assessment of the ISA was that harm to the terrorist's family and their property was a decisive factor to be considered by a terrorist candidate for a suicide attack."[355]

Regulations 119 and 120 of the Israel Defense (Emergency) Regulations, which are the legal basis for issuing demolition orders, are, in fact, intended to enable the military commander to maintain order and security in the area under his command, that is, for immediate operational needs, and not as punishment. Since this is the case, in 1989, the Supreme Court determined that the use of the authority set forth in Regulation 119 (1) does not depend on the conviction of the perpetrator of the crime. The decision to demolish a terrorist's home is an administrative decision. The military commander's reasoning with regard to the value of the evidence before him should be based on the test of the reasonable man.[356] The Israeli security forces have justified the demolition of homes on the basis of Regulation 23 (g) of the Hague Regulations of 1907, which prohibits the destruction of enemy property "unless such destruction is absolutely necessary for the needs of the war."[357]

The demolition and sealing of homes carried out by the security forces led to many appeals to the Supreme Court by Palestinians who felt that they had been punished for no reason: members of the terrorist's family, people who leased the house to the terrorist, neighbors living in the same building or an adjacent building, and others. These appeals were, for the most part, rejected by the court on the basis that this was a legal operational action that could be taken by the military commander in the field.[358]

At the same time, the Supreme Court was aware of the severity of the action and the significant scope of damage caused by the demolition of homes, if only because such an action is irreversible. For this reason, in 1988, the president of the Supreme Court, Meir Shamgar, proposed that in places where immediate military action involving damage to a building was required, the military commander would make do with a reversible action, that is, sealing the building, until a judicial decision was taken regarding the fate of the building.[359] The IDF continued to make wide use of this mechanism; therefore, despite its inclination not to intervene in the operational considerations of the military commander, the Supreme Court set up tests and restrictions for deciding to demolish or seal buildings, including:

1. The gravity of the acts attributed to the suspect living in the building must be taken into account, as well as the existence of verified proof that they were carried out by the suspect in question.
2. The degree of involvement of other residents of the building, usually the perpetrator's family, in his terrorist acts may be taken into account. The lack of evidence of awareness and involvement on the part of the relatives does not in itself prohibit use of this sanction, but this factor is liable to influence, as noted, the scope of the respondent's injunction.
3. A relevant consideration is whether it is possible to see the suspected terrorist's home as a separate residential unit from the rest of the building.
4. It should be clarified whether it is possible to demolish the suspect's residential unit without damaging the other parts of the building or adjacent buildings. If it emerges that this is not possible, then consideration should be given to making do with just sealing the relevant unit.
5. The respondent must take into account the number of people who are likely to be affected by demolition of the building, and who may be assumed themselves not to have committed any crime, nor even been aware of the suspect's acts.[360]

All these questions and tests were discussed repeatedly in many appeals to the Israel Supreme Court.[361] One of the issues that came up time and time again was the terrorist's *link to the residence* slated for demolition. Regulation 119 allows the demolition of a building that was used for carrying out an illegal act, or alternatively the building in which the terrorist lived. However, the decision to demolish the building requires a response to complex questions, such as: is it the terrorist's home? Is it the home of his parents, used as the permanent or temporary residence of the terrorist? Is a rented apartment to be considered as the home of the terrorist? And so forth. In 1986, the Supreme Court determined that the fact that a terrorist lived from time to time in a particular building was sufficient to enable demolition of the building—for example, a building in which he lived for short periods only during vacations from studies.[362] In another decision, taken in 1997, the former president of the Supreme Court, Justice Meir Shamgar, determined that the center of the accused's life was in his village, in the house where his family lived, even if he only went there on weekends when his work was over.[363] With regard to the question of whether, in the terrorist's absence from his permanent residence, his connection with his home is severed, it was determined in 1994 that the decision should be taken according to the nature and the circumstances of the absence. For example, if the absence is due to the terrorist fleeing from the security forces due to fear of arrest, the residential connection is not severed, and the same is true if the absence is temporary, even if at that time the terrorist had an alternative home.[364]

Another issue that the Supreme Court was asked to discuss was the *degree of harm to others* resulting from the demolition and sealing of homes. In addressing this question, the court wanted to restrict the use of the regulation allowing the demolition of buildings, and determine yardsticks with regard to the proportion of damage to be caused to others as a result of the demolition.[365] It is also not reasonable that because a person living in one room in a multi-storey building in which many others also live is involved in terrorism, the entire building should be demolished.[366] However the principle of degree also has another aspect—*the gravity of the crime*, that is, the severity of the act of terrorism. In this context, the Supreme Court has determined that perpetrating terrorist acts justifies particularly severe measures, including demolishing the homes of collaborators.[367] Justice Ben-Dror even opined, in 1985, that the damage caused to those in the terrorist's vicinity because of the demolition or sealing of the building was no different in substance to the damage caused to a family when the head of the family is given a prison sentence and the family remains without its support and breadwinner.[368]

Despite the fact that the demolition and sealing of buildings are essentially punitive acts, the Supreme Court accepted the state's position and underlined once again that the main character of such acts is deterrent.[369] Against this background, the Supreme Court also rejected the claim that it is prohibited because it represents a certain form of collective punishment.[370] According to President

Barak, "from the moment we ruled that this is not a punitive measure but one whose purpose is preventive and deterrent, there is no basis for this claim and it should be rejected."[371]

The Supreme Court was not prepared to hear any attempt to appeal against the effectiveness of the demolition or sealing of houses. Arguments, accompanied by various affidavits, claiming that not only do these actions not prevent terrorist attacks, they even encourage others to carry out attacks, met with a refusal by the Supreme Court even to discuss their substance. The Supreme Court preferred the assessment of the state's experts and considered that it was not necessarily possible to conclude from the fact that the attacks continued that these measures were not effective, because it was impossible to know what would have been the rate of injuries caused had these steps not been taken.[372]

In this context it should be noted that a considerable number of decision makers and heads of the security system in Israel also cast doubt on the efficacy of these steps. However, their criticism did not necessarily arise from the assumption that these actions served as an incentive to others to take revenge and carry out attacks, but rather resulted from the high amount of compensation given by the terrorist organizations to families whose homes were demolished, enabling them to rebuild the house.

The wave of suicide attacks that swept Israel at the end of 1993-1994 caused a large number of deaths and injuries, considerable anxiety among the Israeli public and noticeable difficulty on the part of the security forces to overcome the phenomenon—and reinforced the Supreme Court's unwillingness to discuss the issue of demolition and sealing of buildings. For example, in 1994, Justice Matza stated that the suicide attacks created a new dimension of crazed extremism, and therefore the authorities in charge of security were even entitled to use means such as the confiscation and demolition of the home of a terrorist who had committed suicide. According to him, in contrast with the steps the authorities had taken in the past to avoid damaging the homes of terrorists killed in the course of carrying out attacks, on the assumption that their deaths provided the fullest deterrent to other potential terrorists, adoption of such a policy with regard to suicide bombers as well was liable to negate in advance any chance that people living in the vicinity of the terrorist and knowing of his intentions to carry out a suicide attack would try to persuade him otherwise.[373] In 1997, the president of the Supreme Court, Aharon Barak, explained that although it was not certain that demolition of a terrorist's home was in fact an effective means, in the framework of the limited means remaining to the state to protect itself against "living bombs," this means should not be disparaged.[374]

The suicide attacks and their terrible results have led the Supreme Court to show considerably more flexibility with the principles of degree and the connection to the building in their judicial review of the executive branch with regard to these actions. The principle of degree was discussed by Justice Bach in HCJ 1730/97 *Adel Salem A / Rabo Sabiah v. Brig. Gen. Ilan Biran, Commander of the IDF Forces in Judea and Samaria.* According to him:

> The alternative proposal of the Appellants, that it should suffice the Respondent to demolish only the private room of the terrorist in the home shared with the other members of the family, or seal it up, seems particularly unconvincing when we are talking about suicide attacks. It seems that with regard to a terrorist planning to blow himself up and commit suicide, the fear that afterwards the army will be able to seal up only his own private room, or even demolish it, will not serve as any form of deterrent. In such a situation the Respondent's injunction would lose all meaning.[375]

With regard to the connection with the house, the Supreme Court also found that the deterrent provided support for the need and justification to demolish or seal up a rented apartment used as the home or workplace of terrorists, even if it was owned by someone else. In this context, the Supreme Court determined that the purpose of sealing the room was to deter not only the terrorist himself, but also those around him. To reinforce the court's position in this matter, President Barak also brought up a case in which the owner of a building who rented an apartment to terrorists told them to vacate the building, and even returned the rent they had paid in advance, because he began to suspect that they were using the apartment for terrorist activities. Accordingly, the judge rejected the claim that it was necessary to distinguish between the owner of the building and the terrorists living there as rental tenants.[376]

The problematic nature, confusion, and lack of desire of the Supreme Court to intervene in issues relating to the demolition and sealing of houses are addressed by Justice Cheshin in HCJ 1730/96 *Adel Salem A / Rabo Sabiah v. Brig. Gen. Ilan Biran, Commander of the IDF Forces in Judea and Samaria*:

...In all of these there is nothing to blunt the sense—and it is a very sharp sense—that we are engaged in a matter that is not ours to engage in...the source of this sense of foreignness lies in the fact that the act of demolition of houses under the Defense Regulations has the nature and character of an act of war. And acts of war are not acts that the courts are routinely required to discuss.

Salach Nazal murdered twenty-three people and injured dozens more when he detonated an explosive charge in the center of a bus. "The act of the murderer," I said of him, "was in essence—although not in framework nor by formal definition—an act of war, and to an act that is in essence an act or war, one responds with an act that is also in essence an act of war, and in the manner of war..." Who, and what manner of person, will deny the statement that life and preservation of life, as it is, is of greater importance than other rights? That property rights have to take a back seat to the right to life? And if the military commander is of the opinion that demolition of the home of a terrorist might possibly—even by the smallest of chances—deter another who might also be a terrorist and murderer like his colleagues in Hamas (or Islamic Jihad), how can the court tell him what to do or not to do? War is war: what has the court to do with instructing a military commander what to do and what not to do?[377]

One of the questions arising in the context of demolishing the homes of terrorists is, as noted: is this action, as justified as it may be, also effective in the final analysis, or does it result in a net loss by increasing the motivation of others to carry out attacks? The military advocate general during the intifada (1987), Amnon Strashnov, testified to his vacillations on this subject:

The position of the security community is that the demolition of a home is highly effective and serves to deter and prevent others from carrying out acts of terrorism...it may perhaps be well founded, although this assumption has not been proved with certainty by any empirical study. Acts of terrorism have continued, as we know, despite the demolition of houses.[378]

We can learn about the effectiveness of house demolition and sealing from Chief of Staff Dan Shomron, who reported to the Knesset Foreign Affairs and Defense Committee on November 8, 1988, that "despite the long-term damage caused by blowing up houses, we cannot let the *intifada* continue to rage. We also cannot ignore the fact that this action has a deterrent effect." The minister of defense at the time, Yitzhak Rabin, supported this assessment, and considered that this policy was indeed effective. According to him: "There has recently been a reduction in the throwing of Molotov cocktails as a result of the punitive policy that has been adopted, in the form of house demolitions."[379]

The demolition of houses, as a punitive and deterrent measure, was also used during the Al Aksa intifada (since 2000 and after). Binyamin Ben-Eliezer, former minister of defense, related to this in his speech at the ICT's Second International Conference, which was held on September 11, 2002, at the Herzliya Interdisciplinary Center:

> We've also come to the conclusion that, while the suicide bombers don't worry about their own well being, they do think about that of their family members. For this reason, we have instituted punitive measures aimed at deterring the bombers, by means of disenfranchising or economically damaging their families, along with the people who send them, the dispatchers, and the people who support them. Speaking cautiously, I would like to say that the steps taken to date have built the beginnings of deterrence; we have found that some potential suicide bombers have been deterred, and some have changed their minds about carrying out an attack.[380]

However, the deterrent effectiveness of the demolition and sealing of houses has never been proved: neither by the energetic use made of this measure during the days of the "first intifada" at the end of the 1980s, nor in its individual and selective use after that. Aryeh Shalev indicates two factors that explain, in his opinion, the development that occurred in the purposefulness of this type of punishment and in its deterrent effect: one, the decision by the PLO to provide financial compensation to the families; and the other, the "boomerang effect" involved in this punitive measure, that is, the increasing hatred and rejection of Israel.[381] To this can be added the criticism that this type of punishment provokes in international public opinion. All these have cast doubt on the method's efficacy. The answer to the question of the effectiveness of house demolition on terrorists may be found in the words of Shimon Peres, who said that he did not rule out the demolition and sealing of houses, but proposed making very limited and selective use of this method. "When you use it too much, it loses its effect...it is necessary to be very careful not to erode its effect. So you need to be very selective in number and target."[382] Yaakov Perry agrees and adds:

> There have been places where a house was demolished and this had an effect on peace and quiet in the area, and for a relatively long period. There were places where it had the opposite effect...the more routine it becomes, the more this tool loses its effectiveness. The more it is used in a focused manner...the better the effect that is obtained.[383]

Administrative Punishment

In contrast with judicial punishment, imposed by means of accepted criminal legal proceedings relating to processes of arresting suspects, bringing them to trial and sentencing them, administrative punishment deviates from what is accepted and required in the civil criminal court. In practice, the military commander and supervisor of security are able to impose punishments and remove those who disturb law and order from society for various periods of time without a court order, making use of the authority granted them by primary legislation or secondary legislation to take various steps in order to maintain order and security.

The importance of administrative punishment increases as the terrorism becomes based on ever-wider circles of activists enjoying broad popular support, or at times when terrorist attacks are occurring repeatedly, and when the legal system does not succeed in providing a fitting response to the scope of the problem.

Administrative punishment makes it possible to shorten the prosecution process, to employ means of punishment that do not fall within the norms of criminal legislation, to direct wide-scale punishment simultaneously at many activists, to maintain the confidentiality of sources of information when suspects are arrested and prosecuted, and more. Therefore, the dilemma involved in administrative punishment lies in the very existence of a process of punishment that does not fit regular criminal judicial processes. The accused is not brought before a professional judge, but is punished by administrative order of a senior military commander or someone appointed by him. Furthermore, he does not receive the opportunity to defend himself to the same extent as a regular criminal defendant. Sometimes the person accused is not familiar at all with the charge sheet and therefore does not know exactly what he is being accused of. Even if he does know, for the most part he is not given access to the evidence against him, and therefore is less able to defend himself and refute his alleged guilt.

In the course of its fight over many years against terrorist attacks, Israel has sometimes been forced to take administrative steps in the areas under its control in Judea, Samaria, and the Gaza Strip. The demolition and sealing of houses, discussed above, is one of these administrative measures. Among the other forms of administrative punishment intended to help the military commander maintain order and counter insurgency are: closure and curfew, administrative detention, and deportation. These steps are usually defined as administrative preventive measures, and not necessarily as punitive measures (see Figure 7.2).

Figure 7.2
Punitive Measures in Counter-Terrorism

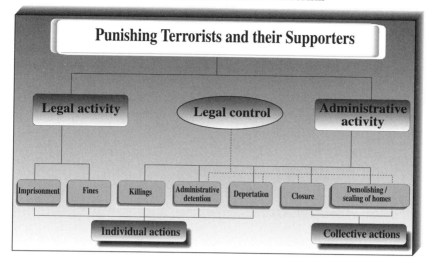

Closure

Closure is imposed, for the most part, after terrorist attacks in Israel, the West Bank or Gaza Strip, or alternatively when the security forces have information about the intention to perpetrate an attack. Sometimes this step is taken with regard to the entire West Bank and Gaza, and sometimes it is limited to only one of these two areas or to a certain city or village. Those who support the imposition of closure consider that even though the closure is not hermetic, it makes it harder for terrorists to enter Israel from the West Bank, and certainly from the Gaza Strip, which is surrounded by a fence, and the Israeli public is more alert and is likely to be better able to identify terrorists since their presence in the streets is more noticeable during a closure. Imposing a closure makes it harder for terrorists to enter Israel in the innocent guise of laborers, makes their movements within Israel harder, and prevents "personal initiative" attacks (which are, for the most part, the result of a momentary impulse on the part of a Palestinian in Israel to carry out an attack, usually making use of cold weapons). Furthermore, according to those who support closure, its imposition is also likely to strengthen the sense of security of the Israeli public. In 1993, then

Deputy Chief of Staff Amnon Lipkin-Shahak remarked in this context:

> The imposition of a closure, and this is a fact, contributes to security. Since imposition of the closure there have been no serious terrorist incidents. In principle, the more it is possible to reduce the number of Arabs staying in Israel, the better the security situation will be.[384]

Those who reject the use of closure, and other similar steps, see this as the imposition of a collective punishment on the Palestinian population in the territories. The argument is that this action is intended, in practice, to put pressure on the civilian population to expose the terrorist organizations and prevent terrorist activity in its midst. These steps, first and foremost the closure, are particularly problematic because of the lack of sufficient sources of livelihood within the West Bank and the Gaza Strip. For this reason, extensive use of the measure causes serious economic harm to the Palestinians. Another claim that is heard against the closure is that it is not at all effective and does not contribute to averting terrorist attacks. In the absence of any physical barrier between the Palestinian population in the West Bank and the Israeli population within the Green Line, the closure prevents Palestinians from earning a living but does not prevent the penetration of terrorists into Israel itself, and certainly does not prevent attacks against Israelis in the West Bank and Gaza Strip. Furthermore, the harm caused to the population because of imposition of the closure increases unrest among the Palestinian public, strengthens support for terrorist organizations and opens the way for acts of revenge even by people who do not belong to a particular terrorist organization.

The Supreme Court has been asked to give its opinion on the relatively wide-scale use made by the IDF of closure and curfew—mainly, as noted, after serious terrorist incidents in Israel or when there is increasing fear of a deterioration of the situation in the territories. For example, after the massacre carried out by Baruch Goldstein in the Tomb of the Patriarchs in Hebron, the Supreme Court was petitioned to issue an injunction "to remove the curfew imposed from time to time" in Hebron. In its rulings, the Supreme Court repeated its decision that it was permitted to impose a curfew for security reasons.[385] However, the Supreme Court emphasized that the military commander must reconsider each time the need to impose the order, with an awareness of the difficulty it causes to the population. The military commander must consider whether and when it is possible to avoid using this measure, or at least reduce its use.[386] In this context, the Supreme Court determined that the longer the state of curfew continues, the greater the burden on state to prove that there is still a real military need justifying its extension.[387] A similar approach was taken by the Supreme Court in relating to the issue of closure, or as it is called by the court—blockade.

The Netanyahu government was set up in 1996 at a time when a closure had already been imposed on the territories for a number of months (since a wave of suicide attacks in February and March 1996). This closure was, in fact, only lifted at the end of 1996, when some 35,000 Palestinians were permitted to come and work in Israel. Arafat claimed that the closure punished the Palestinian population, causing it losses of some $9 million a day.[388] Policymakers in Israel emphasized that the closure was not used by Israel as a means of punishment, but only as a means of prevention, and that it was only imposed when there was a genuine fear of terrorist attacks in Israel, and after it became clear that the Palestinian Authority was not acting to eliminate the attacks. The minister of defense at the time, Yitzhak Mordechai, said: "we do not use closure, heaven forbid, for the purpose of punishment, and when we find that it is possible to lift it, we do so, despite a certain risk involved."[389] The minister of finance at the time, Dan Meridor, also emphasized that Israel "does not believe in closure as a permanent policy."[390]

In response to Arafat's repeated claims that Israel's closure policy harms the basic humanitarian rights of the Palestinian people and causes hunger and a shortage of essential supplies, Netanyahu replied:

> Past experience has shown us that the Palestinian Authority will create a false propaganda impression of shortage of drugs and food. Barefaced lies! There is no shortage! And we will not allow it to happen. They only have to open the door: goods and drugs will come in. We have also allowed the fishermen to go out fishing. We have no interest in harming the Palestinian Authority.... We see the signs, we recognize the formula. "Israel is starving us," as it were. Barefaced lies! There is no hunger.[391]

In retrospect, Netanyahu explained the policy underlying the use of closure, saying:

> I am not a great fan of closures. Closure creates frustration among the population and causes greater damage than benefit. From time to time, I used closure as a supplemen-

tary factor in putting pressure on the Palestinian Authority together with operational activism. I took a very liberal line in terms of days of closure.[392]

It appears that decision makers and experts in fighting terrorism during this period were of one mind about the relative lack of effectiveness of closure in thwarting terrorism. In the absence of a separation fence, physical or geographical obstacles on the ground and sufficient security forces to prevent terrorists who so desired from entering Israel from the West Bank, the damage caused by the closure imposed on hundreds of thousands of civilians, kept from their source of livelihood, was greater than the possible benefits of preventing legal entry to Israel. The head of the Counter-Terrorism Bureau at the time, Meir Dagan, explained the limitations of the use of closure:

> In my opinion, it [closure—BG] has no effect in the war against terrorism…short-term closure is of no significance; long-term closure only does one thing—it creates a sense of discomfort in the terrorist organization, because very few Arabs are walking around in Israel, and so any action appears unusual and therefore there is greater public attention. Is the act of closure in itself effective against terrorism? I doubt it. I can say that most perpetrators have infiltrated into Israel even when there was a closure…. If we relate to actions intended to satisfy the public, this seems to me an effective tool. Because it has an immediate effect on the public's sense of security. It is a classic response. Therefore I, incidentally, have always been in support…[393]

Dagan therefore emphasizes the immediate psychological and morale-raising effect that closure has on the Israeli public, and considers this to be its benefit. However, in this context, it is interesting to note that after the attack at Café Apropo in Tel Aviv in March 1997 only 48 percent of respondents in a countrywide public opinion poll said that in their opinion there should be a permanent closure on the territories in order to prevent attacks, while 44 percent said that this should not be done.[394]

Similar to the step of demolishing terrorists' homes, in this case, too, it seems that the answer to the dispute between those supporting and objecting to the imposition of closure lies in the scale and frequency of its use, its duration and characteristics, and the background and circumstances in which it is imposed. As a deterrent, this measure is of doubtful effectiveness, but it can be justified when it improves preventive capability and strengthens the public's sense of security. After completion of the separation fence between Israel and the West Bank along the 1967 borders, the need for imposing closures in the West Bank will become less pressing, at least those closures intended to eliminate terrorist infiltrations.

Administrative Detention

Another form of administrative punishment is administrative detention, which is anchored in the Fourth Geneva Convention of 1949, dealing with the rights of civilians in an occupied area. In Section 78 of the charter it states that the occupying government is permitted to hold people suspected of subversive actions in administrative detention for an unlimited time, subject to the right of appeal before an authorized body and the requirement to discuss extension of the administrative detention before the authorized body once every six months. According to Leon Shelef, administrative detention is an exception, the need for which is recognized by international norms, and therefore the Geneva Convention takes it into account in the understanding that forces holding an occupied area can expect to come up against various types of resistance on the part of the civilian population that will force them to take exceptional measures.[395] In Israel, administrative detention is imposed on people suspected of harming the security of the state and of the public within the Green Line and in the West Bank and the Gaza Strip.

The attitude of the Israeli Supreme Court to the issue of administrative detention is evident from the words of former president of the Supreme Court Meir Shamgar, in 1998:

> The administrative detainee has not been convicted of a crime and in any case is not serving a sentence. He is imprisoned at the decision of a military administrative authority as an exceptional emergency measure, for absolute security reasons (Section 78 of the Fourth Geneva Convention).... The detention is intended to prevent and thwart a security danger arising from actions which the prisoner is liable to carry out and which there is no reasonable possibility of preventing by regular legal means (criminal proceedings) or by drawing conclusions from past actions with regard to future dangers.[396]

The president of the Supreme Court, Justice Barak, emphasized some ten years later that democratic countries recognize the need for administrative detention as a means of maintaining security.[397]

The status of the administrative detainee is different from that of a prisoner in that the administrative detainee is not obliged to work under the Israeli Prison Act (new version) and Regulations, other than cleaning and tidying the cell in which he is imprisoned. According to former President Shamgar, the trend of those who drew up the Fourth Geneva Convention was to make the conditions of imprisonment of administrative detainees under Section 78 as similar as possible to the conditions of imprisonment of prisoners of war.[398]

In view of the large numbers of administrative detentions made by Israel over the years, it appears that the country's security forces have made considerable use of this measure, over and above the intention of the legislators. This was manifested in a striking manner during the period when Yitzhak Rabin served as prime minister, and in the argument that emerged between him and the government's legal adviser with regard to the need for massive use of administrative detention, including extending the period of detention from six months to one year. Yitzhak Rabin stated, in this context, that he considered administrative detention to be vitally important. According to him, "sometimes, when there is information against certain people, this is the most effective punishment."[399]

The extensive use made of this form of punishment in Israel required the legal system (especially the office of the military advocate general) to prepare accordingly, and adapt the legal proceedings set forth in the regulations to conditions and requirements in the field. One of the main problems faced by the security system was the issue of the "automatic supervision" of administrative detention, by which it was necessary to bring the detainee before a judge, who would examine the circumstances of the detention, within 96 hours of arrest. The fact that the military legal system was unable to fulfill this requirement in view of the large number of detainees led in certain cases to release of administrative prisoners who were not brought before a judge in time. In accordance with a proposal made by the military advocate general, on March 17, 1988, the "Injunction regarding administrative detainees (temporary order) (Judea and Samaria) (No. 1229), 5748–1988" was therefore changed, and afterwards the equivalent injunction for the Gaza Strip was also changed. In the framework of these changes, the duty of automatic supervision by a military judge within 96 hours of the time of arrest was revoked, as was the requirement of a periodic re-examination every three months, but the detainee was given the possibility of appealing his detention before an Appeals Committee. In addition, the authority to issue an administrative detention order was given to all military commanders, not only to the commander of the IDF forces in the region. The change in the orders enabled thousands of Palestinians in the territories to be detained in military detention, and for this purpose a special detention facility was even set up at Ketziot.[400] According to Amnon Strashnov, who served at the time as the military advocate general, the broad application of this punishment did not, in practice, harm proper legal proceedings.

> Even before the military commander signed an order of administrative detention, he had to obtain the opinion of the legal adviser in the region.... It was the obligation of the legal adviser to ensure that information against the detainee was based on more than one source of intelligence, because there is a cross-referencing of information…and that this was reliable and well-founded information.... The guiding principle was that in cases where it was possible to prosecute the suspect before a military court and reveal the evidentiary material in an open process in court, this should be done…[401]

The scale of administrative detentions (many thousands over three years) raises some doubt as to whether the military legal system did indeed have the ability to carry out an individual and close examination of each case of administrative detention. The change in the injunction, and the mass arrests made thereafter, prompted waves of public protest in Israel and abroad, which led, among other things, to a further amendment to the injunction, stating that the judge hearing the appeal of the administrative detainee would have the authority to decide on the appeal, and not just the authority to make a recommendation.[402]

In November 1988, after an urgent need arose to renew the procedure of administrative detention with regard to all the prisoners of the "first wave" of the intifada, six months after their arrest, a demand was made by the security forces to extend the maximum period of the administrative detention order to one year, instead of six months as stated in the injunction. This demand was rejected by the military Advocate General's office, but came up again in August 1989, and in the end the injunction was indeed amended.[403] Among the 14,000 administrative detainees during the intifada, 10,500 detainees submitted appeals against their arrest. Approximately 5 percent of the appeals submitted were accepted by the military judges, most of them by shortening the period of detention by different amounts, and a minority by immediate release of the detainees.[404]

The security community considered administrative detention to be one of the most effective tools available to it in dealing with the intifada, for counter-terrorism and counter insurgency. Many Israeli decision makers emphasized that administrative detention should not be regarded as punishment, but first and foremost as a necessary preventive measure because of the sensitivity of the intelligence information relating to terrorist organizations. According to Lipkin-Shahak:

> Administrative detention is not a deterrent. Administrative detention is a tool which, under the legal restrictions of a democratic country, is necessary when you have information that you cannot use to achieve a conviction. It is obvious to you that administrative detention prevents an attack, frustrates an attack. Therefore I see it as effective and appropriate even today. But here too, it is necessary to talk about the appropriate degree.[405]

Dagan also relates to administrative detention as a necessary evil:

> I think there is no choice. It is not possible in the State of Israel to operate without administrative detention. It is one of the best tools that we have for making use of intelligence information without revealing it to the other side.[406]

In view of this, a country that makes use of administrative detention must take extra care to operate within the framework of steps that are permitted under the provisions of the law and international conventions, and to act according to the procedures of administrative detention verbatim. It must avoid making arbitrary and too frequent use of extreme measures of this kind for purposes for which they were not intended (such as administrative detention of political leaders, and so forth). According to Justice Olshen, who in 1948 instructed that a person be released from administrative detention because he had not been allowed to appeal before the advisory committee:

> It is true that state security justifying a person's detention is no less important than the need to uphold civil rights, but in cases where it is possible to achieve both aims at the same time—neither one nor the other should be ignored.[407]

Deportation

One type of administrative punishment used as a means of enforcing law and order by the military commander is deportation. This is viewed by many decision makers and heads of the security agencies in Israel as an important and effective punitive measure, which should be used to an appropriate degree. However, deportation has been used in Israel in many cases not necessarily against terrorists, but against inciters to violence and terrorism. In practice, this step is intended in principle to remove from the area influential people spreading incitement who are engaged in the political or religious indoctrination of the public and preparing the ground for terrorist attacks.[408]

The Israeli Supreme Court has often been required to discuss the question of the legality of deportation, the argument being that it contradicts international charters prohibiting deportation of the population from occupied territory.[409] According to the Supreme Court, the background to the legislation of Article 49 of the Fourth Geneva Convention was the mass deportation of Europe's Jews to labor camps and death camps during the Holocaust. In the view of the Supreme Court, this article was intended to prohibit arbitrary acts of deportation, but it does not derogate from the obligation of the conquering country to maintain public order in the occupied area and to take the steps necessary for its security.[410]

Despite the Supreme Court's aversion to discussing the question of the legality of deportation on the basis of the Fourth Geneva Convention, the court has deliberated on various issues related to the process of deportation, its stages and its implications. For example, the Supreme Court has determined in a number of rulings that a person should not be expelled if his life, well-being or liberty is in danger in the destination country to which he is being expelled.[411] On the other hand, the Supreme Court ruled that the expellee did not have the right to determine to which country he would be expelled, and that his agreement was not required for deportation to one country or another.[412] The Supreme Court also instructed the security agencies to base their deportation orders on convincing and reliable evidence leaving no room for doubt, and not on rumors and obscure or dubious evidence.[413]

One of the central procedural issues that the Supreme Court was required to discuss was the right of appeal against a deportation order. In Regulations 111 (4) and 112 (8) of the Defense Regulations, the legislators set out a special procedure, which is not recognized in criminal hearings, by which a person slated for deportation will be able to appear, voice his arguments and bring witnesses before a special advisory committee headed by a jurist with the authority to examine the existing information against the candidate for deportation (including privileged evidence) and make a recommendation to the military commander whether to uphold the deportation order or not. If the military commander decides not to revoke the deportation order after receiving the opinion of the advisory committee, the expellee can petition the Supreme Court. The Supreme Court ruled that this special procedure was due to the serious damage and harm caused to the expellee.[414] A serious deviation from this process occurred in the Kawasme affair—the deportation of the mayors of Hebron and Khalkhoul and the Imam of the Al-Ibrahimi Mosque following the murder of six Jews in Hebron on May 2, 1980, as they returned from prayer at the Tomb of the Patriarchs. Immediately after the deportation order was issued, the three were taken from their homes, apparently for a talk with the regional military commander, but in fact they were flown by helicopter to the Lebanese border and expelled, without the possibility of appealing the order before the advisory committee. In a petition submitted to the Supreme Court on their behalf by their wives, the court severely criticized the IDF for not having given the deportees the opportunity to appear before the committee, although it did not revoke the deportation orders. The court chose to return the situation to its previous state and decided to enable two of the deportees to appear before the appeals committee for a hearing on the length of the deportation order.[415]

Whereas in the Kawasme case the Supreme Court was forced to come to terms with a fait accompli, in the case of the deportation of 415 Palestinian Hamas and Palestinian Islamic Jihad activists in December 1992, the court, even before the deportation was actually carried out, prepared the way for a different process of deportation under the heading "temporary deportation order." Below is a description of the incident.

The deportation of 415 Hamas and Palestinian Islamic Jihad activists took place a few months after the Rabin government convened, in December 1992, following a multitude of terrorist attacks leading to the death of five security personnel within two weeks, and against the background of the kidnap and murder of border guard Nissim Toledano by Hamas terrorists. Those expelled belonged, for the most part, to the civil-propaganda and political infrastructure of Hamas—people who were responsible for the distribution of donated money or who served as spokespeople and political activists—and were not necessarily directly involved in carrying out attacks. Rabin saw the deportation as damaging the "upper echelon of Hamas," and not the hard core of terrorist activists.[416] Their deportation was intended to weaken the supportive environment in which Hamas operated, and thus strengthen the peace process and the PLO. Furthermore, the deportation was also intended to demonstrate the government's determination to fight terrorism, and thus calm the public.[417]

The deportation was unique not only in its unprecedented scale, but also in the manner in which it was carried out. Immediately after Toledano's body was discovered, Israel carried out mass arrests in the territories, and arrested around 1,600 Palestinians. The government decided on the deportation of hundreds of Palestinians that same night to Lebanon, for a period of no more than two years, and for that purpose even issued two special injunctions dealing with "temporary deportation" (one applying to the Gaza Strip and the other to Judea and Samaria). Under these injunctions, it was permitted to carry out the deportation immediately and the deportees were given the right to appeal their deportation before special Appeal Committees only retrospectively, after their deportation, by means of a representative (the right to submit an appeal was limited at first to sixty days from the date of deportation, but this time limitation was revoked in January 1993). On the other hand, the general injunctions extended the authority of the Appeal Committees beyond their authority under Regulation 112 (8), and stated that their decision would be binding, and not merely advisory. On the basis of this agreement, 415 personal deportation orders were issued. However, some of the deportees appealed to the Supreme Court, and under an interim injunction from Justice Barak the buses taking them to Lebanon were stopped and in the early hours of the morning hearing of the petitions began. After a hearing lasting fourteen hours, the Supreme Court decided to allow the deportation and revoke the interim order, and the deportees were sent to Lebanon.[418]

Ze'ev Segal is of the opinion that the ruling by the Supreme Court, passed unanimously (and unusually—anonymously), expressed "a rare demonstration of judicial unity."[419] Haim Cohen offers a different explanation, by which this unanimity was perhaps the result of compromise between judges who were uncomfortable with the deportations and judges who were prepared to accept them willingly or for lack of an alternative.[420] The anonymity was therefore intended, according to him, as a cover for the court's confusion.[421]

In any event, the Palestinians took advantage of the deportation to mount an ongoing propaganda campaign against Israel, drawing protest and denouncement from many countries. Reacting to the international condemnation, Foreign Minister Peres responded:

> The Palestinians want us to promise them that there will be no more deportations, but can they promise us that terrorism will stop? On the contrary, let them come to us with a proposal to stop terrorism…. If they stop using knives—we will stop using guns. If they stop using stones—we will stop using punishments like deportation.[422]

On December 18, 1992, the United Nations Security Council passed Resolution 799 condemning the deportation and calling on Israel to ensure the immediate return of the deportees. At the same time, stormy demonstrations spread throughout the West Bank and the Gaza Strip, during which a number of Palestinians were killed and injured.[423] The deportees refused to leave the place to which they had been expelled, and continued living in tents in difficult conditions in Lebanon, with journalists from all over the world providing continuous reports on their situation in the field. Hizballah gave its sponsorship to the deportees, providing them with help and operational training, including military training, preparation of explosive devices, suicide attacks and methods of carrying out attacks.[424] The Lebanese government refused to allow international humanitarian aid to reach the deportees, and on December 25, 1992, the Israeli government also decided not to allow the transfer of humanitarian aid through the area under its control.[425]

International pressure on Israel increased as the media continued to report on life in the tents of the deportees in Lebanon. In January 1993, an agreement was reached between the United States and Israel by which the period of deportation would be shortened to one year. On September 9, 1993, the deportees were returned to the territories. Eight of them remained in Lebanon, apparently fearing that they would be arrested for extended periods on their return to the territories.[426]

This description leads us from the legal question that arises with regard to deportation to the question of its effectiveness. In a manner similar to its approach in discussing other punitive measures brought up for its clarification, the Supreme Court explicitly avoided discussing the question of the effectiveness of deportation. Justice Landau stated in 1980 that "the question of the effectiveness and wisdom of the decision [to expel—BG] that was taken is outside the scope of judicial review and belongs to the sphere of political decision..."[427] In this context, it is particularly interesting to note how decision makers and heads of various systems during this period viewed deportation as punishment. In relating to this question, Shabtai Shavit responded:

> I do not think that it is effective. It is effective in operative terms when you take a trouble-making villain and throw him out. But the trouble he causes you from afar in the transparent world, with the media and the passage of information, I don't know what's worse.[428]

Shimon Peres explained: "It is effective if it is used very infrequently, very collectively, in very small numbers. This deportation of four hundred Hamas people was a mistake."[429] A different position was taken by Peres as prime minister, after a wave of suicide attacks that took place in February and March 1996, when he demonstrated considerable determination with regard to the deportation of terrorists from the territories. At the Cabinet session held immediately after these attacks to discuss Israel's response, the government's legal adviser expressed his objection to deportation as a deterrent action rather than as a preventive measure, and Peres responded: "The closure will continue, the explosions [of terrorists' houses—BG] will continue, workers without permits will be removed, and I also intend to expel family members of suicide bombers, where it is proved that they support terrorism." To the comment by his minister Shulamit Aloni that this was collective punishment, Peres replied: "The attacks are also collective. And they have collective support."[430]

The policy of expelling the family members of suicide bombers announced by Peres back in 1996 was not, in fact, implemented until 2000. At that time, against the background of a wave of terrorist attacks and attempted attacks on an unprecedented scale, the security agencies in Israel were in need of a new deterrent to try and change the considerations of the suicide terrorist. The assessment that the suicide bomber would fear causing damage to his family raised once again the idea of deporting family members. The legal system, by means of the government legal adviser, decided to limit the security system's freedom of action in this sphere, and to permit deportation of members of the suicide bomber's family only in cases in which the family members themselves were involved in carrying out the attack and helping the attacker. This reservation made it possible to obtain the support of the Supreme Court for this punitive measure.

In September 2002, the Supreme Court permitted the deportation from Jenin to the Gaza Strip of Kifah and Intisar Ajouri, the brother and sister of the suicide bomber Ali Ajouri, who blew himself up in the Tel Aviv central bus station. At the trial, held before a panel of nine Supreme Court judges, it was ruled that it was only possible to expel a family member who posed a real danger to Israel, and only on condition that his removal would help remove this danger. In the course of the trial, the representative of the State Prosecutor's office claimed that the new steps that were being taken had a strong deterrent component: "From testaments left by suicide bombers we see that they are anxious that nothing will happen to their families and that they will profit from the act of suicide." According to him, as a result of these steps being taken the terrorist organizations were finding it hard to recruit suicide bombers and many attacks had been prevented.[431]

At a Cabinet meeting held on March 9, 2002, Prime Minister Ariel Sharon instructed the security system to begin preparations to expel the families of suicide bombers from the West Bank to the Gaza Strip, and told them "do not hesitate, this will contribute to deterrence."[432] However, activities with regard to the expulsion of families did not repeat itself.

In conclusion, in the dilemmas relating to the policy of administrative and collective punishment it can be said that in each case where it is possible to use the processes of regular criminal judicial punishment instead of administrative punishment, the former should be preferred. Where there is no choice and there is a clear need for administrative punishment, its use should be as limited as possible, and then only in accordance with the law, for a limited and predetermined time, and under review that is external to the administrative entity imposing the punishment.

8

Dilemmas Concerning Media
Coverage of Terrorist Attacks

Terrorist and guerrilla organizations throughout the world differ from one another in their methods, their aims, the weaponry at their disposal, the extent of outside help they receive, and so on. Therefore, scholars are at odds regarding the very existence of a collective strategy among terrorist organizations.

One school of thought asserts that terrorist organizations operate according to a multi-phase rational strategy, which begins with perpetrating a terrorist attack aimed at achieving widespread media coverage. The media coverage is supposed to intimidate the public, and in this way influence the political perspectives and attitudes of the citizens. The anxiety felt by the nation's citizens will be translated into public pressure on decision makers to accede to terrorists' demands and make decisions that coincide with the interests of the terrorist organizations. This theory perceives the media and public opinion as central elements in the terrorist organizations' attack policy. Another school of thought is doubtful as to the central importance of the media in the terrorists' operational strategy and the extent to which public opinion can influence the attitudes of decision makers, especially on matters of security and foreign affairs.

According to the first school of thought, the written and electronic media play a major role in modern democratic society, among other things, as an agent that mediates between the public and its leadership, and has an impact on shaping public opinion and government decisions. Given the media's importance in modern society, it is a major element in the strategy used by terrorist and guerrilla organizations. This was expressed by Carlos Marighella, who noted that the rescue of prisoners, executions, kidnappings, sabotage, terrorism, and the war of nerves—all these are acts of armed propaganda, carried out solely for propaganda effect.[433]

Terrorist attacks, then, are aimed at achieving maximum coverage in the written and electronic press. Terrorist organizations, aware of the media's importance as a tool for broadcasting their message, do their utmost to attract media attention. As part of this, they act to increase the number of victims in terrorist attacks and escalate the nature of these acts, using means that are increasingly ruthless or terrifying.

Weimann outlines the advantages that terrorists gain from media coverage of terrorist attacks: generating public interest in the terrorists' activities and enhancing their influence; attributing a positive spin to the destructive acts of the terrorist organizations and shaping their image; portraying terrorists as the weak side in the conflict and promoting support for their motives; providing important information regarding counter-terrorism activities, etc.[434] Crenshaw notes that the history of terrorism reveals a series of developments whereby terrorists deliberately choose targets that had previously been considered taboo or locations where violence is unexpected, and the innovation is then disseminated via the international media.[435] Post mentions the fact that terrorists have succeeded in gaining a virtual monopoly over the weapon of the television camera, and in manipulating their target audience through the media. According to Post, terrorist organizations have demonstrated the power and importance of the media and have used this means to highlight the legitimacy of their goals.[436]

This theory postulates that the relationship between terrorist organizations and the media is one of mutual profit. On the one hand, terrorists gain a great deal from the media coverage they receive. The media serve as a stage from which the terrorists broadcast their messages to various target audiences, earning support for the terrorist organization and its actions among its supporters and enhancing its scope and capability far beyond its actual power. Media coverage also helps in gathering vital intelligence information for planning attacks and assessing the offensive intentions of the other side; for imitating successful attacks perpetrated by other organizations; and securing international legitimacy for the terrorist organization while damaging the international image and status of the nation coping with terrorism. On the other hand, terrorists give the media newsworthy and interesting information—drama that involves human lives; a basis for political commentary; human-interest stories on the victims and their families, as well as the terrorists involved in the attack, background coverage, and more. In general, terrorism offers the media gripping stories with an interesting plot, and as a result, they also get higher ratings. Terrorist organizations do not have to do very much in order to attract media attention. It is given to them all too easily, among other things, because of the competition between the different media channels and the desire for financial profit.

Violent incidents (especially terrorist attacks) "sell newspapers" and interest the public. Schmid and De Graff argue that one cannot ignore the fact that the media operate on considerations of profits, which are based on advertising revenue. This revenue depends on the number of television viewers and radio listeners, and newspaper sales. Terrorist acts attract the public's interest, and thus increase sales figures.[437]

As a result of the importance of the media aspect of any terrorism strategy, news coverage may have an impact on the different components of an attack: the target (depending on the symbolism of the target, its security sensitivity, the degree to which it is well-populated, its location, etc.), the duration, the timing, the method chosen. Hoffman stresses, therefore, that modern media play a key role in terrorist activity. Moreover, when the media prepare for coverage and the attack does not take place, it is sometimes forced to justify the money spent by bringing background coverage with a "human interest angle." Thus, there is a distorted focus on the human aspect instead of the overall picture, and the large networks, in fact, become agents that influence the shaping of policy rather than agents that merely report.[438]

Most of the public in the United States identified during the 1980s with the arguments heard against the media regarding their coverage of terrorist attacks. In a public opinion poll conducted by ABC and *The Washington Post* in January 1986, most of the American public (76 percent of those surveyed) felt that the terrorists' success was dependent upon the publicity they received in the media, and that the media sometimes exaggerated terrorist attacks and played into the terrorists' hands by giving them the coverage they were seeking. It was proposed that such television coverage be made illegal, empowering the police to prevent television coverage when necessary. Nonetheless, most respondents felt that media coverage of terrorism serves the public interest, and most believed that television should continue covering terrorist acts even if this led to additional attacks. The vast majority felt that terrorism existed both with television and without it.[439]

This double standard in the public's feelings about the media coverage of terrorist attacks is reflected in academic studies as well. In contrast with the accepted approach regarding the reciprocal relationship between the media and terrorist organizations, another approach was put forth claiming that terrorist organizations do not consider media coverage of their acts to such a large extent, and they certainly do not plan their strategies according to the media. Supporters of this approach rely, *inter alia*, on statements made by terrorist leaders who minimize the media's importance, and at times even attack the media. Moreover, those who side with this theory emphasize that the ability of the terrorist organizations to influence decision makers on political matters by exerting pressure and intimidating the public is not high, and is actually doubtful.

Crenshaw notes in this context that studies conducted with regard to the IRA and the ETA have shown that these organizations find no benefit in media coverage. In reality, they perceive the media as being hostile, prejudiced, and subjective. From their point of view, news reports broadcast through the media are part of the policies of the nations to which they are opposed. Representatives of these organizations claimed the line characterizing the media was one that supported the status quo while exaggerating their reports of the violence so as to damage the organizations' image in the eyes of the public, while at the same time ignoring their non-violent activity.[440] Furthermore, coverage of terrorist attacks usually paints terrorists in a very negative light, which casts doubt on the claim that limiting media coverage reduces the number of attacks.

Hoffman highlights the fact that media coverage sometimes plays a positive role in coping with terrorism. This was the case, for example, when the Unabomber was exposed in the United States following his demand that his ideological manifesto be published in the daily press. The same holds true for the American media's near-obsession with the hostages of the TWA flight hijacked in 1985 which, according to the families of the hostages, kept the issue at the top of the agenda of American decision makers and ultimately led to the release of the hostages.[441] In addition, we must consider the fact that avoiding media coverage of terrorist attacks, or reducing its scope, is liable to cause an escalation in the number of attacks and their nature by the terrorist organizations, in an effort to force the media to cover these acts regardless. And if this were not enough, there is the fear that avoiding media coverage would lead to rumors and that the lack of reliable and up-to-date information would cause widespread, and unnecessary, panic.

Those supporting this theory claim that not only do the media not serve the true goals of the terrorist organization, but even if terrorism also influences the political attitudes of the public through media coverage, it is not at all clear whether public opinion ultimately has any effect on decision makers and their political attitudes. This is because alongside the influence of public opinion, decision makers are exposed to additional—and, at times, contradictory—influences from other sources. Furthermore, even if media coverage of terrorist attacks has an effect on the public and that is indeed translated as pressure on decision makers, it isn't at all clear that this is the influence the terrorist organizations actually hoped for. Quite the reverse, media coverage is likely to arouse public protests that would increase the resources allocated to fight terrorism. Wilensky believes that terrorism does not achieve its goals by employing fear and threats. He claims, on the contrary, that terrorism hardens the population's attitude and leads to counter-terrorism measures.[442] Laquer states that society is willing to suffer terrorism as long as it remains a nuisance. But when a feeling of insecurity begins to spread and when terrorism becomes a genuine danger, people no longer denounce the government for ignoring human rights in order to fight it. Quite the contrary, in such a situation there is increased demand to use more aggressive counter-terrorism measures, without consideration of human rights.[443]

Gur notes that waves of terrorist attacks in Western Europe were accompanied by a rise in public support for taking serious steps against terrorist organizations. According to Gur, waves of terrorism in democratic societies often sow the seeds of its own demise because such violence jeopardizes support for the terrorists, and security forces can then gather intelligence information about them more easily.[444] Hoffman, who bases himself on a study conducted at the RAND Institute in 1989,[445] stresses that in spite of the comprehensive coverage of terrorist attacks by the American media during the five years preceding the study, no support or sympathy was generated among the American public for the attitudes and motives of the terrorists.[446] Gur and Hoffman naturally refer to internal terrorism (which takes place within the nation itself), and their study doesn't necessarily relate to international terrorism (which involves at least two nations), or terrorism that has been "imported" into a country.

Perhaps Abu Iyad, Yasser Arafat's former deputy, can actually bridge the gap between the two opposing theories regarding the question of whether media coverage of terrorist attacks and their influence on public opinion serves the interests of the terrorist organizations or not. In this context, Abu Iyad stated (referring to the attack at the Munich Olympics in September 1972) that one of the goals of the attack was: "To exploit the unusual concentration of media coverage in Munich to give our struggle an international resonance—*positive or negative, it didn't matter!*...[447] In essence, Abu Iyad stresses that in terms of the organization perpetrating the attack, the type of criticism the act evokes is unimportant so long as it succeeds in drawing the public's attention to the problem of the Palestinian people. In other words, it isn't important what the world says about you, the main thing is that they talk about you and are aware of your problems and demands. Hoffman continues this line of thought when he states that the success in achieving the impact you desire is usually measured by terrorists in terms of the amount of publicity and attention garnered, and not in terms of the type of publicity, and whether it is positive or negative.[448]

The Media as Part of the Strategy of Terrorism

The media plays a key role in the strategy of terrorism. Damage from a terrorist attack is usually limited to the scene of the attack itself, but the act also aims to influence a target audience that goes way beyond the victims themselves. The way to reach target audiences and to broadcast the messages the terrorist organization wants to transmit is through the media. Thus, the media serve as a vital means for transmitting messages simultaneously to three different target audiences (see Figure 8.1). For the native population from which the organization originates and activists within the organization itself, the media transmit messages of power; the ability to achieve their strategic goals in spite of their technological inferiority, fewer numbers, and lack of resources; a call to support the organization and join its ranks; and above all—to raise the morale of this target audience. A completely opposite message is broadcast concomitantly to another of the organization's target audiences—the population targeted with terrorism. A terrorist attack is supposed to transmit to this target audience the feeling that they are vulnerable as individuals anywhere and anytime, and therefore their military-economic strength cannot guarantee their lives, their well-being, their health or their property. The message being sent to this audience is usually accompanied by a series of concrete demands, whether political or operational, acquiescence to which would allegedly ensure the end of the attacks and the restoration of peace. With regard to this target audience, the goal of the terrorist organization is to demoralize them and compromise their ability to cope with terrorism. The third message transmitted by the media is geared

Figure 8.1
The Strategy of Modern Terrorism

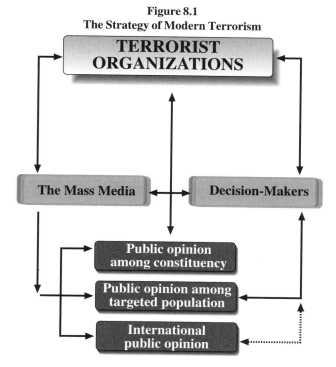

towards international public opinion, that same audience that is not involved in the conflict and observes events from the sidelines. The terrorist organization uses the attack to focus this audience's attention on the conflict in which it is embroiled, the arguments presented by the terrorists and their representatives around the world, and the suffering of the terrorist organization's native population.

Thus, the media serve as a magnifying glass that can intensify the impact of the attack and turn terrorism into an effective tool. Without the media aspect, terrorism remains one more cause of death, one of many, and not necessarily the most important or most dangerous one. Weimann compares the domain of terrorism to a stage. Indeed, almost all of the components found in a theatrical show can be found in a terrorist show, including: a producer—the initiator of the attack; a director—the organizer of the attack; a casting director—who locates and recruits the terrorists for the mission; an audience—the different types of target audiences who observe the attack; the setting—the backdrop chosen to perpetrate the attack; a plot—the story behind the attack, the background and events; a message—the various messages broadcast to the different types of audiences; actors—the terrorists, the victims, and others involved. But beyond all of this, there is the stage. The stage in a theater is usually raised in order to enable a larger and wider audience to observe what is taking place and absorb the message. The stage of terrorism is the media, which serve the terrorist organization in precisely the same way.

The Journalist's Dilemma

In an attempt to justify and explain the way in which the media cover terrorist acts, the media usually cite two main arguments. One is that the media play a major role in the democratic way of government—guaranteeing the "public's right to know." This value necessitates, they believe, media coverage of terrorist attacks without censorship, restrictions, or moral or other type of obstacles. Even if the media act as an essential stage for terrorist organizations and indirectly assists them, their central role in a democracy requires journalists to behave as they do. The other argument, which is held by many in the media, is that in this modern age the main factor that determines the scope of media coverage and its nature is ratings. So long as the public is interested in watching the atrocities of terrorism, there will always be some-one to supply this need and therefore, it is impossible to restrict or change the nature of the media's coverage.

These two statements call for thorough study and examination. On the face of it, the equation that "blood equals ratings" appears correct, but only up to a certain limit. When the public is exposed to images that are particularly harsh—close-ups of body parts, for example, or repeated broadcasts of the death and destruction at the scene of an attack, at least some prefer to turn off the television, switch to another channel, or do something else. This can be con-cluded, for example, from the severe criticism aimed at the media by the public in Israel during the 1990s, concerning the unlimited and unrestrained media coverage from the scenes of terrorist acts, particularly suicide bombings. Such disapproval was expressed in television interviews, calls from radio listeners, review articles in the press, and at times, even from direct contact by citizens to the different media outlets. This criticism ultimately led to positive changes in the nature of Israeli television coverage from the end of 2000 (with the beginning of a wave of terrorist activity and inten-sive violence by the Palestinians, which became known as "the Al Aksa intifada").

The public's demand that reporters cover terrorist attacks in a sober and responsible manner challenges journalists with a very serious dilemma—the journalist's dilemma. This dilemma has two aspects: On one level, the reporter must find the proper balance of his professional obligation as a journalist to cover the events as they happen with the need to respond to the legitimate demands of those in his country who receive this information. On another level, he must find a balance between contingencies derived from com-petition among the many channels and media outlets, and his civic duty not to become a pawn in the hands of the terrorist organizations and assist them, even indirectly, in achieving their short-term and long-term objectives.[449] The call for the media to perform their civic duty is reflected in statements made by Weimann, who declared that along with the public's right to receive precise, genuine, and up-to-date information as far as possible, that is, the public's "right to know," the public also has a "right not to know,"[450] that is, the victim's right to privacy; the right of the public not to be exposed to the personal and intimate details of the terror victims through media coverage that infringes upon their dignity; the right of the public to uphold the state's security secrets that preserve their safety, etc. The journalist's need to cope with these two types of obligations was illustrated most vividly following the terrorist attacks in the United States on September 11, 2001. Television camera crews who covered the horrors of the attack decided at that time to stick small American flags on their cameras, or to cover the live broadcasting vans of the various television networks with American flags or photographs of the missing. Such acts illustrate more than anything else the awareness and responsiveness by American journalists of their two parallel obligations—their professional obligation and their civic duty.

In 1997, the International Policy Institute for Counter-Terrorism at the Herzliya Interdisciplinary Center held a professional conference, called "The Shefayim Conference," which was attended by Israeli media personnel (journalists and editors), and counter-terrorism experts to discuss the media coverage of terrorist attacks in Israel. The goal was to try and find a proper balance between these two obligations (see the Conference Summary, Appendix A). Among recommendations made by conference participants were two main proposals: to avoid close-up images of terrorist victims, and to limit as much as possible the repeated broadcasting of images of death and destruction from the scene of the attack. These two recommendations actually enable journalists to maintain the delicate balance between the journalist's professional obligation and his civic duty. On the one hand, acceptance of these recommendations will help protect the public's right to receive information, since media coverage of the attacks in real time will not be halted. But, on the other hand, without close-up photos of the horrors of the attack, the media will not encourage anxiety and fear and, thus, will not be used as a pawn by the terrorists. Avoiding frequent broadcasts from the scene of the attack will limit the damage to the people's morale from terrorist attacks, and on the other hand, will reduce television viewers' tendency to stop watching or switch to another channel.

The Live Broadcast Dilemma

Among all the different types of media, it would appear that television has the greatest influence on public morale. The terrible images broadcast from the scene of an attack into every home in the targeted nation, and the entire world, serves the propaganda and fear-provoking goals of the terrorist organization more than any other outlet.

Israel's experience during the mid-1990s with regard to television coverage of terrorist attacks is instructive regarding the problem of live coverage at the scene of an attack. The paradox is that through the use of live close-up footage the viewer is exposed, at times, to more horrible scenes than those to which the people at the scene itself are witness. People at the scene are busy carrying out their specific tasks—security, reporting, rescue, recovery—and they are neither interested nor able to actually focus on the particularly horrible images from the scene, such as body parts strewn around the ground or other grisly sights. In contrast with these, when a television cameraman arrives on the scene of the attack who is unaware of the conflict between his professional obligation and his civic duty, he naturally wanders around the scene in search of the most shocking images.

From this perspective, Israel has seen an improvement in its media coverage since the early 2000s. From time to time, if television cameras begin to focus on particularly harsh images during the course of a live broadcast from the scene of an attack, the live broadcast is sometimes suspended and the newscaster or a studio commentator appears on the screen until the camera is no longer focused on the difficult scene. These were correct editing decisions as a result of public criticism.

In this context one must, of course, be careful not to throw the baby out with the bath water. The warranted criticism of the nature of the media coverage must not detract from the importance of media coverage in general, and live broadcasts in particular, when it comes to terrorist attacks. If there is anything more dangerous than irresponsible coverage of terrorist attacks, it is a lack of any coverage. Lack of coverage in real time could lead to the spreading of rumors that are unfounded, and their effect on public morale is liable to be even more damaging and destructive.

To summarize this dilemma, the advantages of live broadcasts of terrorist attacks outweigh the disadvantages, even when the correspondent is unaware of his civic responsibility. When covering terrorist attacks it is possible, and certainly necessary, to employ editorial considerations in real time, to avoid camera close-ups of dead bodies and the wounded, to avoid broadcasting expressions of panic and extreme fear, and to photograph from somewhere slightly removed from the center of the attack.

The Media Coverage of Terrorist Attacks and Its Effect on the Broadcast Schedule

Media coverage of terrorist attacks is, therefore, a natural need of the public who requires ongoing and up-to-date information about security-related events. But even when media coverage of an attack is carried out efficiently, and the delicate balance between journalistic obligation and civic duty is maintained by employing editorial and directorial considerations during the live broadcast, those in the media—especially the electronic media—must determine the precise dosage of media coverage that meets the demands and needs of the public but does not play into the terrorists' hands.

There are important questions to be asked here. How long should the live broadcast be? Should it continue until the last of the victims is evacuated from the scene? Should television continue covering the event until the scene has been cleaned up and life there returns to normal, or should the broadcast end as soon as the picture has been made clear to the viewers and listeners and there is no more new information to transmit to the public? How much should the live broadcast from the scene of the attack impinge on the regular broadcast schedule? Are there certain types of shows that should be avoided immediately following a terrorist attack (variety programs, movies, music, etc.)? Should camera crews be sent to the hospitals to photograph the victims as they are admitted? Should crews be sent to the homes of the victims in order to document their tragedy? And so on. One of the more difficult issues mentioned above is that of frequent and repeated broadcasts from the scene of the attack. These broadcasts are aimed, on the one hand, at filling air time until new information is received from the field, and on the other hand, updating new viewers who joined the broadcast late and informing them of what has taken place.

The key word for all of these questions is, of course, quantity, that is, maintaining the proper balance between the scope of the attack and its damage, and between other events that took place that same day and at the same time. In general, we should aim for the shortest possible coverage and to end the live broadcast from the scene of the attack as soon as all the accurate and comprehensive information about what took place has been transmitted. In a society that suffers from a high frequency of terrorist attacks, one should strive to return to normal as soon as possible, thereby limiting, insofar as possible, the morale-psychological damage the terrorists can inflict on the public through the attack. From this perspective it would appear that the trite comparison between the damage from terrorism and the damage caused by traffic accidents or any other cause of death, can serve as a guideline with regard to proper media coverage and its desired scope. The regular broadcast schedule should be resumed when coverage of the attack has ended, even if the incident has resulted in wounded, and at most the station should avoid broadcasting comedy programs immediately following its coverage of the attack. As a way of symbolizing the end coverage of the terrorist attack and the return to regular programming, the station can consider broadcasting the national anthem. Thus the public will receive the message that the event covered was not just a criminal act, rather it was an act of war aimed at hurting the entire nation, and the anthem will symbolize national unity in the face of this phenomenon. Alternatively, the station can broadcast a slide at the end of the live coverage, a kind of transition, with a minute of silence. Return to routine following a terrorist attack is not meant to offend the dignity of the victims' families or to belittle their tragedy, but is intended as a national message that terrorism will not break the public's will or their ability to withstand terrorist attacks. Within this context, the station must avoid broadcasting scenes of extreme panic during its coverage, and should refrain from sending crews to the hospitals to photograph victims and their families as they arrive at the emergency rooms. This will prevent, among other things, turning the terrorist attack into a "peep show" and invading the privacy of the victims suffering from panic or who were injured and hospitalized. Moreover, such reporting is not newsworthy because it is impossible to obtain information about their condition while they are being admitted to the emergency room.

Interviewing Terrorists and Broadcasting Their Video Tapes

One of the most obvious expressions of the dilemma regarding media coverage of terrorism is the question of broadcasting cassettes produced by the terrorists themselves. Terrorist organizations are fully aware of their critical need to disseminate their message in order to achieve their aims, and therefore they sometimes choose to take a "short cut" and instead of waiting until the media cover an attack or devote some program to the issue of terrorism, they choose to do the work themselves and produce a videotape whose goal is to broadcast their message to the public. These are likely to include cassettes made by suicide bombers before going on their mission, where they spout their ideological doctrine, emphasize their motives, blame the enemy and connect the attack to something they did or didn't do. Thus, they promote the myth of suicide attacks among their native population, and transmit messages of fear to the population in the targeted nation by declaring that they are only the tip of the iceberg, and that many more will follow in their footsteps in the future and perpetrate these types of attacks. Another type of "terrorist tape" is that produced by leaders of terrorist organizations, or their spokesmen. The purpose of these tapes is to clarify to the enemy what it must do and the concessions to which it must agree in order to satisfy the terrorists and ensure the well-being of the citizens. These tapes often contain threats for the future by "exploiting the success" of a recent attack, and sending an ominous message to the public by illustrating the fate of anyone who doesn't acquiesce to the terrorists' demands.

One of the most obvious examples of the importance of the propaganda accompanying a terrorist attack in modern terrorism strategy and the role of terrorist tapes in particular, is Osama Bin Laden immediately following the September 11 attacks. The American public and the administration's decision makers couldn't understand at first why these attacks were perpetrated against the United States. What did these extremists, led by the villain Bin Laden, have against the democratic and liberal American people? This terrorism was perceived by the American public as a product of illogical militantism or irrational behavior. Some went even further, and found it difficult to differentiate between the vast majority of Muslims, who are not necessarily more militant than any other religious group, and the dangerous minority of radical Islamists who believe in the existence of a divine commandment obligating the use of violence and terror to disseminate the militant Islamic ideal throughout the entire world, a minority that believes its religious duty is to kill anyone who does not accept the rule of radical Islam (including a

substantial majority of Muslims, who are perceived by these fundamentalists as infidels).

This, then, was the final goal of Bin Laden and his associates,
and this is what was behind the attacks in New York and Washington. But Bin Laden and his allies know that the task of disseminating radical Islam, that is, actually taking over the world, is no small
matter and certainly cannot be accomplished overnight. Therefore,
it requires a strategy in stages. It is possible to understand the strategy of Bin Laden and the radical Islamic groups cooperating with
him as a three-phase strategy: In the first phase, a radical Islamic
republic would be established in the Muslim countries of Central
Asia and the Middle East (including Afghanistan, Pakistan, the Gulf
States, Jordan, Saudi Arabia, etc.). In the second phase, the territory controlled by radical Islam would be expanded to nations or
regions that already have a Muslim majority, or at least a Muslim
minority, apart from the first group of nations (for example, Bosnia,
Kosovo, Turkey, Chechnya, the Muslim republics of the former
Soviet Union, the Xinjiang province of China, the Philippines, Indonesia, Malaysia, India, and North Africa). In the third phase, the
campaign would spread throughout the rest of the world.

The attacks in the United States on September 11, 2001, were
not aimed, therefore, at bringing down the United States or allowing radical Islam to take over, rather their purpose was to send a
message to the Americans. The attacks aimed at illustrating to the
Americans the ability of radical Islamic terrorism to seriously injure
the United States—its economy, the safety of its citizens, its daily
life—and its determination to do so if the United States did not
initiate a policy that corresponded with the interests of radical Islam. The purpose of the attack in the United States was not to topple
the world's greatest superpower, but rather to awaken the American public to pressure its decision makers into adopting a different
foreign policy. Bin Laden identified the United States as his primary obstacle to achieving the first phase of his strategy—taking
over the Central Asian and Middle Eastern states. Bin Laden probably believed it would be possible to force the United States to stop
its economic, military, or other aid to moderate Arab and Muslim
states in Central Asia and the Middle East, and force them to withdraw their military forces from any territory of the Muslim and Arab
nations in the region. This, Bin Laden believed, would make it easier

for radical Islamic agents in these countries to foment revolution, because without external aid from America the governments in those nations could not give their people many of the services they need (education, welfare and social aid, health, etc.). Without an American military presence in the region, there will be no one to protect regimes that are not radical Islamic regimes.

But the terrorist attacks in and of themselves, serious though they may be, were not enough to achieve this strategic goal and force the United States to amend its foreign policy. To achieve this would require terrorist activity combined with focused propaganda. Bin Laden had already prepared the intricate terrorist attacks in the United States, and the wave of propaganda that accompanied them. Bin Laden had produced video cassettes in advance, which were sent to Arab broadcasting stations, and from these to the American stations, so they could broadcast to the American people the messages of intimidation and threats. In these tapes, Bin Laden repeated his demands from the Americans, which seemed, on the face of things, not to demand a particularly high price in order to ensure the well-being of the American public. Indeed, all Bin Laden asked the Americans to do was safeguard the lives of their sons and daughters serving as soldiers in Arab countries and remove them from all Muslim territory, and to save the American taxpayers' money by stopping aid to what he would define as "reactionary and corrupt Arab regimes."

One of the main reasons Bin Laden did not succeed in achieving his strategic goals was the balanced and responsible position adopted by the American media, which refused to provide a stage for Bin Laden's propaganda messages. The American media avoided broadcasting a significant portion of the tapes sent to them, and the short sections that were broadcast were heavily edited. The terrorist attacks were more than the Americans could bear, but the wave of propaganda that accompanied them dissipated before it was even heard by the terrorists' target audience.

In contrast with this, there are those who feel that it is the obligation of the media to broadcast the messages sent by terrorist organizations as they are expressed through the video cassettes, in their own words and language, just as they should not avoid broadcasting interviews with terrorist leaders and activists. Editorial considerations, in their view, should be made by each and every citizen for himself, and not by some editor or journalist. At best, the tapes can be accompanied, either during or following the broadcast, by professional commentary that can balance the messages and highlight their inclinations.

It seems that an effective strategy for dealing with terrorism requires adopting the American model, as reflected in the coverage of the September 11 attacks. Broadcasts of tapes prepared by terrorist organizations themselves should be kept to a bare minimum, because of the fear that they may contain hidden messages for terrorists in other target nations, and in order to avoid the possibility of enabling the terrorist organizations to use the media as a stage for incitement, intimidation, and brain-washing. On the other hand, to avoid hiding important and updated information from the public, sections of the tape can be broadcast, or better yet—what is contained on the tape can be paraphrased. Regarding interviews with terrorist leaders and their spokesmen, the media should, in any event, avoid accepting dictates with regard to how the interview will be conducted and which questions are permitted or forbidden. The interviewee should not be shown the questions before the interview, and the interview should not be broadcast live for fear that he might exploit the interview for the benefit of the terrorist organization.

Media Response to Invitations from Terrorists

At times, terrorist organizations find direct ways of appealing to the media and using it for their own purposes: occasionally, during extortion and hostage barricade attacks, they demand that the media conduct interviews with them; in some cases terrorist organizations in various parts of the world have taken over radio and television stations to force them into transmitting their message to the public; and in other cases they have invited the media to the scene of an attack even before it took place. In the latter case, the terrorist organization does not trust the media's tendency to arrive on the scene quickly but is interested, by inviting the journalists, in guaranteeing in advance media coverage of the event. At the end of the 1980s, during the Palestinian intifada in Judea, Samaria, and the Gaza Strip, several such incidents took place in which journalists were invited by representatives of terrorist organizations to a certain location, at a given time, but without revealing in advance the reason they were being summoned to that spot. After the fact they realized they had been invited, for example, to cover the execution of Palestinians who were suspected by their comrades of collaborating with Israel. In other cases, the very arrival of the media on the scene was incentive enough for the development of violent action, which probably would not have taken place if not for the presence of the media. In these cases the media is liable to become an agent that provokes or participates in violence and terrorism, instead of an agent that merely reports about terrorist activity, even if this is not intentional.

In contrast with the serious professional and ethical dilemmas that characterize other media-related issues, it seems that in this case the medium in question must take an unequivocal and uncompromising stand, without any ethical or professional struggle. Despite the temptation of getting exclusive information or photos and beating out the competition in the ratings game, responding to the invitation to the site of a future terrorist attack can be considered crossing a "red line" in terms of the media's civic duty and professional obligation. In essence, it implies voluntary agreement to be used as a pawn by the terrorist organization.

Furthermore, while the reporter's civic duty in the context of covering a terrorist attack and broadcasting "terrorist tapes" actually obligates only the media in the targeted nation (because it is impossible to request or demand compliance from journalists who are not citizens of that country), the civic duty not to respond to invitations from terrorist organizations applies to foreign media groups as well, because it is their duty as citizens of the world not to do anything that could provoke a terrorist attack.

Censoring the Media while Covering Terrorism

It would seem that the state's leadership has a convenient tool it can use to simultaneously solve all the media-related dilemmas regarding covering terrorism—it can impose censorship on the media's coverage of terrorist attacks. The state can, using appropriate legislation, prevent media coverage that risks jeopardizing the safety of the nation and its inhabitants. Indeed, there are those who believe that because of the risk involved in terrorism and the importance of the media as a key element in modern terrorist strategy, and in light of the media's unwillingness to recognize their civic duty alongside their professional obligation, the government has no choice but to exercise its authority and censor the media regarding all aspects of covering terrorism. The need to impose censorship may have another explanation—to prevent terrorist organizations from obtaining information concerning the methods, means, capabilities, and intentions of the security forces. Former Prime Minister Yitzhak Shamir expressed his unequivocal support for imposing censorship in certain cases:

> Absolutely. First of all, censorship must prevent publications that are liable to abet the enemy. This should be unrestricted. With regard to anything that can help the enemy— censorship as in war. This is justified: it prevents victims and encourages success.[451]

But the decision to impose censorship is not a simple one, and its benefit is debatable. Firstly, it should be recalled that one of the interim goals of the terrorist organization is to damage the enlightened and liberal-democratic image of the nation against which it is fighting, and thereby compromise its international status. Thus, imposing censorship on the media, even if only in cases of tangible risk to state security in the wake of media coverage that clearly challenges journalistic and civic duty, is liable to serve the terrorist organization's aims. In addition, in this modern era—the age of numerous media channels and where many citizens have home video cameras—it is almost impossible to seal the scene of an attack and prevent photographers from approaching. In this context, we need to take into account that most terrorist attacks occur in crowded urban areas. Even if professional photographers are prevented from reaching the scene of an incident, it is probable that some citizen will film the events and may sell or transmit the photographs to any buyer. These will be broadcast on foreign stations and in many cases, will also be seen in the targeted nation.

There is another risk entailed in imposing censorship on media coverage. As with other issues involving limitations of civil rights, it is easy to define where, when, and under what circumstances one begins to limit freedom of action, but it is much harder to define when the slow or rapid deterioration begins towards the improper and unjustified use of these means by the government for political, personal, or other needs. Moshe Negbi recommends extreme caution when imposing censorship and limiting media coverage, if only because the good of the nation or its national interests cannot be known in advance—not by the government nor by anyone else. He claims there must be a free "opinion market" that enables each one to present his own reasoned opinion and attempt to persuade others. An open and uncensored media— which provides the public with information, facts, and data as well as an expression of protest and criticism—is, therefore, a necessity not to be condemned.[452]

In conclusion, in response to the censorship dilemma, it is best if government leaders do not impose censorship on the media with regard to their coverage of terrorism, but when necessary, when the media ignore their civic obligation, it is possible to appeal to the public and initiate public pressure to demand that the media maintain the balance between civic duty and professional obligation. It seems preferable for the government to avoid taking administrative steps, and to turn the matter over to "market forces." In other words, instead of enacting a law or regulation that would prevent media coverage of acts of terrorism, we should encourage public censure and protest activity on the part of the general public. As previously stated, it appears that this type of protest was productive in Israel, and motivated Israeli television stations to adopt different and more responsible attitudes towards their coverage of terrorism. Yet this is merely a single step, albeit in the right direction, in a long and tiring journey of combining professional obligation and civic duty in an age when terrorism is escalating and intensifying throughout the entire world.

The media must adopt rules for media coverage that will neutralize, or at least minimize, misuse by terrorist organizations of the media stage. They must voluntarily adopt rules such as the principles recommended at the Shefayim Conference held by the International Policy Institute for Counter-Terrorism (see Appendix A)—rules that do not impede the free and ongoing operation of the media, that do not jeopardize the public's right to know, and which take into consideration the impact of competition between the various media networks on ratings. The public must demand civic responsibility from the media in the way they cover terrorist attacks, and punish them for any gross deviation by touching one of the media's most vulnerable areas—through a buyers' boycott or a viewers' embargo.

Doubters who question the public's ability to motivate the media to pursue responsible coverage will say that even if television networks in a particular country decide voluntarily to change the nature of their coverage, such an agreement would not obligate foreign networks and they would continue to broadcast, for example, close-up shots of horrifying scenes. But in contrast with the damage caused by unrestricted media coverage of terrorist attacks by the media of the targeted nation, such coverage by foreign media does not cause any essential damage and occasionally, may even be beneficial for the targeted nation. In order to understand this statement, we must go back to the strategy of modern terrorism and the division into three audiences—the native population, the local (targeted) public, and the international public. From this strategy we can understand that while irresponsible coverage of terrorist attacks by the media of the targeted nation is liable to increase the strategic damage from terrorism, because it harms the public's morale and ability to cope with terrorism, coverage of the horrors with close-ups by foreign media only serves the aims of the targeted nation. This type of coverage illustrates to the world the inhumanity of the terrorists, who are not loath to murder men, women, children, and the elderly in the cruelest of manners. It jeopardizes the international goals the terrorist organization hopes to achieve and reduces its legitimacy and international recognition. Even if a small number of the public targeted by terrorism is likely to be exposed to such broadcasts through cable or satellite networks, the public still has the option of choosing to watch local networks and to prefer the less shocking media coverage of the event—reliable coverage in real time, but without unnecessarily focusing on the horrors of the scene itself.

In this context it is important to remember that in many instances children also watch the news on television, together with their parents, or they are exposed to information while their parents are watching. The ability to watch the news in real time during a terrorist attack without the unnecessarily graphic footage is likely to reduce the damage that is liable to be caused to children from their exposure to the attack.

9

Dilemmas in Coping with the Psychological-Morale Damage from Terrorism

Modern terrorism differs from criminal activity in that it is motivated by political goals. The actions a terrorist commits—murder, sabotage, blackmail, arson, etc.—may be identical to those of the common criminal, but these are all simply means to achieve broader ideological, social, economic, national, or religious goals. In achieving his ultimate political goal, the terrorist passes through a vital interim stage—instilling a paralyzing sense of fear within each individual in the targeted community that he or she could be the victim in the next attack. Terrorism works to undermine the sense of security and to disrupt everyday life so as to harm the target country's ability to function. The goal of this strategy is to drive public opinion to pressure decision makers to surrender to the terrorists' demands, thereby restoring the sense of personal safety they feel has been lost. In this way the target population becomes a tool in the hands of the terrorists to promote their political interests.

In his assessment regarding the importance of terrorism's effect in demoralizing the targeted population, former Israeli Prime Minister Yitzhak Shamir said the following:

> Terrorism can have a highly demoralizing effect. In taking away people's self-confidence, it causes a feeling of defeatism, a sense of "who are we," "what is our strength," "we cannot withstand enemies," "we must surrender," "we must accede to all kinds of demands." This is a negative thing and should be fought against.[453]

The terrorist organization is not necessarily interested in causing the death of dozens, hundreds, or thousands of people in every case. The sole purpose of terrorism is to cause fear among the target population. In fact, the terrorists can ostensibly achieve this objective even without staging terrorist attacks, by ongoing publication of threats and statements in the media, through media interviews and videotapes, by issuing leaflets and all other methods of psychological warfare.

In focusing from the outset upon civilians as the target of its attacks, terrorism violates every international norm of the rules of war. In attacking the civilian "soft underbelly," terrorism turns the home front into the front line. The civilian population is not only a convenient target for the terrorist, but also an effective means to achieve his goals. The random nature of the act of terrorism and the indiscriminate choice of targets contribute to the sense of anxiety. The message conveyed to the public is that anyone, anywhere, at any given moment, could fall victim to a terrorist attack. A threat of this kind undermines the sense of stability and security necessary to maintain the normal life of a civilian population. When every routine activity (going to work or on an outing, planning activities for children or managing life in the home environment) requires calculating in advance the risk of injury, and assessing the necessary actions in order to avoid encountering a possible terrorist attack, one's daily routine becomes fraught with anxiety.

One terrorist organization that understands the strategy of terrorism as psychological warfare and demoralization, and has fine-tuned the method to the level of an art form, is Hizballah in Lebanon. Hizballah has invested substantial resources in planning and executing the psychological-demoralization campaign against Israel, both in guerrilla strikes against IDF soldiers in Lebanon and in terrorist attacks against Israeli communities in the northern part of the country.[454] The organization strove to increase the number of casualties among IDF troops, so as to arouse the Israeli public and motivate it to demand that the government withdraw from Lebanon. To this end, Hizballah made sure to accompany every operational cell it dispatched with a camera crew, which filmed the attack on the IDF and the casualties suffered by Israel, and quickly transmitted the footage to all international news agencies. These film clips were also aired on Israeli television newscasts. At times, Hizballah staged incidents that had not taken place in reality, solely for the purpose of achieving the desired psychological impact. Hizballah also used many other means at its disposal for the purpose of psychological warfare, such as radio stations, television, newspapers, web sites and the like, which it employed to broadcast propaganda to its home population in Arabic, to international public opinion in English, and to Israeli public opinion in Hebrew. As part of its psychological warfare, Hizballah made sure to convey direct messages and threats to various target populations in Israel: Threats to the lives of senior officers on the northern border, threatening messages aimed at soldiers who served on this front, warnings and threats to the soldiers' families, and threatening messages to the population in the northern border communities. In conjunction, Hizballah succeeded in setting "red lines" for Israel, and when these were crossed, Hizballah countered with a harsh response. Collateral damage to a Lebanese civilian or particularly severe damage to Hizballah's operatives or infrastructure led to massive Katyusha rocket fire towards the northern Israeli communities. Residents of the north thereby became hostages to any Israeli offensive activity in Lebanon.[455]

Conventional terrorist attacks (unlike biological and nuclear terrorist attacks, for example) cause relatively contained damage. The number of victims in these attacks is smaller in most cases than the number of victims from other causes of mortality—illness, road accidents, war, and so on. The effectiveness of terrorist attacks lies, as stated above, in their ability to disseminate the terrorists' messages to the organization's various target audiences, primarily that of the country under attack. The public opinion of this population plays a key role in translating these messages into manifestations of personal fear, and in channeling this fear into pressure on decision makers to change their policy in a manner that will conform to the terrorist organizations' interests and aspirations. The success of this strategy, therefore, depends on the terrorists' ability to generate fear that is disproportional and much greater than the scope of the real threat.

Fear caused by terrorism can be classified into two categories: "rational fear" and "irrational anxiety" (see Figure 9.1). Rational fear is, in fact, a corollary of the chance of being harmed in a terrorist attack. This is a fear proportional to the scope of the threat and the probability of its occurrence. In a society exposed to a large number of frequent terrorist attacks, rational fear is a natural phe-

Figure 9.1
Fear of Terrorism

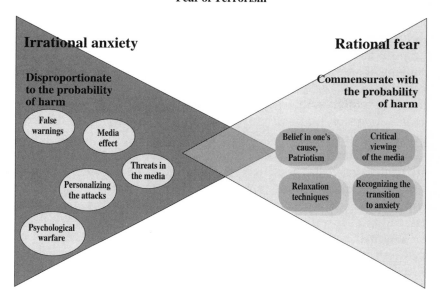

nomenon. This phenomenon cannot be eradicated, and in fact there is no need to make efforts to do so, since it has the positive result of creating awareness in the public to the possibility of a terrorist attack taking place. This awareness assists security forces in thwarting future attacks, locating terrorists and arresting them. However, above and beyond the level of rational fear lies irrational anxiety, which bears no relation to the real scope of the threat posed by terrorism, and is disproportionate to the chances of falling victim to this phenomenon.

Irrational anxiety is the immediate goal of terrorist attacks, and constitutes a necessary condition for the success of modern terrorism strategy. Anxiety is meant to paralyze the individual in the society under attack, neutralize his ability to contribute to society, and disrupt the routine course of his life. Anxiety is intended to change the emphasis in the targeted society from concern for national security to apprehension over the personal and family safety of the individuals in society. Terrorism is intended to cause the individual in the terrorism-stricken society to change his assessments and beliefs as to the importance of his country's interests, values and national objectives, and place in their stead the basic concern for his own welfare and the welfare of his family.

Jenkins emphasizes that terrorism includes a central psychological component—one that is intended for its observers. The targets' identity is usually secondary in importance compared with the primary goal, which is disseminating terror or securing concessions. He concludes from this that the difference between the immediate victims of terrorist attacks and the psychological impact of that attack on a wider public is a fundamental element of terrorism.[456] According to this school of thought, the terrorism's effect on public opinion stems from its immediate threat to the personal security of the individual in society. Lesser contends that the basic principle underlying terrorism, which differentiates it from other types of violence, is its ability to directly compromise one's sense of personal security.[457]

Bandura cites four factors behind the success of terrorism in creating a sense of anxiety in the public: (1) The random nature of the attack—the fact that it is impossible to predict when and where a terrorist attack will take place intensifies the public's sense of anxiety since it feels it is not protected against the danger; (2) The severity of the result—the terrorist attack involves mortal danger, and therefore arouses a relatively high level of anxiety, although the chance of falling victim to a terrorist attack is very small in comparison with the chance of being the victim of a crime, for instance; (3) The sense of lack of control over the situation—people believe that they have no way of reducing the chance of being victims of terrorism (as opposed to traffic accidents, for example). Therefore, despite the fact that the chance of being hurt in an accident is much higher than the chance of being the victim of a terrorist attack, they are more fearful of terrorism; (4) The "soft underbelly" of modern society—the existence of vital services that could cause grave damage to modern society if damaged, such as the media and infrastructures relating to transportation, electricity, water, and the like.[458]

All of these create anxiety in the public which, according to Lesser, is translated into influence on decision makers on issues of national importance. Lesser believes that many of the national objectives in the United States have been undermined due to terrorist acts on its soil, and the issue of America's presence in various locations around the world has been questioned due to attacks on U.S. troops.[459]

In fact, the terrorists wish to bring about the "atomization" of the attacked society, in other words, to turn it from a unified national strong society—united around a common history, culture, language, national interests, values and shared goals—into a weak and paralyzed group of frightened individuals closeted in their homes and devoting all their attention to ensuring personal security.

Terrorist organizations therefore invest great efforts and resources in an attempt to sow anxiety and achieve the desired demoralization-psychological effect in the target population. For this purpose, they continuously monitor media reports of the attacked target nation in order to pinpoint the society's weak points, locate and intensify anxieties, identify social schisms and internal struggles, and harness these to serve their aims. Dissenting views in the public are exploited by the terrorist organization, among other purposes, to undermine the public's faith in the justness of its cause, its values, and its government. Terrorists take advantage of intense emotions in the society being victimized, and exploit them to undercut the society's resilience. Terrorist organizations are aware of the fact that they cannot achieve their objectives solely through their limited physical ability, and therefore psychological warfare takes on supreme importance as a means of accelerating the society's destruction from within. The effectiveness of this war will increase as the campaign becomes longer and turns into a war of attrition comprising many, frequent terrorist attacks, even if the number of victims is limited.

One of the more effective methods for creating anxiety through terrorist attacks is "*personalization of the attack*." This phenomenon is exhibited every time a terrorist attack takes place in a central and bustling location, such as a commercial center, busy street, movie theater, tourist attraction, and so forth. The thought that immediately goes through the mind of the individual from the targeted population is—"I was just there a week or two ago," or "I had just planned to go there tomorrow," or "my wife works on the next block," or "my aunt lives down the road." People in the target population have a natural tendency to search for a personal connection to the attack, and this is precisely the aim of the terrorist organization.

By "personalizing" the terrorist attack, a clear message is conveyed to all citizens who were not part of the immediate victims of the attack, that "it is only by chance that I or someone close to me was not hurt in the attack this time, and therefore it is reasonable to assume that I or someone dear to me will be next in line." These feelings, of course, have no basis in reality, considering the statistical chances of being harmed by terrorism in comparison with other causes of death. In fact, the likelihood of being hit by a moving vehicle while crossing a major street in any city in the world is several times greater than the likelihood of encountering a terrorist attack on the same street. Nevertheless, a very tangible fear results from personalizing the terrorist attack.

Another way to generate fear of terrorist attacks is, as mentioned earlier, through a calculated and coordinated system to disseminate threats and intimidating messages among the target population. For example, after offensive activity against the terrorist organization, or following any other act or omission on the part of the state that displeases the terrorist organization, a spokesperson for the organization issues a threatening message that the organization is about to carry out an attack in retaliation. Hamas spokespersons, for example, have threatened from time to time that their organizations plan to dispatch ten suicide bombers in revenge for a "targeted killing" operation or other offensive action taken by Israel against them. These threats have no significance, of course, aside from being part of a sophisticated campaign of psychological warfare. What reason would an organization have to warn its enemies before staging an attack, except the desire to generate constant worry? The population under attack should ask itself what the meaning of the publicized threat is. Will the ten suicide bombers be sent on their mission within the next ten days? Within the next ten months? Perhaps within the next ten years? (In the latter case, the threat might actually convey a calming message). In the absence of a time frame, a threat of this sort is meaningless. Does the organization's spokesperson wish to say that at the conclusion of the series of suicide attacks he is threatening to execute, the organization intends to disarm and stop using terrorist attacks of this nature? These are, of course, rhetorical questions, which only illustrate how illogical and meaningless is the threat. Yet the public, which is not trained to view the media critically or to process and analyze the threatening messages it receives, tends to accept these threats at face value and become unnecessarily fearful. This is how terrorist psychological warfare operates. The threats can preserve fear of terrorism over time even if attacks are not carried out in practice. However, when an attack does takes place after such a threat is issued, the public could interpret the terrorist attack as part of the realization of the terrorist organization's threat, and say to itself: "Oh no, there are still nine more attacks like this to come." This erroneous interpretation could lead to a state of paralyzing anxiety.

Media professionals, decision makers, and even security officials in countries targeted by terrorism sometimes lack a basic understanding of terrorism as a method of psychological warfare, and all too often play into the terrorists' hands and help intensify the irrational anxiety that is aroused. This is evident in their repetition of terrorist threats and declarations in order to illustrate the scope of the danger and threat to the public, or to justify the need for various counter-measures. For example, a minister, prime minister or head of a security agency could remind the public in his speech that a certain organization has threatened to dispatch a series of suicide bombers. The mere mention of the threat already grants the terrorists a tangible achievement and an unnecessary platform for their messages, and plays into their hands.

Publicizing Intelligence Warnings Regarding a Potential Attack

One of the most important dilemmas faced by security agencies in a country targeted by terrorism is the degree to which they should share with the public warning information and internal deliberations with consequences for public safety. For example, when there is knowledge that a terrorist organization intends to stage an attack in a certain place at a given time, should the public be notified of this, or should the information be kept within the security establishment while taking the requisite preventive steps without issuing a public warning?

Some security officials and decision makers believe it is their public duty to inform citizens about imminent dangers. This was the argument raised by the governor of California when he decided to issue a warning regarding a possible terrorist attack on one of the city's numerous bridges.[460] Security officials who agree with this approach also say that the warning should be issued due to the need to increase public awareness and obtain assistance in preventing planned terrorist attacks. However, it would appear that the decision of politicians and security officials to issue intelligence warnings of possible terrorist attacks is primarily due to a desire to relieve themselves of responsibility for not preventing the attack, as if to say, "I told the people, and therefore I am exempt." In doing so, they hand over to the public the decision of what to do with the information, as well as the responsibility for its fate.

Others believe that publication of an intelligence warning constitutes a severe error in itself, and plays into the hands of the terrorists on several levels at once. First of all, issuing the warning could cause irreparable damage to the intelligence source of the sensitive information. The terrorist organization will make every effort to discover where the security agencies obtained the information on the planned attack. Moreover, when perpetrators of terrorist attacks know that security agencies are in possession of a warning regarding the impending attack, they may divert the attack to another target or to another time that will surprise the security agencies. Yet the damage of issuing a warning is not limited to the intelligence-defensive sphere alone. On the contrary, the main negative effect is the psychological and morale-related damage caused. In fact, publicly issuing an intelligence warning creates a psychological effect similar to that of a terrorist attack even before the attack has occurred. The warning can cause the public to experience tension, pressure and fear when nothing has actually happened. It should be recalled that the security establishment usually receives a substantial number of warnings. Israeli security services stated that they had between forty to fifty warnings of terrorist attacks simultaneously.[461] It should be kept in mind that ultimately most of these warnings do not pan out. Who decides, then, which warning to publicize and which not to publicize? Doesn't the decision to selectively issue warnings of terrorist attacks mislead the public? Furthermore, a sophisticated terrorist organization that studies the targeted nation's policy on issuing warnings could make deliberate use of it to send out idle threats and disrupt routine life in the country.

A public that is used to receiving information on impending attacks through the media, and makes its plans accordingly, could find itself helpless upon arriving in an area where it believes that no terrorist attack is expected, since a concrete warning was not issued regarding it—but becomes the scene of an attack nevertheless. Security personnel who believe that issuing a warning absolves them of responsibility may find themselves bombarded by criticism from the public for an attack that was perpetrated somewhere, for which no warning was issued. In this case the damage could be greater than the gain.

And what of the claim that the warning must be publicized in order to increase public alertness? This claim is groundless, since a public that lives in a country suffering from terrorism is at a high level of alertness in any case, and does not need organized state-sponsored intimidation in order to maintain its vigilance. In addition, public awareness can be increased through other, more effective means, such as education, public service announcements, informational ads, and more.

If so, then what policy should be adopted on this issue? Should a nation refrain in all cases from publicizing warning information? The recommended rule to adopt is that a warning should only be issued when it can be accompanied by concrete guidelines to the public; a list of "do's and don'ts" directly related to the warning. These might include instructions to avoid a certain activity, to refrain from assembling or frequenting a certain area, to take certain protective measures, or any other guidelines instructing the public how to behave in light of the warning that was issued. In the absence of such guidelines, the intelligence information held by the defense establishment should not be shared with the public.

Reinforcing the Public's Ability to Cope

Terrorism is a type of psychological and morale-related battle, and its success and effectiveness are measured in these terms. The difficult and ongoing battle against terrorist organizations may be filled with tactical successes and achievements—averting concrete terrorist attacks; locating, arresting, and killing terrorists; revealing and neutralizing explosives and weapons, and the like. However, despite repeated victories in the battles against terrorism, the state could lose the war if the terrorists succeed in instilling fear among the public and disrupting routine life in the country. This means that the war against terrorism is decided in the public's consciousness, not necessarily on the battlefield.

The question is then asked: Can the public's ability to contend with terrorism be strengthened in a proactive manner? Can the demoralization caused by terrorism be neutralized or reduced? Can the public be informed and educated how to cope effectively with irrational anxiety?

Those who argue against this possibility would say it is impossible to cope with irrational emotions and reactions using rational considerations and explanations. Moreover, some would say that any attempt to disseminate information to the public in the domain of terrorism could "open a Pandora's box" and arouse greater fear than before among people not personally exposed to the horrors of terrorism. As opposed to this criticism, it can be argued that explanatory and educational action aimed at conveying professional information to the public on the issue of terrorism, in an orderly, logical, and consistent manner, would not arouse undue anxiety, but rather immunize the public to the psychological and morale-related damage of terrorism. Even if at a particular moment, the information conveyed to the public increases the fear of terrorism, eventually this information will create "antibodies," or building blocks, that are necessary to build up the mental fortitude to strengthen the public during ongoing exposure to terrorist attacks.[462]

As mentioned above, citizens of a nation targeted by terrorism find themselves exposed to rational fears stemming from the level of real and tangible danger posed by terrorism, but some of them also suffer from irrational anxiety as a result of the psychological warfare and their ongoing exposure to severe terrorist attacks. The informational-educational goal should therefore be reducing the public's irrational anxiety caused by terror. For this purpose, an attempt should be made, first and foremost, to teach the public to identify the borderline between these two types of fear. What is the red line that separates rational and natural fear, which is necessary and understandable in light of terrorism, from the realm of paralyzing and dangerous anxiety that plays into the hands of the terrorist organizations? This red line is, by its very nature, personal and dynamic, and changes according to each person's beliefs and values, his psychological structure, his general tendency to fear various situations, the extent of his previous cumulative experience with dangerous incidents in general, and terrorist incidents in particular, the culture and values of the society in which he lives, and the measure of support and the behavior exhibited by his peer group and society in general. Recognizing this borderline terrorism constitutes a first stage on the path towards enhancing this individual's ability to cope in the face of terrorism.

At the next stage, the citizen can be equipped with information that will clarify to him the characteristics of the terrorists' action; the nature of terrorism as psychological and morale-related warfare; the explicit and implicit messages the terrorist organization is trying to convey to him as an individual in a society suffering from terrorism, in an attempt to heighten the anxiety aroused by terrorism; the manipulation that the terrorists are trying to achieve through the mass media; the scope of the genuine danger posed by terrorism, which is relatively small in comparison to other causes of death; the ability to protect oneself from this danger; and above all—the fact that the citizen, as an individual, constitutes the critical factor that will ultimately decide whether terrorism will win and achieve its goals or whether the terrorists will fail in breaking the determination and resilience of the society and its individuals. Understanding the various aspects of terrorism, as well as recognizing the individual's responsibility in contending with terrorism, will help the individual reduce the degree of irrational anxiety and keep the extent of the threat and the degree of fear of terrorism in perspective.[463]

A citizen who understands the meaning of the "personalization" of a terrorist attack, for example, will say to himself next time he encounters such feeling of "almost being hit" that this feeling is completely baseless. The next time he watches a newscast on television or is exposed to a broadcast threat by a terrorist organization, he will remember the demoralization goals that motivated the organization to publicize this threat and its meaninglessness. This will be an important contribution by the education and information system towards strengthening society's fortitude in the face of terrorism.

The Psychological Impact of Terrorism in Israel and Its Effect on Morale

The effect of terrorism on the Israeli public in the mid-1990s is evident from a statement made by Ehud Sprinzak:

> Between October 1994 and January 1995, Israeli society underwent an extremely severe upheaval. A series of cruel terrorist attacks placed terrorism—usually a tactical hazard that does not endanger national security—at the center of national consciousness and the public agenda. Israel's citizens entered a mental "bunker" of anxiety, and public support for the government plunged in an unprecedented manner.[464]

Binyamin Ben-Eliezer, who was Construction and Housing Minister at the time, described the public mood in February 1995, saying: "Personal security in Israel has dropped to zero, and it is difficult to move on to the next stage of talks with the Palestinians this way. The people have lost faith in the process and we look very bad on the ground."[465] This trend was also expressed in public opinion polls. A poll conducted by the Dahaf Institute in January 1995 showed that the main issue causing public disappointment with the government's performance (36 percent of respondents) was "the continuation of Arab terrorism."[466] In light of the terrorist attacks that took place in Israel, the public was also pessimistic with regard to the future, and estimated that the attacks would continue even if peace agreements were to be signed with all the Arab countries. In the Peace Index survey conducted by Civil Information (*Modi'in Ezrachi*) for the Tami Steinmetz Center for Peace Research in October 1994, 47.5 percent of respondents answered that in peacetime as well, terrorism would continue at its prevent level or even increase, and 40.9 percent believed that terrorism would decrease but not stop, as opposed to only 7.2 percent who believed that terrorism would stop.

In April 1995, Yitzhak Rabin was asked about his assessment regarding the erosion of support for his government due to the terrorist attacks, and his attitude towards the polls indicating this erosion, and replied:

> One would have to be deaf and blind not to understand that an incident such as Beit Lid or Kfar Darom [two large-scale terror attacks—BG] would have a natural emotional effect on the public. I took into account that there would also be painful events in this process...[467]

Rabin did not disregard the feelings of anxiety, and viewed them as an ongoing erosion of the Israeli public's resilience, and particularly their ability to cope with terrorism. However, his conclusion was the opposite of that demanded by the public: rather than delaying or halting the peace process, it was accelerated. Efraim Inbar says:

> Rabin, like other leaders, felt that Israeli society was displaying signs of fatigue, and less willing to bear the results of the protracted war with the Arabs. Rabin compared the reaction of the Jewish population to the Egyptian bombing in 1948 with the Iraqi missile attack of 1991. In 1948, the death of over 30 Jews in the Egyptian bombing did not make an impression on life in Tel Aviv, whereas in 1991 tens of thousands

escaped the city and its suburbs. He ended the comparison by saying that "we've changed." His conclusion was that the Israelis had lost some of their determination and fortitude. His belief that Israeli society had softened expedited the need to successfully complete the peace process."[468]

The heads of the defense establishment at the time also identified a weakness in the public, and repeatedly called upon it to strengthen its resolve in the face of terrorist attacks. In an interview in December 1993, Yigal Pressler, the prime minister's advisor on counter-terrorism at that time, said:

> My message to the citizens of Israel is a double one: On one hand, I would like to call upon them not to play into the hands of the terrorists and not allow terrorism to affect their attitudes, feelings and mental fortitude; on the other hand, I would like to call upon the public not to enter into complacency or euphoria.[469]

Ehud Barak, who was chief of staff at the time, also chose to emphasize in an interview to the press that "in battling against terrorism, there is no choice but to show determination, firmness, patience, perseverance and staying power in the face of the other side's successes."[470] Uri Sagie, then-director of Military Intelligence, explained the terrorist organizations' psychological warfare strategy by saying:

> I don't think the Palestinian organizations believe that terrorism will bring Israel to its knees. Even Hamas has not come to this conclusion. But they are very aware of the damage that it causes to our national mood and the psychological effects that personal terrorism has on us. They live among us. They watch our television. They read our newspapers. There is no doubt that the difficult atmosphere here in Israel encourages them to continue...[471]

Of particular interest is the argument raised by Shabtai Shavit, former head of the Mossad, that there is a reciprocal relationship between the erosion in the public's ability to cope and terrorism. Terrorism, he argues, has caused an erosion in the public's fortitude, but is also the result of this erosion, in a cause and effect relationship.[472]

Benjamin Netanyahu explains in his writings that terrorism, by its very nature, is intended to frighten the public. It is the random choice of an innocent victim that intensifies the anxiety factor and transmits a message that anyone could be the next victim. However, Netanyahu emphasizes that alongside the anxiety that terrorism creates in a democratic society, there is also a reverse effect, that is, feelings of anger and alienation on the part of the citizens.[473]

If so, before coming to power, Netanyahu was aware of the importance of the psychological and morale-related aspects of terrorism. His critics say that he even made cynical use of the public's emotions and anxieties in order to gain a political achievement and beat Shimon Peres in the elections.[474] Lesser made an interesting comment in this context, stating that "Benjamin Netanyahu's victory in the latest elections in Israel was not the result of a referendum on the peace process, but rather the result of a referendum on personal security in light of the large number of terrorist attacks."[475]

The call to the public to stand firm against the challenges facing it, corresponds with the tenth recommendation for formulating a correct counter-terrorism policy, which concludes Netanyahu's book, *Fighting Terrorism*, under the heading "Educating the public."[476] In this section, Netanyahu explains that terrorists use violence in order to erode the resistance of the public and its leaders to their political demands. However, he says:

> The resistance of a society to terrorist blackmail may likewise be *strengthened* by counter-terrorist education.... By preparing terrorism-education programs for various age groups and including them in school curriculum, the government can inoculate the population against the impulse to give in when faced with protracted terrorist pressure. Familiarity with terrorism and its complete rejection would create a citizenry which is capable of "living with terror"—not in the sense of accepting terror, but rather in the sense of understanding what is needed for society to survive its attacks with the least damage.[477]

Nonetheless, this recommendation was not implemented during Netanyahu's term as prime minister, nor did the Israeli education system formally deal with this domain during this period. The only such activity was carried out by the International Policy Institute for Counter-Terrorism at the Herzliya Interdisciplinary Center, which has been sending lecturers to high schools around Israel since 1997 in order to hold information and education activities aimed at strengthening the Israeli public's ability to cope with terrorism by instilling knowledge.

The Morale Component in Decision-Making

During the Al Aksa intifada, since 2000, despite a notable increase in the scope of terrorism carried out in Israel, it appears that the Israeli public learned to adjust to the reality, perhaps for lack of choice and in the absence of other alternatives (due to the dissipation of the peace process). Fear of terrorism remains, but it appears to have become more rational, and manifestations of irrational anxiety seem to have lessened. The public in Israel has learned to live with the "phenomenon of terrorism," and it maintains a routine of work and even leisure at a time when many severe terrorist attacks are carried out.

The connection between terrorism and morale is not unidirectional (the effect terror wields on morale and the public's staying power), but rather bi-directional (public pressure also influences decision-making in the sphere of counter-terrorism). The public, which is demoralized by terrorist attacks, translates its feelings into messages that are directed at decision makers and affect policymaking. Pressures of this sort may arrive both from the public in the country victimized by terrorism and from international public opinion (at times these pressures are different and even contradictory).

The consideration of morale was in many cases an important element of Israel's counter-terrorism policy. For example, the first retaliatory strikes in the early 1950s were carried out, among other reasons, due to public demoralization, undermined personal security, and a desire for revenge—or at least, this is how public attitudes were perceived by Israeli decision makers at that time. The IDF's 101st Unit and the retaliatory strikes it carried out, even when Israel did not take overt responsibility for them, raised morale in the Israeli public and strengthened residents in rural communities. According to Merari, there were periods when Israeli policy achieved a certain measure of deterrence, but in general the retaliatory strikes had a greater impact on the morale of the Israeli public than on the terrorists.[478] In this context, Crenshaw stated that democratic governments that stand for elections must usually respond to terrorist attacks, or risk losing their credibility in the eyes of their constituency. In Crenshaw's opinion, Israel can serve as an example of this. The government carried out a retaliatory strike for every terrorist attack attributed to the Palestinians because the public demanded this.[479]

Governments in Israel have in many cases been forced to shape their policies according to their assessment of the influence of the terrorist attacks on public morale. Indeed, the public in Israel attaches great importance to terrorist threats, both at the level of personal feelings and at the level of national security. Hanan Alon argues that terrorism is perceived as a major threat by the Israeli population. This perception is based on a subjective evaluation by individuals regarding the possibility of being victims of terrorism, and the level of damage to the national image as determined by individuals and reflected within the population.[480]

The fact that Israel is a small country, where most of the citizens have an extremely wide range of acquaintances, also influences the psychological pressures brought to bear on decision makers in Israel in a terrorism crisis. The effects of public pressure on decision-making in Israel were prominently manifested in the Entebbe affair, as described by Rechavam Ze'evi, who was the prime minister's advisor on counter-terrorism at the time:

> There were demonstrations by different elements at the entrance to the Government Center, including people whom Rabin knew had children among the hostages... this certainly had and has an effect. It does not have an effect in Baghdad, but it has an effect in Tel Aviv. It would not have an effect in a tyrannical regime, but here, because of the acquaintances, everyone grew up in the same pot...[481]

Shabtai Shavit explains in this regard that the leader's range of decision-making in the area of counter-terrorism is limited by the boundaries of consent in public opinion. He says that the central problem today in combating terror is not to pass the threshold of public opinion, which is willing or unwilling to accept various counter-terrorism measures; and this threshold, in his estimation, is very low.

> Will this action or that operation be accepted, or not receive the support of public opinion? These things are never said or discussed [in government meetings—B.G.]. They talk in the meetings about how the United States, Egypt or Europe will react, but not whether the people of Israel will provide support or not. But it is always in the background, and it always comes back to the same point of national fortitude and resilience. The greater these are, the easier it is for the leadership to make decisions, and vice versa.[482]

However, public opinion not only determines the range of activity, it also affects the type of measures taken against terrorism, the timing of their implementation, their scope and frequency. In response to the question whether the public's attitudes had an effect on the decision-making process in the sphere of counter-terrorism, former ISA head Carmi Gilon said the following:

> That is an excellent question that I am really answering at the level of conjecture, since no prime minister would admit it: "Listen, the public is feeling down, so let's carry out a grandiose operation." This would never pass, no one would admit it. If you ask me when the chances are higher for approval? Of course it is in a public atmosphere that invites such things. Again, why is this? Because the prime minister speaks in professional and statesmanlike language, but he is ultimately also a political person.[483]

The degree to which the public can influence decision makers in Israel with regard to counter-terrorism may be seen from the fact that most of the decisions regarding the establishment of security units (on buses or in schools) to reinforce the police in thwarting terrorism, in allocating budgets, in changing priorities and instituting structural changes, such as forming a counter-terrorism bureau— have been made at government meetings held immediately following, or in the wake of, multiple-victim attacks in Israel. These decisions reflect an attempt to send a calming message to the public, and to give decision makers themselves the feeling that they are not assuming an attitude of "business as usual" but rather, taking practical steps to prevent terrorism. In this context, Yigal Pressler said:

> Unfortunately, government decision-making on fighting terrorism after an attack is not serious. Most of the decisions are made in an atmosphere of public pressure, hefty budgets are approved, security units are assigned, etc. The real difficulty in realizing the decisions comes several months later, when they are tested in the cold light of reality.[484]

With reference to the influence of the public and public opinion on decision makers in connection to counter-terrorism, Yitzhak Shamir said:

> With everything…it can have either a positive or negative influence. Less so with public opinion polls, but that also has an effect. I had a problem when I needed to deal with it when we were on the offensive. Everyday I read newspaper articles attacking us using all possible arguments, and I had to be able to cope extremely well on two levels: first, personally, I had to tell myself that he was wrong and why he was wrong; and second, to explain this to the public and to my own people. You have to explain things to your own people, it's crucial. That is the entire war of opinions.[485]

Amnon Lipkin-Shahak, former chief of the general staff, also claims that the public had a tremendous impact on the decision-making process with regard to counter-terrorism:

> A great deal. The public has a huge influence. Public opinion has an effect—it's the public, the media…[to what extent?] cannot be measured, at least not accurately, but there is no doubt that the public and the media has an impact on decision-makers. [Towards the extreme?] This is usually in the direction of action, rather than the direction of restraint.[487]

Meir Dagan explains the characteristics of the public's influence on decision makers with regard to the counter-terrorism domain, when he says:

> If there were no terrorist acts, the issue of terrorism would never be discussed by the prime minister. The only thing that places this issue on the discussion table is public

reaction and the effectiveness of the public's response to such events. It forces decision-makers to deal with it.[488]

Dagan's attitude towards public influence on the decision-making process in the counter-terrorism domain is twofold: On the one hand, he believes that public pressure has a positive effect in that it places the issue of counter-terrorism on the decision makers' agenda; however, he highlights the fact that public pressure could have negative consequences, primarily when it follows an attack, because it drives decision makers to make hasty, at times erroneous, decisions, just for the sake of satisfying the public.[489]

Using Offensive Means for Purposes of Morale

Since Israel's policymakers are almost completely in agreement as regards the powerful effect of public opinion on decision-making processes in the counter-terrorism domain, we may ask whether it is proper for this influence to be reflected in offensive action as well. In other words, should offensive means be used in order to enhance public morale? If terrorism is, in fact, morale-psychological warfare, perhaps we should not settle merely for using educational and informational measures and changing that nature of media's coverage of terrorism. Rather, we should take offensive steps in order to illustrate to the public the nation's military supremacy, its ability to respond and the determination of its leaders to defend the lives of its citizens, in order to allow the public to diffuse its anger and realize its desire for vengeance against terrorist organizations, and to generally reinforce their sense of security and feelings of pride.

Detractors would claim that this course of action might quickly deteriorate into the cynical use of offensive action by the nation's leaders for political purposes and inappropriate reasons. For example, they might initiate a military action that makes no operational sense close to an election campaign, solely for the purpose of enhancing the ruling party's standing. Moreover, this type of action would actually endanger soldiers' lives solely in order to satisfy the public and raise morale, but it would be clear from the outset that it has no operational benefit. Add to this the risk of the boomerang effect as a response to military action, and we can see that this type of action may have little benefit. Others will argue that we should not ignore the benefit and the positive influence of a successful military action, and we should not deter from using offensive means for purposes of morale.

It would appear that in this dilemma, the scales tip in favor of the first group—those who criticize offensive action solely for purposes of morale. The morale component is indeed a key element, and it would be wrong to ignore this when deciding the objectives and nature of counter-terrorism action, or when assessing the effectiveness of counter-terrorism policy. But this component should not be expected to fulfill all the expectations of any counter-terrorism policy and it would be wrong to carry out offensive actions for reasons of morale alone. The impact of offensive actions on morale is certainly important and should therefore be taken into account, but only as part of a series of considerations that also include other operational and preventive objectives.

Summary and Conclusions

Coping with the psychological and morale-related impact of terrorism must focus, first and foremost, on a comprehensive educational and informational policy that will target the public's attitude towards terrorism, reduce the level of irrational anxiety, and help to enhance morale and reinforce the individual's feeling of security in the face of the threat. If such a policy is applied, it can help minimize anxiety levels, prevent disruption of people's daily lives due to terrorism, and will reduce its impact on political attitudes and processes.

This type of policy must be directed to three main spheres of activity: the media, the political system, and the public in general (see Figure 9.2).

- *Media charter*—Principles must be determined that will be accepted by the media and on the basis of which rules for covering terrorist attacks can be formulated. As part of this charter, photographers arriving at the scene of an attack should be instructed to avoid direct shots of close-up footage, in order to avoid transmitting horrific images that can increase public fear (but without preventing direct broadcasts from the scene of the attack, which can provide the public with reliable information in real time and thus prevent dangerous rumors from spreading). Furthermore, the media should not keep re-broadcasting pictures from the scene, so that the public can calm themselves and return to their regular routine.[490]
- *Political charter*—A charter between Knesset members and political parties that will set down rules of behavior for politi-

cians following a terrorist attack. It is important to stress that criticism by the opposition aimed at government policy with regard to all aspects of terrorist attacks, including the argument that incorrect policies enhance terrorist activities, is legitimate in a democratic regime. But along with maintaining the opposition's right to criticize the government, several rules of behavior must be defined to illustrate to the public that with regard to terrorism, the country stands united against the terrorist organizations, and this unity is translated as national resilience. For example, the charter will state that politicians may not express criticism at the site of an attack (unless he has an official position that obligates him to be at the scene), so as not to inflame emotions. Another section that can be included in such a political charter should state that Knesset members will avoid granting interviews about the attack until after the victims' funerals.

- *Educational activities*—Enhancing the people's resilience against terrorism requires that we enhance the public's awareness regarding the importance of the struggle's underlying interest. Only a public who is convinced of the need to fight for disputed issues and believes in the justice of its fight will be prepared to bear the burden of the struggle against terrorism—both on the national level and a personal level.

Alongside educational activities, decision makers must formulate a sophisticated information campaign that will neutralize the terrorist organizations' psychological warfare: they must present the true extent of the terrorist threats; explain the terrorists' strategy and how the terrorist organizations are attempting to manipulate the public through their clever use of the media and methods of psychological warfare; clarify dilemmas and difficulties as part of the national effort to cope with terrorism; and illustrate to citizens the need for their involvement in the fight against terrorism. As such, the public must also be given psychological and practical tools that can enhance their personal sense of security, including self-defense training, and be encouraged to join voluntary security frameworks, such as the Civil Guard. A comprehensive educational-informational policy will demonstrate to the public that, in the words of President Franklin D. Roosevelt, "the only thing we have to fear is fear itself."

Figure 9.2
Coping with Terrorism

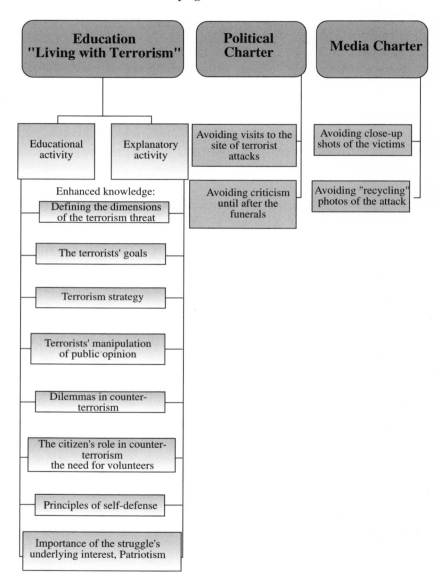

10

Dilemmas Concerning International Cooperation on Counter-Terrorism

On September 11, 2001, the face of international terrorism changed. From that point forward the world faced a new brand of threat, of a scope and severity that was heretofore unknown. To understand the significance of the threat posed by international terrorism, we need to go back to the Afghanistan War (in the late 1970s and early 1980s), when the Soviet army invaded Afghanistan to support the pro-Communist regime against the threat of the Muslim *mujahidin*. The mujahidin called upon their allies from all over the Muslim world to come to their aid in the battle against the world's second greatest superpower. Volunteers came en masse and joined in the fighting throughout Afghanistan. After ten years, the mujahidin and Islamic fundamentalist mercenaries who had come from all over the world scored a stunning victory, and forced the Communist power to retreat unconditionally from Afghanistan. The fundamentalist warriors, flushed with victory, needed no other proof that "God was with them," as if only the hand of God could have changed the balance of power so profoundly and led them to victory.

The Muslim mercenaries who had completed their mission now divided into three groups: one group remained in Afghanistan and its members were united by Osama Bin Laden to form the "Al Qaida" organization. Members of the second group returned to their native countries and joined Islamic fundamentalist terrorist organizations that were already active in those countries (some had been members of these organizations even before volunteering to fight in Afghanistan). Members of the third group also wanted to return home, but they were refused entry by their native governments, who feared their negative and dangerous influence. Armed with this official refusal, they appealed to Western nations for political asylum—which was granted. That is how radical activists spread throughout the Western world, to countries like the United States, Great Britain, Europe, etc. These "Afghan veterans" settled in the West, and in many cases, served as dormant terrorist cells, recruiters, and spiritual leaders who enlisted locals and other Muslim immigrants into the ranks of radical Islam. The problem of international radical Islamic terrorism is not the problem of one individual—Osama Bin Laden, or a single organization—Al Qaida—but rather, is that of a vast, international terrorist network with global reach, which includes activists from different backgrounds living and working in Arab and Muslim nations, as well as in Western states and Third World countries.

The existence of this international terrorist network is not a new phenomenon, nor is it unique to modern history. The world has already witnessed various terrorist networks in the past, headed by the network of Communist and anarchist organizations that operated during the late 1960s and through the 1970s under the direction of the Soviet Union. But the international radical Islamic terrorist base poses an unprecedented threat to the enlightened world, if for no other reason than the dangerous combination of several characteristics that are unique to this group:

- The fundamentalist belief in the divine command instructing the network's members to disseminate their radical Islamic worldview across the globe, through the use of extreme violence and terrorism. The belief in *jihad* (holy war) makes these activists particularly dangerous because if this is the will of God, then neither argument nor compromise is acceptable. What is needed is all-out war. There are those who erroneously believe that the reason for the outbreak of militant Islamic fundamentalism is rooted in the Israeli-Palestinian conflict. However, the roots of radical Islamic terrorism are steeped in religious sources, rather than being based on any particular national conflict. The Palestinian conflict serves merely as lip service for Bin Laden and his associates; in fact, they are not really interested in the fate of the Palestinian people but are cynically exploiting the conflict as a unifying Islamic cause, based on incitement and religious indoctrination. In this regard, Israel is not the cause for the eruption of radical Islamic—on the contrary. Israel is the victim, by virtue of its being identified with the West, and as being a defensive shield that is preventing radical Islam from realizing its objectives and spreading into Europe and the West. The same is true with regard to the negotiations between Israel and Hizballah over the release of the bodies of the three Israeli soldiers and the civilian, Elchanan Tannenbaum, in 2003-2004.

- Extensive global reach based on many Islamic fundamentalist terrorist organizations, as well as dormant cells in various countries—Arab states, Islamic states, and Western states.
- In contrast with members of other terrorist networks in the past—frustrated, middle-class students who decided to be momentary revolutionaries—members of the radical Islamic networks are not novices. Rather, in many cases, they are battle-seasoned warriors who gained their combat experience during the Afghan campaign.
- Personal connections and prior acquaintances among many of the members of these international networks, which originated with their participation in the battles in Afghanistan over many years.
- Members of this network do not hesitate to use the modern terrorist method that has been proven more effective than any other—suicide terrorism. As a result of their extreme religious beliefs, they are even happy to undertake this type of attack, out of their conviction that with such action they will not die at all, and they are certainly not committing suicide (which is forbidden by Islamic religious law), rather, they are carrying out a sacrifice for the sake of martyrdom (*istishad*), guaranteeing them eternal life in Paradise.
- Statements made by leaders of the international radical Islamic terrorist network, and the successful prevention of attacks by others belonging to this system, indicate that these terrorists have no qualms about using non-conventional means if necessary—chemical, biological, or even nuclear weapons—in order to achieve their goals.

The combination of all these characteristics creates an unparalleled level of postmodern threat and danger to the entire enlightened world. So enormous a threat demands that the international community unite its efforts, combine forces, and formulate a new international strategy to fight terrorism. A strategy to combat international radical Islamic terrorism requires concomitant action on four levels:

1. Action against the Al Qaida organization and Bin Laden—Primarily military-intelligence action, started with the international campaign led by the United States in Afghanistan during the months immediately following September 11, 2001. This campaign was surprisingly successful, and ended with the destruction of Al Qaida's infrastructure in Afghanistan, the elimination and arrest of many of its activists, and overthrow of the Taliban regime that had provided the organization with support and protection. But despite the relative success of the military campaign in Afghanistan, the international struggle, even on this first level, is far from over. Bin Laden himself has yet to be caught; many Al Qaida activists escaped Afghanistan to neighboring nations and have spread all over the world, and are continuing to plan and prepare terrorist attacks.

2. The second level on which the international campaign must be waged involves taking action against other radical Islamic terrorist organizations around the Muslim world, such as: Abu Sayyaf and the Moro Islamic Liberation Front in the Philippines; Al-Gama'a al-Islamiya in Egypt, Malaysia, and Indonesia; the Egyptian, Bangladeshi and Palestinian Jihad organizations; Jama'at a-Takfir and al-Hegira in Egypt; the GIA and GSPC in Algeria; GTI in Tunisia; the Army of Muhammad, Lashkar a-Toiba, Harakat ul-Mujehideen and Hizb ul-Mujehideen in India; Hamas, the Palestinian Islamic Jihad, and the Lebanese and Turkish Hizballah; the Islamic Movement in Uzbekistan and Tajikistan; and many more.

In 1998, some of these organizations joined the umbrella organization known as "The World Islamic Front for Jihad Against the Jews and the Crusaders," led by Bin Laden. The campaign against them does not necessarily need to be the job of the Western world or the Americans alone. First and foremost, this is the job of Arab and Muslim countries that are not part of radical Islamic movements. Moderate Muslims must stand at the forefront of the camp fighting radical Islam, not for altruistic reasons—to save the Western world or other religions—but primarily for the sake of their own survival. (The vast majority of Muslims are opposed to violence and militantism. This population is perceived in the eyes of the fundamentalists as infidels, no less than the Jews and the Christians, and perhaps even more so.)

International action against radical Islamic organizations and movements throughout the Muslim world must focus, on the one hand, on military aspects—hitting their infrastructures, stopping their activities, drying up their financial resources—so as to limit their operational capabilities. But at the same time, moderate Muslim nations must restrict the hold these radical movements have secured among the Muslim masses through a constant supply of basic services, such as religion, social welfare, health, and education. As part of this struggle, they must fight to outlaw and shut down the community centers opened by radical Islamic groups, and replace them with centers run by the central government, which will provide for these needy masses without militant indoctrination and fundamentalist propaganda.

Naturally, this task entails a lengthy and difficult process and its results, if and when they appear, will be seen only in several years, perhaps only in future generations. For this reason it is important to act against radical Islamic terrorist organizations throughout the Muslim world on two levels simultaneously: a repeated, ongoing military struggle to reduce their short-term capabilities, after which there will be enough time to tackle the motivation of the organizations' activists and the masses who support them through informational, educational, welfare, and other such activities, the results of which will be reaped in the long term.

3. The third sphere of activity is international action against state sponsors of terrorism. In order for this action to be successful, the enlightened nations of the world must accept two fundamental moral principles. First is the need for an accepted and objective international definition of the concept of terrorism (see chapter 1). This is a direct result of the need to achieve a common denominator that will allow nations to establish a normative international system to combat terrorism. Based on this it will be possible to introduce international charters that will define the range of the nations' commitment to an international war against terrorism in general, and particularly against state sponsors of terrorism. The second moral principle that must be accepted is the need to change the balance of particularistic interests of each of the world's enlightened nations. They must recognize the scope of the threat posed by international terrorism, and understand that fighting terrorism must be the primary objective of every state, a goal that is more important than any other political or economic interest. (See chapter 4 for a discussion of the difficulties and dilemmas involved in effectively coping with state sponsors of terrorism.)

In reality, most of the world's nations claim their opposition to terrorism (based on a definition that suits them), and most of them probably do believe this. But the problem is that in many cases the interest of international counter-terrorism is low on the list of national priorities in these nations, compared with economic, social, political security and other interests. Today, the scope of the danger from radical Islamic terrorism requires a change in the balance of interests among all enlightened nations, and the war against terrorism must become a major and primary goal above all other objectives.

4. The fourth sphere of activity within the international campaign against radical Islamic terrorism is the struggle against terrorist cells located throughout the Western world and in other nations. This refers to the activists and supporters, who have settled in various countries and who, in many cases, have even been granted citizenship. The task of coping with these activist cells falls directly on each of the countries in which they have found haven, particularly in the West. They must adjust their laws accordingly and grant their security forces the necessary means to cope with these dangerous agents. Security forces must follow the illegal activities of the radical Islamic activists, as well as verbal incitement spoken in the local languages and in Arabic, which are often peppered with linguistic arguments and quotes from the Koran that camouflage their true radical intent. Security agencies must make the necessary arrests, and even re-voke citizenship and deport especially dangerous activists in order to weaken the hold of radical Islamic organizations in these na-tions. Special emphasis should be placed on native citizens who have converted to Islam and adopted radical Islamic views, or Muslims born in that nation who have begun to associate with radical agents and frequent their mosques.

This type of international campaign, based on the four elements described above, must be carried out simultaneously on a global level against all those who belong to or support the radical Is-lamic terrorist network, because the scope of the threat necessi-tates an urgent and significant reduction of their operational capability. An essential and fundamental condition for the campaign's success is honest and close cooperation between the greatest possible number of Western and Third World na-tions, in the following spheres:

- Creating a shared normative-legal platform for the interna-tional struggle against terrorism;
- Bilateral and multilateral cooperation in transmitting intelli-gence information and cumulative offensive and defensive experience;
- Establishing joint international frameworks for fighting ter-rorism.

Creating a Joint, Legal-Normative Platform to Combat Terrorism

As stated, the first step in formulating a joint international counter-terrorism policy is to create a normative common denominator in the form of an accepted definition for the term "terrorism." This definition must be as narrow and limiting as possible so that it represents the broadest possible basis for shared agreement, and makes a distinction between the goals of terrorists and their modes of operation, that is, deliberate injury to civilians With such a definition it will be possible to formulate international charters for combating terrorism.

The system of international charters must include provisions that will require nations to act against infrastructures of foreign terrorist organizations located on their territory, and against communities that aid terrorist organizations operating on their soil; charters that obligate nations to fight terrorist financing—raising funds aimed at terrorist activity, money-laundering, and camouflaging funds under the guise of philanthropic social welfare activities; charters that compel banks to divulge information to security forces regarding terrorist organizations or those suspected of involvement in terrorist activity; treaties for extraditing terrorists and their associates; treaties that prohibit membership in terrorist organizations and perpetrating various types of terrorist acts—suicide bombings, extortion attacks, killing, and sabotage; treaties that establish a nation's right to carry out counter-terrorist activity against terrorist organizations on the territory of another nation under certain circumstances; and so on.

A well-developed system of international treaties as described above will provide a broad platform for developing international cooperation in many spheres relating to counter-terrorism. In formulating these new international norms, we must also strive to achieve a common thread with regard to domestic legislation against terrorism, and encourage nations to adopt laws that will make it possible to confiscate terrorist organizations' financial and other resources, prohibit incitement, and prevent expressions of identification with terrorist organizations. There must also be a defined range of what is permitted and prohibited for security forces coping with terrorism—surveillance, wiretapping communications, interrogating terrorist suspects, and procedures for prosecution—that are rooted in a legislative framework that will distinguish terrorism from other types of criminal activity.

Cooperation in Combating Terrorism

International cooperation is therefore a key element in coping with global terrorism. The dilemmas involved in international intelligence cooperation were discussed in chapter 3. But there are many other areas, beyond the intelligence domain, in which exchange of information between nations can contribute greatly in this effort. The experience garnered by various nations with regard to counter-terrorism could be used to help other nations that lack relevant experience in this sphere, making their struggle more effective. This experience may be expressed in the following spheres: a nation's punitive policy—information regarding types of punishment and their efficacy; security policy—security measures at various military and civilian facilities, security methods and special means; how to manage emergency services (police, firefighters, and first aid) at the scene of an attack, by establishing a control and command post at the site of terrorist attacks, the nature of such work, how to coordinate among the various agencies working at the scene, and typical medical treatment methods for terrorist incidents; operating procedures for security forces—how to handle suspicious people and objects, neutralizing explosives, etc.

Information about these and other issues can be transmitted via joint training activities—shared counter-terrorism courses, exchange programs for officers and fighters, tactical drills, strategic education, etc.

Another form of cooperation has to do with sharing technological knowledge. There should be a united effort to develop a variety of technological means: to identify and neutralize terrorists from a distance; intelligence equipment for wiretapping, surveillance, command and control; means for locating and neutralizing explosives, as well as chemical and biological agents; methods for supervising crowds and restoring order. A joint, international technological effort in all of these areas can help improve the final outcome, reduce development costs, and shorten time frames. Joint technological teams can more easily overcome typical technical problems and obstacles on the road to product development, while basing their efforts on technological experience gained in various countries.

Security forces and terrorists are in perpetual competition—who will find advanced technological means and methods of operation to surprise the opponent and overcome the obstacles? According to Lesser and Hoffman et al., terrorists' ability to employ diverse weaponry, whether simple or sophisticated, has often enabled them to get the jump on those fighting terrorism and surmount the security measures they faced. They claim that we must not denigrate the enemy's technological sophistication, nor can we be complacent.[491]

We can compare the development of terrorism to a wave moving along the axis of time. For example, in the late 1960s and early 1970s, there was a wave of airplane hijackings that posed a challenge to security forces. Once security agencies started using technological means (metal detectors at the entrance to aircraft), and adopted new modes of operation—such as placing sky marshals and security personnel in planes to contend with skyjackers even during a flight itself—the incidence of hijackings declined. But as this wave was dying down a new type of air transportation attack made its appearance in the late 1970s and early 1980s, the goal of which was not to hijack the planes but rather to blow them up in mid-air. Now, it was no longer necessary to try and sneak a gun onto the plane and have to deal with security agents during the flight. Now it was enough to load the plane with a cargo of plastic or other type of explosives, sometimes using a "duped passenger" who would get the explosives onto the plane without even being aware of it.

A similar process took place in Israel at the end of the 1970s. At that time, and even earlier, terrorist organizations made numerous attempts to infiltrate into Israel by crossing the nation's borders from a neighboring state (Jordan and Lebanon), in an effort to carry out a hostage barricade attack or murder in an outlying locality. As obstacles and control systems at Israel's borders became more sophisticated, and after Israel had adopted certain methods involving patrol and ambush, as well as invasive preventive action in neighboring states, terrorist organizations found it more difficult to perpetrate these types of attacks. They found a solution in the early 1980s. Terrorists quickly learned they could overcome land-based obstacles and IDF forces by using artillery, which enabled them to "transmit" explosives across the borders without endangering the lives of the perpetrators.

The nature of this "competition" between terrorists and security forces poses a dilemma to decision makers. As might be expected, they are interested in developing new technological means and finding alternative methods of operation that can reduce the scope and damage of terrorist attacks. However, if the success of these improvements in foiling attacks only motivates terrorist organizations to step up their efforts to improve and develop newer, more lethal methods, then perhaps the struggle to effectively fight terrorism is a losing battle. The short-term effectiveness of counter-terrorism measures is liable to become damaging in the long run. Perhaps it is best to allow the terrorist organizations to operate freely so as not to challenge them to improve and develop their means and methods.

This discussion is only theoretical, however, because decision makers cannot honestly make such a speculative decision. The primary obligation of our leaders is to do whatever they can to safeguard the lives and security of their citizens. Moreover, improved counter-terrorism measures may carry a risk of future escalation, but at the same time there is the possibility that scientists and counter-terrorism specialists will find the proper solution, in time to meet the next challenge. Similarly, perhaps a significant decline in the scope of terrorism now can buy leaders some time that will enable them to solve the problem by finding a political solution. Finally, the temporary drop in terrorist activity might give security forces the time they need to deal a severe blow to the terrorist organization, which will find its operational capability dramatically reduced for some time to come.

In light of the above, it is vital that we intensify international cooperative relationships with regard to technological development: establish an international mechanism to facilitate the ongoing sharing of information; set up an database of international goals and needs for counter-terrorism technologies; initiate joint development teams and think tanks, with each nation focusing on areas in which they have a relative advantage; establish international research foundations devoted to funding and promoting technological developments in this sphere; and enable scientists from different nations to employ the special technologies they have to discover new counter-terrorism measures.

Establishing Joint International Counter-Terrorism Frameworks

It has already been mentioned that the scope and nature of terrorism at the dawn of the third millennium constitutes a tangible threat to the peace of modern Western civilization, and poses a serious challenge to the enlightened world. As such, there is a primary need to approach a new level of international cooperation in the effort to confront radical Islamic terrorism. It is no longer enough to improve and enhance international cooperation on the basis of the familiar formula; rather, we must develop a joint international counter-terrorism campaign. *The transition from international co-*

operation to a joint counter-terrorism campaign is not merely a se-
mantic change, but rather, it entails a new understanding regarding the
essence of the struggle and the means needed for coping on an international scale. Naturally, the transition to a joint international campaign does not contradict the need to enhance cooperation as was
described above, but at the same time, it demands that we establish
joint frameworks of action for a more effective international effort,
which relate to almost all spheres and elements of counter-terrorism:

- *Intelligence*—An international intelligence body should be
  established, to which real-time warning data can be chan-
  neled as well as information concerning the movements, intentions, capabilities, and characteristics of terrorist operations.
  This information will be made available to the coalition of
  nations committed to the uncompromising struggle against
  international terrorism, and which will use it to foil potential
  attacks. This international entity is also likely to employ its
  own independent intelligence sources against terrorist agents
  throughout the world.
- *In the offensive domain*—A joint intervention unit should be
  established, as well as international counter-terrorism units,
  which will be available at short notice to nations under attack
  to carry out anti-terrorist missions—to capture terrorists, rescue hostages, etc. Concomitantly, there should be an international unit to handle negotiations with terrorists in cases of
  extortion. The unit members must be well acquainted with
  all aspects of radical Islamic terrorism, including the culture,
  language, religious, decision-making processes, and intellectual characteristics of its adherents.
- *In the defensive domain*—International security units should
  be introduced to help nations contending with an ongoing
  terrorism threat, and to demonstrate international determination and solidarity in the war on terrorism. The units will be
  equipped with the most advanced technological means and
  will be deployed ad hoc in sensitive areas within any nation
  requesting such assistance. They will also help train a security and preventive network in these nations, so that after a
  certain time local units will be able to replace the international ones.
- *Legislative and judicial action*—An international court for
  terrorist crimes should be instituted. The idea is to fill the
  lacuna that presently exists since the establishment of the
  International Court of Justice in the Hague, regarding which
  it had already been stipulated that the court would be authorized to try any person—leader and common citizen alike—
  but only for criminal acts or war crimes, without any mention

of terrorist activity. Instead, an international court for terrorism would focus on trials for terrorists, and would be based on an accepted definition of terrorism and international charters ratified accordingly. This court could also recommend that international institutions develop new international charters, if necessary.

- *Civilian activity*—Terrorism is an interdisciplinary issue more than any other phenomenon. Almost every academic discipline is relevant to one aspect of terrorism or other—political science, international relations, Middle Eastern studies, sociology, psychology, economics, computer science, law, biology, chemistry, physics, and many more. For this reason, the issue of coping with terrorism demands a perspective and analytical ability as broad as possible. The academic system must be prepared by making available all relevant knowledge and information. As part of this effort, an international academic research network should be set up with the finest academic minds, directing them towards research questions that are particularly relevant for prevention agencies, providing them with the necessary financial resources, forging links between different researchers from around the world and conducting working meetings, and helping to build joint academic databases. Such a network has recently been established by this author—ICTAC, the International Academic Community—and it includes about a dozen academic research institutes and professionals from various countries.

- *Educational and informational activity*—To enlist international public opinion in the vital struggle, informational and educational activities must be dovetailed in nations coping with terrorism, and other nations as well. An international framework of experts should be established to formulate joint public relations and educational policies, and to work with education systems in the different nations. It is especially important that this framework offer assistance to education and information systems in Muslim countries as part of the effort to counter radical Islamic indoctrination. International teams will provide Muslim nations with all the help they need to develop curricula and to hold educational activities promoting tolerance, pragmatism, and humanism.

- *Establishing a "League of Nations Fighting Terrorism"*—To promote effective action against terrorist organizations and the states that support them, a permanent, international anti-terrorism institution must be given the authority to identify nations and organizations considered to be involved in terrorism, and determine sanctions and actions to be taken against them. This institution would operate on the basis of a clear and approved mandate. It would include experts from different countries who would study global terrorism and on the basis of their findings, would publish an annual list of nations supporting terrorism. International sanctions could then be adopted against countries included on that list, in accordance with the scope of their support, so as to force them to stop or limit their involvement.

This is a particularly challenging task and would require, as stated, a broad international consensus regarding a definition of terrorism, and a classification of the different levels of involvement. Most likely any international effort in this direction would be doomed to fail, although perhaps some of the goals can be achieved through the establishment of a "League of Nations Fighting Terrorism" by a few countries, with others joining later on.

The United Nations should fulfill this role, but past experience shows that it cannot be expected to lead an effective campaign against international terrorism, and certainly not against specific sponsors of terrorism. In this context, former Israeli president Mr. Chaim Herzog, who also served as Israel's ambassador to the United Nations, said the following:

> It is utterly unrealistic to expect any positive development to emerge from the UN on the subject of terrorism, as on many other subjects. The only hope is for the free nations, led by the U.S., to join together in a convention outside the UN against terror, which provides for international sanctions, a convention by which they will be bound.[492]

The late prime minister of Israel, Yitzhak Rabin, also addressed this issue:

> The response to such international terror must also be international. Nations must find new ways of cooperating against the terrorist network...I propose that this type of cooperation institutionalized and made concrete. Countries that choose to coordinate their activities against international terrorism should create a special international organization for this purpose. Obviously, this organization cannot be created within the framework of the United Nations. It can come into being only if the United States, the most powerful country in the free world, will take the initiative and call for its establishment.... The existence of such an agency might help serve as a deterrent, and possibly an effective means of sanctions and punishment.[493]

Summary and Conclusions

It seems that so long as the world does not change its balance of interests with regard to terrorism, it will not be possible to mount an effective joint, international campaign against it. Only when the nations of the free world understand that their interest in fighting international terrorism is more important than any other interest, will it be possible to begin coordinated and effective steps to force nations such as Iran, Syria, and Lebanon to limit their involvement in terrorism and stop sponsoring such organizations. This step could change the cost-benefit equation for terrorist organizations, and allow the world to fight global terrorism more effectively. However, the nations' balance of interests will change only when terrorism crosses a certain level of damage and the threat increases significantly. In other words, the nations of the world need for "things to get worse" before they will take the initiative. Perhaps the September 11 attacks in the United States served as the watershed in international terrorism. But as of this writing it would appear that, except for the American leadership, and perhaps the British as well, the world has yet to awaken from its complacency.

It appears that only when waves of multi-victim terrorist attacks wash over the nations currently choosing to ignore the severity of the problem, or when there are sufficient signs that the level of global terrorism has increased (with the use of unconventional—chemical, biological or nuclear—weapons), and the risk to world peace becomes more tangible, only then can we expect the nations of the free world to unite together in a genuine and uncompromising struggle against international terrorism.

Summary and Conclusions:
Israel's Counter-Terrorism Strategy

The dilemmas mentioned in this book with respect to counter-terrorism, and the numerous other dilemmas that constantly arise with the need to address terrorist attacks, are ample proof of how complicated coping with terrorism can be—a multifaceted and complex task that requires appropriate training and constant learning from the experience gained by other countries.

The issue's complexity derives, *inter alia*, from the very fact that terrorism is, essentially, an interdisciplinary phenomenon that touches on a range of spheres. Consequently, there are many entities engaged in the fight against terrorism as part of the ongoing performance of their jobs: different government ministries—Defense, Internal Security, Justice, Finance, Foreign Affairs, Education, Interior, Health, and of course, the Prime Minister's Office, as well as various military, intelligence, security and police, tax, immigration, banking, and other authorities. Effective coping with terrorism requires concomitant action in all spheres by these entities, and demands constant and effective coordination among them. If such coordination is in place, this is likely to enhance the efforts to confront terrorism, enabling these agencies to synchronize intelligence information and use it in an effective and focused manner. On the other hand, lack of coordination could lead to a serious waste of resources, counter-productive competition between the various parties, bureaucratic complexity and above all—ineffective efforts in contending with terrorism.

Given the subject's sensitivity and complexity, and considering the natural institutional jealousy between and within the different government and security agencies in protecting the autonomy of their own domains, the person charged with coordinating the war against terrorism must have a strong security and public reputation, and he must draw his authority from the top of the nation's government pyramid—the prime minister. The coordinating entity must be given power to make decisions and allocate resources as a direct result of the prime minister's authority. The coordinating agent must receive constant updates of all security-related activity being conducted, and he must have access to the entire intelligence picture at any given moment. The coordinator will define the intelligence gaps that must be filled with regard to counter-terrorism, and will assign tasks to the relevant bodies in charge of implementation.

Since dealing with terrorism is directly related to all walks of life in the nation—military, social, political, economic, and psychological—it demands a long-term strategic perspective while balancing all of the nation's interests. The decision about what actions to take against terrorism and what means to employ—military or political, dogmatic or conciliatory—must be made not only on the basis of immediate needs, but on the basis of an assessment of how these steps will impact on the nation's long-term objectives, among other things, because terrorism is aimed at damaging these interests.

But does such a strategic perspective necessarily mean defining a clear, written strategy, indelibly etched in stone and passed on from one generation to the next with regard to the way a nation fights terrorism? Most Israeli policymakers who were interviewed for this book were in complete agreement that Israel does not have— nor did it ever have—a written, structured and unambiguous counter-terrorism policy:[494] Rehavam Ze'evi—"There is no such thing as a formal, written policy that goes from leader to leader, from official to official." Shlomo Gazit—"None, there is no strategy. There are ad-hoc decisions, there are ad-hoc reactions." Meir Amit—"I would tend to say there isn't." Yigal Pressler—"No, Israel has no strategy. We operate from one day to the next." Ariel Sharon—"I know of no strategy. I know there are techniques for securing facilities— how to secure things here and there." Sharon adds that in his opinion, a clear policy is needed in this sphere but it should not be made public. Shabtai Shavit—"In my opinion Israel never had a counter-terrorism policy.... I don't know of any system or entity whose job it was or was given a mandate or was put in charge of dealing with this issue on a strategic level—to think, analyze and propose." However, Shavit believes that Israel has had an operational policy, which he places at a higher level than the tactical level. Meir Dagan—"In my opinion, Israel, as with many other spheres, never had a written doctrine on this issue.... The reason there was never a written doctrine is not technical.... People did not want to confine themselves to limitations that would not stand the test of reality." Yitzhak Shamir cautions against having a written counter-terrorism policy when he states that, "We must be careful of doctrines in general. Not everything needs to have a doctrine." Shimon Peres, on the other hand, stresses the point that Israel needs a counter-terrorism policy based on an arrangement with the Arabs. According to Peres, "During my term of office it was very clear that I thought we needed to reach an agreement either with the Jordanians or the Palestinians so they could fight terrorism."

Despite the consensus regarding the lack of a written and structured counter-terrorism strategy, some of those asked believe that throughout its history various Israeli governments did have several underlying principles that represented the positions of the decision makers and policymakers at that time. Yaakov Perry defines this as the "oral law." But an oral law or doctrine may be problematic because since terrorism is a means for achieving political aims, the oral doctrine tends to follow the political world view of the nation's leader, and this inclination is likely to make the job of thwarting terrorism more difficult.

An example of the slant of an oral counter-terrorism doctrine can be seen from Yitzhak Rabin's attitude between 1993 and 1995, when he stated that Israel should fight terrorism as if there were no peace process, and make peace as if there was no terrorism. Carmi Gilon commented on this policy by saying, "It was a working guideline, if you like, but for me, the practical translation of this was Doctor Jekyll and Mr. Hyde." Shlomo Gazit is also critical of Rabin's attitude, stating that this was actually a return to Ben-Gurion's formula towards the British during World War II. Gazit doubts the relevance of such a policy during Rabin's period, just as it was not actually implemented during Ben-Gurion's time ("It's a nice formula but I don't know how correct it was in Ben-Gurion's day. He didn't fight the White Paper beginning in September 1939, in spite of what he said").

When asked to give an example of the underlying principles that typify Israel's counter-terrorism policy throughout the years, some of those interviewed returned to the example of individual offensive action—"targeted killing."[495] But this only illustrates the extent to which Israeli thinking is focused primarily on attempting to find operational methods that will be more effective ad hoc and will help achieve the goal of limiting terrorism and reducing its damage in the present.

From the above it appears that despite the relatively extensive scope of terrorist attacks perpetrated against Israel over the years, Israeli governments have not been able to develop a formal strategy for coping with terrorism. The nation's method has been an admixture of operational measures implemented by virtue of the inspiration of charismatic decision makers who have led the political or security system. These actions were carried out either with the instructions or the approval of the Israeli government, and were usually decided in response to the impact of mass-victim terrorist attacks perpetrated in Israel at a particular time.

Government outcomes in this domain were influenced by inputs from several factors (see Figure S.1): the attitude of security agencies regarding the necessary and recommended steps (IDF, ISA, Israel Police and occasionally the Mossad, and the prime minister's advisor on counter-terrorism or the head of the Counter-Terrorism Bureau); the attitude of various ministers, particularly the defense minister and minister of internal security; and above all—the personal attitude of the prime minister. As stated, government outputs in the counter-terrorism domain are not an operational interpretation of a formal counter-terrorism policy, but rather an attempt to offer a temporary solution to the influences, attitudes, and pressures in the domestic arena (attitudes of pressure groups, the opposition, public opinion and the media with regard to the security situation, the scope and nature of terrorism, the political atmosphere in the nation) and the international arena (in the Israeli case—the relationship between the Israelis and the Palestinians both before and after the signing of the Oslo Accords, Israel's relationship with Arab nations, and its relationship with the rest of the world, especially the United States).

When the policymakers interviewed for this book were asked about their assessment, in retrospect, of the effectiveness of Israel's counter-terrorism measures, the vast majority responded that it would be impossible to point to sweeping achievements of this policy, although in certain areas Israel made significant progress. Rafi Eitan, for example, claims that Israel's political and offensive activity did

Figure S.1
Factors that Influence the Israeli Government in Counter-Terrorism

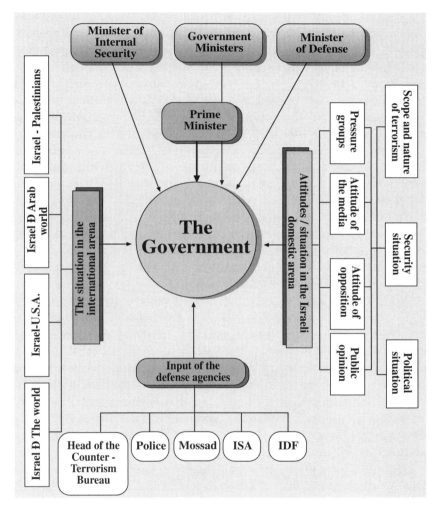

not yield significant results, but its defensive action proved itself. According to Eitan, "The defensive system was always extraordinarily successful. Israel's defensive system is still a success." Shabtai Shavit believes that "Israel has partially achieved its goals." According to him, the question that should be asked is not whether Israeli actions were effective, but rather was there another method

that wasn't attempted, and to this he replies, "The answer as to
whether the policy was correct or incorrect is—there was no other
way. How do you respond to terrorism—should you give in to it?
When you have finally reached the thousandth level of terrorism
do you say, 'I'm ready to give you a Palestinian state, just stop
terrorism'?" Meir Amit believes that Israel's actions to combat terrorism were successful in the main, although not absolutely. Amit
feels that even if terrorism had an influence on political steps, that
influence was "in the realm of the flexibility of counter-measures." Ariel Sharon sums up and states that Israel's counter-
terrorism actions were a success, albeit limited. According to
him, there were "successes for periods of time, breathing space
for certain periods of time." Among the successes that Sharon
mentions he includes the removal of the PLO's military forces
from Lebanon in 1982, and the elimination of *fedayeen* action during the Sinai Campaign. Sharon highlights in this context that with
regard to counter-terrorism activity, "you always have to examine
what would have happened had you not done it. This is a hypo-
thetical question that must be answered."

No one questions the fact that Israel's counter-terrorism activity
has not eliminated terrorism, but was that, indeed, its goal? The
answer to this question would appear to be "no." Israel's goal in
coping with terrorism, during most years of its existence, was not to
eliminate this phenomenon but to limit the scope of the attacks and
minimize their damage. In these terms it would appear that Israel's
counter-terrorism did, in fact, achieve its objective. Israeli security
agencies, led by the intelligence community, have foiled thousands
of terrorist attacks throughout the years and prevented damage to
strategic Israeli interests.

The most prominent disappointment of Israel's counter-terrorism activities has been the failure to understand the phenomenon as
morale-psychological warfare. And consequently, no tools have
been developed to neutralize or, at least, to reduce the morale damage caused by terrorism, and almost no morale-psychological considerations are taken into account in choosing the counter-terrorism
actions Israel undertakes. These types of considerations have been
rejected out of hand with the argument that they are merely political populism,[496] and that the boomerang effect would counteract
the morale success of any effective counter-terrorism measures.[497]

However, despite the difficulty in assessing in advance the influence of any operational step on morale, such an assessment is a fact of reality. Without it, the nation may continue to win numerous battles against terrorism, but ultimately lose the war.

A series of recommendations and principles can be formulated in view of the counter-terrorism dilemmas presented in this volume that should be applied in order to make any nation's counter-terrorism policy more effective:

- *Terrorism as a strategic threat*—Recognizing the strategic significance of the threat of terrorism, and its ability to influence political processes and attitudes. The characteristics of the radical Islamic terrorism network presently deployed throughout the entire world—that these terrorists are professionals in the tactics of terrorism and guerrilla warfare; their motives, as reflected in their radical religious ideology and their belief in God's command to disseminate their version of religion throughout the world using aggressive means; their willingness to die during an attack; and the realistic possibility that they would employ unconventional means in these attacks—make international terrorism the most serious strategic threat to global peace and safety of the world.

- *Goals of counter-terrorism*—The world's nations must define two levels of involvement in coping with terrorism—domestic and international. On the international level, every nation must contribute its share, to the best of its ability, to the international effort to eliminate terrorism in general, and radical Islamic terrorism in particular. Every nation must change its balance of interests and place counter-terrorism above any other economic-political interest. On the domestic level, decision makers of the targeted nation must define counter-terrorism goals on the basis of the scope and nature of the terrorist acts being perpetrated against it. The country must employ firm measures against any attempts at terrorist organization, which includes support and assistance to terrorists on its territory even if they had no intention of perpetrating terrorist acts in that country, but rather in preparation for an attack against another nation; and against the terrorist organization's ongoing administration.

- *Scope of resources allocated to fighting terrorism*—Counter-terrorism efforts must receive resources that correspond with the scope and impact of the threat, in relation to and compared with other challenges, tasks, and threats facing the nation. In this regard, it should be recalled that over-spending on counter-terrorism at the expense of the government's other responsibilities will play into the hands of the terrorists.

- *Neutralizing the terrorism strategy*—Recognizing the different components of the terrorists' strategy and acting to minimize and neutralize terrorism damage with regard to each component: The media—striving for professional, fair, and responsible media coverage of terrorism-related events, such that it does not help the terrorists achieve their morale-psychological aims; public opinion—extensive educational-informational activities should be carried out in order to reduce the anxiety levels concerning terrorism and to strengthen the public's ability to cope; decision makers—limiting as much as possible the political outcomes that are the result of repeated terrorist attacks, and formulating a charter that will outline the desired behaviors of politicians during a terrorist incident.

- *Combining military counter-terrorism measures with political activity*—The military component should not be ruled out as a legitimate and effective means for thwarting terrorist attacks, minimizing their damage, and destroying terrorist organizations. The nation must find the proper balance between constant military-offensive action against terrorist organizations and activity to counteract the motivation of the population that the terrorist organization claims to represent. However, at the same time, nations need to examine the terrorists' demands, the degree to which they are reasonable and legitimate, the extent of the damage to the nation's vital interests if they are realized, and the chance for reaching a compromise solution that is acceptable to both sides. Concomitantly, the nation's ability to prevent terrorist organizations from achieving their goals over the long term must be assessed.

- *Political solution*—The state must avoid allowing terrorist organizations to achieve political success, but whenever negotiations are held in order to reach a political solution, it must be established that negotiations are to be conducted only with those who are not involved in terrorism, and only after terrorism against the nation stops, or concomitantly.[498]

- *Rationality of the terrorist organization*—In general, terrorist organizations should be considered as rational organizations that make cost-benefit calculations, and because of this one can influence their policies and activities.

- *Deterring terrorist organizations*—Given that terrorist organizations are rational, the use of deterrent methods and means is relevant and applicable. However, we must carefully consider the organization's characteristics and match it to the type of deterrent used, the deterrent message being sent, and how this is to be achieved. Furthermore, the nation must examine its ability and willingness to pay the price in case the organization crosses a "red line," as well as the image and impression the terrorist organization has of the nation's capability and determination.

- *Importance of the intelligence component*—It should be clear that the first and primary component of a counter-terrorist policy is intelligence gathering. Accordingly, the nation must invest the resources necessary to gather and process basic intelligence data and tactical intelligence regarding terrorist organizations, if necessary, even at the expense of resources allocated to other components of the war against terrorism.*Actively fighting terrorism*—Nations should not be passive with regard to counter-terrorism. Nations combating terrorism should include an applied offensive component on the basis of optimal conditions for implementing such actions, and not necessarily against the background of terrorist incidents that have taken place.

- *Timing of counter-terrorism activity*—The nation should not be dragged into carrying out counter-terrorism measures specifically following severe attacks. However, nor should morale-psychological considerations be rejected out of hand, in the context of weighing and assessing the advantages and disadvantages of a planned counter-terrorism operation.

- *The boomerang effect*—Nations should not ignore the boomerang effect, which may be the result of carrying out effective counter-terrorism actions. But when assessing the possibility of such a response, the nation should differentiate between organizations for which the main factor limiting their operations is their operational capability (in such cases, despite their desire for vengeance due to the nation's operational action, they will be unable to act on their motivation); and between organizations whose operational capability is greater than their motivation (in which case, we may expect the boomerang effect). Even in cases where the leadership believes that action directed towards the terrorist organization might result in a boomerang effect, such action should not be rejected. The advantages of carrying out any operation should be weighed against the potential damage.

- *Selecting means and objectives within the context of counter-terrorism measures*—In an offensive action, the means used and the attack objective should be carefully examined. The people responsible for terrorism must be located on a local, regional, and organizational level, as well as perpetrators and their associates—individuals, communities, and nations—and they should be punished directly taking care to avoid collateral damage to innocents.

- *Defensive-security actions*—Security measures are the last link in the chain of eliminating terrorism, but when other counter-terrorism components have failed, they become essential. Since security measures require the extensive enlistment of manpower a security network should be based—at least in part—on volunteer recruits who provide back-up for the regular forces during times of heightened tension. Volunteers who take part in a counter-terrorism network can also contribute, among other things, to boosting public morale.

- *Limiting the ethical damage from coping with terrorism*— Making certain that counter-terrorism measures are implemented only within the context of the law of the land and in a manner that corresponds with liberal-democratic values. Any action that contradicts these will play into the hands of the terrorists and legitimize their use of violence. Nevertheless, one must strive towards flexibility and creativity when implementing counter-terrorism measures, and to change and adapt them as circumstances shift vis-à-vis the scope and nature of terrorist attacks. When emergency legislation is required to allow for unusual measures, such legislation should be limited in advance to a specific period of time, its relevant activities should be subject to judicial review, and there should be public-parliamentary supervision.

- *Collective punishment*—Collective punishment should be avoided to the extent possible so that people who are not involved in terrorism, or those who may be "straddling the fence," are not pushed into the cycle of violence. However, in cases where effective counter-terrorism measures conflict with concerns regarding the welfare of populations supporting terrorism, preference should be given to concrete preventive and deterrent measures while limiting the collateral damage from such action as much as possible.[499]

- *Trial procedures and methods for interrogating suspected terrorists*—The rights of suspected terrorists must be protected. Nonetheless, because of the special nature of terrorism and the unique risk to modern society and the democratic state, one cannot reject the option of having special trial procedures and interrogation methods to be used only against those suspected of involvement in terrorism, especially those defined as "ticking bombs" (people who have information that is relevant to preventing concrete future attacks). Notwithstanding the above, even in such cases one must be sure that these special arrangements do not cause significant damage to the suspect. Interrogations must be conducted so as take extra care regarding specified procedures, in accordance with special and individual authorizations on a case-by-case basis, under independent judicial supervision and using overt or covert control methods (video cameras, for example).

- *Defining terrorism*—Expanding the basis for international consensus regarding the struggle against terrorism, and involving as many nations as possible in international charters that prohibit terrorist activity or aiding such activity, are essential for effective international counter-terrorism. For this purpose, there is a need to reach an accepted international definition of terrorism, which distinguishes between the different aims terrorist organizations strive to achieve and the illegitimate violent means they employ. It is necessary to attain international agreement that no aim, no matter how defensible it may be, can justify terrorism.
- *Assessing the effectiveness of counter-terrorism measures*— In conclusion, there is a need to develop advanced qualitative and quantitative indices to examine the effectiveness of various counter-terrorism measures. One can then weigh and assess each planned counter-terror step and ascertain that the advantages of employing that measure outweigh the potential damage.

In summary, the phenomenon of terrorism has spread, turning it into a greater danger to the well-being of all the world's inhabitants. More and more nations are finding themselves victims of this type of violence, and decision makers in the political, security, and commercial spheres are forced to address this problem as part of their system of considerations and decisions. Yet these decisions are often made as an immediate response to terrorist attacks and influenced by public pressure, rather than after an in-depth calculation examining the costs and benefits and based on past experience of that nation, and others.

The dilemmas presented in this book in the various counter-terrorism domains (see Figure S.2) and the models presented for solving these dilemmas are based on Israel's counter-terrorism experience and are aimed at serving as a theoretical basis—and in the future, perhaps even an empirical basis—for assessing and considering the efficacy of counter-terrorism measures, and for making the most reasoned, effective counter-terrorism decisions.

Figure S.2
Decision-Making Dilemmas in the War on Terrorism

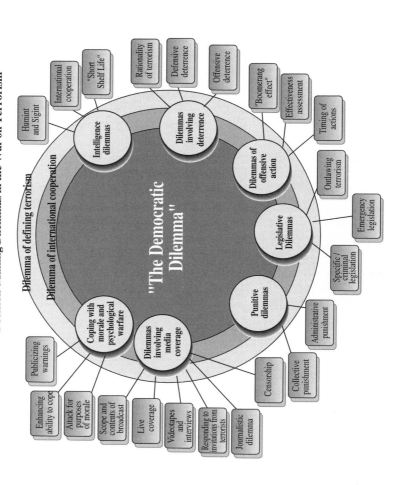

Notes

Chapter 1

1. This was true regarding the Hizballah Movement when it began its relationship with Iran, and with regard to the Palestinian Islamic Jihad Organization and its relationship to the same country.
2. *Ha'aretz*, June 19, 1988.
3. Walter Laquer, *The Age of Terrorism,* Little Brown and Co., Boston, 1987, p. 146.
4. *Yediot Aharonot*, August 18, 1987.
5. *Ha'aretz*, October 22, 1987.
6. http://www.unis.unvienna.org/en/news/2002/pressrels/12989e.htm.
7. Brian M. Jenkins, "Foreword," in Ian O. Lesser, Bruce Hoffman et al., *Countering the New Terrorism.* RAND Project Air Force, 1999, p. *xii.*
8. One of Barzilai's weightier arguments is that the determination that a group of people is a terrorist organization removes, in effect, the basis underlying a serious and considered discussion of its demands and claims (in: Gad Barzilai, "Center vs. Periphery: Rules for 'Preventing Terrorism' as Politics," *Criminal Cases (Pelilim), 8,* 2000, p. 247.) This argument brings us back to the traditional issue of defining terrorism. If terrorism is "the deliberate use of violence against civilians to achieve political aims," we can look positively upon a country's claim that any meaningful discussion regarding the demands of a group using terrorist methods is contingent upon the organization no longer using terrorism (though, not necessarily, violence) in order to promote its interests. Consistently asserting this principle is likely to motivate some terrorist organizations to refrain from using terrorist methods and focus their activities on other, non-violent spheres, or at least to stop directing violence at civilians.
9. Michal Tzur (under the guidance of Professor Mordechai Kremnitzer), *(Emergency) Defense Regulations 1945*, Position Paper No. 16, Israel Democracy Institute, Jerusalem, October 1999, pp. 22, 89.
10. Ibid., p. 89.
11. HCJ 6026/94 *Abd al-Rahim Hassan Nazal et al. v. Commander of the IDF Force in Judea and Samaria,* Verdict No. 338(5).
12. Ehud Sprinzak, "The Psychopolitical Formation of Extreme Left Terrorism in Democracy: The Case of the Weathermen," in Walter Reich (Ed.), *Origins of Terrorism*, Woodrow Wilson Center Press, 1998, p. 78.
13. Martha Crenshaw, "The Counter-Terrorism and Terrorism Dynamic," in Alan Thompson (Ed.), *Terrorism and the 2000 Olympics*, Australian Defence Studies Center, 1996, p. 125.
14. Abu Iyad, *Without a Homeland: Conversations with Arik Rouleau*, Mifras Publications, Tel Aviv, 1983, p. 146.

15. *Hatzav*, November 25, 1986, p. 5. (Originally in *Tishrin*, Syria, November 17, 1986).
16. *Terrorism—The Islamic Point of View.*" Published by the Muslim World League— Secretary-General Makkah al Mukarramah, distributed by the NGO Conference held in Durban, South Africa, 2001.
17. *Hatzav*, February 11, 1987, p. 18. (Originally in *Al-Anba'a*, Kuwait, January 30, 1987.)
18. Ray S. Cline and Yonah Alexander, *Terrorism as State-Sponsored Covert Warfare*, Hero Books, Fairfax, VA, 1986, p. 24.
19. George P. Schultz, "The Challenge to Democratic Nations," in Benjamin Netanyahu (Ed.), *Terrorism—How the West Can Win*, Ma'ariv Library Publications, 1997, p. 18.
20. Benzion Netanyahu, "Terrorists and Freedom-Fighters," in Benjamin Netanyahu (Ed.), ibid., pp. 27-29.
21. Jenny Hocking, "Orthodox Theories of 'Terrorism': The Power of Politicized Terminology," *Politics, Australian Political Studies Association Journal 19(2)*, 1984, p. 109.
22. Benjamin Netanyahu, "Defining Terrorism," in Benjamin Netanyahu (Ed.), supra note 19, p. 9.
23. Benjamin Netanyahu, *Fighting Terrorism: How Democracies Can Defeat Domestic and International Terrorism, Yediot Aharonot*, Tel Aviv, 1996, p. 8.
24. Abu Iyad, supra note 14, pp. 78, 155-156.
25. Albert J. Jongman and Alex P. Schmid, *Political Terrorism.* SWIDOC, Amsterdam and Transaction Publishers, New Brunswick, NJ, 1983, p. 5.
26. Ibid., pp. 29-30.
27. *Ha'aretz*, May 5, 1989 (translation from the Hebrew edition).
28. Michael Stohl and Raymond D. Duvall, cited in *Political Terrorism,* supra note 25, p. 100.
29. Yehoshafat Harkabi, *On Guerrilla Warfare*, Ma'arachot Publishers, Tel Aviv, 1983, p. 27.
30. Ibid., p. 16.
31. Ibid., p. 28.
32. Thomas P. Thornton, cited in *Political Terrorism*, supra note 25, p. 41.
33. Laquer, supra note 3, p. 147.
34. Taken from Professor Sprinzak's remarks at a seminar on "Israel and Terrorism" held under the auspices of the International Center for Contemporary Social Research, Jerusalem, 1985.
35. David Rapoport, cited in *Political Terrorism*, supra note 25, p. 44.

Chapter 2

36. Personal interview with former Prime Minister Yitzhak Shamir, November 18, 1996; personal interview with former Prime Minister Shimon Peres, December 7, 1999.
37. Personal interview with Meir Dagan, former head of the Counter-Terrorism Bureau (and presently, head of the Mossad), December 2, 1999; personal interview with Rechavam Ze'evi, former advisor to the prime minister on counter-terrorism, November 25, 1999; personal interview with Rafi Eitan, former advisor to the prime minister on counter-terrorism, October 30, 1999.
38. Personal interview with Yaakov Perry, former head of the Israel Security Agency, November 28, 1999.

39. Later on in the interview, Shavit explained that an aggressive military solution to terrorism requires that all signs of the enemy's presence in the disputed territory be completely destroyed.
40. Ibid., interview with Shavit.
41. Personal interview with Amnon Lipkin-Shahak, former chief of staff, December 23, 1999.
42. Benjamin Netanyahu, supra note 23, p. 9.
43. B. Pollack and G. Hunter, "Dictatorship, Democracy and Terrorism in Spain," in Juliet Lodge (Ed.), *The Threat of Terrorism*, Wheatsheaf Books, Great Britain, 1988, p. 130.
44. Michel Wieviorka, "French Politics and Strategy on Terrorism," in Barry Rubin (Ed.), *The Politics of Counter-Terrorism: The Ordeal of Democratic States.* School of Advanced International Studies, Washington, DC, 1990, pp. 68, 70.
45. John W. Soule, "Problems in Applying Counter-terrorism to Prevent Terrorism: Two Decades of Violence in Northern Ireland Reconsidered." *Terrorism: An International Journal, 12(1)*, 1989, p. 32.
46. Aharon Yariv, "Countering Palestinian Terrorism," in Ariel Merari (Ed.): *On Terrorism and Combating Terrorism.* University Publications of America, Inc., 1985, pp. 3-4.
47. Interview with Rafi Eitan, supra note 37.
48. Carmi Gilon, *The Israel Security Agency Between the Cracks.* Yediot Aharonot Publications, Tel Aviv, 2000, p. 191.
49. Personal interview with former Prime Minister Benjamin Netanyahu, conducted on December 20, 1999.
50. Crenshaw, supra note 13, p. 124.

Chapter 3

51. David A. Charters, "Counter-Terrorism Intelligence: Sources, Methods, Process and Problems," in David A. Charters (Ed.), *Democratic Responses to International Terrorism*, Transnational Publishers, Inc., New York, 1991, p. 227.
52. Alex P. Schmid, "Terrorism and Democracy," in Alex P. Schmid and Ronald D. Crelinsten (Eds.), *Terrorism and Political Violence.* Frank Cass, London, 1993, p.14.
53. Ken G. Robertson, "Intelligence, Terrorism and Civil Liberties," in Paul Wilkinson and Stewart M. Alasdair (Eds.), *Contemporary Research on Terrorism*, Aberdeen University Press, 1987, p. 555.
54. Charters, supra note 51, pp. 230-233.
55. Allan Behm, "Prevention and Response: How to Get the Mix Right," in Alan Thompson (Ed.), *Terrorism and the 2000 Olympics*, Australian Defense Studies Center, 1996, p. 69.
56. Martha Crenshaw, "Terrorism—What Should We Do?" in Steven Anzovin (Ed.), *Terrorism: The Reference Shelf, 58(3)*, p. 168.
57. Interview with Shavit, supra note 39.
58. Bruce Hoffman and Jennifer Morrison-Taw, *A Strategic Framework for Countering Terrorism and Insurgency*, A Rand Note prepared for the U.S. Department of State, Santa Monica, 1992; George Carver, "Tough Choices Terrorists Force Us to Make," in Yonah Alexander and James Denton (Eds.), *Governmental Responses to Terrorism*, Hero Books, 1986, p. 36.
59. *Ma'ariv*, March 31, 1996, p. 3.
60. Interview with Dagan, supra note 37.
61. *Ha'aretz,* January 24, 1995.

62. *Ha'aretz,* September 13, 1995.
63. *Ma'ariv,* February 8, 1995.
64. *Ma'ariv,* September 1, 1994.
65. This was the case in August 1994, when Israel gave accurate information to the Palestinians concerning the perpetrators of the double murder at the construction site in Ramle (*Ma'ariv,* August 29, 1994); and in February 1995 as well when Israel found out about intentions of the Hamas and Palestinian Islamic Jihad to send a car-bomb from Jericho in order to carry out an attack in Jerusalem (*Ma'ariv,* February 5, 1995).
66. *Yediot Aharonot,* January 27, 1995.
67. *Yediot Aharonot,* September 8, 1995.
68. *Yediot Aharonot,* April 12, 1995.
69. In early September 1995, Daniel Frey was murdered in Ma'ale Michmas, and his pregnant wife was seriously injured, by a terrorist who wanted to clear himself from the accusation of "collaborating" with Israel (*Yediot Aharonot,* September 7, 1995).
70. Personal interview with Carmi Gilon, former head of the ISA, conducted on November 24, 1999.
71. *Yediot Aharonot,* September 8, 1995.
72. *Yediot Aharonot,* November 17, 1994.
73. *Ma'ariv*, September 22, 1995.
74. Ian O. Lesser, Bruce Hoffman et at., *Countering the New Terrorism*, RAND—Project Air Force, 1999, p. 126.
75. Crenshaw, supra note 13, p. 128.
76. Hoffman and Morrison-Taw, supra note 58, pp. 2, 4, 29.
77. Paul Wilkinson, "British Policy on Terrorism: An Assessment," in *The Threat of Terrorism*, Wheatsheaf Books, Great Britain, 1988, p. 52.
78. Virender Uberoy, *Combating Terrorism.* Intellectual Books Corner PVT, Ltd., New Delhi, 1992, pp. 118-120.
79. Allan Behm, supra note 55, pp. 78-79.
80. Interview with Netanyahu, supra note 49.
81. Ibid.
82. Interview with Perry, supra note 38.
83. Interview with Dagan, supra note 37.
84. Interview with Shimon Peres by Hemi Shalev, *Ma'ariv,* May 12, 1995, Weekend Supplement, p. 5.

Chapter 4

85. Yehudah Wallach, *Military Theories and their Development in the 19th and 20th Centuries*, Ma'arachot—Ministry of Defense Publications, 3rd Edition, 1980, pp. 331,334.
86. Yehezkel Dror, *Grand-Strategies for Israel*, Akademon, Jerusalem 1989, p. 132.
87. Lesser, Hoffman, et al., supra note 74, pp. 129-130.
88. Dror, supra note 86, pp. 132, 133.
89. Crenshaw, supra note 56, pp. 170.
90. Jessica Stern, *The Ultimate Terrorism*, Harvard University Press, Boston, 1999, pp. 130-131.
91. Aryeh Shalev said that deportation has a dual purpose: to deter others from provocation and agitation, and to mitigate the damage caused by the deportees (Aryeh Shalev, *Ha'aretz*, April 12, 1988, p. 2).
92. *Ma'ariv*, April 24, 2002.
93. *Ma'ariv*, June 24, 2002.
94. *Yediot Aharonot*, October 6, 2002.

95. Shmuel Gordon, "The Vulture and the Snake: Counter-Guerrilla Air Warfare—The War in Southern Lebanon," *Mideast Security and Policy Studies, 39*, p. 22. Bar Ilan University, Begin-Sadat Center for Strategic Studies, 1998.

96. *Ma'ariv*, April 24, 2002.

97. *Ma'ariv*, October 21, 1994, p. 7.

98. Interview with Gilon, supra note 70.

99. Interview with Shavit, supra note 39.

100. Interview with Dagan, supra note 37.

101. Interview with Peres, supra note 36.

102. Interview with Perry, supra note 38.

103. Cline and Alexander, Terrorism as State Sponsored Covert Warfare, supra note 18, p. 1.

104. U.S. Department of State, *Patterns of Global Terrorism—Overview of State Sponsored Terrorism 2003,* April 29, 2004.

105. U.S. Department of State, *Patterns of Global Terrorism, 2001*, May 2002, p. 63.

106. Yehezkel Dror, *Crazy State—Fanaticism and Terrorism as a Security Problem*, Tel Aviv: Ma'arachot (1974), pp. 125-126.

107. The law, which was ratified unanimously by the U.S. Congress in July 1996, was aimed at imposing damages on foreign companies that invested more than $40 million per year in the oil, gas or petrochemical industries in Iran or Libya. The D'Amato Act obligated the president, among other things, to block the importation of products from these companies into the United States, to prevent the approval of loans exceeding $10 million per year from American financial institutions, and to prohibit American government bodies from purchasing goods from those companies. The law also called upon the president to work with America's allies in order to reach multilateral agreements prohibiting trade and investment in Iran and Libya because of their support for terrorism. (The law was passed in light of a law that prohibited American companies from trading with Libya and Iran, and following ratification of a similar law—the Helms Burton Act—against Cuba.)

"The time has come to take real steps against states that support terrorism. Now the nations of the world will know they have the choice of trading with Iran and Libya, or trading with the United States. They will have to choose." (*Ha'aretz*, July 25, 1996, translation from the Hebrew edition).

The D'Amato Act soon angered the European nations. Words of protest and even threats to retaliate against the United States were heard in various European capitals. An official statement issued by the French Ministry of Foreign Affairs stated that the American law was a gross violation of international trade laws and that France, like its other European partners, would not obey such dictates. "We will take our own steps in retaliation if this law is implemented," said the French Foreign Ministry spokesperson.

Klaus Kinkel, the German foreign minister announced that "the American law and its plans defy the fundamental principles of the International Trade Organization and the Organization for Economic Cooperation and Development, and we hereby state that we will not accept them" (*Ha'aretz*, August 7, 1996).

Not only did the American initiative meet with opposition in Europe. The Japanese government expressed its regret at the ratification of the law, and called upon the United States to reconsider its position. A spokesman for the Foreign Ministry in Tokyo stressed that the law defined rules that apply outside the U.S. jurisdiction, and could jeopardize international trade agreements. Tim Fischer, the Australian minister of trade, announced that his country would take all steps necessary to oppose implementation of the American law. According to him, Australia severely condemns terrorism but "the imposition of sanctions against innocent companies and nations is an erroneous principle, and is liable to jeopardize Australian trade" (*Ha'aretz*, August 8, 1996). The spokesman for the Chinese Foreign Ministry added that "the steps taken by the United States are not compatible with regulations governing international relations, and will solve nothing. No one can systematically use sanctions pressure to solve this type of problem" (*Ha'aretz*, August 8, 1996). Vladimir Andreyev, spokesman for the Russian Foreign Ministry, stated "we need practical steps in order to enhance international cooperation against terrorism, but not unilateral steps that are illegal" (*Ha'aretz,* August 8, 1996).

The claim that the D'Amato Act jeopardized international agreements and trade regulations was not unfounded. The law was, in fact, a secondary embargo on economic companies and therefore jeopardized free international commerce by introducing considerations that could be defined as political, in determining trade procedures. But the law reflected a genuine and more crucial international need. The law aimed at closing the loophole that had allowed companies to bypass international sanctions and embargos that were imposed on states supporting terrorism. Without punishing those who defied international sanctions, they could not be enforced.

The fact that the law could hurt international trade agreements does not derogate from its validity or importance, but only demonstrates the urgent need to amend the trade agreements so they would concur with such a law. The trade agreements had been signed during a time when the degree to which international terrorism would endanger world peace and the safety of the world's citizens could not foreseen. The trade agreements must provide an effective way for combating states supporters of terrorism. The agreements were aimed at regulating international economics, and counter-terrorism measures were aimed at ensuring the safety of the international community.

If any criticism of the D'Amato Act is appropriate, it should actually focus on the high bar set for its implementation—as stated, the law required the imposition of sanctions only against companies that invested more than $40 million per year in Iran and Libya. This sum still left companies too much leeway to continue investing in these countries and maintain extensive economic relationships.

In any case, encouraged by the widespread international support in Iran and criticism aimed at the United States regarding the D'Amato Act, the Iranian oil minister announced that the sanctions would have no effect on his country's oil production. "The petroleum industry has never been in a better position, and I have no doubts about the future," (*Ha'aretz,* August 8, 1996). Ali Akbar Velayati, the Iranian foreign minister, added that his country "was not afraid of the American sanctions, which would have no impact at all on Iran's economic situation," (ibid.). Iran even filed a complaint against the United States with the International Court of Justice in the Hague, and asked the court to approve preventive measures that would keep the United States from implementing the law.

108. *Ha'aretz,* August 6, 1996 (translation from the Hebrew edition).
109. *Ha'aretz,* April 15, 1992.
110. *Ha'aretz,* March 23, 1992 (translation from the Hebrew edition).
111. *Ha'aretz,* May 1, 1992 (translation from the Hebrew edition).
112. *Yediot Aharonot,* October 30, 1986.
113. *Ma'ariv,* October 29, 1986 (translation from the Hebrew edition).
114. *Ha'aretz,* April 1, 1992.
115. U.S. Department of State, "International Community Action Against Terrorism," *Patterns of Global Terrorism 1993*, Department of State Publication No. 10316.
116. *Ha'aretz,* August 24, 1989(translation from the Hebrew edition).

117. *Ma'ariv,* October 29, 1986 (translation from the Hebrew edition).
118. Thus, for example, the United States asked Germany to contact Iran regarding the release of American citizens captured in Lebanon during the 1980s, and Israel asked Germany to make use of its good terms with Iran to help with the return of Israeli MIAs from the Lebanese war and the release of captured navigator Ron Arad. Germany also served as a mediator between Hizballah, Iran, and Israel in the prisoner exchange that took place in 2004. Such requests are liable to be used by nations using a critical dialogue policy as justification of their policy.
119. *Ha'aretz,* August 6, 1996 (translation from the Hebrew edition).
120. Researcher Michael Eisenstadt of the Washington Near East Policy Institute, found that economic sanctions imposed by the United States against Iran succeeded in damaging Teheran's ability to become the dominant military force in the Persian Gulf, and delayed its plans for purchasing nuclear weapons (in "The American Sanctions Hurt Iran's Plans for Nuclear Arms" by Yerach Tal, *Ha'aretz,* September 6, 1996, p. 13A).
121. *Ha'aretz,* September 1, 1993.
122. *Davar,* November 2, 1993.
123. *Ha'aretz,* November 3, 1993.
124. Crenshaw, supra note 13, p.126.
125. Israel Tal, *National Security—the Few Versus the Many*, Dvir Publications, 1996, p. 62.
126. Crenshaw, supra note 56, p. 168

Chapter 5

127. Following the death of Palestinian Islamic Jihad activist Hanni Al Abed, it was announced that "the Palestinian Islamic Jihad in the Gaza Strip was planning to explode a car bomb in Israel. Planning for this attack was in the final stages. Hanni Al Abed, the senior-level Palestinian Islamic Jihad activist murdered when his car blew up, was one of the planners of this attack.... Abed, a chemist by profession, was supposed to plan the placement of the car and to put together the charges that were to be placed in the car. According to these sources, Hanni had planned other attacks together with wanted Palestinian Islamic Jihad activists, among others, three shooting attacks in the Gush Katif region." (*Ha'aretz,* November 4, 1994, p. 1.)
128. *Ha'aretz,* February 17, 1992, p. A-2.
129. *Yediot Aharonot,* April 20, 1988, p. 2.
130. *Ma'ariv,* October 10, 1995, p. 3.
131. *Ma'ariv,* April 2, 1996.
132. The claim that a certain individual attack was carried out for improper reasons or out of inappropriate considerations is often heard by the terrorist organizations themselves, and at times, by spokespersons for the opposition, too. Following the assassination of Black September activist Attaf Besiso (in June 1992), Yasser Arafat stated that "a source who has already proven his loyalty many times over" told him that the Israeli Mossad had recently marked several PLO members as targets for assassination prior to Israel's election day. "They even warned me," Arafat added, "that the Mossad could try an attempt on my life, too." A PLO spokesman said that it was "an operation by the Israeli Mossad aimed at supporting [Yitzhak] Shamir's election campaign, and telling the Israeli people, 'Look, we are very strong, we can protect the people in Israel.' In fact, they killed an innocent man who was a supporter of peace" (*Ha'aretz,* June 9, 1992).

An editorial written in Israel following the assassination of Yihye Ayyash ("The Engineer") stated: "The assassination of arch-terrorist Yihye Ayyash came, perhaps at the wrong time in terms of the Palestinians, but it gives Prime Minister Shimon Peres a significant political boost in his home court. Since taking office, Peres's political statements to Syrian President Haffez Assad have had an appeasing tone, not to mention submissive. Now, regardless of who perpetrated the assassination, Peres can add the title of the one who continues to apply Israel's long arm of justice against its enemies. It is important for Peres not to appear in public as a naïve do-gooder. The assassination exposed an iron fist underneath the silk gloves" (*Ma'ariv*, January 7, 1996, p. 4).

Another editorial had this to say: "Many believed the ISA needed the assassination in order to repair its bad image following the Rabin assassination. Others have said that there are those within Israel's intelligence branches who want to damage the Palestinian Authority and the entire peace process" (*Ha'aretz*, January 7, 1996, p. 2).

In another incident, MK Ron Nachman, head of the Ariel Local Council, charged that the kidnapping of Dirani to Israel (in May 1994) stemmed from political motives: "The prime minister is acting as the party chairman. He took advantage of the military operation and said that by withdrawing from Gaza and Jericho we are sending the military to carry out the real missions. As if defending the nation's residents is not a real mission." MK Moshe Peled from Tzomet also made some accusations: "The timing of the kidnapping by the IDF in Lebanon is political, and stems from a desire to distract public opinion from the Prime Minister's failures within his own party, including the Histadrut elections, the failure to implement the Gaza-Jericho agreement, the murder of the soldiers at the Erez roadblock in Gush Katif—all these were an important factor in his decision to order the IDF into action in Lebanon" (*Ma'ariv,* May 23, 1995, p. 5).

133. Shlomo Aharonson and Dan Horowitz, "The Strategy of Controlled Reprisal—The Israeli Example," in *State and Government 1(1)*, 1971, p. 82.

134. Adherents to this school of thought claim that Israel's reprisal policy leads the region towards a vicious cycle of incident-response-incident-response, while restraint on Israel's part is likely to end this cycle. Their suggestion was to replace the reprisal policy with massive preparations and activity by IDF forces all along Israel's borders, in order to prevent infiltrations and reduce the phenomenon (Zachi Shalom, *David Ben-Gurion, the State of Israel and the Arab World, 1949-1956*, Ben-Gurion Heritage Center, Sde Boker, 1995, p. 180).

135. Minister of Defense Pinchas Levon gave expression to this when he said, "I am authorized to state that our responses are deterrent, highly deterrent. They do not lead to counter-reprisals" (ibid., p. 160).

136. Ibid., p. 160.

137. Hanan Alon, *Countering Palestinian Terrorism in Israel: Toward a Policy Analysis of Countermeasures*, RAND, Santa Monica, 1980, p. 142.

138. Ibid., p. 117.

139. *Ha'aretz,* December 15, 1994.

140. *Ha'aretz,* August 23, 2002.

141. Channel 2, June 24, 2003.

142. Round Table Forum, Israel Democracy Institute, November 25, 1997.

143. *Ha'aretz*, June 13, 2003.

144. *Ha'aretz*, October 6, 1997.

145. Neil Livingston and Dudu Halevy, "Up Close to the Left Temple," *Ha'ir,* August 29, 1997, p. 50 (the article was published in the August edition of *Soldier of Fortune* magazine).

146. *Makor Rishon,* Weekly Supplement, October 10, 1997, p. 22. See also "Eliminating Terrorists as Law Enforcement," *Nativ,* June 1997 issue, p. 9.

147. Crenshaw, supra note 13, p. 125.

148. Ariel Merari and Shlomi Elad, *The International Dimension of Palestinian Terrorism,* United Kibbutz Publishers, 1986, p. 118.

149. Ibid., p. 119.

150. Abu Iyad, supra note 14, pp. 166-167.

151. *Ha-Tzofeh,* September 19, 1994.

152. *Ha'aretz,* November 21, 1994.

153. *Ha'aretz,* January 24, 1995.

154. The exchange between Israel and Jordan following the Mashaal incident included four stages: First, Sheikh Yassin was released to Jordan. Two days later, Yassin was transferred from Jordan to Gaza and twenty additional prisoners were released (nine of them, who were Jordanian citizens, were sent to Jordan and the other eleven were sent to the Palestinian Authority). In third stage, eight terrorists and criminals were released to Jordan; and in the fourth stage, the Israeli agents were released.

155. *Ma'ariv,* Yom Kippur, October 10, 1997, pp. 12-13.

156. Interview with Netanyahu, supra note 49.

157. *Yediot Aharonot,* "Seven Days" Weekend Supplement, April 16, 1999, pp. 34-41.

158. According to the report of the Ciechanover Commission, "Perpetrating the act in Jordan was made on the basis of instructions from its planners: (A) The operation's methods must guarantee that Israel's "fingerprints" would not be left on the operation, so that even if it was successful, nobody would be able to point the finger at Israel with certainty.... The possibility that the operation would fail, and the operational and planning significance of such a possibility, were barely even considered by the planners and those in the Mossad who approved the operation. (B) The peaceful relations between Israel and Jordan, and their establishment, was one of the cornerstones of Israel's policy, and even if something were to go wrong, it would not jeopardize the essence of the infrastructure of that relationship.... All the heads of the intelligence community agreed to these underlying assumptions, as did most of the witnesses who appeared before us..." (*Ma'ariv,* February 17, 1998, pp. 2-3).

159. Danny Naveh, *Government Secrets,* Yediot Aharonot Publications, Tel Aviv, 1999, pp. 169-170.

160. *Yediot Aharonot,* "Seven Days" Weekend Supplement, April 16, 1999, pp. 34-41.

161. *Ma'ariv,* February 17, 1998, pp. 2-3.

162. The six members of the committee were: Yossi Sarid from Meretz; Uzi Landau, Benny Begin, and Gideon Ezra of the Likud; and Ori Orr and Ehud Barak from the Labor Party. All of the committee's members were unanimous in their opinion that an exhaustive war must be waged against terrorism, but Yossi Sarid highlighted the fact that individual assassination must be used more selectively (*Ha'aretz,* March 17, 1998, p. 22).

163. *Ma'ariv,* February 16, 1998.

164. *Ha'aretz,* March 17, 1998, p. B-2.

165. *Ha'aretz,* October 5, 1997, p. A-5.

166. *Ma'ariv,* July 24, 1994.

167. *Ma'ariv,* May 28, 1995.

168. Interview with Netanyahu, supra note 49.

169. Interview with Dagan, supra note 37.

170. Interview with Lipkin-Shahak, supra note 41.

171. *Ma'ariv,* December 14, 1995, p. 6.

172. *Ma'ariv,* November 23, 1993, p. 3.

173. *Ha'aretz*, March 5, 1996.
174. *Ha'aretz*, January 15, 1996.
175. Trends in Terrorism—Post September 11, The International Policy Institute for Counter-Terrorism, September 11, 2002, p. 32.
176. Salah Khalaf (Abu Iyad), Arafat's deputy, claimed in June 1990 that Israel had a list of seventeen top PLO activists who were candidates for assassination, and that "the organization had taken steps to prevent the murder of its leaders. Among others, the leadership cut back on their air travel" (*Yediot Aharonot*, June 19, 1990). Abu Iyad also spoke of himself, that "in general, I avoid visiting public places for security reasons" (*Without a Homeland,* supra note 14, p. 170).
177. The most prominent of these in this regard is Yasser Arafat, whose flight plans are kept top secret and prefers to fly via planes provided for his use by friendly Arab countries, so that any damage to them would be considered a direct attack against those countries. Arafat tends to change his flight plans very often, and changes his destinations shortly before these visits take place (*Yediot Aharonot*, April 9, 1992, p. 2). The fear of a direct attack has also forced the organizations to deploy their offices and the homes of their activists in a variety of regions, rather than concentrating everything in one place. Abu Iyad notes, with regard to operation "Spring of Youth" in Beirut (April 1973): "By disregarding the most basic security rules, Hawatme's people concentrated all the administrative, financial and publicity functions in a single, nine-storey building, as well as an important part of the archives" (*Without a Homeland,* supra note 14, p. 169). This building was one of the targets of that campaign.
178. Thus, for example, following the assassination of Abu Jihad it was decided to increase security around senior PLO officials. Instructions were given to all top-level PLO activists coming to Tunis not to stay in hotels, so as not to register with the reception desks, and whenever possible to stay with colleagues in their homes, which were located in the suburbs of Tunis (*Ma'ariv*, June 9, 1992).

   Following the suicide bombing of Bus #5 in Tel Aviv (October 1994), the German newspaper *Bild* stated that activists from Izzadin al-Kassam Brigades, the military wing of Hamas, were afraid of reprisals from Israel, and that they had escaped to Bulgaria. The paper further reported that Mossad assassination teams, known as "Spearhead," had been given the "green light" to find the leaders of the Hamas military branch and kill them, "based on a list located in the safe in the prime minister's office" (*Ma'ariv,* October 25, 1994).

   Following the assassination of Hanni Al Abed, it was reported that senior members of Hamas and the Palestinian Islamic Jihad panicked and spent the night following the assassination outside their homes—some of them slept in their cars and others had found hideouts (*Yediot Aharonot*, November 4, 1994).
179. Another example of the fear of assassination by Israel felt by senior members of Hamas following the attempt on Rantisi's life was the sudden termination of an interview with a top Hamas official. During the interview, which was broadcast directly from the studios of Al-Jazeera television, a senior official was heard to say, "I must cut this interview short now because I can hear helicopters," and ended the interview (*Ha'aretz*, June 13, 2003).
180. June 13, 2003, at www.nfc.co.il.
181. Abu Iyad tells of an exchange with three senior members of Fatah in Beirut, several days before their assassination as part of Operation "Spring of Youth" in April 1973:

   About ten days before the Israeli raid that took the lives of Kamal Nasser, Yussuf al Najjar, and Kamal Adwan, some friends—including these three and Yasser Arafat—

had gathered in Kamal Nasser's apartment. The three of them, who were about to become martyrs of the opposition movement, lived in the same building.... Did I have a premonition about their tragic death? It is quite possible, because when I arrived and I noticed that there were no guards there or any kind of security arrangements, I told them half seriously and half in jest, "You're really taking chances! Soon an Israeli helicopter will land in the vacant lot across the street and kidnap the three of you." The remark was laughed off but Yasser Arafat repeated the topic and seriously advised them to be more careful about their security. They replied that they didn't want to cause any inconvenience for their neighbors by placing guards too prominently around the building (*Without a Homeland*, supra note 14, p. 169).

182. Guy Bechor, *PLO Lexicon*, Ministry of Defense Publications, Tel Aviv, 1991, p. 175.

183. The fears felt by senior activists in the terrorist organization can be seen from this collection of quotations:

Yasser Arafat—In early 1989 Arafat met with a large group of Israeli reporters, and claimed that Prime Minister Shamir and the security services "want to eliminate me. Instead of negotiating and resolving the problem they pursue me everywhere, follow me and photograph me. I even know the code name of the secret plan to assassinate me—'The Best Hit' they called it" (*Yediot Aharonot*, "Seven Days" Weekend Supplement, December 22, 1989). At the end of 1989, Arafat told reporters who had come to interview him at the Andalus Palace in Cairo, "'The Best Hit' was still on the agenda." Arafat also repeated these words on the British television program "Profile" where he announced that Arik Sharon was the one who wanted to assassinate him (ibid.). In December 1992, in an interview with the Hadash Party newspaper *Al-Itihad,* Arafat accused Israel of planning to kill him, and that was why they had been training in Tze'elim where five IDF soldiers had been killed (*Ha'aretz,* December 11, 1992).

Abu Iyad (Salah Khalaf), in his book *Without a Homeland* (see supra note 14), said that "there is no doubt that the Israelis have not abandoned their plans to eliminate the *Fedayeen* leadership, thinking that this way they can destroy the Palestinian National Movement. From this perspective I am certainly still one of their major targets…" (ibid., p. 175). Abu Iyad said about himself that "despite the constant danger for my life, I do not fear death…[nevertheless] the Divine providence that has protected my life up to now does not exempt me from taking minimal security precautions in order to safeguard me and my family…" (ibid., p. 177).

Abu Jihad—Hanan a-Dik, Abu Jihad's daughter, said in an interview: "During the final months of his life my father lived with the feeling that the Israeli's were always on his trail.... He didn't hide his fears from us. He and I had developed a private kind of black humor.... When he would ask me for something and I was lazy he would scold me with a half-smile: do what I am asking you now, in any case soon I won't be around anymore and you'll be able to do what you want. Two weeks before his death I sat with my mother in the living room of our home in Tunis. The television was broadcasting a report on the funeral of an *intifada* martyr. The pictures were very moving and we both burst into tears. Father came into the room and when he saw us crying he remarked: I hope that after they kill me you won't behave like this…" (*Yediot Aharonot,* "Seven Days" Weekend Supplement, April 22, 1994, p. 6).

Abu Jihad's wife, Intissar, tells that when she complained to her husband about his security arrangements on the eve of his assassination, he replied, "I know, but there is no point in doubling the bodyguards so that 'they' won't know that we're 'on to' them. I have a gun and three loyal bodyguards. I trust them.... And besides…they promised me a new weapon to protect myself" (*Yediot Aharonot,* May 20, 1988). A short time after Abu Jihad's assassination, the British newspapers *The Sunday Times* and *The Observer* reported that four days prior to the assassination Arafat had warned his deputy and other PLO activists against assassination. This warning came in light of an article in the Israeli newspaper *Davar,* stating that the prime minister's counter-terrorism advisor, Brig. General Yigal Pressler, had advised Prime Minister Yitzhak Shamir to order selective assassinations against terrorist organization leaders. According to the report in *The Observer,* Arafat had ordered copies of the paper to be distributed in PLO offices worldwide, along with the warning the Israel was planning a campaign against the PLO leadership (*Ma'ariv,* April 24, 1988, p. 2).

Sheikh Hassan Nasrallah, Secretary-General of Hizballah (in an interview with the Saudi weekly *Al Awsat,* published in London, in June 1996): "The IDF commando unit had planned to kidnap me, and after the Lebanese who followed me were caught…the plan came to life…. The Israel plan was to arrive at my house in a caravan of cars (similar to the one in which he traveled) and to surprise the guards with explosions and kill them, penetrate the house, kidnap me and continue towards the closest sea shore and launch a rubber raft to the Israeli war ships waiting nearby" (*Ma'ariv,* April 2, 1996).

Ali Hassan Salame was one of the planners of the attack against the Israeli athletes at the Munich Olympics. Israel tried to kill him in the city of Lillehammer in Norway, in 1973. But due to a misidentification, a waiter named Ahmed Bushiki was killed instead. Ultimately, Salame was killed in Beirut in 1979 (apparently by the Mossad). His wife, Georgina, said that, "Towards the end he was tired. He was sick of running. And like many others from the Middle East, he believed in the power of destiny" (*Yediot Aharonot,* "Seven Days" Weekend Supplement, February 14, 1990, p. 32).

Attaf Besiso, a Fatah leader involved in the slaughter of the athletes in Munich. Yasser Arafat stated after Besiso's death, "I warned him, just as I warned all of our other senior activists, the Israeli Mossad was after him" (*Yediot Aharonot,* June 9, 1992, p. 2).

Reports in the Palestinian and Arab media also indicate that terrorist organizations were fearful that their leaders would be eliminated. The Jordanian newspaper *Al Dustur* published an article in July 1990, in which it quoted Palestinian sources who claimed that Israel had prepared a plan to murder PLO chief Yasser Arafat and other Palestinian leaders. According to the paper, the intelligence services and Israel's defense minister had prepared "a detailed plan for carrying out these attacks, and are merely waiting for 'the green light' from Prime Minister Shamir." The paper quoted the names of other personalities Israel wanted to murder: Mahmoud Abbas (Abu al Abbas)—head of the Palestine Liberation Front; Hakam Balawi—PLO representative in Tunis; Tayeb Abdel Rahim—PLO representative in Amman; and Abbas Zaki—a member of the Fatah Central Committee (*Ma'ariv,* July 10, 1990). It is no wonder that *The Plot to Kill Arafat,* the book written by Mustafa Bakhri (reporter for the Arab weekly *Kol al Arab* in Egypt), became a bestseller in the Arab world. The book describes the Mossad's attempt to poison Arafat at a meal to which he was invited in the Far East. According to the author, the Israeli prime minister has a "special archives" that documents every hour in the lives of the Palestinian organizations' leaders, their customs and movements: "Israel doesn't leave them alone, follows them, photographs them, tapes them and collects every scrap of information (*Yediot Aharonot,* "Seven Days" Weekend Supplement, December 22, 1989). Thus, the book reflects the fundamental belief among the Palestinians and the Arab world that senior activists in the terrorist organizations were under constant surveillance. The question of whether this is true or not is a secondary issue, so long as this is how they feel. In the words of the former deputy director of the ISA, MK Gideon Ezra, "When people fear for their lives, they are worried about themselves—it's a deterrent" (Round Table Forum, Israel Democracy Institute, November 25, 1997).

184. Albert Bandura, "Mechanisms of Moral Disengagement," in Walter Reich (Ed.), *Origins of Terrorism,* Woodrow Wilson Center Press, 1998, p. 169.
185. Crenshaw, supra note 13, pp. 124-125.
186. Personal interview with former Defense Minister Moshe Arens, on November 20, 1996.
187. Personal interview with Prime Minister of Israel, Ariel Sharon, on September 13, 2000 (at that time Member of Knesset).
188. Personal interview with Yigal Pressler, former counter-terrorism advisor to the prime minister, October 31, 1999.
189. Orly Azzoulai-Katz, *The Man Who Couldn't Win,* Yediot Aharonot Publications, Tel Aviv, 1996, p. 238.
190. Uri Savir, *The Process: Behind the Scenes of a Historic Decision,* Yediot Aharonot Publications, Tel Aviv, 1998, 320.
191. Interview with Peres, supra note 36.
192. Savir, supra note 190, p. 318.
193. Interview with Gilon, supra note 70.
194. Gilon, supra note 48, p. 196.
195. Ibid.
196. Interview with Dagan, supra note 37.
197. William V. O'Brien, "Terrorism—What Should We Do?" in Steven Anzovin (Ed.), *Terrorism, The Reference Shelf 58(3),* 1986, p. 155.
198. Crenshaw, supra note 56, p. 168.
199. Behm, supra note 55, p. 67.
200. Charters, supra note 51, p. 159.
201. Carver, supra note 58, p. 36.
202. Peter St. John, "Counter-Terrorism Policy Making: The Case of Aircraft Hijacking, 1968-1988," in Charters, supra note 51, p. 73.
203. Lesser, Hoffman et al., supra note 74, pp. 120-121.
204. Ian S. Lustick, "Terrorism in the Arab-Israeli Conflict: Targets and Audiences," in Martha Crenshaw, (Ed.), *Terrorism in Context,* The Pennsylvania State University Press, 1995, p. 259.
205. Aryeh Avneri, *Reprisal Raids: Twenty Years of Israeli Reprisals Beyond Enemy Lines,* Madim Library, 1970, Vol. 2, p. 384.
206. Merari and Elad, supra note 148, pp. 115,116
207. Ibid.
208. Shmuel Stempler, "Multilateral Struggle Against Terrorism," *Monthly Survey, 10,* 1972, p. 32.
209. Gad Barzilai, *Democracy at War: Controversy and Consensus in Israel,* Poalim Library, National Kibbutz Publications, 1992, p. 152.
210. Ibid.
211. Aryeh Naor, *Begin in Government: A Personal Testimony,* Yediot Aharonot, Tel Aviv, 1993, p. 245.
212. *Yediot Aharonot,* May 8, 1986, p. 18.
213. Christopher Davy, "Managing Risk and Uncertainty: An Approach to Counter-Terrorist Planning," in Alan Thompson (Ed.), *Terrorism and the 2000 Olympics,* Australian Defence Studies Center, 1996, p. 165.

214. Martha Crenshaw, "The Logic of Terrorism: Terrorist Behavior as a Product of Strategic Choice," in Walter Reich, (Ed.), *Origins of Terrorism,* Woodrow Wilson Center Press, 1998, pp. 14-15.
215. Yariv, supra note 46, p. 4.
216. O'Brien, supra note 197, p. 155.
217. Crenshaw, supra note 13, p. 126.
218. Bandura, supra note 184, p. 169.
219. *Ma'ariv,* December 1, 1994.
220. Personal interview with Shlomo Gazit, former head of Military Intelligence, held on November 7, 1999.
221. Interview with Ze'evi, supra note 37.
222. Merari and Elad, supra note 148, p. 118.

Chapter 6

223. William R. Farrell, *The U.S. Government Response to Terrorism: In Search of an Effective Strategy,* Westview Press, Boulder, CO, 1982, p. 119.
224. Yehezkel Dror, "Terrorism as a Challenge for the Striving of Democracies to Govern," *Terrorism, Legitimacy and Power,* Wesleyan University Press, Middletown, CT, 1983, pp. 71, 79, 80.
225. Schmid, supra note 52, p. 17.
226. Ibid., p. 14.
227. Zeev Laquer, "The Ineffectiveness of Terrorism," *Cyclone (1)* 1976, p. 68.
228. Paul Wilkinson, "Terrorism versus Democracy: Anatomy of a Conflict," *Cyclone (1),* 1976, p. 11.
229. Schmid, supra note 52, p. 18.
230. Boaz Ganor, "Terrorism and Public Opinion in Israel," Master's Thesis, Political Science Department, Tel Aviv University, 1990, pp. 57-58.
231. Stansfield Turner, *Terrorism and Democracy,* Houghton Mifflin Company, Boston, 1991, p. 169.
232. Harkabi, supra note 29, p. 29.
233. K. J. Holsti, *International Politics,* Prentice Hall International Inc., London, 1972, pp. 382-384.
234. Asher Arian, "Public Opinion and the Lebanon War," Memorandum No. 15, Jaffe Center for Strategic Studies, Tel Aviv University, October 1985, p. 4.
235. Interview with Pressler, supra note 188.
236. Interview with Rafi Eitan, supra note 37.
237. Interview with Perry, supra note 38.
238. Peter Janke (Ed.), *Terrorism and Democracy: Some Contemporary Cases,* Macmillan, London, 1992, p. 213.
239. Schmid, supra note 52, p. 24.
240. Patrick Clawson, "U.S. Options for Combating Terrorism," in Barry Rubin (Ed.), *The Politics of Counter-Terrorism,* Johns Hopkins Foreign Policy Institute, 1990, p. 28.
241. Schmid, supra note 52, p. 19.
242. John Danforth, "Terrorism versus Democracy," *International Terrorism*, The Jonathan Institute, Jerusalem, 1980, p. 117.
243. Paul Wilkinson, "Terrorism versus Liberal Democracy: The Problems of Response," *Contemporary Terrorism,* Facts on File Publications, New York, 1986, p. 17.
244. Crenshaw, supra note 13, p. 124.
245. Hoffman and Morrison-Taw, supra note 58, p. 29.
246. Crenshaw, supra note 214, pp. 14-15.

247. Carver, supra note 58, p. 32.
248. Bandura, supra note 184, p. 167.
249. Menachem Hoffnung, *Israel—State Security versus the Rule of Law,* Nevo Publications, Jerusalem, 1991, p. 21.
250. Barzilai, supra note 8, p. 247.
251. Ibid., p. 234.
252. Pnina Lahav, "A Barrel Without Rings: The Impact of Counter-Terrorism on the Legal Culture in Israel," *State, Government and International Relations (33),* 1990, p. 19.
253. Ibid.
254. Robert Moss, "Urban Terrorism: Political Violence in Western Society," *Cyclone (1),* 1976, p. 46.
255. Wilkinson, supra note 228, p. 22.
256. Michael Sthol, *The Politics of Terrorism,* Dekker Inc., U.S.A., 1983, p. 165.
257. Charters, supra note 51, p. 348.
258. In this context, Israel is presented in Hoffnung's book as a suitable research site for examining the impact of a continuous external threat on the functioning of a democracy. This is because, according to Hoffnung, Israel meets two essential and fundamental conditions: Since 1949 Israel has held regular and open elections on both the national and municipal level and since its establishment, Israel has had to face a significant external threat to its existence (Hoffnung, supra note 249, p. 2).
259. Netanyahu, supra note 23, p. 31.
260. Crenshaw, supra note 13, p. 121.
261. Schmid, supra note 52, p. 14.
262. C.A. 4211/91 *State of Israel vs. Al Masri et al.,* Judgments XLVII [5], 636.
263. *Ha'aretz,* March 28, 1995.
264. Ibid.
265. *Ma'ariv,* January 11, 1995, p. 9.
266. Deputy Chief of Staff Amnon Lipkin-Shahak said that "[the issue of] interrogations in the Territories is, in my opinion, an issue that must be addressed.... At the present time it is difficult to interrogate quickly, and interrogations take too long. I know about interrogations, that if it were possible to shorten them legally, we could prevent the terrorist attacks that take place in the interim" (*Ma'ariv,* April 5, 1993).
267. Ilan Rachum, *The ISA Episode,* Carmel Publications, Jerusalem, 1990, pp. 167-168.
268. Amnon Strashnov, *Justice Under Fire,* Yediot Aharonot, Tel Aviv, 1994, p. 339.
269. Rachum, supra note 267, pp. 172, 173.
270. B'Tselem—Israeli Information Center for Human Rights in the Territories, *Interrogation of Palestinians During the Intifada: Ill-treatment, "Moderate Physical Pressure" or Torture?* Jerusalem, March 1991, p. 21.
271. Yaakov Perry, *He Who Comes to Kill You,* Keshet Publications, Tel Aviv, 1999, p. 145.
272. B'Tselem, supra note 270, p. 21.
273. According to Gilon: A "ticking bomb" is what we call a terrorist who knows, for example, that a bomb has been placed in a particular location, and is slated to explode in a short time. According to the guidelines of the Landau Commission, if it is believed that a suspect has such information, it is permissible to use "moderate physical pressure" to get him to reveal the location of the bomb because this is a matter of saving lives. In contrast with this, if a person is suspected, for example, of recruiting people for the Palestinian Islamic Jihad, "moderate physical pressure" may not be used because his act of recruiting does not make him a "ticking bomb" (Gilon, supra note 48, p. 386).
274. *Ha'aretz,* March 11, 1990.

275. Lahav, supra note 252, p. 40.
276. Alan M. Dershowitz, *Why Terrorism Works,* Yale University Press, New Haven and London, 2002, p. 151.
277. HCJ 5100/94 *Israel Public Committee Against Torture et al. versus The Government of Israel et al.*, Judgments, LXVIII[4], 817.
278. Interview with Shamir, supra note 36.
279. Interview with Peres, supra note 36.
280. Interview with Perry, supra note 38.
281. Interview with Gilon, supra note 70.
282. Interview with Lipkin-Shahak, supra note 41.
283. *Yediot Aharonot*, June 15, 1995.
284. Dershowitz, supra note 276, p. 144.
285. Interview with Pressler, supra note 188.
286. Interview with Shavit, supra note 39.
287. Interview with Gilon, supra note 70.
288. Dershowitz, supra note 276, p. 151.
289. Gilon explains the composition of this special ministerial committee and how it functions: During the period I'm referring to, members of the committee were Yitzhak Rabin (Prime Minister and Minister of Defense, who served as committee chairman), Minister of Police Moshe Shahal, and Justice Minister David Libai. Since Rabin was wearing two hats, it was decided that another member should be added to the committee, and that was Minister of the Environment Yossi Sarid. In the wake of the tremendous shock following the bombing of Bus No. 5, the committee approved the requested authorizations. Three months passed and then there was the terrible attack at the Beit Lid Junction. The authorizations were renewed and this was also the case after another three months. By the time I retired from the ISA in February 1996, I had managed to request renewal of the authorizations five times.... Prior to the renewal I would come to the ministerial committee meeting, present statistics on the number of Hamas detainees, detail the number of cases from these interrogations where we had used the special authorizations, and the results. I made it clear to all those involved that from the point of view of the ISA, continued granting of the authorizations was vital in order to foil terrorist attacks before they happened. The ministerial committee would discuss the matter and approve them (Gilon, supra note 48, p. 387).
290. *Yediot Aharonot,* April 27, 1993.
291. Statement No. 4 by the Director of the ISA, p. 3, submitted on May 2, 1993, in conjunction with HCJ 2581/91.
292. Ibid., pp. 7-9.
293. Gilon, supra note 48, p. 18.
294. Ibid., p. 203.
295. Dershowitz, supra note 276, p. 138.
296. *Yediot Aharonot*, December 1, 1994, p. 7.
297. *Ma'ariv*, August 24, 1995, p. 2.
298. Gilon, supra note 48, p. 384.
299. In his book Gilon, described the events as follows: Rabin, naturally, was completely in favor of my position, as Prime Minister, as Minister in charge of the ISA, as Defense Minister and based on his own general point of view. Shahal was very close to Rabin's approach. Libai and Sarid were less vocal in their support for my position, although they also took a pragmatic approach and understood that the ISA was not asking for these authorizations in order to satisfy the alleged sadistic lust of the interrogators, but rather, in order to save Israeli lives, and that is not merely a figure

of speech.....At one of the meetings of the ministerial committee, Rabin grumbled at Ben-Ya'ir, "What kind of Attorney General are you? I need to fight terrorism and you are always telling me what I can't do. For heaven's sake, tell me what I can do, not what I can't do..."Ben-Ya'ir, as always, did not get excited and continued to speak softly and calmly. Rabin turned red, and you could feel that he was about to explode, and then suddenly, he got up, his chair flew back and hit the wall, and he yelled at Ben-Ya'ir, "I can't work like this! The terrorists are blowing us up and you are driving me crazy!" And he stormed out of the room and slammed the door (Gilon, supra note 48, p. 388).

300. *Ma'ariv*, February 8, 1995, p. 15.
301. *Kolbo*, November 11, 1994.
302. *Yediot Aharonot*, May 1, 1995.
303. *Yediot Aharonot*, June 15, 1995.
304. Gilon, supra note 48, p. 390.
305. Ibid., p. 395.
306. *Yediot Aharonot*, August 3, 1995.
307. *Ma'ariv*, September 6, 1995, p. 10.
308. *Ma'ariv*, January 12, 1998.
309. HCJ 5100/94 *Israel Public Committee Against Torture et al. versus The Government of Israel et al.,* Judgments LXVIII [4], 817.
310. Turner, supra note 231, p. 168.
311. Regarding the matter of judicial review of IDF activities in the West Bank by Israeli courts, Shlomo Gazit says: From the outset the Israeli government decided in principle that the military administration would not claim that the Supreme Court had no jurisdiction to discuss actions or omissions in the West Bank, because these are actions conducted outside the state's boundaries. During the early years of Israeli rule, West Bank residents avoided appealing to the Supreme Court, both because they did not believe that an Israeli court could discuss their concerns objectively and for political reasons—an unwillingness to grant legitimacy to the Israeli regime by turning to their courts. After a while this attitude changed and Palestinians began to appeal to the Supreme Court and seek judicial relief there (Shlomo Gazit, *Fools in a Trap—Thirty Years of Israel Policy in the Territories,* Zemora Bitan, 1999, p. 53).

Chapter 7

312. Hoffman and Morrison-Taw, supra note 58, p.71.
313. Peter J. Sacopulos, "Terrorism in Britain: Threat, Reality, Response," *Terrorism and International Journal, 12 (3), 1989,* p. 153.
314. Hoffman and Morrison-Taw, supra note 58, pp 45-55.
315. Sacopulos, supra note 313, pp. 157-158.
316. Soule, supra note 45, p. 31.
317. Hoffman and Morrison-Taw, supra note 58, p. 54.
318. Soule, supra note 45, p. 40.
319. Clawson, supra note 240, pp. 16-17.
320. Christopher Seton-Watson, "Terrorism in Italy," in Juliet Loedge (Ed.), *The Threat of Terrorism*, Wheatsheaf Books, 1988, p. 103.
321. Hoffman and Morrison-Taw, supra note 58, pp. 69-71.
322. Peter Janke, "The Neutralization of the Red Army Faction," in Peter Janke (Ed.), supra note 238, p. 125.
323. Hoffnung, supra note 249, p. 52, 53.

324. According to Michal Tzur, the Defense (Emergency) Regulations—enacted in Israel under Article 6 of the Palestine (Defense) Order-in-Council—1937, passed in England as part of the emergency legislation and with regard to World War II—gave the security services in Israel certain tools for dealing with terrorism, although it was not explicitly stated that this was the purpose of these regulations. The regulations dealt with central issues such as: arresting suspects, deportation, expropriation of property, determining taxes, payment to victims and legal procedures. Tzur emphasizes in this context that most of the crimes detailed in the Defense (Emergency) Regulations are also expressed in the Penal Code or Prevention of Terrorism Act, although sometimes their definition in the regulations is broader, the sanctions are more severe, and a special military court is given jurisdiction, with special legal procedures (Tzur, supra note 9, pp. 9, 14, 21, and 97).

325. Important changes were made to the Act in 1986, including: revoking the articles with regard to setting up a military court under the Act, and revoking the absolute autonomy of the military judicial system by subordinating the Military Court of Appeal to the Supreme Court (Hoffnung, supra note 249, pp. 279-280).

326. Barzilai, supra note 8, p. 238.

327. Article 8 of the Act: "If the government declares, by an announcement in the Official Gazette, that a certain assembly of people is a terrorist organization, this announcement shall serve as proof in any legal debate that this assembly of people is a terrorist organization, unless proven otherwise."

328. A terrorist organization is defined in the Act as follows: "An assembly of people employing, in its actions, acts of violence that are liable to cause death or injury, or threatening such acts of violence…"(Article 1 of the Act).

329. Tzur, supra note 9, p. 5.

330. Barzilai, supra note 8, p. 245.

331. Ibid., p. 247.

332. Schmid, supra note 52, p. 14.

333. Tzur, supra note 9, p. 44.

334. *Ha'aretz*, May 24, 1989.

335. Britain has only outlawed the military wing of Hizballah. See: http://www.homeoffice.gov.uk/terrorism/threat/groups/.

336. Moshe Negbi, *Freedom of the Press in Israel—Values as Reflected in the Law,* Jerusalem Institute of Israel Studies, Jerusalem, 2nd Edition, 1999, p. 126.

337. Ibid., pp. 129-130.

338. HCJ 103/92 *Jouad Boulus et al. v. The Advisory Committee et al.*, Judgments XLV (1), 466.

339. HCJ 672/88 *Muhammad Abdullah al-Labdi v. The Commander of the IDF Forces in the West Bank*, Judgments XLIII (2) 227.

340. Ibid.

341. HCJ 19/86 (HCJ 634/85, HCJ 635/85) *Dr. Azmi Alshouebi et al. v. The Military Supervisor for Judea and Samaria,* Judgments XL (1) 219.

342. See, for example, HCJ 792/88 *Muhammad A / Galil A / Mahdi Matour et al. v. The Commander of the IDF Forces in the West Bank*, Judgments XLIII (3) 542; HCJ 672/88 *Muhammad Abdullah al-Labdi v. The Commander of the IDF Forces in the West Bank,* Judgments XLIII (2) 227.

343. Hoffnung, supra note 249, pp. 24-25.

344. Aharon Barak, *Judicial Reasoning*, Papyrus Press—Tel Aviv University, 1987, p. 506.

345. Crenshaw, supra note 13, p. 121. .

346. O'Brien, supra note 197, p. 156.

347. Rehavam Ze'evi disagrees with the definitions of collective punishment: "We must look for what hurts them, and we do not do this. We are scared, for example, of collective punishment, despite the fact that it works exceptionally well. Disturbances in Beit Fajar will lead to a prohibition against exporting stones via the Allenby Bridge. If there are disturbances in Hebron, the grapes from the Hebron vineyards will not be sent to Jordan! If you say this is immoral, I will answer that it is more than moral, because in this way less blood is spilled, both Jewish and Arab alike. But people object to taking these steps, because it is collective punishment" (Michael Shashar, *Conversations with Rehavam Gandhi Ze'evi,* Yediot Aharonot, Sifrei Hemed, Jerusalem, 1992, pp. 132-133.)
348. Soule, supra note 45, p. 41.
349. Peter Janke, "The Neutralization of the Red Army Faction," in Peter Janke, (Ed.), supra note 238, p. 125.
350. Hoffman and Morrison-Taw, supra note 58, p. 29.
351. Ibid.
352. Shashar, supra note 347, pp. 132-133.
353. Ibid., pp. 115, 117, 128.
354. *Ha'aretz*, February 26, 1990.
355. Perry, supra note 271, p. 230.
356. HCJ 802/89 *Nasman v. The Commander of the IDF Forces in the Gaza Strip,* Judgments XLIV (2) 601.
357. Yael Stein, "Policy of Destruction: House Demolition and Destruction of Agricultural Land in the Gaza Strip," B'Tselem, February 2002, p. 18.
358. HCJ 4112/90 *The Association for Civil Rights in Israel v. The Head of Southern Command,* Judgments XLIV (4) 636.
359. The following are the words of Supreme Court President Shamgar on the demolition of houses: "The demolition of a building is agreed by all to be a very severe and serious means of punishment, and its deterrent value does not detract from its nature as described. One of its main properties is that it is irreversible, that is, it cannot be corrected after the fact" (HCJ 358/88 *The Association for Civil Rights in Israel et al. v. The Head of Central Command et al.,* Judgments XLIII (2) 540).
360. HCJ 1730/96 *Adel Salem A / Rabo Sabiah v. Brigadier General Ilan Biran, Commander of the IDF Forces in Judea and Samaria,* Judgments L (1) 353.
361. In a decision from 1997, Supreme Court President Barak defined six tests for examining the decision to demolish or seal a building: the degree of balance between the seriousness of the terrorist act and the scope of the sanction; the balance between the anticipated damage to the terrorist's family and the need to deter potential future terrorists; the balance between the basic right of all people to their property and the right and duty of the regime to maintain security and public order; the terrorist's link to the building; the size of the building; and the effect of applying sanctions on other people (HCJ 6299/97 *Ali Muhammad Abdullah Yassin et al. v. The Military Commander in the Judea and Samaria Region,* Tik-Al 97 (4) 617).
362. HCJ 897/86 *Ramzi Hana Jaber v. The Head of the Central Command et al.* Judgments XLI (2) 522.
363. HCJ 2006/97 *Maysun Muhammad Abu Fara et al. v. The Head of the Central Command,* Judgments LI (2) 651.
364. HCJ 6026/94 *Abed Al Rahim Hassan Nazal et al. v. The Commander of the IDF Forces in Judea and Samaria,* Judgments XLVIII (5) 338.
365. Justice Bach notes in this context, "the literal text of Regulation 119(1) allows implementation of demolition of buildings on the broadest scale, which is not in line with basic perceptions of justice in an advanced country." And he adds: "We have

therefore determined, in a number of rulings, that the implementation of this regulation shall be restricted, but we must be aware of the fact that by doing so we are not interpreting the regulation but merely imposing limits on the manner in which it is applied and carried out, applying rules of degree and a sense of proportion"(HCJ 1730/96 *Adel Salem A / Rabo Sabiah v. Brigadier General Ilan Biran, Commander of the IDF Forces in Judea and Samaria,* Judgments L (1) 353).

366. HCJ 2722/92 *Al-Amrin v. The Commander of the IDF Forces in the Gaza Strip,* Judgments XLV (3) 699.

367. In a ruling from 1996, Justice Barak also stated the other aspect of the principle of degree in determining that collaborating in the cold-blooded murder of innocent people is a very serious crime. According to him, the crime of assisting in murder also justifies demolition of buildings, after less severe means, such as sealing, have been found to be insufficient (HCJ 2161/96 *Rabhi Said v. The Head of the Home Front Command,* Judgments L (4) 485).

368. HCJ 698/85 *Mazen A / Allah Said Dejalas et al. v. The Commander of the IDF Forces in Judea and Samaria,* Judgments XL (2) 42.

369. HCJ 6299/97 *Ali Muhammad Abdullah Yassin et al. v. The Military Commander in the Judea and Samaria Region,* Tik-Al 97 (4) 617.

370. This claim was also made, among others, by Leon Shelef, who stated: The demolition of a house is a radical deviation from the accepted norms of an enlightened society, because this is a collective punishment…and because it causes irreversible damage…and because the demolition is usually carried out before the suspect has been tried in a proper criminal proceeding"(Leon Shelef, *The Bitterness of Law and the Essence of Government, On the Rule of Law, Method of Government and Legacy of Israel,* Papyrus Press—Tel Aviv University, 1996, p. 124).

371. HCJ 11/97 *Naja'a Arafat Abu Halawi et al. v. Brig. Gen. Shmuel Arad et al.* Tik-Al 97 (3) 111.

372. HCJ 2209/90 *Shouahin v. The Commander of the IDF Forces,* Judgments XLIV (3) 877; HCJ 242/90 *Alkatzaf et al. v. The Commander of the IDF Forces,* Judgments XLIV (1) 616.

373. HCJ 6026/94 *Abed Al Rahim Hassan Nazal et al. v. The Commander of the IDF Forces in Judea and Samaria,* Judgments XLVIII (5) 338. In HCJ 2006/97 *Maysun Muhammad Abu Fara et al. v. The Head of the Central Command,* the court repeated the state's claim that pressure by the families because of the expected demolition was likely to deter terrorists from carrying out similar actions.

374. HCJ 2006/97 *Maysun Muhammad Abu Fara et al. v. The Head of the Central Command,* Judgments LI (2) 651.

375. HCJ 1730/96 *Adel Salem A / Rabo Sabiah v. Brig. Gen. Ilan Biran, Commander of the IDF Forces in Judea and Samaria,* Judgments L (1) 353.

376. HCJ 11/97 *Naja'a Arafat Abu Halawi et al. v. Brigadier General Shmuel Arad et al.* Tik-Al 97 (3) 111.

377. HCJ 1730/96 *Adel Salem A / Rabo Sabiah v. Brig. Gen. Ilan Biran, Commander of the IDF Forces in Judea and Samaria,* Judgments L (1) 353.

378. Strashnov, supra note 268, p. 92.

379. B'Tselem—The Israeli Center for Human Rights in the Territories, *Demolition and Sealing of Houses in the West Bank and the Gaza Strip as a Punitive Measure During the Intifada,* Jerusalem, September 1989, p. 26.

380. Trends in Terrorism—Post September 11, The International Policy Institute for Counter-Terrorism, September 11, 2002, pp. 36-37.

381. Aryeh Shalev, *The Intifada: Reasons, Characteristics and Implications,* Papyrus Press—Tel Aviv University, 1990, p. 129.

382. Interview with Peres, supra note 36.

383. Interview with Perry, supra note 38.

384. *Ma'ariv*, April 5, 1993.

385. HCJ 1759/94 *Anne Srosberg et al. v. The Minister of Defense,* Savir's Summary Repository, Judgments XLIII (18) 281.

386. HCJ 113/90 *Aliya Sa'adi Said Shouwe et al. v. The Commander of the IDF Forces in the Gaza Strip,* Judgments XLIV (4) 590.

387. HCJ 5820/91 *Father Samuel Fanus et al. v. Dani Yatom, Commander of the Central Command et al.*, Tik-Al 92 (1) 270.

388. At the international conference at Davos in February 1997, Arafat claimed that the closure caused Palestinians to lose $7 million a day in revenue (*Ha'aretz*, February 3, 1997). Following the closure imposed on the territories after the attacks in Jerusalem in September 1997, Arafat claimed that the closure caused the Palestinian Authority a loss of between $9 to 10 million a day (*Ha'aretz*, September 14, 1997, p. 4).

389. *Ha'aretz*, November 11, 1996.

390. *Ha'aretz*, January 15, 1997.

391. *Ha'aretz*, August 8, 1997.

392. Interview with Netanyahu, supra note 49.

393. Interview with Dagan, supra note 37.

394. *Ma'ariv*, Weekend supplement, March 28, 1997, p. 16.

395. Shelef, supra note 370, p. 117.

396. HCJ 253/88 *Sajadia v. The Minister of Defense,* Judgments XLII (3) 821.

397. HCJ 7048/97 *Anonymous v. The Minister of Defense,* Judgments LIV (1) 721.

398. HCJ 253/88 *Sajadia v. The Minister of Defense,* Judgments XLII (3) 822.

399. *Davar*, November 14, 1994.

400. Ibid., pp. 66, 67, 70.

401. Ibid., p. 71.

402. Ibid., p. 68.

403. Ibid., p. 70.

404. Strashnov, supra note 268, p. 72.

405. Interview with Lipkin-Shahak, supra note 41.

406. Interview with Dagan, supra note 37.

407. HCJ 48/7 *Al Karbutli v. The Minister of Defense,* Judgments II, p. 5, quoted in Ze'ev Segal, "The Supreme Court and the Hamas Exiles," *Monthly Review, 10,* 1993, p. 34.

408. In its ruling in the Alba affair, the court convicted the accused of publishing articles containing incitement. Thus the Supreme Court set a precedent which, in practice, extended the application of the punishment of deportation, under Article 4(a) of the Prevention of Terrorism Act, from direct incitement to terrorism to all words praising terrorist actions (CA 2831/95 *Alba v. The State of Israel,* Judgments L (5) 221).

409. Thus, for example, in HCJ 698/80 *Fahd Daoud Kawasme et al. v. The Minister of Defense et al.*, it was claimed by the petitioner that the act of deportation went against Article 49, Para. 1 of the Fourth Geneva Convention, stating that "the forced transfer of protected people, individuals or masses, and the deportation of protected people from the captured territory to the territory of the conquering power or to the territory of another country—whether conquered territory or unconquered territory—is prohibited, no matter what the motive" (HCJ 698/80 *Fahd Daoud Kawasme et al. v. The Minister of Defense et al.*, Judgments XXXIV (1) 617).

410. HCJ 97/79 *Abu Awad v. The Commander of the Judea and Samaria Region,* Judgments XXXIII (3) 309, 316.

411. See, for example, HCJ 4702/94 *Kadem al Tai et al. v. The Minister of the Interior et al.*, Judgments XLIX (3) 849; HCJ 17/71 *I' A' Mrar et al. v. The Minister of Defense*

et al., Judgments XXV (1) 142; HCJ 98/85 *Shahin v. The Minister of the Interior et al.* Judgments XXXIX (1) 798.

412. HCJ 4702/94 *Kadem Al Tai et al. v. The Minister of the Interior et al.,* Judgments XLIX (3) 849.

413. HCJ 792/88 *Muhammad A / Galil A / Mahdi Matuor et al. v. The Commander of the IDF Forces in the West Bank,* Judgments XLIII (3) 542; HCJ 159/84 *Abed Al Aziz Ali Shahin v. The Commander of the IDF Forces in the Gaza Strip,* Judgments XXXIX (1) 309.

414. HCJ 497/88 *Shachshir v. The Commander of the IDF Forces in the West Bank,* Judgments XLIII (1) 529.

415. HCJ 320/80 *Kawasme et al. v. The Minister of Defense,* Judgments XXXV (3) 113; HCJ 5973/92 *The Association for Civil Rights in Israel v. The Minister of Defense,* Judgments XLVII (1) 267.

416. *Ha'aretz,* March 31, 1993.

417. Anat Kurtz and David Tal, *Islamic Terrorism and Israel,* Papyrus Press—Tel Aviv University, 1993, p. 175

418. B'Tselem—Israeli Information Center for Human Rights in the Territories, *The Infringement of Human Rights in the Territories 1992/93.* HCJ 2722/92 *Al Amrim v. The Commander of the IDF in the Gaza Strip,* Judgments XLV (3) 699.

419. Segal, supra note 407, p. 35.

420. Haim Cohen, "Legal deportation," *Law and Government, A,* 5753, p. 471.

421. Ibid., p. 474.

422. *Al Hamishmar,* March 26, 1993.

423. Aviva Shabi and Ronnie Shaked, *Hamas—From Belief in Allah to the Path of Terrorism,* Keter, Jerusalem, 1994, p. 21.

424. *Yediot Aharonot,* December 1, 1994, p. 7.

425. B'Tselem, supra note 418, pp. 61-63.

426. Ibid.

427. HCJ 698/80 *Fahd Daoud Kawasme et al. v. The Minister of Defense et al.,* Judgments XXXV (1) 617.

428. Interview with Shavit, supra note 39.

429. Interview with Peres, supra note 36.

430. Ilan Kfir, Ben Caspit and Hanan Crystal, *Suicide: A Party Gives Up Its Authority,* Avivim (Ma'ariv Edition), 1996, p. 142.

431. *Yediot Aharonot,* August 27, 2002.

432. *Yediot Aharonot,* March 10, 2003.

Chapter 8

433. Robert Cooperman and Daryl Trent, *Terrorism: The Danger, the Reality, the Response,* Ma'arachot, 1982, p. 268.

434. Gabriel Weimann, "The Theater of Terror: Effects of Press Coverage," *Journal of Communications,* Winter 1983, pp. 38-45.

435. Crenshaw, supra note 214, pp. 14-15.

436. Jerrold M. Post, "Terrorist Psycho-logic: Terrorist Behavior as a Product of Psychological Forces," in Walter Reich (Ed.), *Origins of Terrorism,* Woodrow Wilson Center Press, 1998, p. 40.

437. Alex P. Schmid and Janny De Graaf, *Violence as Communication: Insurgent Terrorism and the Western News Media,* Sage Publications, London, 1982, p. 69.

438. Bruce Hoffman, *Inside Terrorism,* The Columbia University Press, New York, 1988, pp. 132-133.

439. Ronald H. Hinckley, "American Opinion Towards Terrorism—The Reagan Years," *Terrorism: An International Journal 12(6)*, 1989, pp. 394-395.
440. Crenshaw, supra note 13, p. 128.
441. Hoffman, supra note 438, pp. 147, 154.
442. Wilkinson, supra note 77, p. 42.
443. Lacquer, supra note 227, p. 68.
444. Ted Robert Gur, "Terrorism in Democracies: Its Social and Political Bases," in Walter Reich, (Ed.), *Origins of Terrorism,* Woodrow Wilson Center Press, 1998, p. 102.
445. Hoffman, supra note 438, pp. 143-144.
446. The American study examined the public's attitudes towards terrorist attacks on American targets, and thus it is no wonder that the media's reporting did not arouse any sympathy towards the terrorist organizations. But this raises the question of whether people who are not the target of terrorist attacks and are exposed to comprehensive media coverage of the attacks and their background stories, for example, a French audience, would respond in the same way. In other words, suicide bombings in Israel certainly do not arouse sympathy towards the terrorists in Israeli public opinion, but doesn't the American public ask itself what motivates a young person to perpetrate a suicide attack?
447. Abu Iyad, supra note 14, pp. 158,165 (emphasis is mine—B.G.).
448. Hoffman, supra note 438, p. 176.
449. Joseph Draznin, *News Coverage of Terrorism: The Media Perspective,* doctoral dissertation, University of Maryland at College Park, 1997, UMI Microform 9816453, pp. 182-185.
450. Gabriel Weimann and Conrad Winn, *The Theater of Terror: The Mass Media and International Terrorism,* Longman Publishing/Addison-Wesley, New York, 1993, p. 295.
451. Interview with Shamir, supra note 36.
452. Negbi, supra note 336, pp. 1-5.

Chapter 9

453. Interview with Shamir, supra note 36.
454. It should be noted in this context that similar to terrorist attacks aimed at civilians, a guerrilla strike aimed primarily at soldiers is also meant to achieve the psychological-demoralization effect of anxiety among the combatants and/or their families, and the public on the home front.
455. Following an Air Force bombing on a Hizballah training base at Ein Dardara, Lebanon, in June 1994, residents of the north entered their shelters independently, and one Kiryat Shemona resident even said to the press, "we don't need slides or a PA system. As soon as we heard about the IDF operation, we knew we would spend the coming nights in shelters and security rooms" (*Ma'ariv*, June 3, 1994).
456. Jenkins, supra note 7, p. v.
457. Lesser, Hoffman et al., supra note 74, p. 96.
458. Bandura, supra note 184, p. 168.
459. Lesser, Hoffman et al., supra note 74, p. 86.
460. *The Guardian*, November 2, 2001.
461. *Yediot Aharonot*, July 30, 2002, January 6, 2003.
462. Ofra Ayalon and Mooli Lahad, *Life on the Edge 2000—Stress and Coping in High Risk Situations*, Nord Publications, Haifa, p. 190.
463. The International Policy Institute for Counter-Terrorism at the Herzliya Interdisciplinary Center has been implementing this method for years with various target audiences in Israel—placing a special emphasis on activity with youth, teachers, and

educators in high schools—and has received favorable responses from the groups participating in the seminars.

464. Ehud Sprinzak, *Israeli Society v. the Challenge of Muslim Terrorism*, Center for Special Studies in Memory of the Fallen of the Israeli Intelligence Service, Tel Aviv, 1997, p. 2.

465. *Ma'ariv*, February 1, 1995, p. 12.

466. *Yediot Aharonot*, January 20, 1995, p. 3.

467. *Ma'ariv*, April 14, 1995, Passover supplement, pp. 2-3.

468. Efraim Inbar, "Yitzhak Rabin and Israel's National Security," *Yitzhak Rabin and Israel's National Security—Special Memorial Issue*, Mideast Security and Policy Studies, Begin-Sadat Center for Strategic Studies, Bar Ilan University, 1996, pp. 33-34.

469. "*Hakol Diburim*," (*It's All Talk*), Israel Radio Reshet Bet, December 13, 1993.

470. *Ma'ariv*, June 3, 1994.

471. *Yediot Aharonot*, April 5, 1993, p. 6.

472. Interview with Shavit, supra note 39.

473. Netanyahu, supra note 23, p. 18.

474. This criticism raises an interesting question of how much the opposition can allow itself to criticize the government's counter-terrorism policy. It is clear to all that criticism in this sphere is legitimate, but it appears that the manner of conveying the message should be considered. Even the harshest of allegations spoken from the Knesset podium, or even in the media, are the natural right of an opposition that is interested in replacing the government. This is not true of voicing criticism shortly after a terrorist attack, or at times even at the site of the attack itself. Criticism of this sort could inflame tempers and cause others to employ violence against innocent people.

475. Lesser, Hoffman et al., supra note 74, p. 9.

476. In this section Netanyahu bases himself on the essay of the writer of these lines, and references it: "Counter-terrorism—New Directions," *Emdat Mafteach*, Jerusalem, Shalem Center, 1995, pp. 7-10.

477. Netanyahu, supra note 23, pp. 146-147.

478. Merari and Elad, supra note 148, p. 116.

479. Crenshaw, supra note 13, p. 124.

480. Alon, supra note 137, p. 107.

481. Interview with Ze'evi, supra note 37.

482. Interview with Shavit, supra note 39.

483. Interview with Gilon, supra note 70.

484. Interview with Pressler, supra note 188.

485. Interview with Shamir, supra note 36.

486. Interview with Rafi Eitan, supra note 37.

487. Interview with Lipkin-Shahak, supra note 41.

488. Interview with Dagan, supra note 37.

489. Dagan illustrates his statement on the public's influence on policymakers: "For example, following terrorist attacks they decided to set up bus security units. Did this disrupt terrorist activity? The answer is no. It was about calming public awareness. I don't denigrate that, but the question is what could we have done with the 30 or 50 million shekels? If I were the one deciding priorities, this would be the last thing I would invest in. I would achieve better results if I were to invest in other things. Therefore the need to satisfy the public because of the impact of the media is, for us, highly 'counterproductive.' I cannot say this with complete confidence. I can say that it places the need to fight terrorism on the public agenda. It obligates us to understand that we need to act all the time, and it helps us organize the resources and readiness

[so that] when we are ready [operationally—B.G.] to move against a terrorist organization [we can] realize it. But there is still an internal contradiction, because ultimately what we do following an attack is not what we should be doing, that is, the purpose of the action is merely to humor the public" (interview with Dagan, supra note 37).

490. Brig. Gen. Yaakov Amidror, who served as head of the Research Department of the IDF's Intelligence Branch, said: "To the best of my judgment, the way we deal with terrorism contributes to its influence on us. If we were capable, whenever there was a terrorist incident, to grit our teeth, publicize the event without screaming headlines, without color, without close-ups of the dead and wounded and without pouring out endless words over meters of paper and kilometers of film, terrorism would be less successful. Perhaps there would even be less terrorism. Because terrorism feeds on and is strengthened by the publicity it receives" (*Ha'aretz,* May 12, 1995).

Chapter 10

491. Lesser, Hoffman et al., supra note 74, p. 34.
492. Chaim Herzog, cited in Benjamin Netanyahu (Ed.), *International Terrorism: Challenges and Response,* The Jonathan Institute, Jerusalem, 1980, p. 56.
493. Yitzhak Rabin, "An International Agency against Terrorism," in Benjamin Netanyahu (Ed.), *Terrorism: How the West Can Win,* New York: Farrar, Straus & Giroux, 1986, pp. 183-185.

Summary and Conclusion

494. All of the quotes cited in this chapter are taken from the personal interviews conducted with the persons mentioned, unless noted otherwise.
495. Yigal Pressler, for example, stated that "In the past, until Oslo and somewhat afterwards, the goal was always to cause harm to commanders and individuals and this had an impact—undoubtedly. All the operations we carried out in the past, and even to date, against organization leaders and networks—this has a tremendous effect. Either it brings about a lengthy halt to the bombings or they begin to think differently" (interview with Pressler, supra note 188).
496. At times, out of political and foreign affairs considerations, leaders have attempted to sidestep the need to act against terrorism with the argument that the only possible effect such a step would have would be on morale. Thus, for example, "high level" political sources were quoted in the Israeli press, in October 1995, following the harsh attacks against Israel in Lebanon by saying that "there was no intention of initiating operations that might bring about public calm but would do nothing for the situation in the field." At the same time, Prime Minister Yitzhak Rabin stated at a government meeting that we were against creating any "linkage" between negotiations with Syria and what was happening on the northern border (*Yediot Aharonot,* October 17, 1995, p. 11).
497. The "boomerang effect" is, indeed, relevant and should be taken into account as counteracting any morale benefit. But in many cases it is possible to determine whether there will actually be a boomerang effect following certain counter-terrorism measures. Even in cases where it is believed that the boomerang effect will, indeed, take place, this should be weighed against all of the goals and advantages of the proposed action, and the decision should be made on the basis of a cost-benefit analysis.
498. A political achievement by a terrorist organization is likely to motivate and arouse more radical groups and organizations to employ terrorism in order to achieve aims that are even more extreme.

499. Ariel Sharon said in this context, with regard to methods employed in the Gaza Strip during the 1970s, "First of all, the population must not be harmed. I, for example, did not permit entry into schools, but we conducted a parents' meeting and we would explain to parents their responsibility for their children (interview with Sharon, supra note 187).

Appendix A

Conclusions of the "Shefayyim Conference" of the
International Policy Institute for Counter-Terrorism
June 7-26, 1997

Terrorism and the Media Panel

1. Participants at the Shefayyim Conference from the International Policy Institute for Counter-Terrorism (ICT) at the Interdisciplinary Center in Herzliya, in conjunction with the Counter-Terrorism Bureau of the Prime Minister's Office—which includes academics, former and current security experts, psychologists, media specialists, and others—reiterate that:

    A. Terrorism is designed to undermine the moral strength of Israeli citizens and disrupt their way of life. Its threat and damage to persons and property is demoralizing and causes psychological damage

    B. Terrorist attacks are meant to achieve political aims: changing policies and influencing political moves. To achieve these aims, terrorism seeks widespread media coverage, in its effort to reach various target populations and spread fear and anxiety throughout the Israeli public.

    C. All agencies involved in shaping Israeli public opinion (including politicians, public figures, media people, academics, educators, etc.) must contribute their share to minimize the morale-psychological damage of terrorist attacks.

    D. Methods and guidelines must be formulated that will, on the one hand, enable the media to continue playing their vital role in a democratic society to report to the public freely and without external interference and, on the other hand, to reduce the damage to people's sense of personal safety and to public morale.

In the light of these underlying principles, the conference participants believe the following operative steps should be promoted:

1. Participants at the Shefayyim Conference believe that an ongoing, two-way relationship should be established between defense agencies and the government, as represented by the Counter-Terrorism Bureau, and the media, on matters relating to terrorism.

For this purpose, an authorized body should be created, to which media representatives can turn for reliable, on-line information regarding terrorism, both during terrorist attacks and on a regular basis. It should be noted that during the discussions at the conference, the Counter-Terrorism Headquarters agreed in principle to the creation of such a body.

2. Participants at the Shefayyim Conference call upon members of Israel's electronic media and the press—editors, journalists, publishers, and owners—to establish an ad hoc committee of media personnel to formulate technical rules regarding media coverage of terrorist attacks, during and after their occurrence. The International Policy Institute for Counter-Terrorism is prepared to assist in the creation of such a committee by providing technical support and professional advice.

3. In this context, conference participants recommend that this journalists' committee discuss ways of preventing the demoralization and the psychological and operational damage caused to the public and individuals due to the following:

During the course of an attack—
   A. Taking close-up pictures of the dead or injured in the area of the attack.
   B. Broadcasting or reporting from the area about extreme signs of panic and anxiety.
   C. Recycling the trauma by repeatedly and frequently transmitting pictures and sounds from the scene.
   D. Disclosing procedures, operational techniques, and deployment of security forces in the area of the attack.

Following attacks and on a regular basis—
  A. Photographing and broadcasting extreme expressions of mourning and anxiety from funerals and from victims' homes.
  B. Dramatizing terrorist attacks and expressing admiration for their perpetrators (on their determination, their professionalism, their willingness for self-sacrifice, etc.).
  C. Broadcasting propaganda cassettes from terrorist organizations (tapes from the scene, tapes made by suicide attackers, or showing kidnapped victims, etc.).
  D. Drastically changing program schedules in the electronic media.

4. In this context, participants at the Shefayyim Conference also recommend the following:
  A. Training reporters on methods for covering terrorist attacks under pressure.
  B. Informing the public regarding the ways in which terrorist organizations attempt to manipulate Israeli public opinion, and about the relatively low probability of being injured in a terrorist attack as compared with other factors (road accidents, etc.). This can be accomplished by using professional commentary by relevant experts, and through ongoing contacts, during and after attacks, with the coordinating body to be established for this purpose by the Counter-Terrorism Headquarters.

5. Participants at the Shefayyim Conference are aware of the impact that public statements made during and after mass terrorist attacks have on the Israeli public. In this regard, the International Policy Institute for Counter-Terrorism will seek to formulate guidelines concerning the behavior of public figures during such events, and make these available to the appropriate institutions.

Participants on the Media Panel at the Shefayyim Conference

Prof. Yonah Alexander—The Inter-University Center for Terrorism Studies
Mr. Guy Bechor—*Ha'aretz* newspaper
Mr. Ron Ben-Yishai—*Yediot Aharonot* newspaper
Mr. Avyatar Ben-Zadaf—Former editor of *Ma'archot,* Media Studies Unit, Bar-Ilan University

Dr. Eli Carmon—Haifa University

Mr. Avi Dagan—Member of the Counter-Terrorism Bureau, Prime Minister's Office

Gen. (Res.) Meir Dagan—Head of the Counter-Terrorism Bureau, Prime Minister's Office

Mr. Boaz Ganor—Academic Director, International Policy Institute for Counter-Terrorism

Mr. Micha Gilad—Psychologist, Emergency Center, Kiryat Shemona

Mr. Carmi Gilon—Former director of the ISA

Mr. Ronen Hoffman—Director-General, International Policy Institute for Counter-Terrorism

Dr. David Kimchi—Chairman of the Board, International Policy Institute for Counter-Terrorism

Mr. Aharon Klein—*Time*—Time-Life News Service (passing on Para. 3C)

Dr. Mooli Lahad—Director of the Emergency Center, Kiryat Shemona

Prof. Ariel Merari—Head of the Political Violence Research Unit, Tel Aviv University (passing on Para. 3C, with special emphasis on Para. 3B—"It is the public's obligation to know all relevant details concerning a terrorist attack, without special dramatization.")

Dr. Yossi Olmert—Former Head of the Government Press Office

Ms. Sharona Recanati

Prof. Uriel Reichman—President, Interdisciplinary Center at Herzliya

Prof. Barry Rubin—Begin-Sadat Center for Strategic Research, Bar-Ilan University

Dr. Yehuda Shaham—Emergency Center, Kiryat Shemona

Ms. Galit Shaltiel—Psychologist, Emergency Center, Kiryat Shemona

Mr. Shabbetai Shavit—Former Head of the Mossad, Chair of the Board of Governors, International Policy Institute for Counter-Terrorism

Dr. Yigal Shefi—Defense Studies Program, Tel Aviv University

Mr. Zalman Shoval—Former Israeli Ambassador to the United States

Prof. Ehud Sprinzak—Political Science Department, Hebrew University, Jerusalem

Mr. Nachman Tal—The Center for Strategic Research, Tel Aviv University

Mr. Ehud Yatom—Member of the Counter-Terrorism Headquarters

Dr. Mina Zemach—Director, "Dahaf" Research Institute

Appendix B

Recommendations by Participants in the Conference on International Cooperation on Terrorism

The International Policy Institute for Counter-Terrorism

27 March, 1997

ICT Policy Paper on Countering International Terrorism

1.   The International Policy Institute for Counter-Terrorism asserts that terrorism is not solely a domestic problem of individual countries, but rather an international phenomenon that endangers world peace and threatens the lives of its inhabitants.

2.   Due to the international effects of this phenomenon, it is the duty of all nations to cooperate in all fields related to counter-terrorism.

3.   In order to combat international terrorism, members of the international community need:

A. To declare that no political goal justifies the use of terror-(herein defined as an intentional violent attack on the lives of civilians aimed to achieve political goals).

B. To enhance international cooperation in the field of counter-terrorism.

C. To formulate and enforce joint international policy against governments sponsoring and actively participating in terrorism.

D. To advocate international agreements regarding terrorism in order to significantly impede the activities of terrorists.

E. To deepen cooperation among intelligence and law enforcement agencies; and to share expertise in the field of counter-terrorism.

F. To jointly develop new technologies in order to strengthen special counter-terror units.

G. To dry up existing financial sources of terror organizations; to prohibit the raising of funds and the transfer of capital to terror organizations.

H. To prepare for the threat of unconventional terrorism - nuclear, biological, and chemical - and to jointly declare that any attempt by a terror organization in planning, threatening or carrying out an attack will be prevented by the actions of the entire international community.

I. To formulate international policy focusing on the psychological aspects of terrorism, through international seminars, joint press conferences and mock trials of terrorists.

J. To unite against extremist groups that manipulate religious or secular doctrines from whatever quarter in order to promote, assist, initiate and execute terror attacks.

K. To set up international research funds to be used to promote policy research in the field of counter-terrorism.

Mr. Bernd Schmidbauer	Amb. R. James Woolsey	Amb. Edward Djerejian
Mr. Shabtai Shavit	Dr. David Kimche	Prof. Uriel Reichman
Prof. Haim Shaked	Mr. Aharon Scherf	Ret. Gen. Meir Dagan
Mr. Ronen Hoffman	Mr. Boaz Ganor	

329

Index